Alexander Pope

European University Studies

Europäische Hochschulschriften
Publications Universitaires Européennes

**Series XVIII
Comparative Literature**

Reihe XVIII   Série XVIII
Vergleichende Literaturwissenschaft
Littérature comparée

Vol./Band 39

PETER LANG
Berne · Frankfurt am Main · New York

Deirdre O'Grady

||

Alexander Pope and Eighteenth-Century Italian Poetry

PETER LANG

Berne · Frankfurt am Main · New York

CIP-Kurztitelaufnahme der Deutschen Bibliothek

O'Grady, Deirdre:
Alexander Pope and Eighteenth-Century Italian
Poetry / Deirdre O'Grady. – Berne; Frankfurt am
Main; New York: Lang, 1986.
    (European University Studies: Ser. 18, Comparative Literature; Vol. 39)
    ISBN 3-261-04089-0

NE: Europäische Hochschulschriften / 18

© Peter Lang Publishers Ltd., Berne 1986
Successors of Herbert Lang & Co. Ltd., Berne

Printed by Lang Druck Ltd., Liebefeld/Berne (Switzerland)

TABLE OF CONTENTS

INTRODUCTION

Alexander Pope in Eighteenth-Century Italy

The purpose of this study is to demonstrate Alexander Pope's popularity in eighteenth-century Italy and to examine the literary genres
with which he was most closely associated. Although there was a
deep interest in English literature and customs during the "settecento", many made their first acquaintance with Pope through translation, and it is for the reason that a comparative study of translations occupies a considerable part of the present dissertation. His
most translated work was *An Essay on Man*. It had eight known
translators, and many reprints. It indicated a taste for the fusion of
poetry and philosophy, and also the failure of the Italian reading
public to insist on precise choice of language and coherence of
thought when dealing with philosophy or theology. *Eloisa to Abelard*
had only three known translators during the eighteenth century, the
most outstanding of which was Antonio Conti. The same can be said
for *The Rape of the Lock*. Its translators and imitators immortalise
Belinda, Savioli's "minacciata inglese", whose lock becomes symbolic
of the eighteenth-century "bel mondo", of sophistication, frivolity
and decadence in turn. A consideration of translators, imitators and
places of publication indicates that interest in Pope stemmed from
three main centres: Venice, Florence and Naples. The latter had long
been a centre of philosophic aspiration, and the social and intellectual activity which surrounded the residence of the British Ambassador both there and in Venice accounts for the popularity of British
authors, language and customs.

It may come as a surprise that there were no eighteenth-century
translations into Italian of *Imitations of English Poets, Elegy to the
Memory of an Unfortunate Lady*, the *Epistles, Satires* or *The Dunciad*. There were, however, translations of the *Pastorals, Windsor
Forest, Messiah, Ode on St. Cecilia's Day*, the *Essay on Criticism*
and the *Moral Essays*. Such titles reveal the prevailing cultivation

7

of arcadian simplicity, "buon gusto" with regard to literary works and personal behaviour, and some religious fervour. The *Pastorals* were translated by Ermidio De Vincenti (Naples) and Giammaria Pagnini (Parma 1780). The latter archieved fame both as poet and translator of Classics. His approach can be defined as Neo-Classic, in that he avoids the more minute scale of the arcadian world, to create a work of larger proportions, with an elegiac limpidity of tone pointing to the approaching era of pre-Romanticism. Pagnini also translated the *Ode on St. Cecilia's Day*, which was published in Parma in 1800. *Windsor Forest* was translated into Italian by Alfieri and Benvenuto da San Raffaele, while *Messiah* ad as many as five translators in the eighteenth century, including Agostino Paradisi, whose work appeared in 1759, and Angelo Dalmistro (1794). Other translators of *Messiah* are Benvenuto da San Raffaele, also known as Robbio da San Raffaele, Filippo Litardi, and Marco Osvaldo Fassadoni.

One of Pope's most read and translated works remains the *Essay on Criticism*, which in eighteenth-century Italy was synonomous with a handbook for literary taste and critical approach. It had six translators including Alfieri, who revealed misunderstanding of the original, and whose version is in prose, and incomplete. Antonio Pillori's version is perhaps the most read. It dates from Florence 1759, is dedicated to "Sua Eccellenza, il Signor Conte di Northampton, Barone Compton di Compton, pari d'Inghilterra". Pillori refers to Pope as the "maggior poeta del secolo". The next version to appear was that of Gian-Paolo Ricolvi of Turin, whose efforts published in 1778 have been hitherto ignored. Gian-Vincenzo Benini's work was published in Padua in 1792, and two further versions demand our attention: those of Gozzi (1758), and Cesarotti, entitled "Saggio sulla filosofia del gusto" (1785). The Venetian writer Gasparo Gozzi was unfamiliar with the English language. His work entitled *Li principj del buon gusto, ovvero saggio di critica, poema inglese del Sig. Pope ora per la prima volta fatto italiano da Gasparo Gozzi*, was published by Zatta in Venice in 1758. The poet claims that the work is a translation. In an address to the publisher Gozzi requests: "Fate a modo mio: Stampatelo. Son certo che gradirete. . ." On close examination, however, the work bears little direct resemblance to the *Essay on Criticism*, and in my opinion can be regarded as a poem "after Pope" rather than a translation in the accepted sense. Cesarotti's "Saggio sulla filosofia del gusto", a prose essay, is referred to by Donald B. Clark in his essay "The Italian Fame of Alexander Pope", as the fourth translation of the *Essay*.

The *Moral Epistles* of Pope were, it appears, only twice translated during the "Settecento" - by Cerretesi de ' Pazzi (Milan, 1756), and by Marco Osvaldo Fassadoni in 1795. Nonetheless, it must be admitted, in the light of the works translated, and the number of editions of a work such as *An Essay on Man*, that Pope's popularity and significance in eighteenth-century Italy remains undisputed.

Pope first became known in Italy as a poet engaged in the communication of philosophic thought, and not surprisingly it was his *Essay on Man* which was most read and translated during the early eighteenth century. Amongst his earliest admirers were Francesco Algarotti (1712-1764) and Saverio Bettinelli (1718-1808). It is his precision and classical discipline which appeals to the former, while Bettinelli regards him as the most accurate of poets. He refers to his achievement in the following terms: "Quest'uomo ha saputo abbellire e dar forza alle più alte insieme e più necessarie massime della morale dell'uomo, temperando mirabilmente la più bella poesia colla filosofia più pregiata". In a letter addressed to Domenico Fabri, Bettinelli lists his favourite authors: Lucan, Cicero, Virgil, Petrarch, Ariosto, Racine, Boileau, Fontanelle and Pope. However, the earliest poetic tribute to Pope was on the occasion of the birth of the first son of Lord Holdernesse, British Ambassador to Venice, and the voice raised in praise was that of Carlo Innocenzo Frugoni. The year was 1744, and the title of the poem was "L'ombra di Pope". It was the first of many poetic tributes, there followed the "Ombra di Pope" by Lorenzo Pignotti in 1782 and another poem of the same title by the Abate Godard in 1790. Frugoni dedicates the poem to the first born "di Milord Holderness, Ambasciatore Straordinario di Sua Maestà Brittanica alla Repubblica di Venezia". It is also included in *Poemetti e sciolti del secolo XVIII* (Venice, 1790). Frugoni writes not only in praise of Pope, but also stresses the influence of the English poet's writings on his own work. Through the mouth of the British Orpheus, crowned with laurel wreath, he compliments himself on his own poetic achievement.

9

A further tribute is paid in 1757 by the Abate Giulio Perini, in a sonnet celebrating Anton Filippo Adami's translation of the *Essay on Man*. This was the most influential of the many translations of the work. It was reprinted no less than eight times in the course of the century. The sonnet in question was published as part of the 1757 Venetian edition, and bears the title "In lode della traduzione del poema di Pope fatta dall'illustriss. Sig. Cav. Anton Filippo Adami". While the poem represents an appraisal of the translator's ability, the tribute to Pope cannot be overlooked, as it serves as an indication of his popularity and the esteem in which he was held:

> A piè della fredd'urna, ove giacea
> Pope, famoso all'uno, e all'altro polo.
> Quei che potè sovra degli altri il volo
> Stender sublime alla pendice ascrea.
>
> Nel rinnovarsi in me la trista idea
> Della perdita sua, colmo di duolo.
> Poiché di largo pianto aspersi il suono
> Fra i singulti, e i sospir così dicea:
>
> O gran Lume dell'Anglia, ombra immortale,
> Lascia gli Elisi, e dalle torbid'onde
> Di Lete scendi in sen dell'alma Flora:
>
> Quivi potrai veder qual forza, e quale
> Raggio su te nuovo cantor diffonde,
> E ben dirai, che non sei morto ancora.

The vision-poem "Ombra di Pope" by Frugoni no doubt was the source of the work of the same name by Lorenzo Pignotti — (1739-1812). However, as early as 1759 Pignotti referred to Pope in terms of his composition of *The Rape of the Lock* in "La tomba di Shakespear", in the following lines:

> E quei che il furto della chioma bionda
> seppe cantare in sì soavi tempre.

His poetic tributes did not end in 1782 with the publication of "L'Ombra di Pope", which appeared with the title "L'Ombra di Pope, poemetto in versi sciolti alla Nobilissima Dama Maria Isabella di Somerset Duchessa di Rutland", and was published in the volume as *Favole e Novelle del Dottor Lorenzo Pignotti, in Pisa l'anno MDCCL XXXII per Francesco Pieraccini*. However, his most significant work as regards the English poet's inspiration and influence is *La treccia donata*, a mock-heroic work in imitation of *The Rape of the Lock* — published in Florence in 1808. Of all Pope's imitators, it is in my opinion Pignotti who plays the most significant part in Italian literature, as his contribution to the mock-heroic genre in Italy cannot be overlooked.

If further proof were needed of the impact of the work of Alexander Pope on Pignotti, one need but briefly refer to the latter's *Lettere sopra i classici*, and in particular to Letter IV. In the preceeding letter the writer had referred to Locke and the theory of the association of ideas, and this introduces the point that Pignotti did not favour metaphyiscal poetry. This disapproval did not extend to the poetic expression of the philosophical, the best example of which proves to be Pope's *Essay on Man*, which, he believed would be more excellent if metaphysics did not play such a dominant part.

As can be observed, historians, philosophers, poets and critics sang the praises of Pope during the Settecento. The historian Carlo Denina regarded him unsurpassed in strength of expression and in nobility of ideas. Giuseppe Baretti in the Frusta Letteraria No. XXIV attacked both Chiari and Vicini for attempting a translation of Pope, who he stressed "scriveva con forza di stile, con varietà e con sodezza di pensieri".

Alexander Pope's popularity is not surprising when one considers the world of the "Settecento" and its fusion of the philosophical and frivolous, the minute elegance and precision portrayed in turn by Metastasio and Rosalba Carriera, Goldoni and Longhi, and the philosophic awareness of the "istruiti" during the "età dei lumi". However little study has been carried out on Pope in Italy. Yet critics have never refrained from making passing references to his influence and contribution. Giacomo Zanella in *Paralleli letterari* (Verona, 1885) stated that Antonio Conti, as a translator of Pope, wished to introduce into Italy the metaphysical poetry that Pope had introduced into England. There follow two studies which link the names of Pope and Parini. The first by G. Agnelli, *Precursori e imitatori del Giorno* (Bologna, 1888) names Giovanni Battista Mutinelli, Gaetano Gutterez, and Durante Duranti as principle exponents of the social satire, but surprisingly ignores Angelo Talassi and Lorenzo Pignotti. F.

11

Rodriguez, in his *Vita di Lorenzo Pignotti* (Florence, 1896) comments that Pignotti, versed in English literature, was influenced by Pope's *The Rape of the Lock*. Augusta Serena, in *Appunti letterari* (Rome, 1903) makes the interesting comment that Pope's Eloisa as she appears in translation, is the mouthpiece of pre-Romantic ardour. Two important works which catalogue English authors translated into Italian during the eighteenth-century are Arturo Graf, *L'Anglomania e l'influsso inglese in Italia nel secolo XVIII* (Turin, 1911), and Giulio Natali, *Il settecento*, II (Milan, 1944). Neither work provides critical assessment of the translations, or attempts to investigate the intention of the translator. There are short articles on the subject by Francesco Viglione, "Luigi Cerretti e Alessandro Pope," in *Vittorio Cian — i suoi scolari dell'università di Pisa* (Pisa, 1909), U.E. Varzan, "La fortuna di Alessandro Pope in Italia" in *Rivista d'Italia*, XXIII (1920), Donald B. Clark, "The Italian fame of Alexander Pope," in *Modern Languages Quarterly*, XXII (1961) and Giovanna Gronda, "Tradizione e innovazione; le versioni poetiche di Antonio Conti," in *G.S.L.I.* LXXXVII (1970).

The only lengthy study to appear on Pope in Italy is that of Giovanni Lenta. Entitled *Pope in Italia e "Il riccio rapito"*, it was published in Florence in 1931. It does not provide a detailed account of translations, nor does it provide anything resembling a comparative study of versions. His assessment of similarities between Pope and Pignotti are limited to similarities of situation, without regard to imagery or symbolism. There is no mention of Pignotti's acquaintance with *The Dunciad*. By far the most significant contribution to date on Pope, his translators and imitators, is provided by Giovanna Gronda in her edition *Antonio Conti, versioni poetiche* (Bari, 1966). She makes linguistic comments on five different manuscripts of his translation of *The Rape of the Lock* and has discovered and published Conti's own composition *Abelardo ad Elisa*, an epistle written by Conti intended as a reply to *Elisa ad Abelardo* which he translated from Pope. Gronda does not however provide a critical assessment of Conti's composition or attempt to link it to the poetic climate of the time. Further reference to Pope as a translator is made by George E. Dorris in *Paolo Rolli and the Italian circle in London, 1715-1745* (The Hague, 1967).

The present dissertation provides the first general analytical study of Pope's impact on eighteenth-century Italy. It is divided into two main sections, Section I deals exclusively with *The Rape of the Lock*. Section II treats of *An Essay on Man* and *Eloisa to Abelard*. I have chosen these three works for special consideration, since I believe them to have been of most interest to the eighteenth-century "letterati". *The Rape of the Lock* was quickly identified with the miniature world of the Italian "bel mondo", and Belinda, in the guise of Silvia, Lisetta, Lucinda and Aurilla soon found her way into the Italian boudoir. Pope's Eloisa is seen isolated from the gothic world of the English poem, as the exponent of pre-Romantic ardour and conflict. The result is a dialogue of deprivation and despair, with the nun pleading for the expression of, rather than the silent suppression of the will. *An Essay on Man* cannot be regarded as an influential work, but the number of versions and reprints demonstrates the popularity of the subject and content.

Since the title of the dissertation reads: *Alexander Pope and Eighteenth-Century Italian Poetry,* I have sought to identify the three poetic works with the Italian literary climate of the time. It is for this reason that the poetry of "buon gusto", eighteenth-century manners and objects are afforded close consideration. In the case of Talassi and Pignotti an appendix containing unpublished letters is provided. As regards the former the way of life of the extemporary poet is explored, and biographical details of both are set straight. Part I treats of:

Translations and their influence on eighteenth-century poets reproducing the "bel mondo".

Elegance alongside decadence, with "buon gusto" yielding to "cattivo gusto" in the poetry of the Tupé.

Outright imitations of *The Rape of the Lock* containing an attack on the object of decorum — the lock, wig or feather. Its symbolism varies from that of virginity and pride to society at large and infidelity.

The pursuit of the lock provides a journey through society in miniature, convoyed with chiselled classical precision: it touches the mock heroic satire conveyed with biting irony. Finally, with the world of

Lorenzo Pignotti, one enters the realm of the fairytale. Such a demonstration of the "poetry of the lock" has not hitherto been attempted.

Part II contains:

The first comparative study of some of the most outstanding versions of *An Essay on Man*. There is also reference to some attempts at imitation of the work.

A detailed study of the totally neglected eighteenth-century poetry of the cloister, which I have defined the "poesia di monacazione".

I have then attempted to consider the work of Antonio Conti as a more daring aspect of that poetry.

Finally I have referred to imitations of Pope and Conti.

The result, I trust, is an acclamation of the eighteenth-century fame of Pope, his popularity and direct and indirect influence on literary output.

I would like to thank all who offered help, advice and encouragement while the work was in preparation. A special word of gratitude is due to Rev. Professor E.F. O'Doherty and Professor Conn Ó Cleirigh of University College, Dublin, and to Professor Andrea Tossi of the Italian Cultural Institute. I would also like to thank the staff of the following libraries who continually came to my aid: the Biblioteca Marciana, Venice; the Biblioteca Comunale, Pistoia; the Biblioteca Ariostea, Ferrara, with special thanks to Dr. Capra for his personal assistance; the Biblioteca Civica, Bassano del Grappa; the Biblioteca Nazionale, Florence. Finally, I would like to express my gratitude to the staff of the Main Library, University College, Dublin and to the Istituto di Letterature Medioevali e Moderne of the Università Cattolica del Sacro Cuore, Milan.

Deirdre A. O'Grady
July, 1983

PART I

CHAPTER I

Eighteenth-Century Translations

During the age of Queen Anne (1702-14) English society witnessed a marked shift from liberalism to restraint with the cultivation of calculated and refined elegance. This can be illustrated with reference to the social satires of both periods: the wit of Dryden's *Absalom and Architophel* and *MacFlecknoe* vastly differs from that of Pope's *The Rape of the Lock*. In the latter, one witnesses the projection of every aspect of early eighteenth-century social life, with Pope satirizing "mildly and genially, the restrained and refined manners of the upper classes by sending Belinda to a fashionable party at Hampton Court, where ministers of State do 'sometimes counsel take — and sometimes tea'".[1] Such a social satire received acclaim not only at home, but also in France and Italy. The eighteenth-century reader perceived a fusion of two civilisations: while the wit and humour is British, the verbal decorum and visual ornamentation represents Italian social frivolity — the dressing table, the card game and hypocondria were all part of a decadent world taking its main fashionable influence from France. It is therefore not surprising that in *The Rape of the Lock* Italians found a work which appealed, amused and with which they could identify. It was translated and imitated, and in many cases where slavish imitation was avoided it remained a model of technical ability and social awareness to poets reproducing the "bel mondo".

The first Italian translator of *The Rape of the Lock* was Antonio Conti whose version was written in 1724,[2] but not published until 1751. It was not in fact seen in Italy until 1756, when it appeared in *Prose e poesie*, II, (Venice, 1756) edited by Toaldo. The first translation printed in Italy was that of Andrea Bonducci. It is dated Florence 1739, entitled *Il riccio rapito poema eroicomico del Signore Alessandro Pope tradotto dall'inglese in verso toscano*, Firenze MDCCXXXIX. This was reprinted in 1750 in Florence and Venice, and again in Naples in 1760. In 1804 Gian Vincenzo Benini's version was published. While English was studied, and English literature was much cultivated during the eighteenth century, the majority of readers in Italy made their acquaintance with Pope and *The Rape of the Lock* through translation. It was Bonducci's which made the initial impact since it made its appearance in Italy seventeen years before that of Conti. Brian Moloney in his study of relations and contacts between Italy and Tuscany in the eighteenth-century, makes the point that at the middle of the century little English was known in literary circles, thus forcing interested parties to rely on translations of literary works. "Andrea Bonducci, who in 1739 translated Pope's *The Rape of the Lock*, and Antonio Cocchi who kept part of his diary in English were the exception rather than the rule. Pignotti was in all probability right when he said that before about 1750, little English was known in literary circles."[3]

There can be little doubt that Bonducci admired English customs and institutions. Apart from his mastery of the English language and his translation of Pope, tribute is paid to that country in his sonnet on the death of Queen Anne. This is contained in M/S Palatini 1081[4] of the Biblioteca Nazionale, Florence. Bonducci pays the following tribute:

> Cinto d'alga e di spume in grave ammanto
> Sul Britannico suol corre il Tamigi,
> E convertito in ondeggiante pianto
> Dalla sua foce il duol porta a Parigi.
> Ne' Franchi lidi ripercosso e franto
> Con fluttuoso suon dice a Luigi:
> Piangi o monarca, il mio caduto manto
> Che al tuo − per divertir litigi
> Anna Stuarda l'eroina forte
> A cui quest'onda mia lambiva il piede
> Colse al colpo fatal d'iniqua sorte.
> Or tu, che sei il suo volere Erede,
> Dona ad onta al fato e alla morte,
> Al mondo pace, e agli Anglicani Fede.

Over the years Bonducci's translation of *The Rape of the Lock* has been praised for its precision and fluency rather than for its poetic value. Carducci in his *Storia del Giorno* calls it "andante se non elegante"[5] while Antonio Conti advised: "chi vuole una esatta traduzione del testo si attenza a quella stampata a Firenze, e non si tenza alla mia". . .[6] Giovanni Lenta also stresses Bonducci's fidelity to the original but its poetic inferiority to Conti's version: "è fedelissima. . . ma non sempre felice nella struttura del verso. Essa è molto più ligia al testo di quella del Conti, ma è precisamente la versione alla quale il Conti indirizzava i lettori che avessero desiderato una esatta conoscenza del testo".[7] Donald Clark in his short article "The Italian Fame of Alexander Pope" in *Modern Languages Quarterly* XXII (1961) pp. 362-3 refers to the Naples (1760) edition as the second of Bonducci's to appear — "The structure of his verse is not happy, and he freely expurgated all passages which might offend Italian ears. On the whole, however, the translation is faithful. His rendering of Ariel's speech (Canto II, 123 ff), beginning "Whatever spirit, careless of his charge", illustrates his fidelity to the original".

Bonducci's translation is dedicated "all' illustrissima Signora Elisabetta Capponi Grifoni". It contains an address to the Muse[8] and an appraisal of the translation by the Abate Giuseppe Buondelmonti — Lettera dell'illustrissimo Signor Abate Giuseppe Buondelmonti, scritta sovra il presente poema all'abate Andrea Bonducci". Buondelmonti[9] bases his praise on Bonducci's ability to faithfully reproduce the original, rather than on any outstanding original poetic gifts: Bonducci is one "che ha potuto sì fedelmente e sì nobilmente non ostante le diversità delle due lingue, rivestire col poetico linguaggio Toscano le immagini e i sentimenti, che rendono l'originale ammirabile"[10], he is one who can translate "con esattezza insieme e leggiadria nella nostra volgar favella i bellissimi versi di un felice ingegno Britanno che merita la lode di sommo poeta, e di eccelente filosofo".[11] The judgment pronounced by Buondelmonti on Pope as poet and philosopher, and his consideration of the poet-satirist as opposed to the pure philosopher proves valuable when one attempts to arrive at a critical assessment of the translation, and an analysis of the translator's technique. Buondelmonti states:

La differenza tra il Poeta ridente ed il serio Filosofo nel distruggere i falsi pregiudizi, che danno il vantaggio a una cosa sopra un'altra, consiste in questo, che il Filosofo direttamente dimostra, che quelle opinioni speculative, e pratiche, nelle quali si supponeva una grandissima differenza dalle

17

opinioni erronee, o dannose, sono egualmente che altre poco, o niente stima-
bili, ovvero cattive, o si paragonino colla verità, o colla utilità. Ma il Poeta
burlesco, o colui, che vuole eccitare il riso, e produrre l'istesso effetto sceglie
dei mezzi termini obliqui, e fra questi il più efficace, ch'io conosca, è quello
di provare l'uguaglianza delle prefate cose supposte inequali, col dipingere
in una maniera, che faccia conoscere la convenienza vera, che è fra esse,
come utilissime cose riconosciute per indifferenti, o perniciose, e col rappre-
sentare, come verissime, le proposizioni generalmente credute false; Questo è
ciò, che maravigliosamente ha eseguito il Sig. Pope: questo è ciò che i valenti
comici antichi, e moderni hanno usato molte volte, ed in questi principal-
mente consiste il ridicolo, che ha fatto tanto onore a Luciano, a Rabelais, al
Signore de la Fontaine, all'Autore dei viaggi del Capitan Gulliver, a Butler e
ad altri che farebbe troppo lungo il mentovare[12].

Buondelmonti's final praise of Pope's ability brings to light the
esteem in which the English poet was held, and the critical awareness
of his readers in Italy as early as 1739: "questa qualità di adattare lo
stile ai differenti soggetti e alle loro diverse modificazioni senza esser
prosaico, basso e nojoso è una delle principali doti, che rendono il
suo nome, ed i suoi scritti così famosi al presente, e che gli renderan-
no nei secoli avvenire superiori all'invidia ed immortali".[13]

In taking a critical approach to Bonducci's translation, bearing in
mind the outstanding qualities of Pope's mock-heroic writing, one
becomes increasingly aware of the Italian's shortcomings as a poet:
he does not succeed in recreating the qualities of the "poeta ridente"
expressed by Buondelmonti. Perhaps Bonducci's weakest point lies in
his inability to successfully unite two contrasting elements of style —
the light and serious, the satirical, and the profoundly philosophical.
For this reason the figure of Belinda never really comes off. Bonducci
never succeeds in conveying the sense of the incongruous. One also
finds an inability to condense concepts, thus resulting in a playing-
down in the climatic moments. For these reasons Bonducci's translation does not rank as a piece of eighteenth-century elegance. It lacks
lightness, subtlety and wit. In Pope's original, while one finds the
poetic identification of reality and fancy, the truth of every situation
is made extremely clear. Not so in Bonducci's translation, the comical
is often rendered serious. Nonetheless this is in many ways a successful version. While the subtlety and complexity of the original is often
lost, Bonducci's work creates impact in the serious passages. His

drawing of caricatures provides the highlights of the work. The *Rape of the Lock* is the mock-heroic "par excellence" which presents the "bel mondo" of its writer's day on both miniature and magnified scale. The "perfect" world of the boudoir and of Hampton Court vies with the near grotesque world of the Cave of Spleen. There does, however, exist within this poem yet another dimension — the cardboard world of the cards brought to life in order to illustrate the "social battle" of Belinda in another key:

> Belinda now, whom thirst of fame invites,
> Burns to encounter two adventurous knights,
> At ombre singly to decide their doom;
> And swells her breast with conquests yet to come.
> (Pope, *The Rape of the Lock*, Canto III. 25.8.)

Such an episode, I believe was most successfully translated into Italian by Bonducci. It provides another aspect of the fantastic within Pope's world. As opposed to that of any substance, one finds oneself in the world of stock-characters, resembling those of the improvised theatre. "Less than heroes, Pope's beaux are also less than men; but they are certainly practised in the "whole art" of their intricate warfare. It is, by convention as by hyperbole, an "unequal fight" — the men worshipping and pleading for favours, the ladies dispensing mortal wounds and withholding their cure."[14] Husbands receive far less dedicated attention or social prominence than beaux or lap-dogs, and as in Restoration Comedy, assume a supporting role. The lap-dog, as Cunningham points out[15] is on a par with the lover, to be petted, fretted over, or discarded. *The Rape of the Lock* is, then, a mock-heroic epic of which genteel society is the protagonist. It is also a work of profound moralising whose apparent superficiality decorates a spectrum of activity pointing finally to contemplation of Being as opposed to Behaviour.

On reading Bonducci's translation one is at once aware of an ability to capture movement. This is most apparent in Ariel's speech in Canto I. The circular movement of the spirits and the indication of space is imaginatively recaptured:

> Or sappi dunque, che al tuo corpo intorno
> Vola di spirti innumerabil schiera,
> Lieve milizia del più basso cielo;

> Questi agli squardi tuoi benchè nascosi
> Stanno sempre su l'ale, altri sospesi
> Sul dipinto palchetto il volo fermano,
> Ed altri al corso circolare intorno
> S'aggirano confusi a mille a mille.[16]

> Know, then, unnumbered spirits round thee fly,
> The light militia of the lower sky:
> These, though unseen, are ever on the wing,
> Hang o'er the box, and hover round the ring.
> (Pope, *The Rape of the Lock*, Canto I. 41-44).

Bonducci takes eight lines to Pope's four — obviously the condension of concepts evades the translator. Yet the word choice is entirely successful — "al tuo corpo intorno/Vola di spirti innumerabil schiera — più basso cielo" clearly conveys the flurry of the spirits in open space. Continuity of movements is also indicated by the position in the sentence and verbal weight given to "stanno sempre". The giddy flight, and the maiden's uncertainty of direction is captured by the terms "Cammino incerto, misteriosi laberinti, dubbiosi passi, l'intricato cerchio". The following passage is a literal translation which splendidly captures the spirit of the original:

> I Silfi son, che il loro cammino incerto
> Per misteriosi laberinti guidano,
> Ed essi son, che i lor dubbiosi passi
> Seguono ognor per l'intricato cerchio,
> E con nova follia fanan l'antica.[17]

> Oft when the world imagine women stray,
> The sylphs through mystic mazes guide their way,
> Through all the giddy circle they pursue,
> And old impertinence expel by new.
> (Pope, *The Rape of the Lock*, Canto I. 91-94).

Once again, in the passage describing the making of coffee, it is Bonducci's power to visually convey movement which strikes the reader. His gift for gentle exaggeration is also here employed — the atmosphere assumes an exoticism which will be reproduced later by eighteenth-century poets depicting customs, conversation and social activity. A study of Conti's version of the same passage reveals more refinement and sophistication, resembling the eigthteenth-century miniature, yet Bonducci's lines come nearer to the eroticism of Pope's original:

> Ma già di tazze, e di cucchiari intorno
> Coronata divien la ricca tavola;
> I grani del Caffè arsi, e rinchiusi
> Odonsi sgretolare, e il mulinello
> Si rivolge veloce in tondi giri.
> Su sfavillanti altari del Giappone
> La lucerna d'argento omai s'inalza;
> I focosi del vin spirti fiammeggiano,
> Dagli argentei beccucci i grati umori
> Scorrono, e intanto la Chinese terra
> Riceve nel suo sen l'onda fumente:[18]

> For lo! the board with cups and spoons is crown'd,
> The berries crackle, and the mill turns round:
> On shining altars of Japan they raise
> The silver lamp; the fiery spirits blaze:
> From silver spouts the grateful liquors glide,
> While China's earth receives the smoking tide:
> (Pope, *The Rape of the Lock*, Canto III. 105-110).

One notes that Bonducci takes eleven lines to Pope's six. The constant use of the letter f — "focosi, fiammeggiano, fumante and sfavillanti" contribute to the oriental atmosphere of the passage. If the mock-heroic "par excellence" evades Bonducci, his technique with regard to the identification of being and space is quite remarkable. When Pope relies on the abstract to convey such a concept, Bonducci approaches the translation in physical terms. This is best illustrated with regard to the following passage: —

> Con soave passaggio andammo poi
> Gl'immensi spazzi ad abitar dell'aria.
> Nè creder già, che quando alcuna donna
> L'estremo spirto fuggitivo esala
> Tutte le voglie sue vadano sotterra:
> Ad altre vanità successe a quelle
> Ella pure ha riguardo, ed alle carte
> Presiede ancor — benchè giocar non possa.[19]

> Thence, by a soft transition, we repair
> From earthly vehicles to those of air.

Think not, when woman's transient breath is fled,
That all her vanities at once are dead;
Succeeding vanities she still regards,
And though she plays no more, o'erlooks the cards.
(Pope, *The Rape of the Lock*, Canto I. 48-53).

Pope's lines 48-49 are by far more gentle than Bonducci's "The soft transition" and "earthly vehicles to those of air" indicates a dissolution of the human substance leading to the identification of the being with space and air. Bonducci, in introducing the verbs "andammo" and "abitar" allows the reader visualise a physical passage from earth to space. Then having almost bodily transported the individual from earth to the spheres, Bonducci avoids repetition and adds subtlety and variation. Pope relies on verbs of action and finality, but the translator uses those implying presence, allowing for continuity in space. So Pope's "is fled", "dead", "regards", "plays", "o'erlooks" is rendered by "l'estremo spirto fuggitivo esala", "voglie", "ha riguardo", "presiede". The final result, though achieved in a totally different manner, rekindles the spirit of the original, and achieves the same effect as does Pope's passage.

The Rape of the Lock abounds in decorative and ornate passages. In Bonducci's hands, those of a "semi-serious" nature can be numbered amongst his most successful. In the following extract, the social glitter of the original is maintained. Yet a literal rendering is avoided. The word groups are well chosen, and a sense of the original is preserved:

Non con più di splendor, con più di gloria
Del purpureo Ocean s'alza dall'onde
All'eterea pianura il Sol nascente,
Di quel che fuor del caro albergo uscita
La gloriosa Rival de'raggi suoi
Dell'argenteo Tamigi entro nel seno.[20]

Not with more glories, in th'ereal plain,
The sun just rises o'er the purpled main,
Than, issuing forth, the rival of his beams
Launch'd on the bosom of the silver Thames.
(Pope, *The Rape of the Lock*, Canto II. 1-4).

Ed ecco omai, che tolto il vel spiegata
Stà la Tolette, ed ogni argenteo vaso
In ordinanza misteriosa è posto.
Pria d'altro ufficio la devota Ninfa
Cinta di bianchi lini, e nuda il capo
Del lusso femminile i Numi adora.

Celeste immago appar nel terso specchio,
A questa ella si volge, e gli occhi suoi
Indrizza a questa; dell'altare al lato
L'inferior sacerdotessa stando,
Le sacre cerimonie dell'orgoglio
Incomincia tremante:[21]

And now, unveil'd, the toilet stands display'd,
Each silver vase in mystic order laid.
First, robed in white, the nymph intent adores,
With head uncover'd, the cosmetic powers.
A heavenly image in the glass appears,
To that she bends, to that her eye she rears;
Th'inferior priestess, at her altar's side,
Trembling, begins the sacred rites of pride.
(Pope, *The Rape of the Lock*, Canto I. 121-128).

In the above quoted passages, it is Bonducci's skill as a translator which is in question. It must be remembered, however, that an Italian reading public would have accepted *Il riccio rapito* as a poem in its own right. Bonducci's poetic gifts, as well as those of mere literal translator, are, I believe, apparent in the above introductory passage to Belinda's toilette. "Spiegata/stà la Tolette", "cinta di bianchi lini" and "lusso femminile", while accurately translating Pope's lines are original poetic utterances. Here the ceremonial display of the dressing-table and the self-adoration of the nymph assume classical proportions, but in doing so, lose some of the wit of the original.[22] "The sacred rites of pride" for Bonducci become so seriously oriented as to lose their mock-heroic spirit. The same can be said for the act of the rape of the lock itself — that is to say, the lightness of touch is lost and the act resembles real life rape. In the game of ombre sequence the cards become "larger than life" figures.

Bonducci is most successful when transforming comic characters to caricatures. This once again bears out the statement that the Italian translator was unable to bridge the gap between the comic and the serious. However, the Baron and the card figures are his most successful creations: historically I believe them to be of much significance. They represent for the reader the first encounter with the English eighteenth-century mock-heroic genre. They illustrate for the first time in the eighteenth-century, the destruction of an object of adornment which has a personal and political significance, and bring to Italian poetry the popular game of Ombra,[23] which will later prove a favourite activity in the poetic representation of a day in the life of an eighteenth-century lady or gentleman.

The figure of the Baron is one of Bonducci's most successful creations. Though an ardent, amorous being, he is drawn as one following the dictates of his head rather than his heart. As the poem progresses he emerges as the villain of the piece, a Machiavellian operator, rather than the daring cad of *The Rape of the Lock*. Bonducci captures the stages of the Baron's materialising thoughts, provides a clear-cut objective assessment of his situation, and triumphantly declares coffee the final enlightening force:

> Del chiaro scintillar de'biondi Ricci
> Un ardito Baron meravigliossi,
> Gli mirò, gli bramò, desio li venne
> Di farne acquisto; in tal pensier costante.
> La maniera tra se medita, e volge
> Di rapirli con forza, e con inganno:
> Che se l'evento favorevol segue
> Le travagliose cure d'un amante,
> Pochi son quelli, che da lui ricercano,
> Se per forza, o per frode il premio ottenne.[24]

> Th'adventurous baron the bright locks admired;
> He saw, he wish'd, and to the prize aspired.
> Resolved to win, he meditates the way,
> By force to ravish, or by fraud betray;
> For when success a lover's toil attends,
> Few ask, if fraud or force attain'd his ends.
> (Pope, *The Rape of the Lock*, Canto II. 29-34).

Bonducci uses the indefinite article in place of Pope's definite. He condenses the Baron's reaction into three stages as in the original: "gli mirò, gli bramò, desio li venne" — "He saw, he wish'd, and to the prize aspired". His alternatives are stated in one line — "Di rapirli con forza, econ inganno". Four lines further down he changes "inganno" to "frode" thus achiving alliteration as in the original: — "Pochi son quelle, che da lui ricercano,/Se per forza, o per frode il premio ottenne". Bonducci's first line prepares for the clarity in tone of the passage to follow — "del chiaro scintillar de'biondi Ricci". These lines perform the verbal function of clarifying the passage to come.

The Baron's altar to love is not as wittily transposed as one might expect, which goes to render his pursuit of the lock all the more serious, and his character all the more cunning:

> Ad Amore un altare alzò composto
> Di dodici ben grossi alti volumi
> Di Romanzi Francesi, ornati d'oro;
> Su questi ei pone tre Giartiere, e un guanto,
> E de'suoi primi amor tutti i trofei/
> Con un foglio amoroso il rogo accende
> E tre caldi sospir dal cor traendo,
> Cresce col soffio la vorace fiamma.[25]

> — to Love an altar built,
> Of twelve vast French romances, neatly gilt.
> There lay three garters, half a pair of gloves;
> And all the trophies of his former loves:
> With tender billet-doux he lights the pyre,
> And breathes three amorous sights to raise the fire.
> (Pope, *The Rape of the Lock*, Canto II. 37-42).

At this point in the translation the Baron enters the world of the caricature. While the first three lines are in keeping with the spirit hitherto established, the lines "Su questi ei pone tre Giartiere, e un guanto/E de'suoi primi amor tutti i trofei" are awkward. The fusion of the scheming qualities and those of the comic remove the Baron even further from the world of the mock-heroic. With the effect of the coffee he rises to a new level of astuteness —

> Ora il Caffé,
> Che maggio senno agli Statisti inspira.
> E ai loro occhi socchiusi il tutto scopre,
> Al cervel del Baron miste tramanda
> Con i vapori suoi novelle astuzie
> Per far conquista del bel Riccio.[26]

Coffee (which makes the politician wise,
And see through all things with his half-shut eyes)
Sent up in vapours to the baron's brain
New stratagems, the radiant lock to gain.
(Pope, *The Rape of the Lock*, Canto III. 117-120).

The constant use of the letter "s" — "senno", "Statisti", "occhi socchiusi", "scopre", and the placing of "novelle astuzie" at the end of the line brings the reader into visual contact with a shrewd scheming statesman. His cry of victory while providing a climax to the entire episode, is in Bonducci's translation far more effective than the lines marking the cutting of the hair. Thus for the translator the real triumph belongs to the Baron, while the lines pronouncing the final severing of the lock fall rather flat in Italian:

E all'incontro fatal delle due punte
Si separò dalla leggiadra testa
per sempre ahiemè, Per sempre il Sacro riccio.[27]

The meeting points the sacred hair dissever
From the fair head, for ever and for ever!
(Pope, *The Rape of the Lock*, Canto III. 153-54).

There can be no doubt that for the Italian reader the Baron's cry of victory forms the high point of the poem:

Corone di trionfo ora circondino
L'onorate mie tempie, il vincitore
Gridò contento, il glorioso premio
È in mio poter; finchè dell'onde, i pesci
O dell'aria gli augelli avran diletto.
O d'aureo cocchio a sei le Belle Inglesi;
Finchè letta sarà la nova Atlantide
E delle Dame ai deliziòsi letti
D'ornamento farà piccol guanciale; ...[28]

Let wreaths of triumph now my temples twine,
(The victor cried) the glorious prize is mine!
While fish in streams, or birds delight in air,
Or in a coach and six the British fair,
As long as Atalantis shall be read,
Or the small pillow grace a ladies bed. . .
(Pope, *The Rape of the Lock*, Canto III. 161-166).

At this point it could be argued that the true significance of the entire poem has been misunderstood by Bonducci. The subtlety of mock-heroic genre has fallen flat, the humour of word play is not rendered in Italian. In its place we find the comic situation verging on the grotesque, yielding to black comedy. Bonducci's *Riccio rapito* is in its lighter moments burlesque, rather than an illustration of a tantalising and sophisticated world.

In the game of cards, however, Bonducci's kings and queens are more lively and life-like than those of Pope. It can be said that the latter at this point is the victim of his metre. The figures are static, dignified and restrained:

> Behold, four Kings in majesty revered,
> With hoary whiskers and forky beard;
> And four fair Queens, whose hands sustain a flower,
> Th'expressive emblem of their softer power;
> (Pope, *The Rape of the Lock*, Canto III. 37-40).

Bonducci succeeds in creating larger than life cardboard images, which exist outside the mere game of cards. Their form, disposition and movement is conveyed in terms of pomp and ceremony. In English we witness a seriousness of subject treated with a lightness of touch. Here we find exaggerated dignity:

> Ecco, che quattro coronati Regi
> In Venerabil maestate appajono,
> Gravi nel ciglio, con canuti baffi,
> Con lunga barba biforcata, e quattro
> Belle Regine, a cui ridente fiore
> Stà nelle mani, misterioso Emblema,
> Che la più grata lor potenza esprime.[29]

The "extra" life conferred on the figures by Bonducci is created by the use of two words "appajono" which conveys presence and movement, and "ridente fiore" which transfers the human quality from the being to the object in its hands, achieving both touches of delicacy and caricature. The use of "grata" and "potenza" within the same line suggests a paradox which transfers the figures to the realm of the fairy-tale. Quaintness of touch is further added as the battle begins. Belinda is the force behind the game, though the action resembles real war:

Ed ecco, che al conflitto ella già move
I neri Mattador, che nel sembiante
Simili sono ai condottier dei Mori
Di color basanè: prima in valore
L'invincibil Spadiglià due trionfi
Schiavi conduce spolverando il piano:
Altrettanti Maniglia a ceder sforza,
E scorre vincitrice il verde campo.[30]

Now move to war her sable Matadores,
In show-like leaders of the swarthy Moors.
Spadillio first, unconquerable lord!
Led off two captive trumps, and swept the board.
As many more Manillio forced to yield
And march'd a victor from the verdant field.
(Pope, *The Rape of the Lock,* Canto III. 47-52).

It is in passages such as these that the translator can be judged a literary figure in his own right. Never approaching the qualities of a great poet he nevertheless objectively mirrors eighteenth-century life, with a touch of cynicism, and indulgence in black comedy. Where, however, calculated elegance, restraint and cultivated mannerisms reign supreme, he simply does not possess the refinement of technique to express Pope's balance, parallelism, antithesis, juxtaposition and zellegma, all employed in the service of incongruity which is the cornerstone of the mock-heroic genre.

For Pope, love is seen both as a game and a battle. Conquest is illustrated as both a political and social achievement. His work can be interpreted on several levels. Bonducci's generally has only one level of interpretation. This is the reason he is most acceptable in serious and comic passages bordering on caricature and the grotesque. Having seen some examples of this, let us now concentrate on some passages in which the translator, rather than the poetic satirist is at large.

Pope achieves his effect in the opening of *The Rape of the Lock* by allowing his contrasts to fall in the same lines, i.e.

What dire offence from amorous causes springs,
What mighty contests rise from trivial things,
(Pope, *The Rape of the Lock*, Canto I. 1-2).

Say what strange motive, goddess! could compel
A well-bred lord to assault a gentle belle?
O say what stranger cause, yet unexplored,
Could make a gentle belle reject a lord?
In tasks so bold, can little men engage,
And in soft bosoms dwells such mighty rage?
(Pope, *The Rape of the Lock*, Canto I. 7-12).

Bonducci, partly because of the difficulties involved in condensing the Italian language, and partly because he attempts to reproduce Pope's feigned rhetorical style, entirely sacrifices lightness and wit. He is not capable of placing opposites in the same line, and because he does not stress the contrast when it is eventually expressed, the spirit of the work is lost. It becomes reduced to the level of a classroom translation, of much help to the student of English with difficulty in understanding the original.

A study of the following passages by Bonducci brings to the fore the difficulties involved in translation and the demands placed upon the translator, as linguist, poet and critic.

Narrami, O Diva, qual motivo strano
Spinse nobil Signore a fare oltraggio
A una bella; disvelami l'ascosa,
E più strana cagion, per cui potea
A un Milord una bella esser ritrosa.[31]

A così ardite imprese i picciol'uomini
Osano cimentarsi, e sì potente
Sdegno n'petti delicati alberga?[32]

On some occasions, as in the following quotation, Bonducci succeeded in achieving balance by allowing a line to each alternative:

Oh se tutta impiegar la notte in danze
E tutto il dì nell'acconciarsi il crine,
Contra il vajol fosse efficace incanto,[33]

Oh! if to dance all night, and dress all day,
Charm'd the small-pox, or chased old age away;
(Pope, *The Rape of the Lock*, Canto V. 19-20).

Another difficulty facing the translator of the mock-heroic is that of ensuring that the true state of affairs is clearly conveyed. Bonducci does not always do so — once again the technical difficulty of writing fantasy and truth becomes too much. In the following quotation, zellegma is not achieved:

> Noto non è se dalla nostra Ninfa
> Di Diana sarà rotta la legge,
> O se scoppiando fenderassi in mezzo
> Fragil vaso chinese; o se macchiato
> Sarà il suo onore, o il suo novel broccato;[34]

> Whether the nymph shall break Diana's law,
> Or some frail china-jar receive a flaw;
> Or stain her honour or her new brocade;
> (Pope, *The Rape of the Lock*, Canto II. 105-107).

Once again Bonducci has provided a competent literal translation, without humour, or wit. Only a new choise of metre could provide the fast moving effect of Pope:

> Qui tu grand'Anna, a cui tre Regni omaggio
> Prestano obbedienti, alcune volte
> Prendi consigli, ad alcun altre il Tè.[35]

> Here thou, Great Anna! whom three realms obey,
> Dost sometimes counsel take — and sometimes tea.
> (Pope, *The Rape of the Lock*, Canto III. 7-8).

In order to confer his own personal stamp on his translation, it appears that Bonducci overdramatises certain incidents. It must be said that at times such overdramatisation is artistically successful in isolation, but that the poetic unity of the poem, and the original tone is lost. Here Bonducci creates an eroticism not present in the original:

> Che qualunque in beltà chiara donzella,
> Che gl'impuri dell'uomo amplessi fugga,
> E il virginal suo fior casta conservi,
> Divien d'alcun di noi dolce piacere.[36]

> . . . . whoever fair and chaste
> Rejects mankind, is by some sylph embraced:
> (Pope, *The Rape of the Lock*, Canto I. 67-68).

In the same manner, the description of the ball is overdramatised: —

Chi le assicura dall'amico infido,
Dall'ardito galante, e da i loquaci
Squardi nel giorno, e da i discorsi fatti
Placidamente nell'orror di notte?[37]

What guards the purity of melting maids,
In courtly balls, and midnight masquerades,
Safe from the treach'rous friend, the daring spark,
The glance by day, the whisper in the dark,
(Pope, *The Rape of the Lock*, Canto I. 71-74).

My final and most serious criticism of Bonducci's translation is that
on occasions the sense of a passage is obscured, thus reducing the
lines in question to artless expressions. Such passages lay claim
neither to translation or poetry. This I believe to be the case with
regard to the following lines:

Quale offesa crudel nasca da Amore,
Quai da lieve cagion forti contrasti
Sorgan, Io canto. Questo carme, o Musa,
Devesi a Tirsi, e può Belinda ancora
Degnarsi in questo di fissar lo sguardo.[38]

What dire offence from amorous causes springs,
What mighty contests rise from tirvial things,
I sing-this verse to Caryll, Muse! is due:
This, even Belinda may vouchsafe to view;
(Pope, *The Rape of the Lock*, Canto I. 1-4).

Deh riconosci de'bei pregi tuoi
La sublime grandezza, e non volere
Sovra oggetto terren fissare i lumi:
Vi sono arcane verità, celate
All'orgoglio dei dotti e solamente
Disvelate ai fanciulli, ed alle vergini –
Spiriti dubitanti a tali cose
Niuna fede daran, ma gl'innocenti,
E le belle le avran sempre per vere.[39]

Hear and believe! they soon importance know,
Nor bound thy narrow views to things below.
Some secret truths from learned pride conceal'd,
To maids alone and children are reveal'd:

31

What though no credit doubting wits may give?
The fair and innocent shall still believe.
(Pope, *The Rape of the Lock*, Canto I. 35-40).

The real significance of Bonducci's Il *riccio rapito* is that it is the first Italian translation to appear of Pope's *The Rape of the Lock*, and before the appearance of Conti's version it had been reprinted in Florence and Venice in 1750. For seventeen years it was the sole Italian rendering available. It therefore provided readers of mid-eighteenth century with their first impressions of Pope. The influence of such a work can therefore not be underestimated. Bonducci introduced a poem to the Italians, which became extremely popular. The appearance of Antonio Conti's translation can be seen as a transformation of the work in question from light burlesque to rococo elegance.

II

Antonio Conti played a key role in introducing English letters into Italy. His translation of *The Rape of the Lock* was indeed most influential. His verbal grace was such, that while avoiding a literal rendering in the manner of Bonducci, he succeeded in bringing to his Italian version all the poetic sophistication of Pope. Although the translation did not appear in Italy until 1756, in the second volume of *Prose e poesie* edited by Toaldo, there exists a version which was printed in London in 1751.

> Esso è il risultato di un costante lavoro di revisione e di correzione compiuto in tre distinte fasi, nello spazio di sedici anni, dalla prima stesura nel'24 in Francia all'ultima probabilmente sollecitata dalla stampa Italiana; La lunga rielaborazione conferma il perdurare dell'ammirazione e del gusto contiano per questa poesia anche quando erano venute meno l'influenza del grande amico del Pope, quel Lord Bolingbroke che lo aveva aiutato a compiere la prima redazione, . . .[40].

Conti's English sojourn was for him decisive, since it marked the change in his interests from primarily scientific to literary. In 1715, we are informed by Toaldo[41] Conti was attacked by asthma, and while resting in Kensington began to write a poem on Newtonian philosophy. At the same time he became acquainted with Katherine Sheffield, Duchess of Buckinghamshire, whose husband's *Essay on*

Poetry he translated into Italian. He then went on to translate Milton, Dryden, Pope, Prior and Swift. By 1718 he had begun to consolidate his English interests: "By then he had gained a fair knowledge of English letters, probably much of it through his acquaintance with English writers. It may well have been from knowing Pope that he conceived the idea of translating *The Rape of the Lock* and *Eloisa to Abelard* into Italian,. . ."[42]

Conti's ability to recapture the delicacy and miniature elegance of Pope can be attributed to his attention to detail, and his classical preparation:

> Correzioni, varianti e innovazioni testimoniano un senso di insoddisfazione e di autocritica non comune nei traduttori del tempo. Un'altra affinità culturale accomuna il poeta inglese ad il letterato italiano: il profondo interesse per il mondo classico. Il Conti, grande ammiratore della cultura greco-latina del Pope, sapeva bene quanto Omero e Virgilio avessero educato il gusto e l'arte dell'autore del *Rape of the Lock*. Il traduttore non si limita dunque a riprodurre, ma partecipa direttamente alla rielaborazione in senso eroicomico della tradizione epica, senza esitare a fare autonomi ricorsi agli originali classici.[43]

In his "prefazione del traduttore", Conti touches on the various comical aspects of the poem and states that the baron is its hero:

> L'azion del poema è il rapimento del riccio, poiché a questo si riferiscono le custodie, e le paure de'Silfi, il sacrifizio, il trionfo del barone ed il coraggio col qual osa resistere alla eloquenza del cavalier di Piuma, alle minacce di Talestri, a'lamenti di Belinda, e finalmente all'assalto nel quale è rinversato con un dito a terra. Il Barone perciò è propriamente l'eroe del poema, poiché egli è quello che per mezzi comicamente difficili conduce a fine una impresa grande per le circostanze con cui l'accompagna il poeta.[44]

This critical approach and observation is revealed in his projection of character and presentation of incidents: he states that Pope includes: "tutto ciò che da varietà e magnificenza al poema eroico. Non è però l'eroico introdotto che un certo velo per cui trasparisce un comico tanto più caro, quanto più satirico, e satirico, che nella azione e ne'caratteri più che nelle frasi e ne' riflessi consiste."[45] That Conti had made a detailed study of Pope's rhyme scheme there can be little doubt — "idee inglesi colorite all'italiana" owe their success to his precision in word choice, ability to condense concepts, attention to verbs and the placing of emphasis at the same point in the line as in the original. To this can be added a certain originality of concept, and an impression of continuity which seldom allows the tone to fall flat. As opposed to Bonducci's figure, Conti's baron is a philosopher demonstrating the art of conquest, while life and personality is conveyed to the locks which compete amongst themselves and assume an intrinsic life force. The world of social frivolity is brought alive with the employment of light imagery, refined ornamentation and decoration. He is thus most successful in lines concentrating on feminine artifice, combining arcadian elegance with clear perception of human motives.

Conti's achievement of lightness of touch illustrates his ability to do just what Bonducci could not — condense concepts, place words conveying space and movement at the end of the line, so preserving the sense of the original. This ability can be illustrated with reference to the passage describing the function of the sylphs:

> Sappi dunque che a te vola d'intorno
> Falange innumerabile di spirti,
> Agil milizia del più basso cielo;
> Amanti, ed invisibili ministri
> Stanno su l'ali in tuo servigio pronti[46]

> Know, then, unnumbered spirits round thee fly,
> The light militia of the lower sky:
> These though unseen are ever on the wing,
> (Pope, *The Rape of the Lock*, Canto I. 41-43).

One observes that here Conti has avoided a literal translation. His placing of "vola d'intorno" and "pronto" at the end of lines allows for the indication of space and movement. Conti's precision and attention to the original metre, and verb position in *The Rape of the Lock* allows him as far as possible to let the stress fall at the same point as in the original. This is particularly true of the passage dealing with Clarissa's presentation of the scissors:

> Nel tempo che il Baron medita il furto
> Clarissa trasse con accorto vezzo
> Da fodro scintillante arma a due tagli
> Ed al Baron cortesemente l'offre.
> (Così le donne ai cavalieri antichi
> Offrir per le battaglie o lancia o spada).[47]

> Just then, Clarissa drew with tempting grace
> A two-edged weapon from her shining case:
> So ladies, in romance assist their knight,
> Present the spear, and arm him for the fight.
> (Pope, *The Rape of the Lock*, Canto III. 127-30).

One is at once impressed by Conti's word choice — "accorto vezzo", "fodro scintillante", "cortesemente" — one notices that "accorto vezzo" and "tempting grace" both fall at the end of a line. The positions of "two-edged weapon" and "shining case" is reversed in the translation but they occur within the same line, as is the case in the original. One further notes that in the following passage "stende", "spiega" and "inchinava" each occur at the same point as in the original:

> Con riverenza ei prende il dono e stende
> Su la cima de'diti il breve ordigno;
> E al collo di Belinda indi lo spiega
> Appunto allor ch'ella inchinava il capo
> Sul torrente odoroso.[48]

> He takes the gift with reverence and extends
> The little engine on his finger's ends;
> This just behind Belinda's neck he spread,
> As o'er the fragrant steams she bends her head.
> (Pope, *The Rape of the Lock*, Canto III. 131-4).

One could almost call Conti's version a "Venetian" translation, though the "silvery" quality of Pope is captured by light imagery and ornamentation. No aspect of the ladies social life escapes him, and he well captures appearances, glances, sensations and nocturnal enterprises. Conti's translation becomes a mirror of Italian eighteenth-century life, the most successful passages are those reproduced by major and minor poets of the "bel mondo". For Conti, Belinda will prove the centre of social activity and so the passages most memorable in his work reproduce the dressingtable, the various objects of feminine adornment, nocturnal exploits, the coffee table, the ball, and the final reminder that old age is but a step away. It is as though Conti in his phrasing of "idee inglesi colorite all'italiana", was indeed to such an extent reproducing the society to which he was accustomed that the scene is English merely in name, as can indeed be said of some of Antonio Canal's views of the Thames. The subject is London, but the spirit is Venetian. So Conti paints and brings to life the world so aptly described by Natali:

> Il Settecento amò le donne, dirò così, artificiali. Noi ci estasiamo dinanzi ai loro ritratti, illudendoci di ammirare la freschezza del colorito, lo splendore delle capigliature di quelle dame, e risentiamo il fascino della bellezza settecentesca, senza pensare che quella bellezza era tutta fittizia: alti "tupè" incipriati pieni di penne e fiori, di perle e diamanti, visi impiastricciati di belletto e sparsi di nei, che avevano un loro galante linguaggio. . . Ecco la donna pupattola d'Arcadia. . .[49] Parucca incipriata a arricciata, biancheggiante intorno alla faccia accuratamente rasa, giubba gallonata e giustacuori di seta ricamati con le lattughe dì trìne al petto e ai polsi, tricorno sotto il braccio per non guastar l'acconciatura. Spadino senza lama; gingilli tintinnanti, calzonetti, calze di seta, scarpette con fibbie d'oro o d'argento. Ecco il degno cavalier servente.[50]

In order to maintain the necessary degree of artifice and decorum there needs to be an apparent freeness of expression and fluency which conceals the attention to every minor detail and the constant re-elaboration:

> Il risultato è una traduzione senza sforzi, dallo sciolto ritmo armonioso, concreta ed elegante nella lingua e nella forma della descrizione, come di chi ha visto e ben conosce le cose che disegna, ma non dimentica mai di star descrivendo oggetti di canto e di vagheggiamento poetico, sì che la realtà si trasfiguri nei versi del poeta come in quelli del traduttore non per astrazione o paludamento letterario, ma per ironica, aristocratica contemplazione.[51]

Thus the glances, blushes and amorous flutterings of hearts and fans are reproduced in a spontaneous manner in Conti's work:

> A questo è quel che di buon'ora infetta
> L'alma de le fanciulle, ahi questo è quello
> Che a gli occhi insegna a misurar con arte
> Gli sguardi, e a ricoprir le guancie a tempo
> Di rossor comandato, e verso il vago
> A palpitar i tenerelli cori.[52]

> Ei serba de le facili fanciulle
> La purità ne le regali danze,
> Ne le notturne mascherate, a fronte
> D'amico traditor, d'amante audace;
> Ei le preserva da l'occhiate il giorno,

O da ì bisbigli ne l'oscuro, o quando
Incontro amico il lor desio riscalda,
O pure le titilla il ballo, il canto.[53]

Tis these that early taint the female soul,
Instruct the eyes of young coquettes to roll,
Teach infant cheeks a bidden blush to know,
And little hearts to flutter at a beau.
                    (Canto I. 87-90).

What tender maid but must a victim fall
To one man's treat, but for another's ball?
When Florio speaks, what virgin could withstand,
If gentle Damon did not squeeze her hand?
(Pope, *The Rape of the Lock*, Canto I. 95-98).

With regard to word grouping, the first passage cannot be regarded as successful as the second. The concept of "measured" glances well conveys, however, the point to point plan of the female seductress. It balances with "tenerelli cori", rounding off the section and at the same time restoring a note of innocence. This daring innocence is further conveyed with the choice of "facili fanciulle". The entire social scene is set with the terms "regali danze", "notturne mascherate", "amico traditor", "amante audace": contrasting situations are indicated – the dignity of the "regali danze" is complemented by the term "amante audace" which conveys informality.

The above mentioned ability to convey continuity prevents the tone from becoming monotonous. This is seen in Conti's treatment of Belinda as the central figure in social events. His effect of duration is cleverly achieved in the following passage describing Belinda at the tea-party:

Mentre tazze frequenti in giro porte
Prolungano il piacer del bel convito,
I Silfi non men ch'api a fior novello,
Volan intorno a la guardata Bella."[54]

At once they gratify their scent and taste,
And frequent cups prolong the rich repast.
Straight hover round the fair her airy band;
(Pope, *The Rape of the Lock*, Canto III. 111-113).

Noteworthy is the word choice "in giro porte/prolungano il piacer del bel convito". Time is identified with movement, while the word "piacere" is synonymous with the way of life projected throughout the entire poem. At this point Conti's work departs completely from the realm of translation:— it becomes a piece of spontaneous creativity. In consideration of the influence of Pope on Italian literature one must make the point that Conti's *Il riccio rapito* occupies first place. It cannot be regarded merely as a translation, but as a poem in its own right "after Pope". The work abounds with Conti's original, highly poetic inventions, as, for example, the analogy between Belinda surrounded by Sylphs, and bees around a flower. This from the visual and poetic viewpoint is highly successful. Belinda belongs linguistically to the group of "donne vaghe" of eighteenth-century opera, brought to life by Paisiello and Pergolesi. Unlike Bonducci's projection, Conti's Belinda is completely successful. Through a personification of refinement and manners, the fusion of innocence and wantoness, pride and humility and poetic poise makes her person one of Conti's greatest poetic creations:

> Ne le sue gancie è contemprato il latte
> A le rose. D'intorno al lidio collo
> Sorvolano le Grazie e la splendente
> Croce ch'ei porta maestà gli accresce.
> Sotto i biondi capei, negli occhi neri
> Lieta sfavilla la rinchiusa luce,
> Qual lampo in cielo oscuro ei fere e passa,
> E con l'attività de l'alma scopre
> Gl'instabili pensier, gli erranti affetti.
> Non schiva ella è negli atti, e se rigetta
> Non offende o rattrista, e alcun non osa
> Cercar lusinghe, de'sorrisi pago.
> Non men che il sole i riguardanti fere,
> Ma come il sol a tutti splende eguale.
> Senza sforzo è cortese, senza orgoglio
> E baldanzosa e senza fasto altera,
> E se mai cade in femminile errore,
> Sol che miri il suo volto, il tutto obblii.[55]

> Fair nymphs and well-dressed youths around her shone,
> But every eye was fix'd on her alone.
> On her white breast a sparkling cross she wore,

Which Jews might kiss, and infidels adore.
Her lively looks a sprightly mind disclose,
Quick as her eyes, and as unfix'd as those:
Favours to none, to all she smiles extends;
Oft she rejects, but never once offends.
Bright as the sun, her eyes the gazers strike,
And, like the sun, they shine on all alike.
Yet graceful ease, and sweetness void of pride,
Might hide her faults, if belles had faults to hide:
If to her share some female errors fall,
Look on her face, and you'll forget them all.
(Pope, *The Rape of the Lock*, Canto II. 5-18).

Conti, as he stated in the introduction, believed the Baron to be the real hero of *The Rape of the Lock*. In his hands he becomes rather a dashing, and only slightly treacherous character. He is introduced with a literal translation of Pope. Conti uses the minimum number of words and relies on the strength and effect of verbs:

Un ardito Baron vide i bei crini,
Gli ammirò, gli bramò, volle acquistarli;
Medita tutte l'arti, e al fin prefigge
Rapir a forza od assalir con frode;
Ché, se l'amante ottien ciò che desia,
Poco gli cal se frode adopra o forza.[56]

Here all Pope's humour and irony is captured. The Baron appears a Machiavellian who makes a study of all manners of conquest and finally succeeds as a result of his own expediency. Pope's figure merely "meditates the way", while Conti meditates "tutte l'arti". In the original, Canto III. 1. 116-20 one reads:

Coffee (which makes the politician wise,
And see through all things with his half-shut eyes)
Sent up in vapours to the baron's brain
Now stratagems, the radiant lock to gain. . .
(Pope, *The Rape of the Lock*, Canto III. 117-20).

Conti confers on the coffee the means of sharpening the wit and the intellect, leading to a higher plane of knowledge. The key words here are "l'intelletto aguzza"; "socchiusi lumi", "arcani svela". In contrast to Bonducci's figure, this Baron is an enlightened being, who through Machiavellian expediency arrives at conquest. While it has been

39

stressed that Bonducci's version was successful, it was so in the achievement of an impression akin to that created by the cards. Conti's more academic approach is developed in the lines describing the coffee:

> Caffè, che tanto l'intelletto aguzza
> De'politici e a' lor socchiusi lumi
> Arcani svela a'prenci stessi ignoti.

By using the term "lumi" for eyes, Conti is subtly using an eighteenth-century poetic term to convey both poetry and enlightenment. His translations of "fops" by "cicisbei" at 1.104 and "learned pride" in Canto I. 37 by "Cartesiani e Newtonisti" also illustrate his total identification of the world of *The Rape of the Lock* and that of his own Italian society.

I have stressed the importance of the Baron as a poetic creation of Conti. One finds also that in his version, the lock itself becomes an active force of pride and decorum. While Pope states that the locks "well conspired to deck/With shining ringlets the smooth ivory neck". (Canto II. 21-22). Conti, instead of presenting the locks as "conspiring" to embellish Belinda's neck, makes them compete with each other. Thus feminine ambition is directly transferred from the individual to the object of adornment.

> Ad esterminio de l'umana gente
> Due ciocche di capegli ella nutriva,
> Che torte gentilmente in onde eguali
> Pendevan le di dietro e del bel collo
> Concorreano ad ornare i molli avorj.[57]

Following the cutting of the hair, Conti, in keeping with Pope, conveys to the "sister lock" a bird-like quality:

> Or solitario l'altro riccio siede,
> E nel destin del suo compagno amato
> Prevede il proprio, e rabbuffato chiede
> La forbice fatal.[58]

> The sister-lock now sits uncouth, alone,
> And in its fellow's fate forsees its own;
> (Pope, *The Rape of the Lock*, Canto IV. 171-2).

40

The "sister-lock" is the "compagno amato" which previously competed with and now laments the passing of its twin. It is this projection of life through the "piccole cose della vita" which renders Conti more than a mere translator. And while one observes this introduction of novelty, he never totally departs from the spirit of his master. Can Antonio Conti then be called original poet and translator? A consideration of the following passages demonstrates his claim to both titles:

> Non con più glorie negli eterei campi
> Sul purpureo oceano il sol s'innalza,
> Di quel che la rival de'suoi bei raggi,
> Uscendo lieta del paterno albergo,
> A l'argenteo Tamigi in sen discese
> Accompagnata da vezzose Ninfe
> E da garzoni riccamente adorni;[59]

> Not with more glories, in th'ethereal plain,
> The sun first rises o'er the purpled main,
> Than, issuing forth, the rival of his beams
> Launch'd on the bosom of the silver Thames.
> Fair nymphs and well-dressed youths around her shone,
> But every eye was fix'd on her alone.
> (Pope, *The Rape of the Lock*, Canto II. 1-6).

Here one witnesses Conti the translator at his very best. His version comes close to literal, he manages to create the images projected in the original by means of his vocabulary, creating light imagery, i.e. "gloria", "il sol", "de'suoi bei raggi', "lieta", "argenteo Tamigi". The social reflection of this miracle of nature is seen in the adorned beauty of lords and ladies, wonderfully expressed by Conti by the terms "vezzose ninfe" and "garzoni riccamente adorni". Belinda occupies a central position, not only in being central to the seven line passage, but also because she is visually placed between her "paterno albergo" and the "argenteo Tamigi". Further movement is conveyed by the words "in sen discese". Conti can be said not merely to have translated or transferred the poetry from one tongue to another, but to have brought the scene to life in the Italian language.

In Pope's poem, the toilette occupies a primary position. It is the object with which self-beautification is identified. Conti, instead, allows Belinda to remain protagonist of the canto, and the "dressing-table section" becomes part of the narrative in which Belinda is drawn as the principal image.

> Del letto uscita ella s'invia là dove
> Stanno su la teletta argentei vasi
> In un ordine mistico disposti.
> Pria vestita di bianco a capo nudo
> Adora le cosmetiche potenze.
> Celeste immago ne lo specchio appare
> A cui ella si piega e gli occhi volge.
> Una minor sacerdotessa a lato
> De l'ara giace, e supplice e tremante
> Di vanità comincia i sacri riti.[60]
>
> And now, unveil'd, the toilet stands display'd,
> Each silver vase in mystic order laid,
> First, robed in white, the nymph intent adores,
> With head uncover'd, the cosmetic powers,
> A heav'nly image in the glass appears,
> To that she bends, to that her eye she rears;
> Th' inferior priestess, at her altar's side,
> Trembling, begins the sacred rites of pride.
> (Pope, *The Rape of the Lock*, Canto I. 121-8).

It can be argued that in Conti's translation of the above lines a certain amount of wit is lost — the concept of the toilet unveiled and displayed is lost, while the self-adoration of the nymph is highlighted. There is no other object described which can distract attention from Belinda and her reflection. But while the wit is here undermined, the irony of the situation is emphasised with "giace e supplice e tremante/Di vanità comincia i sacri riti."

Conti's *Il riccio rapito* could indeed be sub-titled "A day in the life of an eighteenth-century Italian lady". There is no doubt that his was the most influential version and that (as will be seen and discussed), it exercised a wide influence on Italian poetry. The passage dedicated to the sylphs, the Court, the tea-party, the game of cards and the cave of spleen will become favourite poetic topics. The cutting of an object of adornment, be it a "tupé" — a lock — or a feather, as in the case of Talassi's *"La piuma recisa"* will become symbolic of attack on a society sporting frivolity and relentless pleasure.

Il riccio rapito is a delightful portrait of a world in which service and aristocratic customs are highlighted. The lady is accompanied by her "cicisbeo",[61] and precise attention to social glitter and the reminder of approaching old age are very much part of the eighteenth-century Italian scene, and their appeal was, as will be seen, immediate.

Conti's knowledge of English customs, fashions and literature, is shown in his notes to the poem. His preparation was complete, his artistic output forms a harmonious unity. His translation conforms to an eighteenth-century Italian creation steeped in the philosophy and idealogy of his time.[62] Conti the philosopher was immediately aware of Pope's implications and how he adapted the natural taste of his time to the projection of a precise and classical image of life:

> Si noti poi che nel periodo inglese il naturale gusto del pittorico e della realtà tradotta in immagini figurative e sensibili entro un colorito rilievo di figura e canto, venne accresciuta dall'esperienza di una cultura più empiristica, dal contatto con un'arte (Addison e Pope) classicistica e razionalistica, ma attentissimo alla realtà sensibile, tesa a captare e tradurre in elegante, classica concisione, impressione della realtà, a descrivere nitidamente ambienti, oggetti, persone, magari in funzione satirica, ma sempre con il compiacimento della rappresentazione perspicua e ben rilevata.[63]

Conti infused classicism and philosophic thought into his translation. The renewed eighteenth-century interest in Renaissance ideals is seen in Conti's opening, in the already discussed felicity of expression and harmony of structure, and in the drawing of the Baron as an intellectually orientated Machiavellian. Pope's opening lines, obviously inspired by Milton, are translated by Conti in lines resembling the catalogue opening of Ariosto's *Orlando furioso*:[64]

> What dire offence from amorous causes springs,
> What mighty contests rise from trivial things,
> I sing —
> (Pope, *The Rape of the Lock*, Canto I. 1-3).

> Canto l'offesa, la vittoria, e 'l pianto,
> Lo sdegno, la battaglia, e la sconfitta,
> Pel riccio tronco, che diè tanta briga
> A' Silfi, a' Gnomi, a l'Ipocondria, al Cielo
> Onde al fin risplendette astro novello.[65]

That Pope's mock-heroic qualities were identified with the classical revival was recognised in Italy as early as 1737. This can be seen with reference to the dedication on a 1737 edition of Tassoni's *La secchia rapita*. The edition is entitled *La secchia rapita*, poema eroicomico del Sig. Allessandro Tassoni, con le dichiarazioni del Sig. Gasparo Salviani accresciute, ed ammendate dal Sig. Abate Marchioni, in Osford, nel Teatro Sceldoniano MDCCXXXVII.[66] Pope's work, then, is a testimony of literary taste and ideological trends during the early "Settecento".

Bonducci's translation is helpful to the student of English, and his frequent exaggerations contribute to the burlesque aspect of his work. However, such concentration on certain aspects of the work robs the piece of poetic unity, it lessens the bite within the satire, and leads to the creation of figures similar to those from the Italian "Commedia dell'arte". "The intention of the poet is spontaneous, primary, graphic; that of the translator is derivative, ultimate, ideational."[67] Perhaps the highest praise one can voice with regard to Conti's translation is that one is not immediately aware of its derivative aspect.

III

The third relevant translation is that of Gian. Vincenzo Benini.[68] It cannot be considered influential within the eighteenth century since it did not appear until 1804. However, it is worthy of consideration. In his "Discorso del traduttore", Benini criticises Conti's translation in the following terms:

> Crediam bensî un dovere quello di ricordare a'nostri Lettori che questo medesimo Poema fu pure in versi sciolti tradotti dal dottissimo abate Conti, e di far loro nel-tempo-stesso sapere che trovasi nella di lui traduzione delle diversità e delle lacune considerabili. Forse l'abate Conti avrà ei tratta la traduzion dalla sua prima edizione che fu riformata in seguito, come appar dall'edizioni susseguenti.[69]

It cannot be argued that Benini makes good any possible omission on the part of Conti. His version is awkward, unpoetic and unattractive. It is reasonably successful in passages of clearcut statement, where elegant turn of phrase is not demanded. This is the case as regards the opening of the poem which is both forceful and effective:

44

Un'offesa crudele e un fier contrasto
Che d'amor nacque e da uno scherzo ardito
Io m'accangio a cantar. Musa, i miei versi
A Carilo consacro, e mi lusingo
Che degnerà di leggerli Belinda.[70]

What dire offence from amorous causes springs,
What mighty contests rise from trivial things,
I sing — This verse to Caryll, Muse! is due:
This, even Belinda may vouchsafe to view;
(Pope, *The Rape of the Lock*, Canto I. 1-4).

The tone is declamatory. The subject of the poem is presented in a clear and uncomplicated manner. However, the result is one of flatness and finality, which in no way prepares us for the fantastic world of belles and beaux. The translator, without the subtlety of the original has presented the dual theme of *The Rape of the Lock*: love and games — "fier contrasto/Che d'amor nacque e da uno scherzo ardito". This awkwardness of approach, lacking in grace and elegance essential to the miniature world of Pope, leads to long descriptions, explanations and narrative, leaving no place for the intuition of the reader. It is true that Pope has merged fact and fantasy, that he fuses the "filagree world" with that of brutal reality:

It is a world in which business goes on and criminals are hanged for all that Belinda is preparing to sit down to ombre. This momentary glimpse of the world of serious affairs, of the world of business and law, of the world of casualness and cruelty, is not introduced merely to shrivel the high concerns of polite society into ironical insignificance, though its effect, of course, is to mock at the seriousness with which the world of fashion takes its affairs.[71]

In fusing the light with the serious, Pope's ability with words impresses. Rather than by what he says, we are intrigued by how he says it. Such is the case with the following extract:

Whether the nymph shall break Diana's law,
Or some frail china-jar receive a flaw;
Or stain her honour or her new brocade;
Forget her prayers, or miss a masquerade;
Or lose her heart, or necklace, at a ball;
Or whether Heaven has doom'd that Shock must fall.
(Pope, *The Rape of the Lock*, Canto II. 105-110).

Benini is unable to kindle the spirit of the original and rise to Pope's highly sophisticated humour. Instead we are left with mere facts, which weigh heavily, altering the tone of the passage:

> No, non si sa se romperà Belinda
> Le leggi di Diana od una tazza,
> Se il core o il vezzo, se un brillante o un nastro
> Se macchierà l'onore o il suo ricamo,
> Smarrirà nella danza, o se trafitta
> Fia d'aspro detto o da una spilla, o se
> Cadrà Mirino od un guancial dal letto.[72]

Benini attempts to assume Pope's technique with "cadrà Mirino od un guancial", but his placing of the verbs "macchierà", "smarrirà" and "cadrà" at the beginning of the line, in my opinion overloads the concept, and robs the poetry of the essential lightness. The same weakness, I believe, is demonstrated in the following moralising passage in Canto V. Pope stresses preservation by good sense, his emphasis is on continuity. Here the translator has missed the point:

> Funesta gloria, se lo spirito perde
> Ciò che acquista beltà, e se non ponno
> Gli uomini dir, nel rimirarci in volto,
> Ella è prima in virtù come in bellezza!
> Se l'ingegno e lo studio e l'arte e l'opra
> Che usiamo noi per affilar i dardi
> De'nostri vezzi, ed appagar il fasto
> Del nostro cor, difender ci potesse
> Dalle ruine che i scorrevoli anni
> Fanci agli occhi, alle guancie, al petto, al crine.[73]

> How vain are all these glories, all our pains,
> Unless good sense preserve what beauty gains;
> That men may say, when we the front-box grace,
> 'Behold the first in virtue as in face!'
> Oh! if to dance all night, and dress all day,
> Charm'd the small-pox, or chased old age away.
> (Pope, *The Rape of the Lock*, Canto V. 15-20).

Pope, with regard to the concept of preservation arrives at a subtle duplicity of intention: he illustrates how by good sense virtue can be preserved, while underlining the fact that no amount of cosmetic treatment or reckless enjoyment can turn back the clock on time.

These opposites and identifications fail to come across in the Benini work, continuity is not stressed, while a certain amount of exaggeration is employed in the lines "Se l'ingegno e lo studio e l'arte e l'opra /Fanci agli occhi, alle guancie, al petto, al crine". The movement, charm and activity conveyed by the juxtaposition of "night and day" in Pope and the alliteration as regards "dance", "dress" are missing, as is the fusion of possibility with the inevitable in the lines: "Charm'd the small-pox, or chased old age away". Gian-Vincenzo Benini, I believe, is unable to objectively assess and reproduce specific linguistic functions in Pope, nor is he able then to identify his effort in its totality, with the original. In the following passage he aims merely at a literal translation:

> Sappi dunque che a te giransi intorno
> Legioni innumerabili di spirti
> Agil milizia delle basse sfere
> Che, invisibili sì ma fidi, ovunque
> Trovansi teco ossia che vegli o dorma
> O pensi o scriva, o canti o giuochi, o vada
> Alla corte, al teatro, al parco, al corso:
> Un sì nobil corteggio in mente volgi,
> E non più mirerai che con dispregio
> L'aurea lettica e i gallonati paggi.[74]

> Know, then, unnumbered spirits round thee fly,
> The light militia of the lower sky:
> These, though unseen, are ever on the wing,
> Hang o'er the box, and hover round the ring.
> Think what an equipage thou hast in air,
> And view with scorn two pages and a chair.
> (Pope, *The Rape of the Lock*, Canto I. 1. 41-6).

The first seven lines do in fact reproduce Pope's passage faithfully. The word choice is often apt, as in the case of "agil milizia", "basse sfere", "nobil corteggio", but the translator fails to condense his thoughts, and is unable to reproduce the equivalent of "Hang o'er the box, and hover round the ring". The lines:

> Trovansi teco ossia che vegli o dorma
> O pensi o scriva, o canti o giuochi, o vada
> Alla corte, al teatro, al parco, al corso:

47

give way to monotony, while the concluding lines of the passage which in Pope create mild ridicule, in Benini appear both awkward and senseless. Giacomo Zanella calls this translation by Benini "roba da fuoco".[75] While not sharing his view completely, one must admit that it is the least satisfactory of the eighteenth century versions as a result of its lack of poetic freedom. However, it is not without its more successful moments, as I believe reference to the "toletta" sequence, the coffee making, and the passage introducing the Baron demonstrates. It is in the latter passage that I find Benini at his best: concise, poised, snappy and above all successful in capturing the spirit of Pope:

> Un ardito Baron vede i bei ricci,
> Li vede, li contempla, e ammira e brama
> E medita di farne il grande acquisto,
> Usando della forza o delle frode;
> Che i desir suoi pur che l'amante ottenga,
> E l'una e l'altra, indifferente, adopra.
> Th' adventurous Baron the bright locks admired;
> He saw, he wish'd, and to the prize aspired.
> Resolved to win, he meditates the way,
> By force to ravish, or by fraud betray;
> For when success a lover's toil attends,
> Few ask, if fraud or force attain'd his ends.[76]
> (Pope, *The Rape of the Lock*, Canto II. 29-34).

It can be argued that at this point Benini had Conti's translation before his eyes[77] — there is a certain similarity with regard to word choice, i.e. "ardito Baron", "medita". Conti translates "a lover's toil" with "ciò che desia", Benini with "i desir suoi"; yet Benini's turn of phrase is fluent, spanning the entire psychological disposition of the Baron — "Li vede, li contempla, e ammira e brama — E l'una e l'altra indifferente adopra".

The same precision and conciseness combined with oriental splendour pervades the description of articles on the dressing-table. Pope manages to create the impression of "shrinking" both elephant and tortoise in order to create for them a new refinement of existance. Benini, on the other hand, by exaggerated exotic imagery provides the beauty aids on a larger-than-life scale, the pins become squadrons. Set for action to protect against the wear and tear of everyday life, powders and pastes unite in the defence of the nymph:

Qui brillan ne'scrignetti indiche gemme;
Là olezzan ne'cristalli arabi odori;
La tartaruga e l'elefante in varj
Pettini si trasformano; di spille
Veggonsi e d'aghi lucidi squadroni,
E confondosi insieme e polvi e paste
E, colla Bibbia, romanzeschi fogli.[78]

This casket India's glowing gems unlocks,
And all Arabia breathes from yonder box.
The tortoise here and elephant unite,
Transformed to combs, the speckled and the white.
Here files of pins extend their shining rows,
Puffs, powders, patches, Bibles, billet-doux.
(Pope, *The Rape of the Lock*, Canto I. 13308).

Benini has here succeeded in combining the light and the serious. Pope's 1.138 points to dainty confusion, the translation points to a more concious effort: "E, colla Bibbia, romanzeschi fogli". The exotic aura of 1. 133-4 contrast with the silver of the pins within the jewel-case. The same exoticism is present in Benini's lines on coffee-making, though there is the effect of fragmentation, as though the translator was not capable of conceiving the passage as a unified whole. Each line is divided in terms of concept, which conveys a certain lack of complexity:

Ma di chinesi tazze ecco coperto
Un piccol desco: crepitar già sode
Il molinello; l'arabo legume
In polve cade; azzurra fiamma sorge
Su giapponese altar; bollente l'acqua
La polve attende, il liquor bruno è pronto
Che diletta due sensi; argenteo vaso
Lo porge alla brigata: a sorso a sorso
Si bee con pause necessarie e grate;
Si loda Moka e si censura il Mondo.[79]

For lo! the board with cups and spoons is crown'd,
The berries crackle, and the mill turns round:
On shining altars of Japan they raise
The silver lamp; the fiery spirits blaze:
From silver spouts the grateful liquors glide,
While China's earth receives the smoking tide:

At once they gratify their scent and taste,
And frequent cups prolong the rich repast.
(Pope, *The Rape of the Lock*, Canto III. 105-112).

Pope's passage can, I believe, be termed as descriptive narrative. Benini's falls into the category of descriptive demonstration, comprising of the colourful demonstration of a series of objects, i.e. "un piccol desco", "il molinello", "l'arabo legume", "azzurra fiamma", "giapponese altar", "bollente acqua", "argenteo vaso". Once again the miniature world of Pope yields to a broader and less delicate civilisation.

Benini's translation cannot be defined as totally literal or poetic. At times it verges on the absurd, while on occasions, as has been illustrated, it can be both forceful and effective with apt word-choice. When the pervading mood of the original is not recaptured the result often creates an impression of exaggeration and fragmentation. One must bear in mind, however, that each translation marks a point in the continued life of the original. To Gian-Vincenzo Benini belongs the dubious distinction of presenting Pope to nineteenth-century readers. His translation appeared at a time when Pope's Italian popularity was beginning to wane. Soon *The Rape of the Lock* would be seen as a period piece and a mere reflection of rococo delicacy. Pope's reputation in Italy was wide, particularly in his own century — the eighteenth century. The nineteenth-century reaction against rationalism, in Italy as in England, somewhat diminished the great poet's fame, but the process was considerably slower in Italy. Admiration for him continued strong past the middle of the nineteenth century. One must, however, bear in mind that the final significance of the translators of Pope cannot be assessed merely by considering them in relation to their original, or by criticising the translation techniques employed. They must also be seen in the light of their influence on the various literary genres and their contribution to poetic language.

In *Preromanticismo italiano* Walter Binni pinpoints the pre-Romantic translations as the source of a new poetic language. The original work, its transference to the Italian tongue and its stylistic influence mark a new trend in imagery and thought: "con limitazioni che privano i testi originali della loro vera forza di novità;"[80]

I traduttori costruirono le loro opere (e molto spesso anche tale spunto potè mancare alla loro personale cultura) ed offrirono al pubblico italiano dei pastiches bizzari che pure furono capaci di iniziare una nuova maniera poetica, di dare il primo urto ad una lingua poetica vissuta in un clima di equilibrio di calma che questa prima ventata romantica incrina.[81]

Beyond all shade of doubt, Binni believes that in eighteenth-century literature, in the new pursuit of fantasy tempered by Classicism, the projection of mythology, added to social grace, finds its influence in pre-Romantic translation. He openly refers to the influence of Pope in this respect:

E si veda come nel classicismo razionalistico popiano gli italiani potessero assorbire stimoli ambiguamente preromantici (Abelardo ed Eloisa, Le quattro stagioni) e, ad ogni modo, stimoli ad un classicismo ricco del senso della realtà che operò soprattutto a metà secolo, e un gusto dell'evidenza sensoriale meno presente nella Arcadia metastasiana e cartesiana.[82]

The most striking aspect of Pope's *The Rape of the Lock* and of Conti's translation is the use of scale to convey the precision of the miniature. This, I believe, is reflected in the classical minuteness of the works of Ludovico Fontana Savioli and Parini. Conti's contribution has indeed been to demonstrate society in miniature, which readers immediately identify with the eighteenth century. What must be remembered is that Conti's translation, dating from his English sojourn, represents the reproduction in Italian of the English genre of Pope first appearing in 1713, and in a revised version in 1714. Shortly after its appearance in Italy in 1756, there follows a sequence of poems representing the "bel mondo". Savioli's *Amori* appeared in 1758, followed by a revised version in 1765. In the meantime, Parini's *Il mattino* and *Il mezzogiorno* had made its appearance in 1763 and Muttinelli's *La sera* in 1767. This was followed in 1768 by Durante's *Il mattino d'Elisa*, while Vittorelli's *Il tupé*, symbolised for the first time an entire society by an object of artifice and embellishment, the "tupé"-lock or wig. Close influence of Pope can also be noted in Clemente Bondi's *La moda* of 1777, while the mock-heroic *La piuma recisa* of Angelo Talassi and *La treccia rubata* of Lorenzo Pignotti are examples of the lengthy mock-heroic genre based on Pope.

The translations of Bonducci and Conti can be regarded then as significant with regard to the reproduction of the English social satire in eighteenth-century Italy, and also with regard to their influence on eighteenth-century poetic genre and language. Benini's version comes too late to be regarded as a significant work, but it is of historic value as an eighteenth-century exercise presenting Pope at a time when the social graces and gaiety of *The Rape of the Lock* were but a memory.

Notes to Chapter I

1 G.S. Rousseau ed. *Twentieth Century Interpretations of the Rape of the Lock* (London, 1969) p. 3.

2 G. Toaldo, "Notizie intorno la vita e gli studi del Sig. Abate Conti", in *Prose e poesie*, II (Venice, 1756). pp. 62-63. Although the translation was prepared for publication in 1739, it did not appear until 1756, in the second volume of Toaldo. Conti's version was published in England in 1751 under the following title: *Il riccio rapito, poema del Signor Alessandro Pope tradotto d'inglese dal Signor Antonio Conti patrizio veneto*, in *il Conte Gabali ovvero ragionamenti sulle science segrete tradotti dal Francese da una Dama italiana*, Londra, Dal Pickard, MDCCLI. It was reprinted in 1800: *Il riccio rapito*, poema eroi-comico di Alessandro Pope, (London, Parma, 1800). Two MS drafts exist: 1) MS Bocchi n. 58/S3-100-F in the Biblioteca Comunale in Treviso 2) MS Manin 1354, Priuli n. 189, t. VII in the Biblioteca Comunale in Udine. For some accounts of Conti's life see the *Vita* prefaced to the second volume of *Prose e poesie* (Venice, 1756) pp. 1-308; G. Brognolino, "L'opera letteraria di Antonio Conti" in *Ateneo Veneto*, XVII, (1893) pp. 162-79 327-50; XVIII (1894) pp. 137-209, 260-310, 49-84; Delmac Hamm, "Conti and the English aesthetics" in *Comparative Literature* VII (1956); Nicola Badaloni, *Antonio Conti − un abate libero pensatore tra Newton e Voltaire* (Milan, 1968).

3 B. Moloney, *Relazioni tra la Toscana e l'Inghilterra nel settecento* (Florence, 1969) p. 151.

4 "Per la morte della maestà della Regina Anna d'Inghilterra," Florence, Biblioteca Nazionale, MS Palatini 1081. The printed catalogue names the MS as Palatini 1107XX.

5 G. Carducci, *Storia del Giorno*, p. 125.

6 A. Conti, *Prose e poesie* II (Venice, 1756).

7 G. Lenta, *Pope in Italia e "Il riccio rapito"* (Florence, 1931).

8 "Vanne ad Elisa, e a rimirar t'appresta
Donna bella qual Diva,
Che incerverisce, e avviva
Illustri cori con accesi strali,
E pigre menti alle bell'opre desta.
Inchinati a costei
Nata da semidei
Per soave piacer di noi mortali,
Ove quasi in sua fede
Bellezza, ed onestà splender si vede".

9 Giuseppe Maria Buondelmonti, b. Florence 1713, d. Pisa 1757. Orator philosopher and poet. Suspected of being a member of the Masons. Bib: G.M. Mazzuchelli, *Scrittori d'Italia* II, IV (Brescia, 1763); F. Inghirami, *Storia della Toscana* (Fiesole, 1844); F. Sbigoli, *Tommaso Crudeli* (Milan, 1884).

10 A. Bonducci, *Il riccio rapito* (Florence, 1739). p. 7.

11 Ibid. p. 5.

12 Ibid. pp. 15-17.

13 Ibid. p. 21.

14 J.S. Cunningham, Pope, *The Rape of the Lock* (London, 1961).

15 Ibid. p. 57.

16 A. Bonducci, op.cit., p. 30, 1. 2-9. The 1739 edition provides no line references. For the convenience of the reader however I provide line references for the page in question.

17 Ibid. pp. 33-34. p. 33, 1. 23-6, p. 34, 1. 1.

18 Ibid. p. 54, 1. 16-26.

19 Ibid. p. 30, 1. 17-23, p. 31, 1. 1.

20 A. Bonducci, op.cit., p. 38, 1. 1-6.

21 Ibid. pp. 35-6, p. 35, 1. 18-26, p. 36, 1. 1-3.

22 See Ferruccio Ulivi, *Settecento neoclassico* (Pisa, 1957) pp. 191-3 for a comparison between Bonducci and Conti in the final passage of Canto I.

23 See Venice, Biblioteca Marciana, MS CL. 9, n. 404, col. 7018 (anon.) "Il gioco dell'ombra".

"L'Ungaro, il Franco ed il Prussiano, in tre
giocano all'ombre, il terzo ha la Spadiglia
casco disse ai compagni: ei casca asse.
– – – – – – – – – e una maniglie.
Gioca Teresa, ed ei le taglia un zè.
Sopra ciò si lusinga, e si consiglia
ma il re di Francia a trionfo si diè.
Grida il crasso mi do, ma non la piglia.
Ha giocato il Prussian a mattadori
ha il cont'ombre in Tonacca e in suo periglio.
Non ha Trionfi, e non ha base agl'ori
ed il Franco Signor darà il codiglio–".

24 A. Bonducci, op.cit., p. 40, 1. 6-15.

25 Ibid. pp. 40-1, p. 40, 1. 20-6, p. 41, 1. 1.

26 Ibid. p. 55, 1. 10-15.

27 Ibid. p. 57, 1. 18-20.

28 Ibid. p. 58, 1. 7-14.

29 Ibid. p. 50, 1. 18-24.

30 Ibid. p. 51, 1. 7-14.

31 Ibid. p. 28, 1. 1-5.

32 Ibid. p. 28, 1. 6-8.

33 Ibid. p. 75, 1. 1-3.
34 Ibid. p. 45, 1. 8-12.
35 Ibid. p. 48, 1. 10-12.
36 Ibid. p. 32, 1. 1-4.
37 Ibid. p. 32, 1. 13-16.
38 Ibid. p. 27, 1. 1-5.
39 Ibid. pp. 29-30, p. 29, 1. 19-26, p. 30, 1. 1.
40 G. Gronda, "Le versioni poetiche di Antonio Conti" in *G.S.L.A.* 147 (1970) p. 307.
41 *Poesie e prose* (Venice, 1756) p. 37.
42 G. Dorris, *Paolo Rolli and the Italian Circle in London, 1715-1744* (The Hague. Paris, 1967) p. 215.
43 G. Gronda, "Le versioni poetiche di A. Conti", op. cit., pp. 308-9.
44 A. Conti, Udine, Biblioteca Comunale MS Manin 1354, Priuli n. 189, T. VII, published in G. Gronda, *Antonio Conti, versioni poetiche*, (Bari, 1966) p. 617. In my references I adher to the eighteenth-century convention of providing capital letters at the commencement of each line.
45 Ibid.
46 G. Gronda, *Antonio Conti, versioni poetiche*, op.cit., p. 43, 1. 55-59.
47 Ibid. p. 59, 1. 158-63.
48 Ibid. p. 59, 1. 164-8.
49 Giulio Natali, *Il Settecento* I (Milan, 1964) pp. 64-65.
50 Ibid. p. 65.
51 G. Gronda, *A. Conti, versioni poetiche*, op.cit., p. 584.
52 Ibid. p. 44, 1. 111-6.
53 Ibid. p. 45, 1. 120-127.
54 Ibid. p. 58, 1. 138-141.
55 Ibid. p. 48, 1. 9-26.
56 Ibid. p. 49, 1. 39-44.
57 Ibid. p. 49, 1. 27-31.
58 Ibid. p. 68, 1. 218-21.
59 Ibid. p. 48, 1. 1-7.
60 Ibid. pp. 46-7, 1. 178-87.
61 G. Natali, *Il Settecento* I, op. cit., pp. 58-60.
62 For a study of Conti as philosopher and thinker see: Nicola Badaloni, *Antonio Conti, Un abate libero pensatore tra Newton e Voltaire* (Milan 1968).
63 Mario Praz, *Storia della letteratura inglese*, op.cit., p. 39.
64 "Le donne, i cavalier, l'arme, gli amori,
   Le cortesie, l'audaci imprese io canto".

   Orlando Furioso, edited by Caretti (Milan 1954) p. 19.
65 G. Gronda, *Antonio Conti, versioni poetiche*, op. cit., p. 41, 1.
66 The dedication reads: "Al Sig. Pope Poeta Famosissimo. Fra tutte le opere del Tassoni questa vien universalmente commendata; sì per l'invenzione del tutto nuova appresso i Moderni, e l'ingegnosa tessitura che gl'inten-

denti vi ammirano, sì per l'artificosa mescolanza del grande e del burlesco, donde nascono insieme (non so dire qual maggiore) diletto, e maraviglia. Questo vago componimento par che sia naturale indirizzarlo all'Autore del leggiadrissimo poemetto *La treccia rapita*. Sì grandi, ma sì diverse son le bellezze che campeggiano in quelle due opere, che sarebbe difficile assai il farne un paragone. In quanto agli Autori, cospicua in vero è la differenza. Il Tassoni non inoltrossi più avanti nella poesia, pago della fama che gli recò la sua Secchia, laddove Voss. stimolata da nobil estro andò cogliendo nuovi allori, non essendo *La treccia rapita* ch'un raggio dello splendore che le vostre immortali fatiche hanno dato al gran nome di Pope. Si degni Voss d'accettare cortesemente questa correttissima edizione del Tassoni; e mi sia lecito, benchè non abbia l'onore di conoscer un vostro pari, di sottoscrivermi con osservanza. Di Vossignoria illustrissima, Umilissimo Servo Giovanni Fabro". One notes that since no Italian translation of Pope was in circulation at that time, the literal translation of the title is used rather than the one which later entered common usage, i.e. *Il riccio rapito.*

67   Walter Benjamin, "The task of the translator", an introduction to the translation of Baudelaire's *Tableaux Parisiens,* in *Illuminations* (Fontana) (Glasgow, 1973) pp. 76-7.

68   Gian Vincenzo Benini, in Arcadia Creofilo Sminteo, b. Bologna 1713, d. 1764. Doctor, writer and translator. Best known for his translations of the latin poem *La sifilide* by Fracastoro, and of Alexander Pope: *Saggio sull'uomo* (Venice, 1788), *Principi del buon gusto* (Padua, 1792), *Eloisa ad Abelardo* (1804), *Il riccio rapito* (1803). editions: *l Capi d'Opera di Alessandro Pope* (Venice, 1825); unpublished autographed letters to the abate Giovanni Brunacci, Padova, in Forlì, Biblioteca Comunale (MS Piancastelli).

69   *Capi d'Opera di Alessandro Pope,* II (Venice, 1825) p. 235. This edition does not provide line references. For the convenience of the reader, line references per page will be given.

70   Ibid. p. 155. 1. 1-5.

71   Cleanth Brooks. "The case of Miss Arabella Fermor", in *Pope, A Collection of Critical Essays,* edited by Guerinot. (New Jersey, 1972). p. 110.

72   G.V. Benini, *Capi d'Opera di A. Pope,* op.cit., pp. 133-4. p. 133, 1. 20-24, p. 134, 1. 1-2.

73   Ibid. p. 165, 1. 13-22.

74   G.V. Benini, *Capi d'Opera di A. Pope,* op.cit., pp. 118-9. p. 118, 1. 17-24, p. 119. 1. 1-2.

75   G. Zanella "Alessandro Pope e Antonio Conti" in *Nuova antologia,* II XXXIV (1882). p. 18. Reprint (Verona, 1885).

76   G.V. Benini, *Capi d'Opera di A. Pope,* op.cit., p. 129, 1. 8-13.

77   "Un ardito Baron vide i bei crini,
     Gli ammirò, gli bramò, volle acquistarli;
     Medita tutte l'arti, e al fin prefigge
     Rapir a forza od assalir con frode;

Chè, se l'amante ottien ciò che desia,
Poco gli cal se frode adopra o forza."

G. Gronda, *A. Conti, versioni poetiche*, p. 49, 1. 39-44.
78 G.V. Benini, *Capi d'Opera di A. Pope*, op.cit., p. 124, 1. 6-12.
79 Ibid. pp. 143-4. p. 143 1. 17-24. p. 144. 1. 1-2.
80 Walter Binni, *Preromanticismo italiano*, (Rome, Bari, 1974) p. 129.
81 Ibid., p. 135.
82 W. Binni, *Classicismo e neoclassicismo nella letteratura del settecento* (Florence, 1963).

CHAPTER II

The Eighteenth-Century Poetic Miniature

1

Pope's influence on eighteenth-century Italian literature is considerable, his cultivation of the world of the miniature sets up a double view of a play-world which has the smallness of scale and fineness of organisation of a work of art. The dressing-table sequence, reproduced again and again in Italian literature represents both social order and self-adornment. "Belinda's world. . .is preoccupied with ceremonies. These are sometimes beautiful, sometimes absurd, never innocent. . . At the dressing-table Belinda prepares for conquest".[1] The same ritual and ceremony is identified with the Sylphs, who also find a place in the writings of Pope's imitators. They guard ephemeral beauties: china jars and honour. These translucent, fluttering spirits presume, and assume that a coquette's life is "pure game". Other aspects of this "pure game" are seen in social activities such as the tea-party, the game of ombre and the sheer boredom of it all. The final ambiguity is contained in the fact that hair, the lock, or the "tupé", as the case may be, must be guarded. It symbolises honour, defended by Sylphs acting for social convention. It cannot be kept forever, and at a certain point must be discarded. Towards the end of the century, in the hands of Angelo Talassi and Lorenzo Pignotti, the ornament becomes synonomous with pride, stupidity and the artifice of a decadent society wallowing in its final spell of glory.

Such a literature coincided with the publication in Italy of Conti's *Il riccio rapito*. In the light of such a fact, the influence of Pope cannot be ignored:

Eppure, nonostante il ritardo con cui esse furono pubblicate, le traduzioni contiane e quella del *Riccio rapito* in particolare ebbero un loro circoscritto ma concreto influsso sulla poesia italiana. Costituirono all'interno di una tradizione letteraria arcadica e classicistica un' apertura senza urti, un passaggio che nel suo essere e rimanere quasi inavvertito, apportava alla stilizzata poetica italiana forme e contenuti nuovi che essa poteva accettare: un gusto più preciso e concreto della parola e della cosa, una tensione di ironia ed una adesione più diretta nei confronti della realtà osservata sia pure attraverso la mediazione letteraria, più attentamente e da vicino; il che si rivela anche sul piano linguistico nella precisione e nell'arricchimento del contemporaneo vocabolario poetico.[2]

The task of conveying a sense of morality to the world of the rococo miniature belongs to Parini, who in *Il giorno* combines the sensitivity and precision of Pope, with biting irony. For him the "bel mondo" and its social occasions no longer appear a sophisticated game, but corruption and decadence. Prior to the appearance of the first part of *Il giorno*, namely *Il mattino*, the first edition of Ludovico Savioli's *Amori* came into print:

Sull'incontro di uno sviluppo più deciso del rococò (passato nella moda più vulgata delle cosîdette arti applicate e proprio nei termini di una società più chiaramente francesizzante dopo quella più incerta del primo Settecento, più meridionale e ancora ricca di magnificenza spagnolesca ed imperiale) e di una mentalità illuministico-sensistica nella sua divulgazione più galante ed edonistica e di una lettura di classici da boudoir (più Ovidio ed Orazio e gli elegiaci che Pindaro od Omero) appoggiata alla nuova passione per i cammei e per le pitture ercolanensi, l'esperienza poetica di Ludovico Savioli rappresenta senza dubbio un momento essenziale nella cultura letteraria settecentesca.[3]

Savioli was born in Bologna in 1729. He was educated at Jesuit schools, and privately by Ferdinando Ghedini and Angelo Michele Rota. In 1744 he entered Arcadia with the name of Lavisio Eginetico. In 1758 he published the first twelve "canzonette" entitled *Amori*, in Venice. While his education was purely classical, some of his poems bear witness to his interest in English literature. *Il passeggio* contains a reference to Addison's *Spectator*, while *La disperazione* projects gloom and melancholy akin to Young. *Il mattino* and *La maschera* bear witness to Savioli's reading and study of Pope.

Il passeggio contains a delightful reference to that object of utility and decorum which came into its own in the eighteenth century — the fan. It is seen as the inviter of breezes, the delicate mistress of movement, the technique of which is indicated and illustrated in the English paper *The Spectator*:

Risvegliator di zefiri
Ventaglio avea la manca,
Onde solea percotere
Lieve la gota bianca.
Ne'moti or lenti, or rapidi
Arte apparia maestra;
Lo Spettator dell'Anglia
Così le Belle addestra.[4]

Savioli's reference to *The Spectator* is as a result of an article by
Addison which appeared in the paper No. 102, of June 27, 1711,
which stated that ladies were armed with fans, as were gentlemen
with swords. It went on to say that in order that ladies be trained in
the proper use of the fan, the writer had founded an academy, which
would impart the most fashionable movements and gestures in vogue
at Court.[5] Savioli's world, in the *Amori*, is that of mannered frivolity
and refined extravaganza, rendered "serious" and intellectually
orientated by classical references, and mythological associations. Yet
in *Il passeggio* Savioli never departs from the world of the cameo and
miniature:

Nei suoi *Amori* (1765), che godettero di un'immensa fortuna, i riti e le varie
vicende delle avventure galanti, i sospiri, le civetterie, e le gelosie delle da-
mine incipriate, l'eleganza dei salotti, i segreti della toeletta, il fascino del
teatro e delle danze, il passeggio e la villeggiatura, tutto il rituale raffinato
insomma della società elegante del Settecento, messa da parte la finzione
pastorale, preferisce avvolgersi in un tenue velo di grazie classicheggianti e
riflettersi trasfigurato nella serena gentilezza delle rievocazioni mitologiche.[6]

Emotion is curbed and restrained in an atmosphere of delicate simplicity. Harmony of sight and sound and the lately experienced fires
of love render the poet powerless to express his true feelings. Refined
restraint is provided by the metre, first used by Rota, Savioli's teacher in 1746, and believed by the same the most suitable for translating
Roman elegies.[7] The projection of emotional restraint is, I believe,
well illustrated by the quotation of the following lines:

Quei vaghi occhi cerulei
Movea frattanto Amore;
Rette per lui scendevano
Le dolci note al core.

Come potrei ripetere
Quel ch'a me udir fu dato?
Dal novo foco insolito
Troppo era il cor turbato.[8]

When *Il mattino*, (the third of the *Amori*) first appeared in 1758, it did so with the title *Alla fanciulla che si adorna*. By the time it made its second printed appearance, Parini's *Il mattino* had already been published two years previously. While not containing a word-for-word reproduction of Pope, nevertheless the breaking of dawn, the ritual at the mirror, the dressing of the hair and the identification of the lady with dawn – (Pope compares Belinda to the Sun) reflect the spirit and world of Pope. The opening lines of *Il mattino* emphasise the importance of light in the poem, the contrast of light and shade, and the emergence from nocturnal prison:

Già col meriggio accelera
L'ora compagna il piede,
E già l'incalza, e stimola
Nova, che a lei succede.
Entra la luce, e rapida
Empie le stanze intorno:
Il pigro sonno involisi,
Apri i begli occhi al giorno.[9]

By means of refined precision, Savioli has succeeded in creating an atmosphere of activity and an impression of space: the verbs "accelera", "incalza", "stimola" create bustle, coming to a climax in the lines:

Entra la luce, e rapida
Empie le stanze intorno:

The impression of space is achieved by "empie le stanze intorno". The only indirect reference to human presence also continues the light imagery. One records that the penetration of light occupies the opening section of *The Rape of the Lock*. However universality on a miniature scale is arrived at in *Il mattino* with reference to the chocolate consumed on wakening: Pope achieved the same effect with reference to coffee-making, and to the articles on the dressing-table:

On shining altars of Japan they raise
The silver lamp; the fiery spirits blaze:
From silver spouts the grateful liquors glide,
While China's earth receives the smoking tide.
The Rape of the Lock (Canto III. 107-110).

This casket India's glowing gems unlocks,
And all Arabia breathes from yonder box.
The tortoise here and elephant unite,
Transform'd to combs, the speckled and the white.
The Rape of the Lock (Canto I. 133-6).

Japan and China unite with regard to grinding and pouring coffee. India and Arabia appear side by side in minute, ornate caskets. Savioli's lines contain a simplicity, and demonstrate an art concealing art which render Pope's lines in comparison, exaggerated.

Cinese tazza eserciti
Beata il suo costume,
E il roseo labbro oscurino
Le Americane spume.[10]

From this point in the poem the classical references abound, and the genteel lightness of the lines is somewhat diminished. The Graces assist, resulting in the transformation of the "ninfa" into a grace:

S'erge segreto un Tempio
Dell'ampie coltri a lato:
Là tue bellezze aspettano
Il sacrifizio usato.
Vieni, sia fausta Venere,
Gli uffizi Amor comparta,
Le Grazie in piedi assistano;
Tu sederai la quarta.[11]

In other words, the miniate world of *Il mattino*, rather than becoming totally identified with the eighteenth-century "bel mondo", achieves perfection by identifying with the world of classicism. The temple of beauty has replaced the "toletta" and the lines on hairdressing provide the final contact with society of the day:

Ma già tuo dolce imperio
La fida ancella invita;
Ella s'appressa e all'opera

Stende la destra ardita.
Già dal notturno carcere
I crini aurei sprigiona
Ed all'eburneo pettine
Gl'indocili abbandona.[12]

While for Pope, and some later Indian imitators, the "bel mondo" of
the Settecento provided the setting for situations of amorous intrigue,
Savioli saw it merely as the point of departure. Perfection in his
world consisted of the identification with the lifeless and timeless,
and the transformation of the "belle" into a finely chiselled statuette. "La società settecentesca vi è ritratta solo superficialmente, con
l'aerea ed inconsistente grazia che essa stessa suggeriva, e tende a farsi
sempre più astratta nel continuo riferimento mitologico che l'appe-
santisce di improprie decorazioni, seppellendola nei fronzoli di cui
essa certo non difettava."[13]

Il mattino or *Alla fanciulla che si adorna* has an historical significance. Following closely on Conti's *Il riccio rapito*, and in keeping
with its first Canto, it describes the beginning of a day in the life of a
lady. If *Il mattino* reflects the spirit of Pope, *La maschera* represents
an entire scene from *The Rape of the Lock*, with the reproduction of
some of his lines and a comment on the fate of "la minacciata inglese". The lock becomes for Savioli "la maschera", worn by the girl,
literally seen as an object of pride, and symbolising virginity. Pride is
finally conquered by love, but its cutting against the maiden's wishes
is seen as a punishment for a refusal to fall in love. *La maschera* contains Savioli's interpretation of *The Rape of the Lock*, and stresses
the passing of youth, as does Pope's poem. It consists of 76 lines
and the references to *The Rape of the Lock* begin at line 44. To that
point it is an appraisal of beauty and its fleeting quality, abounding
in classical references:

A che lo sguardo immobile
Nella parete hai fiso,
E sulle braccia appoggiasi
Languente il caro viso?
Godi, se sai, ché t'aprono
L'aspetto e gli anni il campo:
Ahi! le bellezze passano,
La gioventude è un lampo.[14]

Savioli takes his departure from the static image, and extends his vision to an Ovidian view of life. The second stanza originates in Ovid, *Art of Love* (11. 113-6):

> Forma bonum fragile est,/quantumque accedit
> ad annos/fit minor et spatio carpitur ipsa suo:
> Nec violae semper nec hiantia lilia florent,
> Et riget amissa spina relicta rosa.

From an abstract view of being, Savioli turns his attention to the world of the carnival, held in ancient times in honour of Bacchus, and identifies it with Venetian festivities: —

> Festeggia a gara il popolo
> Dell'ebbro Dio sull'orme:
> Le vesti ora si cangiano.
> E i volti in mille forme.
> Di queste una sull'Adria
> Dall'indolenza nacque:
> Di libertà lo studio
> Vi si conobbe, e piacque.[15]

The sense of immediacy is lost with the classical association and the use of the abstract "indolenza" and "libertà", yet the world of the mask is perfectly evoked in the lines:

> Festeggia a gara il popolo —
> Le vesti ora si cangiano.
> E i volti in mille forme.

The central image in the poem remains the lady of the opening stanza, identified with classical beauty and activity, and for the second section of the poem with Belinda, the heroine of *The Rape of the Lock*. As in Pope's poem, she is guarded by Sylphs, who provide Savioli with a new genre of mythology deriving not from the classical legends of Greece and Rome, but from Le Conte de Gabalis (1670), by the Abbé de Villans. In *La maschera* they are thus introduced:

> Mille a te Silfi accorrono
> In sulle lucid' ali,
> Diva progenie aerea,
> Che sfugge occhi mortali.

Ne'più remoti secoli
Giacque oziosa e oscura;
Oggi del sesso amabile
Commessa è a lor la cura.[16]

In 1756, Antonio Conti's version appeared for the first time in Italy. His introduction to the Sylphs is as follows:

Sappi dunque che a te vola d'intorno
Falange innumerabile di spirti,
Agil milizia del più basso cielo;
Amanti, ed invisibili ministri
Stanno su l'ali in tuo servigio pronti.[17]

Andrea Bonducci, whose work appeared as early as 1739, renders the same passages in a slightly less controlled manner:

Or sappi dunque, che al tuo corpo intorno
Vola di spirti innumerabil schiera,
Lieve milizia del più basso cielo;
Questi agli sguardi tuoi benchè nascosi
Stanno sempre su l'ale, ...[18]

The concept of transparency and invisibility, present in Pope, is achieved by Savioli in addition to an impression of industry created by the verb "accorrono". The shortness of the stanza and the metre creates the effect of both precision and simplicity. The unreal world is further illustrated in terms of a visual description which can merely be visualised in the imagination, given the invisibility of the spirits. They are further removed from real life in terms of time and space and shadow, providing continuity of the nebulous quality achieved with their introduction: i.e.

Nei più remoti secoli
Giacque oziosa e scura;

Savioli's technical ability to condense to miniature proportions various elements of time and space is what bestows on his *Amori* the precision of classicism, the grace of the rococo, and the lightness of the fantastic. His world spans ancient and "modern" mythology, and introduces history within the world of mythology with the words "nei più remoti secoli". The object, as regards the Sylphs is also within the realm of the abstract and the ephemeral, the latter in the case of vapours, dust, coloured stones and flowers, the former in the case of the lady's honour:

> Gelosi custodiscono
> I nèi, l'acque odorate,
> I vari fior, le polveri,
> Le gemme, e l'onestate.[19]

To this point Savioli's efforts have been concentrated on the creation of the "vignette" or "statuette". He now departs from these stylistic devices and predominence is given to the narrative, as the story of Belinda and her lock is told. Three stanzas pinpoint the stages of the incident. The sylphs guard, but are powerless in the hands of fate. Belinda's lock was fashioned by Love and Art, but falls victim to the conqueror's scissors. The condensation of the narrative provides a "story" within the appraisal of beauty. It is extremely effective as it also carries the concept of the "mask" of the title to a further level of symbolism. From the Greco-Roman disguise, one passes to that of Venetian theatrical and social custom, while Flora and her pose as the queen of the Amazons is referred to at lines 29-36. Finally the lock itself is seen as a symbolic mask which is torn away by one desiring closer acquaintance.

The second stanza,[20] dedicated to Belinda, derives its principal influence from Bonducci's translation of Pope. One observes the choice of vocabulary "collo eburneo", "crine aurato". Savioli describes the lock in the following terms:

> Scendea sul collo eburneo
> Parte del crine aurato,
> Per mano delle Veneri
> Ad arte inanellato.[21]

Bonducci, translating directly from Pope, refers to two curls. His style is more expansive, but he is obviously the source of the above lines:

> . . .Ninfa sì bella
> Per tormento mortal dell'uman germe
> Nutria due Ricci, che in leggiadra guisa
> Le pendevano dietro in onde uguali,
> Ed all'eburneo delicato collo,
> Colle dorate tremolanti buccole
> Maestoso crescean novo ornamento.[22]

The circumstances or manner of the cutting of the lock is not described, it is merely told as a "fait accomplit", but yet it serves as both a warning and illustration of what may come to pass in the life of the lady of the poem. The immediacy of the action is demonstrated in the following lines:

> Cadde improvvisa vittima
> D'insidioso acciaro.[23]

The poem ends on a note of exortation to the young lady to participate in the social life of her world. Once again the concept of approaching old age is ambiguously identified with night, with social gaiety which yields to permanent darkness. From the world of the cameo, mythology and eighteenth-century intrigue, Savioli finally verges on the world of social graces and customs of the "Settecento". It is in a poetic world of such social activity that the lock is cut, while youth is still ripe. With use of the vowel "o", movement and continuity is implied, contrasting with the static image of the lady in the opening lines, and her implied intention to preserve the lock forever:

> Ma sorgi omai. S'involano
> L'ore, e la notte avanza:
> Vuoti i teatri affrettano
> La sospirata danza.
> Tu pensierosa or dubiti,
> Gemi, e non hai parole;
> Poi ti dorrà che rapido
> Turbi le veglie il Sole.[24]

The final message is that of *The Rape of the Lock*

> But since, alas! frail beauty must decay
> Curl'd or uncurl'd, since locks will turn to grey
> Since painted, or not painted, all shall fade,
> And she who scorns a man must die a maid.
> (Canto V. 25-8).

Reference to *Il mattino* and *La maschera* reveals beyond all doubt that the source of both "canzonette" is Pope's poem. They are directly linked and correspond to passages in Cantos I and II of *The Rape of the Lock*. It cannot be denied, however, that the cultivation

68

of miniature perfection is Savioli's prime intention. The fusion of eighteenth-century manners and mannerisms with classical mythology and static figures completes the world:

> Per Savioli, come del resto per Rolli, il classicismo è l'unica dimensione possibile in cui rendere l'immagine di un mondo elegante e gaudente, che amava specchiarsi e ammirarsi nei graziosi quadretti di una mitologia minuta e delicata, come in questa canzonetta sul mattino della donna, che è un tema dal risveglio di Belinda nel *Riccio rapito* a quello del "giovin signore" nel *Mattino* frequente nella poesia settecentesca.[25]

It is interesting to consider Savioli's comments on his own work. He is aware of the forced logic in transforming "la Bella" to a Grace, while the former still demands adornment by the Graces. Yet it would appear that Savioli's world contains its own logic which supports the achievement of plastic and conceptual perfection. The lady, far from fighting a losing battle against time, in *Il mattino*, is the personification of beauty itself. Savioli expresses his qualms with regard to the view of his readers in the following terms:

> Non so poi, se possa piacere quel tratto di Poetica adulazione, per cui egli fa sedere alla toletta la Bella, chiamandola quarta delle Grazie. In senso Mitologico, le Grazie non hanno bisogno di adornarsi e una Grazia che ne ha bisogno, non è più Grazia.[26]

Once again with regard to the criticism of *La maschera* one finds the writer aware of his fusion of mythology, the activities within the "bel mondo" and the tale of Belinda:

> Ho voglia di dir di mal di questa, che mi piace molto, nè so perchè. Mi sembra un composto di pezzi bellissimi, che non vorrebbero essere accozzati insieme. ... In fine l'annunziare con tanta serietà que'Silfi, o il loro uffizio, gravemente soggiugnendo, che sono Divinità venute alla moda dopo essere state per molti secoli oziose e oscure, mi presenta un'idea ridicola in istile eroico. Questo ridicolo s'accresce non poco quando appena dopo aver narrato, che codeste Divinità hanno in cura il bel sesso, e ne custodiscono gli ornamenti e l'onestà, racconta subito il Poeta la infelice storia del Riccio di Belinda da Silfi sì mal difeso. Il Rato è sopra, dic'egli, ma vi vuol altro. Buon per Voi mia bella Amica che l'onestade vostra è difesa da una vigile e ferma virtude, e non dai Silfi.[27]

Savioli's adaptation of Pope's world then is purely for artistic purposes. The reproduction of eighteenth-century manners is not of profound social or moral significance. It aids Savioli in the communication of the age-old cliche "Gather ye rosebuds while you may". Historically speaking, it is of importance. It marks the entry of the world of Pope into Italian literature. It is not biting social irony, contained in Dresden china refinement, as in the case of Parini's *Il giorno*, neither is it the poetry of fashion and frivolity, nor can it be regarded as contributing to the "poetry of the lock" which will be discussed later at length. It merely marks the recognition by Savioli of the artistic possibilities of the world of *The Rape of the Lock*, which he places on a par with that of Greco-Roman mythology, and which he uses in the creation of a world of symetric perfection inhabited by Gods and Graces, which by virtue of the precision and perfection of their artistic form, assume the beauty of the statuette.

II

With the advent of Giuseppe Parini, the duplicity and double standards of the "bel mondo" are given prominence in tones of scathing irony which never destroy or even detract from the fashionable and artistic perfection of the society under scrutiny. Parini's view is perfectly controlled, his irony pointed, conveying a sharper outline to his figures and incidents, distinguishing them from the more "classical types" of the world of Savioli's *Amori*. Parini's world is in constant motion and bustle, the eighteenth-century "little people" assume an intrinsic face, which the invisible hand of their creator points towards calculated ignorance of the lot of the greater section of society.

As early as 1763, Parini's *Il mattino* was considered alongside *The Rape of the Lock*. In the *Frusta letteraria* of October 1st 1763, Giuseppe Baretti, in an exhortation to the poet to complete the work states: "Dacci il quadro finito, che te ne avremo obbligo, e contrapporemo senza paura i tre canti del tuo poema al *Lutrin* di Boileau, e al *Rape of the Lock* di Pope, massimamente se ti darai l'incomodo di ridurre i tuoi versi sciolti in versi rimati.[28]

The opinion that Pope was Parini's source was widespread in France during the nineteenth-century. In a letter to Vincenzo Monti Madame de Stael had declared: "Parini que je viens de lire tout entier, *Le matin* et *L'apres-midi*, ce Parini qui fait de tours de force avec les mots comme Marchesi en fait avec des notes, m'a bien peu interessée, c'est une imitation de le *Boucle enlevée* de Pope, c'est une ironie continuelle sans veritable gaité." Some years later Sismondi in his *Littérature du midi de Europe* identified the Italian poet with Pope and was severely criticised by Carducci for such an affirmation. Moreover, Carducci objected to the association with Savioli which Sismondi had made, namely that Parini "est l'egal de Savioli, et comme lui l'emule de Anacréon lorsqu'il chante l'amour".[29] Sismondi in addition to recognising Pope's influence on Parini, praises the Italian poet's precision in depicting the nobility "avec de l'esprit, de l'elégance, de la finesse" and "en ornant de toutes les graces de son pinceau cette vie effeminee."[30]

Both Giacomo Zanella, and Zumbini[31] share Sismondi's view that *Il giorno* is an imitation of *The Rape of the Lock*. Such judgment provoked the following response from Carducci: "Il Sismondi affermò riciso — nel *Giorno* il Parini imita *Il riccio rapito* — che per uno storico è correr troppo: se non che il Sismondi troppo anche mostrò di conoscer poco e gustar meno la poesia del Parini, dicendolo eguale al Savioli, ed emulo d'anacreonte."[32] Zumbini had believed that it was Conti's version which was of most consequence in the introduction of Pope to the Italians, and that both settings and personalities in Parini's poem resemble those of Conti's version of Pope: "Mi limito a dire che la prima parte del *Giorni*, cioè *Il mattino* è tutta ricalcata sul primo canto del poema inglese e specialmente sull'ultima parte di esso canto. Il Giovane Signore è nel poema italiano, un personaggio che corrisponde perfettamente alla Belinda del poema inglese."[33] The subject is also discussed by Giovanni Lenta in *Pope in Italia*,[34] Maria Rosa Catalano in *La fortuna del Pope in Italia*,[35] and by Mario Fubini,[36] while a present-day critic, Giovanna Gronda, stresses the historical and social significance of the translations of Pope into Italian: "le traduzioni dal poeta inglese testimoniarono un rapporto tra società e letteratura più diretto e più concreto di quanto si avesse esperienza in quegli anni in Italia."[37] She dismisses the possibility of Parini being an imitator of Pope, but makes a revealing comment with regard to Pope's influence on the Italian literary scene of the "Settecento": Non d'imitazione infatti si tratta, ma di una prospettiva letteraria, di una forma poetica di cui Conti traducendo il Pope dava esempio in Italia e nella quale il Parini avrà potuto trovare spunti e consonanze alla sua ispirazione.[38]

Our first consideration is to illustrate Parini as master of the rococo world of the miniature, as one capable of refraining from his contained irony in order to preserve the beauty and artifice of a world acceptable only in the figurative arts, where social and moral considerations do not at once come to the fore. It is in the following passage that he reveals himself master of gallantry and manners:

> Ed ecco in un baleno
> I damigelli a'cenni tuoi star pronti,
> Quanto ferve lavoro! Altri ti veste
> La serica zimarra, ove disegno
> Diramasi chinese: altri se il chiede
> Più la stagione, a te le membra copre
> Di stese infino al piè tiepide pelli.
> Questi al fianco ti adatta il bianco lino,
> Che sciorinato poi cada e difenda
> I calzonetti; e quei d'alto curvando
> Il cristallino rostro in su le mani
> Ti versa acque odorate, e da le mani
> Il limpido bacin sotto le accoglie.
> (*Il mattino*, 270-82).

In freely constructed poetry Parini succeeds in maintaining the symmetry of the miniature, while allowing for a greater freedom of movement of object. The elegance is arrived at largely by the use of diminutives (damigelli, calzonetti) and the references to articles of dress and their practical function. He succeeds in combining luxury with utility, while allowing the object of adornment to occupy the principal place in the passage. Thus while scurry of movements is indi-"serica zimarra", "bianco lino", "cristallino rostro" and "acque "serica zimarra", "bianco lino"; "cristallino rostro"; and "acque odorate". In this way mobility of subject/object, and a freedom of expression leads to a widening of horizons opening up an entire world of activity beyond the limitations of the "poemetto didascalico". "Non è una giornata del Giovin Signore, è la vita del Giovin Signore."[39]

Parini was inhibited, however, from attaining the universality which he sought, by the very nature of the tone and style of his *Il giorno*. The world of *Il giorno* is the little world of the "Settecento", inhabited by the expressions of rococo, untouched by the weighty moralising of their creator: "Ma ecco che a Parini, al di là dell'ironia, si schiude la scena rococò di un interno di palazzo aristocratico, alla cui grazia aggiunge la favola galante ed elegante di amore, ingegnoso creatore di aiuti per i suoi fedeli.[40]

The description of the dressing-table, the hairdresser at work and the ensuing battle between Nature and Art, resulting in the triumph of art, are derived from Pope with regard to subject, and circumstance.

> Ecco te pure.
> Te la toilette attende: ivi i bei pregi
> De la natura accrescerai con l'arte:
> Sì che oggi, uscendo del beante aspetto
> Benificar potrai le genti, e grato
> Ricompensar di sue fatiche il mondo.
> (*Il mattino*, 484-9).

> Stuolo d'Amori
> Invisibil sul foco agita i vanni,
> E per entro vi soffia, alto gonfiando
> Ambe le gote. Altri di lor v'appressa
> Pauroso la destra, e prestamente
> Ne rapisce un de'ferri: altri rapito
> Tenta com'arda in su l'estrema cima
> Sospendendol de l'ala, e cauto attende
> Pur se la piuma si contragga o fume:
> Altri un altro ne scote, e de le ceneri
> Filigginose il ripulisce e terge.
> (*Il mattino*, 494-504).

It cannot be claimed that Parini follows Pope, or any of his translators, line for line. Yet the *Amori* perform functions similar to the sylphs guarding Belinda, the scene at the dressing-table derives from the concluding passage of *The Rape of the Lock*, Canto I. *Il mattino*, 484-9 in spirit is akin to the Conti translation, as can be ascertained with reference to the following quotation:

Già la beltade imperiosa ha cinte
l'armi sue lampeggianti, e ad ogn'istante
Nuove lusinghe la sua faccia acquista.
(Conti, *Il riccio rapito*, Canto I. 199-201).

The mood continues at the conclusion of the Canto:

Stannole intorno affacendati i Silfi:
Chi adorna il capo, chi comparte il crine,
Chi la manica piega e chi la veste;
E per opra non sua Lisca si loda.   (Conti, Canto I. 206-9).

Parini's gentle irony is not apparent, but in terms of comparison with Conti's passage, one is aware that the Italian translator is referring to Belinda, while Parini speaks of the "Giovin Signore". Then the lines:

Benificar potrai le genti e grato
Ricompensar di sue fatiche il mondo.

ring ironically — it becomes the equivalent of "Belinda smiled, and all the world was gay". In the second quoted passage from *Il mattino* Parini conveys on the attendants the attributes of "amorini". They are bees, and spirits of the air, uniting the classical, natural and folkloristic. Further variety of movement is created by the use of the singular alongside the subject "altri", and the contrast between the concept of invisibility and the close-up vision of their activity. The physical attributes create the impression of winged humans: "Stuolo d'amori", "Agita i vanni/E per entro vi soffia, alto gonfiando/ambe le gote".

It is as though Parini sought to unite beings with the atmosphere in order to create the concept of invisibility. It is at this point that the Italian poet verges on the realistic, which can have no permanent place in his poetry. Just as the "Giovin Signore" is a prisoner of parks and palaces, so does Parini remain a prisoner of his own poetic style: "È in questo il limite della poesia pariniana: una poesia dalle già prepotenti tendenze realistiche, che non trova una sua via perchè la poetica l'infrena."[41]

The tendency towards realism marks the essential difference between the poetry of *The Rape of the Lock*, of Savioli's *Amori* and Parini's *Il giorno*. The miniature world of Pope and Savioli seeks no existence beyond the confines of Hampton Court and classical mythology. Savioli's portrayal of the temple of beauty and of hair-dressing contains vocabulary which could be the source for Parini's lines. The former's imagery is more minute, more precise and more complete. Where one pinpoints, the other describes:

> Ma già tu dolce imperio
> La fida ancella invita;
> Ella s'appressa e all'opera
> Stende la destra ardita.
> (L. Savioli, *Il mattino*, 37-40).

> Ella frattanto ornavasi
> Pari all'eterne dive,
> E il caldo ferro iliaco
> Torcea le chiome argive.
> (L. Savioli, *Il mattino* , 57-60).

The entire operation takes only two lines in Savioli:

> E il caldo ferro iliaco
> Torcea le chiome argive.

Parini's description takes four and a half lines. Early in Parini's *Il mattino* the servants and attendants appear as three-dimensional creatures, later they are seen as sylphs similar to those of *The Rape of the Lock*. Parini's sylphs are winged, feathered ministers in thousands; Conti, translating Pope, sees them as invisible winged ministers:

> Amanti ed invisibili ministri
> Stanno su l'ali in tuo servigio pronti
> (Pope/Conti Canto I. 58-9).

Parini's sylphs are:

> Mille alati ministri alto volando
> Scoter lor piume, onde fioccò leggera
> Candida polve che a posar poi venne
> Su le giovani chiome, e in bianco volse
> E il biondo e il nero e l'odiato rosso.
> (Parini, *Il mattino*, 834-8).

Savioli's sylphs are:

> Mille a te Silfi accorrono
> In sulle lucidi ali,

> Diva progenie, aerea,
> Che sfugge occhi mortali.
> (L. Savioli, *La maschera*, 45-8).

The duties of such creatures are to guard, apply powder, and there can be little doubt that the inspiration comes from Pope. Their gossamer-like substance, beating wings, and soft feathers provided the material from which Parini, and later poets depicting the "bel mondo", borrowed. The fact that word-for-word borrowings cannot be established, does not in my opinion discount the argument that Pope was one of Parini's sources for *Il mattino*. The following passage from Conti's translation of Pope, is I believe, the basic description from which Parini derived his physical and impressionistic description of the Sylphs:

> Il lucido squadron corre a le vele,
> E dibattendo l'ali in alto crea
> Molle bisbiglio, che rassembra a basso
> Di zeffiro spirante aura soave.[42]
> (Conti. *Il riccio rapito*, Canto II, 74-7).

Light, and ethereal substance, sonically resembling a gentle whisper on a balmy breeze, is the subject of the above passage, while tenuous feathers, and liquid forms are described in Conti's translation, Canto II, lines 78-83, which directly follow the above quoted lines.

> Spiegano al sol le tenui piume i Silfi,
> E chi s'immerge ad aurea nube in seno
> E chi su l'aria tremolando posa.
> Ma non può ravvisar occhio mortale
> Le loro forme trasparenti, i corpi
> liquidi e mezzo ne la luce sciolti.[43]

Parini, as has already been stated, is not content to remain within the world of the figurine, as was illustrated with relation to use of movement. In the same way, his sylphs, servants and attendants are not permanently human or supernatural, but share the qualities of the birds of the air, butterflies, fairy folk and domestic employees. Parini has adapted the world of Pope and Savioli to his own fantasy, linguistic and moral needs. With regard to elegance, one finds in setting up a comparison between Conti's dressing-table and that of Parini, that it is the former who is more precise, orderly and sophisticated. Yet the articles in each are more or less similar. While the polished exotic combs in Conti's translation bring both elephant and tortoise into the world of the miniature on a similar level, Parini creates a more gentle and even effect with the introduction of the swan. In both poems there exists the unveiling of the monument of beauty, verging on the ceremonial. Conti's lines at once convey a note of order and organisation.

> Ell'apre innumerabili tesori,
> Rari tributi dell'intiero mondo,
> E raccoglie da ognun con somma cura
> Qualche spoglia, e la dea ne veste ed orna,
> Qui splendon ne'scrignetti indiche gemme
> E là l'Arabia olezza in pinti vasi:
> La tartaruga e l'elefante a gara
> Si trasformano in pettini macchiati
> E bianchi. D'aghi qua fulgide file
> Si stendono in bell'ordine disposte;
> Là paste, polvi, Bibbia e dolci fogli.[44]
> (Conti, *Il riccio rapito*, Canto I. 188-99).

In Parini's *Il mattino* the "indiche gemme", "pinti vasi", "pettini macchiati e bianchi", "aghi", "fulgide file", "paste", "polvi", "Bibbia e dolci fogli" became "nappi eleganti", "morbide piume", "vapori", "polvi". His touch is more gentle, sweeter, and more colourful, his mood more tender. Where Conti is in keeping with his poet Pope-detached, Parini appears to indulge in his own creation and delight in the beauty of his own tone, at this point more lyrical than elegant. This is particularly true of the concluding lines of the passage below:

> A l'altro lato con la man rosata
> Como e di fiori inghirlandato il crine
> I bissi scopre ove d'idalii arredi
> Almo tesor la tavoletta espone.
> Ivi e nappi eleganti e di canori
> Cigni morbide piume, ivi raccolti
> Di lucide odorate onde vapori,
> Ivi di polvi fuggitive al tatto
> Color diversi ad imitar d'Apollo
> L'aurato biondo o il biondo cenerino
> Che de le sacre Muse in su le spalle

Casca ondeggiando tenero e gentile.
(Parini, *Il mattino*, 520-21).

Though departing here from the "diamond edged" classicism which has become synonomous with his poetry, Parini's expression is far from that of the spoken language. One is of the impression that every utterance is removed from the world of communication, even within the "bel mondo". Parini leans heavily on classical influences, literary inversions ("serica zimarra", "tiepide pelli", "fiammanti brage", "aureo cocchio", "brun cioccolatte". It would appear that he was indirectly influenced by Pope by the time he came to write *Il mattino*. Bonducci's translation of *The Rape of the Lock* had a wide circulation, Conti's version had appeared in England and Italy, and Ludovico Savioli had brought a first edition of *Amori* into print. The influence of Pope on Savioli is there for all to see: his *Il mattino* (or as it first appeared, *A una fanciulla che si adorna*) is based on Canto I of *The Rape of the Lock*. *La maschera* not only refers to Belinda's fate, but provides a "masked" interpretation of Pope's poem. With regard to use of vocabulary it would appear that Bonducci's version has been studied, while the grace and precision of the "canzonette" has much in common with Conti's lightness of touch. That Parini has read Savioli is clear from the sequence of events in *Il mattino* and from some vocabulary in common already illustrated.

In searching for similarities and differences on a social and moral level, it must be pointed out that while Parini's "Giovin Signore" is a product of genteel society, Parini's irony with regard to his behaviour and his moralising brings his protagonist into conflict with the world at large, which extends beyond the eighteenth-century draperies of polite society. While Pope demonstrates the temporary triumph of Art over Nature, Parini indicates that such art, is in fact artifice, to be shattered by the voice of the moralist. Such a voice removes the poet from the miniature world created and bestows on him the moral duty of revealing the hypocrisy hidden behind elegant screens and fashionable decor.

In his attitude Parini reveals himself a world removed from Pope and Savioli. As one aware of the need for reform and a new social structure, he identifies with the latter half of the eighteenth century, despite the fact that his best poetry depicts to perfection the world which he will reject. One must also bear in mind that fifty years have elapsed between the publication of *The Rape of the Lock* and Parini's *Il mattino*. "Giovin Signore" is the projection of social decadence in an enlightened society; while Pope can sneer, scorn and deride Belinda, he is also capable of laughing with her. Interpretations of *The Rape of the Lock* vary, nor can we state that its understanding and appreciation lies in any one interpretation. Parini's satire is more cruel and destructive, leaving no place for laughs. Instead it raises the serious questions of being and existence and their weight within and outside of "il bel mondo":

> Il Giovin Signore è un filosofo nel senso più moderno e più elegante, cioè più forestiero del vocabolo, le grandi scoperte e le grandi conquiste della scienza non affaticano forse troppo del loro peso la sua mente, ma poichè la moda volge propizia alla scienza, perchè tutto ha da portare il suggello della filosofia all'astronomia, alla meccanica, poichè in queste aride discipline le muse istesse sono andate a rintracciare nuove grazie.[45]

Although one observes that Parini's *Il mattino* (1763) and *Il mezzogiorno* (1765) follow an already established poetic and classical tradition, their forcefulness was of greater immediacy than that of the classical compositions of "arcadia classica". The first two sections of *Il giorno* represented the first full length biting social satire directed against the Italian nobility of the "Settecento". It is not surprising that it set a vogue for satires on social decorum, but what must be borne in mind is the fact that all the social satires verging from the mock-heroic to the burlesque, and descending to the grotesque, do not take their inspiration solely from Parini. It can be said that the name of the Lombard poet became identified and associated with a certain genre, but as it will be seen, an important source behind all the so-called "pariniani" is the figure of Alexander Pope. The subject chosen by those poets exploring and exploiting the "bel mondo" of the day varies from aspects of social life such as social games, coffee parties and social conversations, to the use of an object of decorum, the lock, the feather, the wig, as a symbol of the entire society. The principal poets dealing with the latter type of satire are Vittorelli, Talassi and Pignotti.

That Parini would have imitators and followers was only to be expected; but that a third section of his *Il giorno* would be written by another, and published with the two works by Parini in 1767 seems little short of outrageous. Yet this is precisely what happened, to quote Agnelli:

> Per questo dissi che si sarebbe potuto scommettere e vincere che qualcuno, a quella terza parte del poema, avrebbe pensato per lui. Infatti il Mutinelli premessa la dichiarazione pudibonda ch'egli era stato indotto ad imitare, con non biasimevole audacia, l'esempio del premiero poeta della bellezza e dalle novità delle idee leggiadre e spiritose innalzi l'araldo dell'umilità.[46]

Agnelli's judgment of Mutinelli's achievement is harsh; after a resumé of the contents of the work he states:

> Questo lamentatio Muttinelliano è dunque una palese ricalcatura de'due precedenti poemetti pariniani, da gli episodi grandi a i minori, da le considerazioni di filosofia satirica — onde si stabilisce, con l'intervenir del piacere la differenza delle classi sociali — ai consigli dati al giovine eroi su la lettura dei libri francesi, su la piacevol gallica favella, ch'ei deve prediligere.[47]

Agnelli then asks "sapete che cosa è negli sciolti del Mutinelli? Le contorsioni, quelle a punto che dovevano apparire meretrici di poetica robustezza a chi mancava forza vera".

Mutinelli, a Veronese poet and imitator of classical verses, published his imitation of Parini in 1767. Entitled *La sera*, it appeared in Venice, with the stamp of Graziosi along with Parini's *Il mattino* and *Il mezzo giorno*. The preface reads as follows:

> Comparvero alla luce *Il Mattino* ed *Il Mezzo-giorno* per la prima volta in Milano, e furono di poi ristampati parecchie volte a Venezia; segno evidente che se anco *La Sera* ai primi due di mano fosse successa, sarebbe stata senza' dubbio dal Pubblico cortesemente aggradita.
>
> S'invogliò pertanto di questo soggetto anche un Giovane Veronese, e in brevissimo tempo non per desiderio di gloria, nè per derogare punto alla giustissima onorevole fama del primiero Poeta condusse a fine l'ultimo Poemetto, che si desiderava, indi consigliato dagli amici, e da parecchi letterati, cui aveva commesso l'esame del suo componimento, deliberò finalmente di renderlo universale col mezzo delle stampe, incerto per altro dell'esito, che doveva incontrare per essere d'Autore di verso, e questi d'età giovanile. Uscî dunque *La Sera* in Verona dai Torchj dell'Erebe di Agostino Carattoni, e fu subito qui in Venezia ristampata incontrando appresso gli amatori della Poesia compatimento ed applauso, così che facilmente avrà potuto l'Autore da per sè stesso esperimentare, non aver egli mal collocato l'opera sua coll'essersi accinto a questa difficile impresa.[49]

80

With regard to physical description and sartorial refinement Mutinelli's hero is an exact replica of that of Parini. His description of the game would however appear to be derived from *The Rape of the Lock*. There is in common the ambition of the protagonist, the moral battle and the attitude to defeat:

Mutinelli describes the game thus:

> Dunque Signor ti piaccia armar la mano
> D'asta lunga e possente, indi adattando
> I crini in miglior guisa, il nastro, il fido
> Anello tuo pegno di pace, e i bianchi
> Manichetti finissimi volgendo
> Sfida pur un tuo pari al gran cimento;[50]

The object of decoration, and love-token in Mutinelli's poem conforms to the sparkling cross worn by Belinda in the English poem. Above all it is the mood, however, which I feel conforms to Pope's following lines:

> Belinda now, whom thirst of fame invites,
> Burns to encounter two adventurous knights,
> At ombre singly to decide their doom;
> And swells her breast with conquests yet to come.
> (*The Rape of the Lock*, Canto III, 1. 25-8).

The games table resembles the battlefield, in both poems the moves are demonstrated in mock-heroic fashion. One witnesses the battle in miniature and heroic combat seen as a pastime in the manner of medieval times:

> Piccola variata tavoletta
> Su cui segnar dei combattenti i colpi,
> Voi cominciate pur con gare opposte
> Immago finta a suscitar di guerra,
> E in mezzo al vario strepito confuso
> De la turba ondeggiante ognun sul campo
> Di nobile sudor bagnato il volto
> Co l'armi i colpi appresti, i passi mova,
> Vada, torni, si volga, intorno giri,
> E pensi accorto a le nemiche offese.[51]

Mutinelli attempts to create effect by the continued use of the vowel O, and the indication of circular movement, which will later be substantiated by the description of the balls. The entire atmosphere is created on a small scale with an apt choice of vocabulary: i.e. "combattenti i colpi", "gare opposte", "strepito confuso"; Finally a circular activity is achieved: "i passi mova/Vada, torni, si volga, intorno giri". This world of Mutinelli represents yet another level of the miniature, with conquest, ambition, victory and defeat transformed and directed towards objects rather than people. It marks the turning of this world towards lifeless objects which illustrates the lack of spontaneity with which society behaves. The gaming-table along with the "Tupé" will later become symbols of a lifeless and degenerate world bordering on the decadent and grotesque.

The "velvet" world of the battlefield is also the centre of activity in Canto II of *The Rape of the Lock*. Pope refers to the "velvet plain" and the "verdant field", as almost a reminder of the make-believe world in which the activity takes place:

> And party-colour'd troops, a shining train,
> Drawn forth to combat on the velvet plain.
> (Pope, *The Rape of the Lock*, Canto III. 43-4).

> As many more Manillio forced to yield,
> And march'd a victor from the verdant field.
> (Pope, *The Rape of the Lock*, Canto III. 51-2).

The victory of the "Giovin Signore" is conveyed in a series of verbs covering the step by step movement of the game. At this point Mutinelli's poem, I believe, resembles a translation, in that it appears to be lacking in genuine spontaneity of expression. Every word and its function appears to have been premeditated; yet the final effect is surprisingly unpoetic, leaving the impression of flatness, and lack of complexity. In addition the dramatic narrative weighs heavily in the following passage, destroying the lightness and sophistication which marked earlier passages:

> Ma tu, Signor con l'occhio, attento allora
> Guarda che l'armi tue dirittamente
> Portin danno al nemico, e rintuzzando
> L'orgoglio altier de l'avversaria turba,
> Il fianco piega, il piè lancia e distendi,
> Abbassa il capo, indi lo sguardo drizza
> Sopra il colpo prefisso, e lieve lieve

Movendo l'asta in pria cauta prepara
Danno al nemico, finchè poi scoppiato
Altamente lo strepito e l'armi
S'urti palla con palla, e queste insieme
Vadan tornin tondeggino percosse
Con vario giro nel trascorso campo,[52]

One witnesses an overloading of verbs, which provide action without imagery; the sole successful effect, it seems to me, being created by the collision of the balls, providing a circular effect of object and motion. The desire for victory of the "Giovin Signore" it appears, is borrowed from Conti's translation of Pope. Belinda directs movement, and the effect is rather mechanical, as in the case of Mutinelli's lines:

L'industriosa ninfa con gran cura
Le sue squadre rivede e grida: "Sia
Picche il trionfo", ed il trionfo è picche.
Le ciglie aguzza su le carte, guarda
I combattenti, e'l ciel, si morde il labbro,
E al fin con occhio bellicoso move
I neri mattador simili in pompa,
Ai condottier de l'affricane schiere.[53]
(Conti, *Il riccio rapito*, Canto III, 58-65).

The defeat of the "Giovin Signore" and vindication of his position reveals social pride, while Belinda's reaction to defeat in *The Rape of the Lock* demonstrates pride of a different nature. Mutinelli's passage is an emulation of Parini's style. It is far more weighty than Conti's lines, but lacks the uniformity found in the translator's work. The below quoted passage from Mutinelli's *La sera* reveals a less than evenly welded simile with an exaggerated identification of the bull and the hero of the piece. The concluding lines of the passage shatter the refinement of atmosphere and manners hitherto cultivated, and end on a note of drama which is out of keeping with the piece:

che se talvolta
Te pur affligge aspro destino, e devi
Alcuna de le tue stanche falangi
Cedere prigioniera, allora acceso
D'ira e dolor feroce agita il capo,
Fremi, grida, minaccia e con altr'armi

> Tosto riacquista i già perduti colpi
> Col vendicarti, qual feroce Tauro
> Che, perduto pugnando il destro corno
> S'irrita maggiormente a la battaglia,
> E avendo i fianchi del suo sangue aspersi
> Alzando il capo, e l'animoso collo
> Infuriato torcendo ottiene poi
> Sul nemico atterrito anche il trionfo.[54]

In contrast Conti's touch is consistently light, the world of the miniature is constant whatever the mood, while the translator also succeeds in infusing a note of suspense with the lines "Pure come ne'casi
disperati avviene, pende il destino da un azzardo solo."[55] (Canto IV.
1. 116-8). Once again the figure of Belinda comes to light in a new
guise:

> A tale aspetto di repente tinge
> Le guance virginali un vivo sangue,
> E la donzella attonita già mira
> La vittoria, che a lei scherzava intorno,
> Ne le fauci cader o tra gli artigli
> De la riposta o di Codiglio . . .[56]
> (Conti, *Il riccio rapito*, Canto III, 111-6).

The blood imagery in each poem is used in order to create drama and
colour within the piece. Conti's lines present the gradual flush of
colour to the ladies face in a convincing poetic manner. Mutinelli, on
the other hand, creates gore that reveals both a lack of taste and
artistic ability. Conti describes the triumph of Belinda in an echo of
musical acclamation which resounds throughout her own miniature
world:

> La ninfa in festa empie di grida il cielo:
> La valle, il bosco e'l canal lungo eccheggia.
> (Conti, *Il riccio rapito*, Canto III. 124-5).

It has been seen that the world of Parini is one of golden chariots and
brilliant jewels supported by the conventions of classicism and flaw-
less poetic technique. Pope's filagree world is perfect in every detail
and unlike that of Parini's contains its own universality. Mutinelli, I
believe, is of historical, if not artistic importance, in that he carries
the description of eighteenth-century social games a step further. Not

84

a gifted poet, he tends towards figurative imagery rather than conveying personal experience through eighteenth-century usages and manners. Conflict is seen in terms of the game-table, an inanimate object of activity, manipulated by the rich and powerful. Mutinelli's is a world without spontaneity, inspiration or sentiment. Man has already become a mere object, if a decorative one, in his world.

Mutinelli's style combines refinement and awkwardness. The "Giovin Signore" is seen in terms of "Cavalier servente" and bull, hardly a happy alliance, which sounds somewhat discordant even in critical reference. He does illustrate the taste for poems dealing with a day or an evening in the life of the nobility. To Parini is due the popularity of the title *Il mattino*. Although it contains material already in vogue as a result of the popularity of Pope and his translators, and the poet Savioli, Parini is the first to use the title. Savioli's revised version of *Alla fanciulla che si adorna* became *Il mattino*. Mutinelli went a step further by proceeding to *La sera*. The tradition is followed by Durante Duranti, in the following years with his *Il mattino d'Elisa*, and later with *L'Uso*, in which the rococo world with its ritual and ceremony is once again portrayed. Durante Duranti is described by Agnelli as:

> Forse il più pretensioso e il peggiore dei pariniani, non tanto per la forma, poi che osserva giustamente il Baseggio 'non gli si può negare spontaneità di verso' quanto per la contenenza, povera di satira, gonfia di livore e negli episodi priva in modo assoluto di novità.[57]

The poem mirrors the frivolity of Elisa as she prepares to face the day. The work itself bears no close resemblance to *The Rape of the Lock*, but it does contain a reference to Belinda's "message" in the following lines:

> Paventai che intanto il Cavaliere
> Di Belinda rinnovi il caso acerbo
> Col rapirti alcun Riccio alto sporgente.

Such a reference could have been derived from Savioli's *Il mattino*. This seems most likely when one considers that Elisa, like Belinda, is protected by sylphs, who, as a result of their negligence with regard to Belinda's well-being, have doubled their attention in the defence of Elisa:

Resi infelici dal premiero pianto
Validi troppo or ti proteggono.

By the time Duranti's works had circulated, the "poesia satirica del costume" was regarded as an eighteenth-century genre. Reference must also be made to Gian Carlo Passeroni (1713-1803), who, in his *Cicerone*, a work purporting to deal with the life of the Roman Orator, in reality criticised and ridiculed social defects: "Nel secolo XVIII la satira del costume fioriva più rigogliosa che mai, con varietà grande di toni, di forme e di modi . . . La tendenza a notare gli abusi e a suggerire i rimedi era nello spirito del secolo illuminato, e prenunziava quella rigenerazione della coscienza italiana che la filosofia e la critica venivano iniziando".[58] From the social satire dealing with a day in the life of the nobility, their customs and usages, grew the consideration of life itself in its various stages. Duranti's *L'Uso* is such, spanning the gallantry, marriage and old age of a gentleman. The work is divided into three section, *Il nubile, Il maritato* and *Il vedovo*.[59] It was completed in 1779, as is revealed in Duranti's letters in the Biblioteca Civica at Bassano del Grappa. To his friend the Abate Golini, he wrote in 1778, saying: Ho fatto *Il nubile*, che è la prima parte, *Il maritato*, che è la seconda; ora sto architettando anche *Il vedovo*, che sarà la terza e che fatta stamperò poi in appresso.

In January 1779, Duranti was still at work on the third section, and previous to its completion, refused to occupy himself with any other business. This he stated in a letter to Leopoldo Caldani: "Chieggo pienissime scuse al mio Sig. Leopoldo se mi trovo in una dura necessità di non poter secondare, alle sue troppe per me onorevoli ricerche. Quanto mi pesa questa disgustosa circostanza! Io presentemente sto travagliando dentro alla terza parte del mio *Uso* risguardante *Il Vedovo*. Debbo assolutamente finirla entro quaresima, e, distraendomi in altra materia, ciò mi riuscirebbe inesiguibile."

Duranti's work however, lacks freshness, sparkle and literary inspiration. Of the same nature is the work of Giulio Trento. He can be regarded as the least effective of the "pariniani". His imitation of Parini is clear, as is the fate of Pope's poetic legacy: "La coquette non è la Dama del Giovin Signore; la classe sociale, che in essa vien precipalmente satireggiata, non è la nobiltà del *Giorno*. Lucinda è la Signora della borghesia, che per voler vivere splendidamente, per voler gareggiare con le dame nobili e colte e doviziose, cade nel ridicolo, finisce nel fondo dell'abiezione, e vi trascura la famiglia, la società".[60]

Trento, who was born in 1732, studied at the Seminary of Treviso, and later at the University of Padua. Though he originally intended becoming a doctor, he soon abandoned his medical studies and dedicated himself to literature. He taught literature at Castel franco, there he established a printing press which he later transferred to Treviso. Serena calls him: "letterato fecondo, facile editore di sè stesso".[61] Trento's poem *"La coquette"* can be regarded as a skit on Parini's *"Il giorno"*: "Quest'uomo colto e dabbene geloso osservatore delle buone tradizioni morali letterarie linguistiche della sua gente, spettatore amareggiato dalla trionfante corruzione del costume, del gusto della lingua d'Italia, quest uomo pensò d'esalare la sua sarcastica indignazione in un poemetto d'imitazione pariniana *La Coquette*".[62]

Trento was one who cherished native contributions to European culture. Referring to his works, he states: "Spesso ho citati i nostri, poco i stranieri, non perchè io non li abbia letti, o non li pregi, ma quasi per risgarare certi nuovi pedanti che fanno torto alla nostra nazione, togliendo ad essa la lode del Teatro, per coronarne i francesi".[63]

Trento realised the paralysing effect that the slavish imitation of English and French writers had had on Italian poetry. He also was aware that the adoption of English and French customs and fashions had conferred both on society and literature a superficiality and poverty of expression, which stilted all creative and social individuality. However, the criticism and ridicule of poetry and society of the time does not justify the lack of taste in presentation and vulgarity of content. Serena justly comments: "Quanta vil gente! e quanto in basso caduta! I protagonisti e la società del *Giorno* pariniano, al confronto sono esempi di civili e private virtù." He then asks: "Dove precipita questa gente veneta del moribondo secolo XVIII? Non si accorge che è presso lo sfacelo della famiglia e della patria."[64]

Donna Lucinda of *La coquette* is the personification of stupidity, ignorance and amorality.

> Era Lucinda un fior di giovinezza,
> E di beltade; semplice e tranquilla,
> Temprava al senno altrui l'ingegno e l'opre
> Ed i piaceri; di ragione al fianco
> Stava il mite pudor, difesa e schermo
> Al debil intelletto.[65]

In place of refinement of taste, with regard to behaviour and dress, inhabitants of this world are recognised for their vulgar display of money, and the showy objects it can buy. An English lover is easily discerned:

> Fra tutti si distingue un milord
> dal brillante anello, dalle molte sterline.[66]

Trento's work illustrates the deterioration of artistic standards in the "poesia del bel mondo". The wit and control of Pope, reproduced by Conti to reflect the Italian social sophistication and philosophic awareness of his time, and the classical culture which pervades each section of Parini's work has yielded to an intellectual stagnancy reproduced in lines devoid of lasting artistic value. Trento's *La coquette* survives as a mere illustration of the decadence into which the genre which it attempted to contribute to, had fallen.

He thus carries the rococo world of the miniature from the sharp-edged irony of Parini to the world of the "borghesia" where refinement and manners have no historical constituent part. The comic in Duranti, in the hands of Trento[67] borders on the grotesque. Deprived of "buon gusto", the "bel mondo" or what is left of it, lacks both strength of precision, and the forcefulness which justified its poetic existence.

Notes to Chapter II

1 J.S. Cunningham, Pope, *The Rape of the Lock*, op.cit., p. 47.
2 G. Gronda, *A. Conti, versioni poetiche* (Bari, 1966), p. 585.
3 W. Binni, *Classicismo e neoclassicismo nella letteratura del Settecento* (Florence, 1967), p. 54.
4 *Il passeggio*, 1.53-60 in *Lirici del Settecento*, edited by Bruno Maier, (Milan-Naples) 1969, p. 300-303.
5 See Mario Praz, *Joseph Addison, Lo Spettatore* (Turin, 1943), pp. 95-6.
6 Natalino Sapegno, *Disegno storico della letteratura italiana* (Florence, 1948), p. 394.
7 "È la quartina di settenari, di cui il primo e il terzo sono sdruccioli e sciolti, il secondo e il quarto piani e rimati fra di loro. See N. Sapegno, *Disegno storico della latteratura italiana*, op.cit., p. 297. See also Stella Cilario, *Ludovico Savioli, monografia* (Prato, 1902); A. Baccolini, *Vita ed opere di L.S.* (Bologna, 1922); A. Momigliano, *Cinque Saggi* (Florence, 1945). B. Croce, "Intorno al Savioli" in *Critica*, (1944).
8 B. Maier, *Lirici del Settecento* (Milan, 1959), p. 303 1.69-76.
9 Ibid. p. 304.
10 B. Maier, *Lirici del Settecento*, op.cit., p. 304. 1.9-12.
11 Ibid. 1. 13-20.
12 Ibid. p. 306, 1. 36-43.
13 Ranieri Schippisi "L'Arcadia" in *Le correnti, I*, edited by Marzorati (Milan, 1969), p. 537.
14 B. Maier, *Lirici del Settecento*, op.cit. p. 319. 1. 1-8.
15 Ibid. p. 320. 1. 13-20.
16 Ibid. pp. 321-22, 1. 44-51.
17 G. Gronda, *Versioni poetiche*, op.cit., p. 43, 1. 55-8.
18 A. Bonducci, op.cit., p. 30, 1. 2-6.
19 B. Maier, *Lirici del Settecento*, op.cit., p. 322, 1. 53-6. Note the similarity of Savioli's lines to Pope's original.
   "Our humbler province is to tend the fair,
   Not less pleasing, though less glorious care:
   To save the powder from too rude a gale,
   Nor let the imprison'd essences exhale;
   To draw fresh colours from the vernal flowers,
   To steal from rainbows, ere they drop in showers".
                         (Canto II, 1.91-6).
20 See Maier, *Lirici del Settecento*, op.cit., p. 322, 1. 57-60.
21 Ibid. p. 323, 1. 61-4.

22 A. Bonducci, op.cit., p. 38.
23 Maier – *Lirici del Settecento,* op.cit., p. 323, 1. 67-8.
24 Ibid. p. 223, 1. 69-76.
25 G. Savoca, "L'eleganza edonistica di L. Savioli Fontana" in *Il settecento,* op.cit., p. 347.
26 Savioli's criticism of the *Amori* is contained as notes to *Amori del Sig. Conte Ludovico Savioli Fontana, Senatore Bolognese con aggiunta di altre sue poesie e di alcune lettere critiche sopra gli Amori all'eccellenza di Vittoria Corsini Odescalco, Duchessa di Bracciano,* Piacenza, MDCCLXXXIX. He entitles the critical pages "Lettere critiche d'una Dama e d'un suo Amico sugli *Amori* del Sig. Conte Ludovico Savioli Fontana, Bolognese".
27 Ibid.
28 See G. Baretti, *Frusta letteraria,* edited by L. Piccioni, (Bari, 1932).
29 Sismondi, *Litterature du midi de Europe* (Paris, 1813), Ch. XXII, pp. 80-81.
30 Ibid.
31 B. Zumbini, in "Giornale napoletano della domenica", 5 febbraio (1882).
32 G. Carducci, *Storia del "Giorno"* in *Parini maggiore, Opere,* XI, (Bologna, 1907) pp. 106-122.
33 B. Zumbini in "Giornale napoletano della domenica", op.cit.
34 G. Lenta, *Pope in Italia,* op.cit. pp. 42-52.
35 M.R. Catalano, "La fortuna del Pope in Italia" in *Annali della Facoltà di Magistero dell'Università di Messina* (1941) XVIII, pp. 83-100.
36 M. Fubini, *Il Parini e il Giorno* (Milan, 1951-2), pp. 249-304.
37 G. Gronda "Le versioni poetiche di A. Conti", in "Giornale storico della letteratura italiana" LXXXVII (1970), pp. 304-5.
38 Ibid. n.p. 307.
39 Domenico Petrini, *Dal barocco al decadentismo* (Florence, 1957), p. 239.
40 Ibid. p. 205.
41 Ibid. p. 241.
42 G. Gronda, *A. Conti, versioni poetiche,* op.cit., p. 50.
43 Ibid.
44 G. Gronda, *A. Conti, versioni poetiche,* op.cit., p. 47.
45 E. Bertana, *Gli intendimenti della satira pariniana* (Verona, 1892), p. 26.
46 G. Agnelli, *Precursori e imitatori del Giorno* (Bologna, 1888), p. 47.
47 Ibid. p. 53.
48 Ibid. p. 54.
49 Mutinelli, *La sera* (Venice, 1767), ppxi-xii.
50 Ibid. p. CLXXIV, 1. 17-22. The edition supplies no line references. For the convenience of the reader, line references per page are supplied.
51 Ibid. p. CLXXV. 1. 1-10.
52 Ibid. p. CLXXV. 1. 11-23.
53 G. Gronda, *A. Conti, versioni poetiche,* op.cit., p. 56.
54 Mutinelli, *La sera,* op.cit., p. CLXXVI, 1. 5-18.

55 G. Gronda, *A. Conti, versioni poetiche*, op.cit., p. 57.
56 Ibid.
57 C. Agnelli, *Precursori e imitatori del Giorno di Giuseppe Parini*, (Bologna, 1888), p. 75.
58 V. Rossi, *Storia della letteratura italiana*, III, p. 179.
59 Durante discusses his efforts in compiling the work in his letters 1778-9. See Bassano del Grappa, Biblioteca Civica, Epistolario B. Gamba, XII-A-13/1920, and XII-A-13/1921. The first letter is addressed to: Ill.^{ssmo} e Rev.^{e mo} Sig. Colmo,

> Monsignor Don Antonio Golini,
> Vicario Monastico,
> Bassano.

Golini Amato.   Brescia, 12 Aprile 1778.

Se io mi fossi imaginato che il garbato Padre Romelli invece di portarsi così in pochi giorni come mi asserì, avesse resoluto spendere un mese in viaggio, avrei spedito il mio poemetto a voi per il corriero piùttosto che valermi del mezzo suo; La cosa è andata così contro il mio desiderio. Lo volea, che fosse de'primi a leggerlo, e sarete forse degli ultimi − per verità arrabbio contro tanta tardanza; perchè con questa ne soffre l'amicizia mia verso di voi, ed anche il mio amor proprio. Cos' è mai di quel buon Cassinense? Egli ha preso la via di Mantova. Andreasi lo avrà trattenuto: e intanto il mio *Uso* sarà stato giacente: il mio Golino lo avrà aspettato: avrà anche mormorato contro l'autore negligente: lo avrà accusato di poca amicizia e che so io. E pure la colpa non è mia, anzi ho dovuto discapitare anche per un altro verso, cioè sul canto essenziale sulla gola, che sapete essere uno de'miei vizi favoriti. Nella lettera, che era unita al poemetto vi era anche non so quale ricordanza di certe ciambelle di codeste vostre monache. Voi avrete aspettato il mio *Uso*; io le ciambelle; e certo delle due aspettazioni la mia non era inferiore alla vostra. Ora non posso più reggere all'impazienza, non dirò già delle ciambelle, che questo è uno scherzo, ma dibbene all'altro punto del ricapito del mio poemetto. Sai vedermi dunque adunque su questo particolare. Qui, è stato accolto, e sp − oltre la mia aspettazione: e da molte laude viene ricercato. Ho fatto *il Nubile*, che è la prima parte, *il maritato* che è la seconda: ora sto architettando anche *il vedovo*, che sarà la terza; e che fatta stamperò poi in appresso. Il vostro giudizio sulle prime due mi sarà di forse stimolo ad eseguirla. La mia famiglia vi riverisce; amatemi, state sano e crederrmi. Adio Adio −

> Il Vostro Duranti.

The above letter reveals an openness of approach, and readiness of humour in keeping with the "bel mondo" projected in his work. The second letter reveals pressure of work, and determination to finish the third part of *L'Uso*, along with a resoluteness of character. It is addressed to Sig.^{re} Leopoldo Caldani of Padova.

Amico Sig. Colmo,

Chieggo pienissime scuse al dev. mio Sign. Leopoldo, se mi trovo in una dura necessità di non poter secondare, alle sue troppe per me onorevoli ricerche. Quanto mi pesa questa disgustosa circostanza! Io presentemente sto travagliando dentro alla terza parte del mio *Uso* risguardante *Il vedovo*. Debbo assolutamente finirla entro quaresima, e distraendomi in alora materia, ciò mi riuscirebbe inesiguibile. Ella siccome affatto gentile scusi di grazia l'impossibilità mia di servirla, come farò in ogni altra occasione. Oltre a ciò ho tanti affari non miei per le mani che sono veramente oppresso. Torno a dire, imploro la sua ben nota gentilezza per scusarmi: e qui con pienissimo scusa ed amicizia mi raccomando nella sua grazia.

Di. V.S. 11mo,

Brescia di 21 Gennaio 1779.

Duranti.

60 A. Serena, *Varietà letterarie*, op.cit. p. 168.
61 Ibid.
62 Ibid. p. 161.
63 G. Trento, in *Nuova raccolta di operette italiane* (Treviso, 1795).
64 A. Serena, *Varietà letterarie*, op.cit., p. 164.
65 See G. Trento, *Nuova raccolta di operette italiane*, op.cit.
66 See G. Trento, *Nuova raccolta di operette italiane*, op.cit.
67 For correspondence of Giulio Trento see Bassano del Grappa, Biblioteca Civica, MS Gamba, XI. C. 14. MS Remondini XXII. 5.
    The condition of the letters is extremely poor, making reading most difficult.

CHAPTER III

Bondi, Colpani and the poetry of social grace

To Savioli, Parini and the exponents of society on a miniature scale, the daily ritual and customs constituting their entire world provided the subject-matter of their poetic vision. Two further poets specialising in social refinement and sophistication are Clemente Bondi and Giuseppe Colpani. These constitute the artistic survival of the "bel mondo" long after its day-to-day reality had become but a memory. Rather than take a general view of life within the context of a particular social stratum, they are drawn to the illustration of the place of objects in the enactment of customs. Their work highlights the minuteness of, amongst other things, the stove, the clock, the mirror, the fan, and could be regarded as isolating the tools and utensils of self-adornment, coffee-making and self-deception, in an effort to draw attention to the fragility and delicacy of a passing era. Their work, however, also illustrates the survival of a literary "genre" introduced by Bonducci and Conti, which allows for the fusion of Nature, Science, Philosophy and Art, combined with Volterian wit and Cartesian profundity.

Clemente Bondi[1] was born in the village of Mozzano Superiore, in the province of Parma, of Rannuccio and Lisabetta Gennari, on June 27, 1742. When he was twelve, his father died, and an uncle, Don Carlo Bondi, took care of him, providing for his studies at Parma until he reached the age of eighteen. Bondi studied at the Jesuit College of Mantua, and in 1760 entered the Congregation. He then taught at Padua until the suppression of the Order in 1773. His sister Bianca, had in the meantime become a Benedictine nun. In the same year as the suppression of the Order, Bondi made his first impression as a poet. His first poetic work was *La giornata villereccia*, published in Parma in 1773. There followed *La felicità* (Venice, 1775) *La moda* (Padua, 1777), *Le conversazioni* (Padua, 1778). Bondi also translated Virgil (*Aeneid* and *Georgics*) and Ovid (*Meta-*

morphosis). After the suppression of the Jesuits in 1773, Bondi acted as tutor to the Zanardi family at Mantua. Later he moved to Milan where he remained until the arrival of the French in 1796. His remaining years were spent at Brunn as Librarian, and at the Court of Vienna, where he was the last laureate poet.

In the *Giornale letterario d'Italia*, 1789, page 366, a reference to Bondi's technique reads as follows: "Nobiltà di verso sciolto spogliandolo di quel gonfio e ridonante che gli aveva dato Frugoni: che il suo stile sempre sostenuto e terso è simile a quello di Virgilio . . . che nel genere descrittivo non ha forse chi l'agguagli per la castità dei colori e che esatto pittore della natura non l'ha caricata giammai di adornamenti superfini."

La giornata villereccia is a delicately poised account of a day in the life of a young nobleman. It is built around life in a country villa, as opposed to Parini's urban setting. Interesting from the point of view of students of Pope, are the lines devoted to the preparation of coffee, which occur in Canto II, stanzas 30-31-32. These lines in their turn provide a stimulus for Lorenzo Barotti, also a Jesuit (1724-1801), who does not have the poetic grace of Bondi. Bondi stresses the importance of coffee in the day of a lady or gentleman, its taste and effect. There is a detailed account of its preparation:

> Chi di lor nel fornello, atto a tal uso
> Fa foco, e soffia nel carbone ardente;
> E chi nel cavo rame il caffè chiuso
> Volge intorno abbrostendo, infin che sente
> Misto col fumo il grato odor diffuso,
> E de'granelli il crepitar frequente;
> Dal foco allor il toglie, e il gitta fuore
> Vestito a bruno di novel colore.[2]
> (Bondi, *La giornata villereccia* II, 30).

Bondi's technical precision in the presentation of a succession of images conveys a ritualistic effect: the first image presents the utensil and the lighting of the flame; this is closely followed by the circular movement described in the lines:

> E chi nel cavo rame il caffè chiuso
> Volge intorno abbrostendo;[3]

Finally Bondi appeals to the sense of sight, sound and smell with "misto col fumo il grato odor diffuso." The order is continued with the readiness of the coffee:

> Altri in ordigno addentellato il trita
> E polvere ne trae minuta e molle:
> Altri l'occhio e la man pronta e spedita
> Sul vaso tien, che gorgogliando bolle.
> Fin sopra l'orlo in un momento uscita
> L'occhiuta spuma pel calor s'estolle;
> Ma poi lascia il liquor purgato e mondo
> L'impura feccia, che ricade al fondo.[4]
> (Bondi, *La giornata villereccia* II, 31).

Finally the coffee is served. The stanza ends on a note of utility: its purpose has social and practical implications: it counteracts the effects of overindulgence in another liquid:

> L'opra è compiuta; e su le mensa è presta
> Già la bevanda in porcellana fina:
> Silvio il zuccaro infonde, e destro appresta
> Le colorate tazze dalla Cina:
> Indi colma, e fumante or quella, o questa
> Con gentil atto a ognun porge e destina.
> Gustanla a sorsi; e la bevanda amara
> Poscia corregge il rosolin di Zara.[5]
> (Bondi, *La giornata villereccia* II. 32).

Bondi's coffee-making reveals a poetry of objects, odours and sounds, all possessing an intrinsic activity, as though the hand of the artistic had disappeared leaving "fornello", "cavo rame", "grato odor", "vaso", "carbone ardente" to operate independently. This is the poetry "delle piccole cose" uniting minuteness of object and precision of activity. Collective human activity is completed and the beverage is ready for consumption, a name identified with the genteel society is introduced:

> Silvio il zuccaro infonde, e destro appresta
> Le colorate tazze dalla Cina.

Refinement of style goes hand in hand with refinement and purity of concept. The coffee is the purveyor of equilibrium, correcting the heady effect of red wine.

Pope's lines in *The Rape of the Lock* describing the tea-party are more concise. Yet they can be summed up in terms of preparation of beverage, its gratification and effect:

> For lo! the board with cups and spoons is crown'd,
> The berries crackle, and the mill turns round:
> On shining altars of Japan they raise
> The silver lamp; the fiery spirits blaze:
> From silver spouts the grateful liquors glide,
> While China's earth receives the smoking tide:
> At once they gratify their scent and taste,
> And frequent cups prolong the rich repast.
>
> (Pope, *The Rape of the Lock*, Canto III,
> 1. 105-112).

Bonducci's translation highlights the crackling of the coffee beans and the movement of the mill:

> Ma già di tazze, e di cucchiari intorno
> Coronata divien la ricca tavola;
> I grani del Caffè arsi, e rinchiusi
> Odonsi sgretolare, e il mulinello
> Si rivolge veloce in tondi giri.
> Su sfavillanti altari del Giappone
> La lucerna d'argento omai s'inalza;
> I focosi del vin spirti fiammeggiano,
> Dagli argentei beccucci i grati umori
> Scorrono, e intanto la Chinese terra
> Riceve nel suo sen l'onda fumante:[6]

Conti's version is nearer to Bondi's style than that of Bonducci. The former's statements are clear-cut, though not lacking in delicacy, as those of Bonducci:

> Ma di tazze e cucchiaî già si corona
> Picciola mensa, il molinetto gira,
> Il caffè crocchia. Argentea lampa s'alza
> Su giapponese altar. Bolle lo spirto
> De l'acqua arzente con azzurra fiamma,
> Il liquor esce da l'argenteo becco,
> E la terra cinese in sé riceve
> La fumante marea grata a'due sensi.[7]
>
> (Conti. *Il riccio rapito*)

Bondi's world is very much that of Pope, though in his preface to *La giornata villereccia* the Italian poet denies the influence of either Italian or foreign models. Nevertheless his interest in English customs can be seen with reference to *La giornata villereccia*, and in *"L'orologio"*. The direct influence of Pope is apparent in *La moda*, while Parinian sarcasm is displayed in *Il cavalier servente*.[8]

In the preface to *La giornata villereccia* Bondi explains his motive for writing the work, stressing his own originality: "Così la brama di compiacervi, a cui son debitore di ogni leggiadra immagine, che verseggiando per avventura mi si è destata, potuto avesse altresì le poetiche grazie somministrarmi, e lo stile, onde esporla, ed ornarla con dignità. Ciò almeno, di che mi lusingo, si è di non avere per l'una parte i poeti nostri italiani con pedantesca imitazione ricopiati, nè mendicanti per l'altra da straniero idioma barbari vezzi e peregrini colori."[9]

Bondi can be regarded as a typical exponent of eighteenth-century social thought, precisely and elegantly expressed, social frivolity alternated with more serious scientific or philosophic principles. A good example of this is "L'orologio". From the precise, measured activity of the coffee-making in *La giornata villereccia*, one passes to a movement of no less precision — that of time measured by a minute and perfect mechanism, in keeping with the scale and order of Bondi's poetic world. The miniature clock is the globe itself, revolving to mark light and shade in turn. Time abides on its wheels. Yet its face is that of a machine, the object symbol of a philosophic system, mathematically dividing time and being into space, and resounding with the fleeing of every hour:

> Che poi distinti su la faccia esterna
> Volubil freccia in numeri descrive.

Yet the passing of time is not seen as something terrifying, the indicator of old age. It is seen within the context of the little world where all things bring sweetness and pleasure — it is a "macchinetta gentile", which will hopefully signal at least one happy hour for the poet. The sonnet by Bondi points to a scientific interpretation of time and life itself:

O d'Anglia nata su l'estreme rive,
Macchinetta gentile, onde l'eterna
Virtù motrice, misurando alterna
L'ore diurne, e della luce prive.
Su le tue ruote assiso il tempo vive,
Ed i tuoi giri equabili governa,
Che poi distinti su la faccia esterna
Volubil freccia in numeri descrive.
Escon divise intanto ad una ad una
L'ore fugaci e, mentre fuor sen vola
Col suono accusa il suo partir ciascuna.
Deh! fra tante, che t'escono dal seno,
Macchinetta gentile, un'ora sola
Segna, un'ora per me felice almeno.[10]

In the preface to three volumes of his poems published in Vienna in 1808, Bondi stressed that his poetic compositions constituted for him a mere pastime: "Figlie di un ozio pacifico, e di una libera immaginazione e serena, tutte o la maggior parte risentonsi, e nelle immagini, e negli argomenti, della tranquillità dei tempi, e dell'animo, in che furono composte." Bondi, in *La moda* and *Le conversazioni* reveals himself the successor of Pope, and to a lesser extent of Parini: "Ma anche questi due poemetti sono espressione caratteristica di uno spirito oziosamente moralistico, sostanzialmente estraneo al processo di rinnovamento sociale che andava maturando specie in ambiente lombardo – (nella prefazione alle *Conversazioni* scriveva: 'Tutti ho dipinto in astratto i miei caratteri copiati solo dalla natura, e per ciò stesso d'ogni paese e, più o meno, d'ogni conversazione'.

While Pope's subject can be defined as society, and Parini's as "a day" in the life of a young gentleman, Bondi's subject is fashion, as his opening lines reveal. Pope's venue is London, Parini's Milan. Bondi addresses his poem to fashion, the daughter of the Seine in *La Moda*:

O della Senna multiforme figlia,
Dove le grazie, ed il buon gusto han nido,
E le inerzie gentili, instabil Dea,
D'abito varia, e di color, nè mai
Somigliante a te stessa, o sol costante
Ne l'incostanza tua, Proteo novello,
Cui le femminee menti Idolo, e Nume,

> E d'ogni lor pensiero arbitra, e guida
> Di consenso crearono, e col nome
> Distinsero di Moda;[12]

As in the case of Pope, Savioli, Parini and, as will be seen later with regard to Vittorelli, the dressing-table, the mirror and the various beautifying essences contained in miniature jars, represent an important part of *La Moda*:

> Presso la stanza nunzial risiede
> L'elegante ritiro, onde risorte
> Dal letto appena agli esercizj usati
> Le tue devote scarmigliate accoglie.
> Tutto è sacro là dentro. Alla parete
> S'appoggia il breve altar, cui bianco lino
> Tutto circonda, e fino al piè discende;
> Poi sovra steso colorato il copre
> Serico velo. Ma di tanti arnesi,
> Che ingombran l'ara, e chi potrebbe appieno
> Tutti ridire i varj nomi, e l'uso?[13]

The place is sacred, the "toletta" is an altar to beauty.

As in the case of Pope, his translators and Parini, minute attention to detail is employed in the description of the miniature vases, urns and bottles containing artificial aids to beauty. The mirror is also highlighted — it plays an important role in this poetry of objects:

> S'alza nel mezzo consiglier fedele
> Ampio cristallo, cui d'argento adorna
> O vernicata almen liscia cornice.[14]

The objects on the "toletta" are mysterious in themselves; Pope had referred to a "mystic order". Amongst the objects is the Saviolian "eburnei pettini", "a cui/raro è l'ordin dei denti, a cui più denso". While Pope sees the purpose of such aids as contributing to beauty, Bondi sees them as instrumental in conducting a battle against old age, and illustrative of the consequent battle between Nature and artifice. One observes a close relationship between Pope and Bondi in the following passage:

> Sparse d'intorno a lui varie di mole,
> Giaccion urne diverse; e qual di bianca

Polve è ripiena, qual di bionda; questa
Serba i finti capelli, e quella i crini,
Ingombro immenso: altre conservan chiuse
Le odorate manteche, a cui diverso
Donan i fior nome, e fragranza; ed altre
Han dentro accolto un infinito fascio
D'aghi forcuti, morbidi cuscini
Di colorata seta alzan sul dorso
La selva poi delle minori spille.
D'ufficio varj e di figura han loco
Qui pur gli eburnei pettini, ed a cui
Raro è l'ordin dei denti, a cui più denso.[15]

Ma quei, che ascosi, in più riposta parte
Temon la luce, e de'profani il guardo,
Misteriosi vasi, unguenti, e polvi
Chiudono in seno; di virtù possente
Reliquie insigni contro il tempo, e contro
La nerezza, e il pallor; ma grave fora
Delitto imperdonabile gli occulti
Arcani investigarne, e al vulgo ignaro
Con lingua incauta palesarne i riti.[16]

One observes, however, that in both Vittorelli and Bondi, there is
concentration on the false hair, and on the introduction of colour
into the realm of the "toletta", i.e. "cuscini di colorata seta". The
final description of the hair-style at the conclusion of *La moda*, will
have much in common with a similar passage in Vittorelli's *Il tupé*.
As Savioli and Parini do, Bondi dedicates the entire morning to the
self-adornment of his protagonist:

Pur dalla noja di lungh'ore ei giova
A difendere almen; chè breve tempo
Non basta al culto tuo, ma d'ogni giorno
Tutto il Mattino nei misterj augusti
Devotamente si consacra, e perde.
Nè a profanar la santità del loco
S'apre l'ingresso mai del picciol tempio
A straniero pensier. Lungi le cure,
Lungi i consigli della fredda sempre
E incomoda ragion. Solo qui regna,
Il Desio di piacer, scaltro idoletto,
Che ogni donna ha nel cor, che nuove ognora
Meditando conquiste, ogni arte adopra

Onde abbellirsi, e si compiace, e cauto
Di natura i difetti emenda, o cela.[17]

The sheer joy in his own deliciously frivolous expression, which is found in Pope, is here missing. Savioli's fusion of physical and classical beauty is nowhere to be found. Instead there is the conscious awareness of an artificial world, and an artifice bordering on the ridiculous. As do Savioli and Parini, Bondi also presents the servants as sylphs, bees, or winged creatures, ever on the wing, carrying coloured vapours and cloths in order to decorate and ornament the "bel mondo". The introduction of rich colour is in fact a new device of Bondi's. It will later be identified with Talassi, when the silver quality of Pope's original, and the rigid classicism of Savioli and Parini will have disappeared, yielding to the colourful fantasy of the fairy-tale:

Cento, ministri suoi, volan ronzando
Per l'aer sacro instabili, e leggeri
Variopinti capricci, in varie cure
Occupati e divisi. Altri d'un nastro
Suda intento al lavoro, e in mille guise
Variando lo emenda; altri dà forma
A enorme riccio, e increspalo; chi gli aghi,
E chi ministra i crini; uno si specchia
Nelle gemme brillanti, e giaccion altri,[18]

The movement of the servants are likened to the activities of birds and bees:

Quasi nuvolo d'api in ampio nido,
Nel cavo seno d'una cuffia, e alcuno
Come augel nella frasca, in su la cima
Siede di lunga tremolante piuma,
E l'alterno piegar del sottil gambo
Con tremule ali e timido seconda.[19]

In the world of Bondi, the hairdresser has become the priest of fashion, and with the description of his ceremonial arrangement of the hair, the style becomes more and more similar to that of Vittorelli.[20] The exaggerated artifice is referred to as "turrita mole", "piramide", "mausolei superbi", "marmorea mole". Such fine ridicule is compared to the natural beauty of Nice, who has no need of such ornamentation. The poem concludes with the contrast between Nature and Art;

101

the latter illustrated in the course of the poem from the personal and visual view-point. The seductress uses wiles in behaviour and decoration in order to trap the unsuspecting.

The lines depicting the work of the hairdresser are lacking in spontaneity and naturalness. They become identified with the world depicted. One doubts Bondi's originality when one refers to Parini and Savioli, and considers its similarity to the work of Vittorelli written four years previously:

> Pien del suo nume il Sacerdote intanto,
> Di bianca cinto polverosa veste,
> E di pettine armato, agile affronta
> Le sciolte treccie, e con esperta mano
> Pria le turba e disordina, poi dopo
> Le raccoglie increspando, e le compone
> E il bipartito crin, non senza ajuto
> D'ampio volume di straniere chiome
> Alza e dà forma alla turrita mole.[21]

The hairdresser, the "sacerdote" is armed with a catalogue of models to be copied and admired. The style becomes the precise imitation of that most pleasing to the lady:

> Ma fra tanti dissimili modelli
> Qual scegliere a imitar? Cento diversi
> In picciol libro ne incidesti, O Dea.
> Quelli non già, ma te consulta e segue
> Con scrupolosa man l'oracol tuo;
> Donando ai crini quella forma esatta,
> Che ultima piacque a te. Nè men tu sola
> Decider dèi su i cumulari fregi,
> Che ornano aggiunti la composta chioma,
> Qual più convenga, ed in qual nuova foggia,
> Se di Batavi lini, o se di veli
> Il variato ognor bizzarro intreccio;[22]

In Bondi's poem, however, there are no literary references, and few technical devices in attempt to convey complexity and subtle symbolism to the "tupé". The ridicule is not so obvious as in Vittorelli's *Il tupé*, as will later be seen, and this leaves the latter part of the poem without a clear-cut character:

Sotto gli auspicj tuoi tutta si compie,
Onde quasi piramide sul fronte
In trionfo l'ostentano le ornate,
Di fuori almeno femminili teste.
In simil guisa i Mausolei superbi
Ergon nei templi la marmorea mole
Di simulacri adorna, e di trofei,
Raro lavoro di scalpello industre;
Mentre nel vacuo sen chiudono intanto,
Poco cenere sol, silenzio, ed ombra.[23]

The ordered clarity of Bondi's observation is apparent in *La moda*, particularly in the description of articles on the dressing-table, and again he shows himself the poet of objects in the passage depicting the dressing of the hair. The poverty of subject matter is admitted by Bondi in the preface to *Le conversazioni* when he states: "Si studiano gli abbigliamenti, e si trascura l'erudizione e il sapere, fino a persuadersi di fare una figura nei circoli assai brillanti, se vi si porta un abito che fermi gli occhi, e riscuota un elogio."[24]

La moda so reveals attention to objects i.e. (la toletta, il tupé), without the literary and classical references which rendered *Il giorno* so perfect in its own right. *La moda* is without the lightness and delicacy of *La giornata villereccia*; it is as though Bondi had in the former work stripped the world of Bonducci, Conti, Savioli and Parini of genteel ornamentation, both visual and stylistic, leaving the mere objects, with an occasional addition of colour to dazzle momentarily. One could say that the basic theme of *La moda* is that expressed at the conclusion: the contrast between nature and art, and the stupidity of those who dedicate themselves to the pursuit of the artificial. The latter point was made clear with reference to "le ornate/di fuori almeno femminili teste". The message of the poem is directed towards society:

. . .Lascia gli strani
Equivoci ornamenti a lor, che vane
Di risvegliare il languido desio,
Studian le scene seduttrici, e gli usi
Degnansi, e i fregi ricopiarne almeno.
Te la Natura liberal distinse
Con larghi doni, onde chiaman non dèi

L'arte in soccorso, che al natio difetto
Supplisce è ver, ma nol compensa mai.[25]

I do not believe that Clemente Bondi constitutes an essential factor in the development of the poetry of the "bel mondo". I do, however, hold that his poetry is illustrative of taste and society in the late "Settecento". There is little originality in his work: his subjects are drawn from Pope and his translators, his world can be said to be that of Parini, and the grotesque image of the "tupé" finds its counterpart in the poem by Vittorelli, as will be seen later. Yet Bondi is a talented and imaginative poet, whose main concern was the expression of a genteel society. This is clearly illustrated in the preface to Le conversazioni, 1778: "Le Conversazioni erano un tempo una ricreazione di spirito, una distrazione di mente o dagli studi, o da altre cure più serie: precedute dalla fatica si prevenivano col desiderio, dalla rarità stessa animate non languivano taciturne, e limitate a spazio discreto non terminavano colla sazietà. Oggi per molti son divenute una occupazione e un impiego. Tutto il giorno è diviso nel giro eterno di visite successive —: ogni ora quasi ha le sue proprie; il mattino si usurpa le confidenti e segrete, al tardo sol si protraggono quelle di semplice formalità, e le lunghe sere si riserbano quelle di costume, o d'impegno:. . .[26]

Bondi remains for us then the poet of miniature objects varying from the china cup to the clock, and from the jars of paste and powder to combs, mirrors and fans. As has been seen, he was poetically active in the second half of the eighteenth century. On his departure from Italy, and with the coming of the Romantic era, he ceased to depict a set of fashions already dead. Towards the end of his life he admitted a loss of poetic inspiration. In a letter to Giuseppe Bombardini he admits his anti-poetic malady — "Dal Sig. Conte Caldogno ho ricevuto il gratissimo regalo del saggio della di lei poesie. Egli mi ha ritrovato fatalmente incomodato dalla stessa malattia anti-poetica che mi ritarda il piacere di farmene favola lettura, giacchè i miei occhi non mi permettono di farla da me" . . .[27]. Four years later in 1821, he died in Vienna, the last to occupy the position of poet laureate.

The poetic figure of the late eighteenth century whose work automatically classifies him alongside Bondi, is Giuseppe Colpani, a contributor to *Il caffe* in 1764, who spread its ideas and fashions in poems such as "Il gusto" and "Il commercio". Though not an admirer of Parini, he is nontheless an exponent of "il mondo pariniano". Yet his contacts with the English literary world in general, and the influence of Pope in particular, can be said to have exercised an important influence on his choice of topic. He was born in Brescia in 1739, and died in 1822. His interest in English happenings, personalities and his admiration of *The Rape of the Lock* is what draws us to consider his compositions as direct influences of the work and popularity of the English poet. Historically his role in the passage from arcadian Classicism to Neo-Classicism is significant.

Opinions have been divided with regard to the poetic worth of Colpani's compositions. Gaetano Fornasini, having referred to the poem *L'occhio*, praises Colpani as a poet, and refers to his studies of English writers: "Ora, un autore che scrive così parmi che senza opposizione abbia diritto alla giù giusta lode, anzi niuno, io credo, mi darà faccia di eccedere i limiti del vero, s'io lo dirò poeta classico in questo genere di comporre in cui la filosofia viene ingentilita dalle grazie. Se non che i tratti filosofici che di frequente risplendono ne'suoi versi quà e là facendo sentire lo studio ch'ei metteva in Lucrezio, in Pope, e in altri celebri scrittori della inglese pensatrice nazione, talora non bastano a temperare la voluttà che per ogni lato vi traspira.[28]

Fornasini also stresses that Colpani has not merely studied foreign authors and thinkers, but has also absorbed the culture of some of Italy's contemporary poets, and also that of Voltaire: "Dalle Opere sue si rileva inoltre come egli godea dell'amicizia degli scrittori più colti della sua patria, e com'era in corrispondenza e famigliarità coi più celebri letterati d'Italia e fuori; e tra questi particolarmente coi Verri, coi Frisi, coi Beccaria, coi Carli, coi Rezzonico . . . e lo stesso Voltaire.[29]

While Fornasini is complementary in the extreme, the Count Gnoli ignores his poetic talents, or rather what he believes to be a lack of them, in order to underline his historical significance: "Il Colpani, lo ripeto non è davvero un poeta, ma è un documento importante alla storia, una illustrazione preziosa alla poesia pariniana: poichè di quanti verseggiatori italiani dello scorso secolo mi son capitati fra mano, nessuno vale a darci un'idea così compiuta di quel che fosse quella parte di nobiltà colta, filosofica, infranciosata, che passeggiava tranquillamente con un sorrisetto volteriano, sull'orlo di un vulcano che mugghiava; nessuno comprende così interamente in un sistema d'elegante epicureismo la filosofia e la moda, la galanteria e la scienza.[30]

Binni sees him as one attempting to spread the ideas of *Il caffè* in two manners — "con una singolare divaricazione fra le forme
più discorsive di veri poemetti didascalici"

and

"il gusto di canzonetta savoliana esercitato con sommaria e scialba eleganza su temi mondani e galanti."[31]

Colpani's attitude to England and the English race can be summed up as follows: he saw them as a non-gallant race of philosophers, hampered by a certain melancholy identified with the foggy British climate. As opposed to Savioli, Parini, Vittorelli and Bondi, it is the latter aspect of *The Rape of the Lock*, namely the lines dealing with Spleen, and the brief references to the coffee-party, which will become the subject of his poetry. One could say that Colpani finds material for philosophising within such a world, rather than in an atmosphere of reckless gaiety. His poem *L'Emilia*, it is true, can be said to be modelled on *Il mattino*, but at this point in the century the lack of originality is painfully obvious. Yet Colpani is also a poet of minute objects, coffee drinking, "buon gusto" and crystal chandeliers, although he rates all in relation to their utility and commercial value.

That Colpani considered *The Rape of the Lock* the greatest of its genre he states in his *Ottavi niente poetici*:

Nel tuo, Pope immortal, Riccio Rapito,
Dal men galante popolo del Mondo
Il più galante Poemetto è uscito.

He wrote a sonnet on the death of the princess Charlotte of England which concluded:

Fra l'Elisie Ombre illustri Ombra immortale
Vanne alla grande Elisabetta accanto
A lei per genj e per grand'Alma eguale.

He is also the writer of a sonnet entitled "A Wellington e Bluchen", and in "I compensi – anacreontica" refers to boredom, melancolia or hypochondria which he associates with the English:

No non temer, che un'Anglica
Malinconia ricetto
Mai trovi entro il mio petto,
Nè che abbattuto veggasi
Sotto il destin nemico
Il tuo fedel Amico;

La noja, delle vacue
Menti perpetuo albergo,
così da me dispergo
E gli anni, che con rapido
Volo crescendo vanno,
Soavemente inganno.
Così Natura provida,
Se a toglierci non vale
L'inevitabil male.
Pur lo compensa e tempera:
Ne'in porgermi conforto
Il saggio Pope ha torto.[32]

The malady which Pope's contemporaries called "spleen" (vapours, hypochondria and hysteria were other names which they applied to it) had had a long history in medical tradition. Its theoretical existence had been due, ultimately, to Galen and Hippocrates, the ancient Greek phyiscians whose authority had dominated medieval and renaissance medicine. In England it has been a fashionable complaint for over a century when Pope wrote *The Rape of the Lock*. Until rather late in the seventeenth century it had been called melancholy.[33] In "I compensi" Colpani is attempting to define his own personality. The lines create the impression of artlessness – the statements are clear-cut without complexity or sophisticated turn of phrase. The rhyme scheme, in my opinion, combined with the total lack of imagery in the first quotation, makes for a simplistic affect. The second quotation purports to the abstract communication of melancholia, but Colpani here succeeds in merely being obscure. It appears that melancholia was identified with England during the eighteenth century. Dreariness, vapours and clouds are contrasted with the Italian sun, as in "L'Ipocondria",[34] dedicated to the Signora Marchesa Castiglioni, nata Litta:

Il chiaro cielo Italico
È questo pur, ch'io miro:
Non la grave dell'Anglia
Nembrosa aria respiro:
Eppure cede alle mia
L'Inglese Ipocondria.[35]

Qual mai perverso, ed invido
Vento dalla Brittana
Region vaporifera
Il mal, che sì m'affanna.
Sulle gelate penne
Recando, a me sen venne.[36]

The contrast is well conveyed in the opening stanza, with "Italico" and "Anglia" occurring at the end of the line, and the juxtaposition of "miro" and "respiro". The movement of the "ipocondria" after the manner of winds is also well expressed, and the lack of complexity or veiled message on the part of the poet here makes for clarity. Nonetheless it is my opinion that the level of poetry does not rise above that of mediocrity. One is in fact reminded of the extemporary poet, or improvisor, whose rapidity of composition and attention to obvious rhyme is inclined to rob the poetry of creative force or depth.

It is true, however, that there is a connection between the second stanza of "L'Ipocondria" and Pope's *The Rape of the Lock*, Canto IV.

Swift on his sooty pinions flits the gnome,
And in a vapour reached the dismal dome.
No cheerful breeze this sullen region knows,
The dreaded east is all the wind that blows.
(Pope, *The Rape of the Lock*, Canto IV. 18-21).

The same simplicity of diction and concept is employed by Pope, movement is conveyed in both stanzas, and perhaps its weakness could be defined in terms of the obvious. As Pope supplies a detailed account and demonstration of individuals suffering from Spleen, so also does Colpani describe the biological condition of one suffering from "Ipocondria". Once again one is aware of Colpani's ability as a quick-thinking writer of verse. In the lines describing "Noia", "Ipocondria" and other aspects of nervous depression, he is far removed from the world of grace and manners. It is as though Colpani, as later will be seen in the work of Pignotti, sought to produce the basic human functions alongside the assumed and contrived mannerisms of his time. Such expressions are never devoid of humour, as will be seen in the lines quoted below. The symptoms of "Ipocondria" are, according to Colpani, as follows:

> Le viscere irritabili
> Con fiero dente morde,
> Ed or distratte, e rigide
> Come vibranti corde,
> Or le ritiene in forte
> Gordian nodo contorte.

> Cosî al chilific organo
> L'opra compir non lassa,
> E l'importun rigurgito
> Della indigesta massa
> Sino alle fauci estreme
> Spinge, gorgoglia, e freme.

> S'alza dal fondo torbido
> Nebbia di vapor densi,
> Da'cui fumi letargici
> Giaccion torbidi i sensi,
> E degli uffizj usati
> Par, che si sian scordati.[37]

Stanza iv recalls Pope's Cave of Spleen, where individuals resemble bottles and tea-pots and suffer from far-fetched illusions. In Colpani's poem the inside, with rumbling and gurgling, resembles vibrating chords, making strange music indeed. We are now in the realm of poor satire, which in a longer work would have the virtue of providing variety and speeding the descriptive narrative. In a poem of the nature of Colpani's, it merely reduces all to the level of the farcical.

The second attribute of British social life found in the work of Colpani is coffee making. He dedicates his poem "Il caffè" to "le donne inglesi". The poem contains descriptions of the beverage, finely prepared, its preparation, and a final appraisal of the British as a race of philosophers. The influence of Pope is clear in Colpani's poem, terms such as "grato vapor", "caldo umor", "fumoso prandio", "fermentati spiriti", seem inspired by Pope's original "grateful liquors", "smoking tide", "fuming liquor", rather than by Bonducci's or Conti's translation. The spirit and lightness of touch appears to conform very much to the "coffee" passage in *The Rape of the Lock*.

> Già la versata, O Fillide
> Nereggiante bevanda
> Ti sta dinanzi, e il vivido
> Grato vapor tramanda.[38]

> T'offro la colma ciotola
> Dal sottoposto argento:
> Tu il caldo umor delibane
> A facil sorso, e lento.

Its effects are described in the following terms:

> Dopo il fumoso prandio,
> Che serve nelle vene,
> Ai fermentanti spiriti,
> Quanto propizio or viene![39]

> S'ei morde l'irritabile
> Fibra co' sali aguzzi,
> Or fia, che l'acre stimolo
> Dal cibo si rintuzzi.[40]

Pope's oriental atmosphere is retained by Colpani in the lines:

> Fer coll'argilla docile
> La tazza alabastrina
> Gli abitator dell'ultimo
> Giappone, o della Cina.[41]

The poem ends with a tribute to the British race:

> Prega, che un voto unanime
> Il tristo uso condanni,
> E il grande esempio stendasi
> Dai liberi Britanni.[42]

> Un popol di Filosofi
> L'Europa ammiri in voi
> Come i Romani furono
> Un popolo d'Eroi.[43]

In "Il caffè", as also in "Lo specchio", Colpani reveals himself the poet of gracefulness in depicting the miniature. Unlike in the already quoted works describing hypochondria, there is the pointed portrayal of objects, actions and effects, while philosophic and scientific significance is conveyed. As will be seen in "La toletta", "Il cioccolatte" and "Il commercio", Colpani has broadened his horizons from the mere confined activity within the "bel mondo", to consider coffee making, reflection, and trade from the point of view of business and utility.

In the first stanza of "Il caffè", the address to Fillide places the reader in the world of Arcadia. The entire visual effect of the coffee is conveyed in stanza ii. The dainty world of the miniature is seen in iv with the description of the cup, which draws attention not only to the place of origin of the piece but also to the inhabitants, once again providing associations between peoples by means of the object of utility and decoration:

> Fer coll'argilla docile
> La tazza alabastrina
> Gli abitator dell'ultimo
> Giappone, o della Cina.

The final tribute to the British takes the form of a salute to a race of philosophers, the fatherland of Pope, whose oriental atmosphere he succeeds in recapturing in reference to the coffee-cup. In the same way the decorative, useful object, based on a scientific principle, becomes the point of departure in the illustration of the grace and charm of an era in "Lo specchio".[44] Here the image of the hairdresser is seen as a "maestro" of ideas directed at beautification and conquest. The poem is addressed to Fillide, and stanzas i and ii bring together the sublime and the ridiculous, the contrast between fashionable and philosophical speculation:

Al profumato, e nitido
Stranio Garzon, sì destro
Di quell'Arte maestro
Onde l'arguto pettine
Sugli ordini novelli
Edifica i capelli,
A lui, che mentre s'agita
In Francia il gran pensiero
Di ricompor l'Impero,
Venne alle Belle Italiche
Con grazie Parigine
A ricomporre il crine.

The hairdresser is "profumato", "nitido", an artist and philosopher, armed with an "arguto pettine" with which he constructs his creations. His person and work is drawn with precise clarity and precision of touch, while in the final line, the elegant fashion for which he stands is communicated merely by two words "grazie Parigine". In these lines Colpani comes close to the style of Bondi, precise, clearcut and controlled. Later in the poem, by means of light imagery and symbolism, he demonstrates the scientific principle by means of which the mirror operates:

Madre di bei fenomeni,
Quella virtù traluce,
Onde un raggio di luce,
Respinto dalle solide
Parti, con legge eguale
Al suo cader, risale.
E gli oggetti moltiplici
Fansi all'occhio presenti,
Perchè su lor cadenti
I raggi a lui rimbalzano,
Seco recando in vago
Furto la tolta immago.
La stessa nostra immagine
All'occhio si dipinge,

Immediacy and swiftness of movement is achieved with the repeated use of the letter "r" — "raggio", "respinto", "risale", as in the concept of exchange of images with "rimbalzano", "recando". Colpani, in demonstrating the function of the mirror, does not depart from the poetic world created at the opening of the poem. A further dimension is added by the poet with reference to nature, and the stream which provides the rustic maiden with a natural mirror, devoid of the decorations and ornamentation of that of Fillide:

> La Forosetta semplice,
> Assisa in sulla sponda
> Di cheta, e limpid'onda,
> Così allo Specchio guardasi,
> Che a lei senz'altra cura
> Apparecchiò Natura.

Nature, art, artifice and industry, then, form the world of Colpani, as a late eighteenth-century poet alive to the complex functions of literature and not satisfied to remain imprisoned in the world of, and on the same scale as, the statuette. Like Parini, he was aware of the various dimensions on which Being and Existence could be probed, but while Parini was conscious of it first and foremost within the realm of the individual, Colpani sees it with regard to commercial activity. This is particularly so with regard to "La toletta"[45] and "Il ciocolatte". The luxury and frivolity reproduced by Bonducci and Conti, ironically assessed by Parini, and minutely and precisely drawn by Bondi, in the hands of Colpani, have become both useful and necessary. Murano crystal, precious silver, and china combine to raise a hymn of praise to Art and Industry:

> Quante alla sola tua vaga Toletta
> Arti diverse i lor tributi offriro!
> Per te sudar nelle fornaci ardenti
> Del Veneto Murano i fabri ignudi
> Sul non fallace e nitido cristallo,
> Nell'immagine tua lieto e superbo
> Di mostrarti talor quanto sei bella.
> I ricchi a fabbricar lucidi vasi
> Piegò il docile argento in varie forme
> Un novello Germano: o con novella
> Arte, per te sulla Misniaca argilla

Fur da mano Sassonica creati
I Chinesi lavori... [46]

Art and industry also facilitates the coming together of nations and cultures −

O con novella
Arte, per te sulla Misniaca argilla
Fur da mano Sassonica creati
I Chinesi lavori.

Colpani also has here the ability to confer personality on the various objects by the apt choice of adjective: i.e. "fornaci ardenti", "nitido cristallo", "lucidi vasi", "docile argento", and later on in the poem "vivace arancio", "soave gelsomine". The adjectives "ardenti", "nitido", "lucidi", convey varying degrees of light, thus highlighting and illuminating the object in question. Thus each object possesses an independent personality, added to an activity in collaboration with the other articles on the dressing-table. We are now only one step removed from the open appraisal of material gain as a result of the divulgation of art:

Così vive il Commercio, e tutte a gara
Servon l'Arti, e l'industria al piacer nostro. [47]

From the aforementioned examples one can conclude that Colpani used the set cameos of the "Settecento" to create a poetry of social activity, while at the same time introducing business and finance to this world. This can be clearly illustrated by means of two passages from "Il cioccolatte". [48] The first quotation shows the world of the miniature and the custom of chocolate drinking:

Nella Chinese tazza alto spumante
Ecco il salubre, o vezzosetta Nice,
Nettare American. Stendi all'amica
Mattutina bevanda animatrice, [49]

The second quotation praises trade in providing tributaries in order to serve the lady who has given herself over to pleasure. In place of sylphs one finds various races competing in order to provide the tasty and tasteful:

Or, mercè del moltiplice Commercio
Quante non vedi tributarie genti
Ministre al tuo piacer? Per te col vivo
Francese il taciturno Anglo gareggia:
Per te il lento Fiammingo, il grave Ispano
Suda, e il biondo German.[50]

Colpani the poet then has produced, in the pursuit of the "bel mondo" poetry, the good, bad and indifferent. Belonging to the first category are surely "Il caffe", "Lo specchio", and "Il commercio". Opinions indeed differ with regard to the worth of "La toletta" and "Il cioccolatte", while there can be little doubt with regard to the worth of "L'ipocondria". Colpani, at his best, however, was capable of writing in the manner in which he described the work of a friend, the Conte Giuseppe Urbano Pagani Casa — with "il sentimento, l'immaginazione e la grazia".[51] In the same letter, he refers to his work as "miei piacevoli nienti poetici", while in his correspondence to the Abate Golini of Bassano del Grappa, he refers to his "piccolo niente poetico."[52] His images have the finesse of wedgwood, his vision is far-seeing, and his life-span, embracing the periods of Arcadia, Enlightenment, Neo-Classicism and early Romanticism, conferred on him a wealth of literary and political experience.[53]

A final consideration of the "coffee poets" brings us to illustrate some of the work of Lorenzo Barotti, a Jesuit and native of Ferrara. His poem "Il caffe"[54] provides a classically moulded account of coffee-making, describing the operation in terms of a sacred ritual, reminiscent of Savioli with regard to elegant attention to detail. The poem was written in 1781. Barotti combines the world of Savioli and Pope, with the classical cameo, and the raising of the flame, in the making of coffee, reminiscent of Pope in *The Rape of the Lock.*

Frattanto alcune coppie d'Amoretti
Dalla Dea deputati a tal fattura
A'grani del Caffè cerniti, e schietti
Davano insiem la debita cottura.
Altri il fuoco, con mantici, o soffietti
D'attizzar nel fornello avean la cora.
Sicchè la fiamma dalle accese brace
Ognora si levasse alta, e vivace.[55]

Barotti works with both diminutive and the magnified in terms of the "amoretti" and the flame. He attempts to combine purity of expression and concept. The water is drawn, not from a well but from a stream assuring its purity:

> Altri cosî polverizzato, e fino
> In giusta dose (e ben sapean qual era)
> Facevanlo bollire in un ramino
> Detto poi dal suo nome Caffettiera,
> Con acqua, che non pozzo, ma un vicino
> Fonte porgeva lor lieve e sincera.[56]

Barotti has created his own small world in which all is pure, perfect and beneficial; in this respect he has much in common with the poets already quoted and referred to. It must be stated however, that the changing face of the eighteenth century can be viewed through the activity of the ladies and their "cicisbei", and that although all is seen on a very small scale, there is no lack of clarity of message, or of care, in the accurate drawing of a situation.

One could speak of artistic decadence, a decadent aspect of Arcadia, and its visual projection in terms of the rococo. From the purity of Savioli, and the social mission of Parini, one finds in the work of Clemente Bondi, an isolation of objects of utility and decorum, in such a way that they assume an independent activity. The hand of the writer seems to have completely disappeared, leaving the dressing-table with its articles, and the clock, to become the subject matter of the poems. Most important is Bondi's emphasis on the utility of certain objects, combining the functional and the frivolous. This concept is carried further by Giuseppe Colpani, who reviews objects in relation to their commercial value. Flourishing trade, industry and competition between various races, and the commercial value of art and artifice mark the subject matter of Colpani's work, along with his identification of melancholia and hypochondria with the English race. Thus the poetic miniature reflects social change in a society which will finally succumb to the French Revolution.

The poetic miniature, it must also be stressed, is poetry of incidents and objects derived from Pope's *The Rape of the Lock*. It is a world of sylphs and hairdressers, *Ombre* and hypochondria, with pride of place going to the realm of the "toilette" and the art of coffee making. The final impression is that the entire poetic world, because of its fragility, cannot possibly endure. The atmosphere of game, or "villeggiatura" must, like all good things, come to an end.

Notes to Chapter III

1 Clemente Bondi, (in Arcadia Metabo Prianeo).
Born 1742 at Mozzano Superiore, died Vienna, 1821. Taught in Jesuit
school at Padua. Later went to Mantua as tutor to the Zanardi family, and
to Milan until the arrival of the French in 1796. In the same year, Bondi accepted the post of librarian at Brunn, moved to Neustadt, and finally to
Vienna as poet laureate. Died there on June 30, 1821. In addition to his
lyric poetry, he also wrote fables and translations of Virgil's *Georgics* and
Aeneid, and Ovid's *Metamorphosis*. The most complete edition of his poetry
is that in three volumes, published in Vienna in 1808.
Editions: *Poesie diverse di C.B.* (Padua 1776; *Poesie di C.B.* vol. 2 (Padua,
1778); *Versi di C.B.* (Lucca, 1778); *Poemetti e rime varie di C.B.* (Venice,
1778); *Poesie di C.B.* (Parma 1779); *Opere edite e inedite in versi e in prosa
di C.B.*, vol. 7 (Venice, 1798-1801); *Poesie di C.B., Parmigiano* vol. 2 (Florence, 1808); Critical works: A. Donati, *Poeti minori del settecento*, (Bari,
1912-31), pp. 187-250; A. Pezzana, *Intorno a Clemente Bondi, Epistola*
(Parma, 1821); Angelo Ottolini, "Una canzonetta del Parini sconosciuta, in
Archivio storico lombardo, ser v.a. XLVIII, 1921, pp. 185-90; F. Baldenspor-
ger, "Le poete Bondi et Jacques Delille" in *Revue de litterature comparee*,
111, 1, 1923; B. Croce, "Verseggiatori del grave e del sublime" and "Clemente Bondi", in *La letteratura italiana del Settecento*, op.cit., pp. 361-2
and 363-374; Bondi, Forlì, Biblioteca Comunale, MS 154-155, contains a
selection of Bondi's poetry. Part 1, pp. 131-8 contains: *A Gertrude morta
per impeto d'amore; Per monaca incorotta dopo morte; Il passaggio del Pò;
La lontananza; La vanità dei piaceri; Per mondani; Per celebre botanico;*
The second part of the MS contains at pp. 427-35: *Il languore; Il risentimen-
to; La pace; L'indifferenza; Nice elettrizzata; L'impazienza; Offerta pastorale per nozze; La distrazione; L'ambasciata in occasione d'infreddatura;*
Bondi's correspondence is to be found in Forlì, Biblioteca Comunale, MS
Piancastelli; it contains letters to Paganino Sala, Marcantonio Miniscalchi,
Jacques Blanchon, and to the burser of the Seminario di Parma to whom he
sends 400 scudi. The letters are all autographed and do not contain any literary references nor throw any light on his poetry.
The Biblioteca Trivulziana, Milan, contains poems by De Rossi, and Bondi,
in an 'opuscolo' entitled *Poesie varie, 1789.* All poems are written by the
one hand, and the poem of most interest to the present study is *Il ventaglio.*
See Milan, Biblioteca Trivulziana MS Trivulziana Cod. 880. An autographed
letter is to be found in the Biblioteca Civica, Bassano del Grappa, in Autografi Remondini IV. 18. The letter, was written from Vienna four years
prior to his death.

2 *Scelte poesie italiane* (Milan, 1822), p. 51.

3 Ibid.

4 Ibid.

5 Ibid. p. 52.

6 A. Bonducci, *Il riccio rapito*, op.cit., p. 54, 1. 16-26.

7 G. Gronda, *Versioni poetiche*, op.cit., p. 58, 1. 130-7.

8 Femmina di costumi, e di maniere,
   E d'esercizio sol maschio è di sesso,
   Non marito, non celibe, ma spesso
   L'uno e l'altro per genio e per mestiere.
   Supplemento diurno, il cui dovere
   E di star sempre a l'altrui moglie appresso;
   Ed ha per patto e complimento espresso
   Noiarsi insieme le giornate intere:
   Che legge quando sa, cuce e ricama,
   E dieci ore del dì molle indolente
   Serve or d'ombra, or di corpo a la sua dama.
   Questo è lo strano indefinibil ente,
   Quell'anfibio animale, ch'oggi si chiama
   Per tutta Italia cavalier servente.
   In Clemente Bondi, *Opere*, (Venezia, 1798).

9 C. Bondi, *La giornata villereccia* (Parma, 1773).

10 "L'orologio", in *Poesie diverse di Clemente Bondi* (Padua, 1776), p. 11.

11 Giuseppe Savoca, "Satirici e giocosi" in *Il Settecento*, op.cit., p. 593.

12 *Poesie di Clemente Bondi*, I (Vienna, 1808), p. 193, 1.1-10.

13 Ibid., p. 206.

14 Ibid.

15 Ibid., pp. 206-7.

16 Ibid., p. 208.

17 Ibid., p. 209.

18 Ibid., p. 209-10.

19 Ibid., p. 210.

20 A detailed discussion of Vittorelli's work is provided in the following chapter.

21 *Poesie di Clemente Bondi*, I. (Vienna, 1808), p. 210.

22 Ibid., p. 211.

23 Ibid., pp. 211-12.

24 C. Bondi, *Le conversazioni*, (Padua, 1778).

25 *Poesie di Clemente Bondi*, I. op.cit., p. 213.

26 See note 21

27 See Bassano del Grappa, Biblioteca Civica, MS Remondini IV. 18.

28 Gaetano Fornasini in *Ultime poesie del cavaliere Giuseppe Colpani con l'elogio dell'autore* (Brescia, 1823), p. 14.

29 Ibid., p. 17.

30 D. Gnoli, *Studi letterari.*
31 E. Cecchi & N. Sapegno, *Il Settecento* (Milan), p. 525.
32 *Ultime poesie del cavaliere Giuseppe Colpani,* op.cit., pp. 47-54. Also *G.C. Poesie,* V. (Venice, 1794), pp. 59-66.
33 Lawrence Babb, "The Cave of Spleen" in *Review of English Studies,* Vol. 12 (1936), p. 165.
34 G. Colpani, *Poesie,* V, op.cit., pp. 59-66.
35 Ibid., p. 59.
36 Ibid., p. 59.
37 Ibid., pp. 60-61.
38 *Opere del Cavaliere Giuseppe Colpani di Brescia,* III, (Vicenza, 1789), p. 169.
39 Ibid.
40 Ibid., p. 170.
41 Ibid., p. 171.
42 Ibid., p. 175.
43 Ibid.
44 See *Opere del Cavaliere Giuseppe Colpani,* V, op.cit., pp. 37-45.
45 See G. Colpani, *Opere del cavaliere Giuseppe Colpani di Brescia,* II, (Vicenza, 1784), p. 84. Here an appraisal of frivolity is expressed, and its contribution to trade stated:

"Io l'elegante lusso, io le brillanti
Frivolità delle inventrici Mode,
Anima del Commercio, amo ed apprezzo.
Indarno avrebbe il Savonese Tisi,
Sull.intatto Ocean sparse le vele,
E dei tesori Americani aperte
Alla sete Europea le ricche fonti
Invan dal Franco, e dal Brittano lido
Sciolto, e dal Texel l'animoso abete
Ricondurria le stranie merci in porto,
Se fra le varie Nazioni industri
Non le spargesse il florido Commercio,
E l'util Lusso, e la cangiante Moda".

46 Ibid., p. 85.
47 Ibid., p. 87.
48 *Opere del Cavaliere Giuseppe Colpani di Brescia,* II, op.cit., pp. 49-57.
49 Ibid., p. 49.
50 Ibid., p. 53.
51 Bassano del Grappa, Biblioteca Civica, Autografi Gamba XII, a. 28.

Amatissimo Sig. Conte,

Mi sono ieri consegnate le sue opere, e la gentilissima lettera, che le accompagna. Le leggerò tutte con quel piacere medesimo, con cui alcune di esse che avea già letto, e in tutte egualmente ammirerò, da lei con somma felicità riusciti, e come direbbe Orazio, amichevolmente conservati, il sentimento, l'immaginazione e la grazia. M'affretto intanto a contestarle per sì prezioso dono, la mia giusta riconoscenza mi riserbo a presentarle, benchè in troppo svantaggioso contraccambio per lei, i miei versi, quando sian fatti in una nuova edizione raccolti. Non disaggradisca intanto l'ultimo de'miei piacevoli nienti poetici, che le prometto. Vengono con esso i più sinceri sentimenti di vera stima, e di grato animo, co'quali ho l'onore di professarmi,

di Lei, Sig. Conte, Umil[issimo] Dev.[issimo]
servitore.

Giuseppe Colpani.

This letter demonstrates a simplicity of diction and naturalness of expression which indicates self-contained humility. It also illustrates a kindly disposition and readiness to praise the work of a friend and colleague.

52 Ibid. undated letter.

Sign.[re] Ab[te] Golini Onoratissimo,

Questa volta non voglio meritarmi gli obbliganti rimproveri, ch'ella mi fece sul mio ritardo nel mandarle le cose mie, ieri è sortita quest'ultima, ed oggi mi do il piacere di spedirgliela. Gradisca con la solita gentilezza il piccolo niente poetico, se le parrà che ne vaglia la pena. Con lui vengono i più vivi sentimenti dell'antica stima, che conservo per lei: ella per me conservi l'antica amicizia,
e credi inalterabilmente —

Suo devot[issimo] Servit[re] ed amico,

Colpani.

53 In addition to works quoted, see also with reference to Colpani: G. Dandolo, *La caduta della Repubblica di Venezia*, appendice, (Venezia, 1857). *Memorie dell'accademia di Scienze, Lettere e Arti Agiati* "Rovereto, 1901-5). "Il caffe", introduction and notes, L. Collino, (Turin, 1930).

54 *Il caffè*, poemetto di Lorenzo Barotti (Verona, 1821).

55 Ibid., Canto II, XLII, pp. 42-3.

56 Ibid. Canto II, LLIV, p. 43.

CHAPTER IV

Jacopo Vittorelli and the poetry of the "Tupé"

In *The Rape of the Lock* the curl is the symbol of love, pride in virginity, and of eighteenth-century society itself. Savioli saw the lock as "la maschera", a symbol of personal and social pride. For both Mutinelli and Durante, the decoration of the hair was a mere convention. With the work of Giacomo Vittorelli[1] the hair covered with a "tupé" becomes identified with time and space. Its proportions, bordering on the grotesque, are seen as bridging the gap between the natural and supernatural, and artifice is treated with light humour and ridicule. Vittorelli lived from 1749 to 1835, spanning a variety of literary tastes, trends and tendencies from Arcadia, Enlightenment, Neo-Classicism to Romanticism. Yet above all he stands for the decadence of the pre-revolutionary society which he depicted in his poems such as *Il naso, Lo specchio* and above all *Il tupé.* Antonio Piromalli refers to him as one "il quale non ebbe evoluzione spirituale e artistica e rappresentò la decrepitezza dell'Arcadia."[2] For Vittorelli, love appealed above all to the fantasy, it was a game which was "un divertimento occasionale che riesce a simulare nell'abilità tecnica della modulazione melodiosa un sentimento che non è altro che un'intima finzione, e pertanto falso e gracilissimo; il che conduce a porre il Vittorelli fuori di ogni possibilità di valutazione positiva."[3] If it can be said with conviction that an over-all positive assessment of Vittorelli's poetry cannot be made, one can at least stress the poet's role within the decadent, artificial society which was his self-chosen poetic world. One can state his positive qualities within that realm, and the historical significance of his poetic output.

Of noble and well-to-do stock, born at Bassano del Grappa in 1749, Vittorelli studied at the Jesuit Collegio dei Nobili at Brescia where he remained from 1761 to 1770.[4] On completing his education, he returned to Bassano, where he made the acquaintance of the leading literary figures of the time, and was admitted to the Accademia degli Intraprendenti. This is the period of *Il tupé* (1772), *Lo specchio, Il naso, Il farnetico* and *I maccheroni* (1773). In 1787, as a result of a quarrel with his father, Vittorelli left Bassano for Venice, where he held office under Girolamo Ascanio Molin, State Inquisitor for the Republic, and was named "Straordinario collazionista per uso dei nuovi codici veneti civili e criminali sotto la immediata ispezione dello eccelso Consiglio dei Dieci". In Venice, Vittorelli made close friendships with Giovanni and Ippolito Pindemonte with Gritti and Lamberti, and proved an assiduous frequentor of the salon of Giustina Renier-Michiel. In 1796, on the death of his father, he paid a short return visit to his home town. A letter of that period reveals the difficulty in making the short journey from Venice to Bassano: "Io sono in una confusione grandissima, e mi figuro lo scompiglio di tutti voi altri. Io non parto certamente da Venezia se io non vengo assicurato da voi di poter venire e di poter agire."[5] Vittorelli resided in Padua, returned to Venice, where he lived from 1798 to 1802, while from 1809-1814 he held the position of Director of the College and School of Santa Giustina at Padua.

Vittorelli's letters reveal a mild, gentle disposition of one who, feeling abandoned by friends and fortune, was given to expressions of self-pity. Totally apolitical, he disliked the confusion and hardship inflicted by revolutions, and sought to serve with loyalty and dedication any office bestowed upon him. Many of Vittorelli's letters are undated. In one to Ascanio Molin, he comments on happenings and his hopes to return to Venice within a few days. It would appear from the content of the letter that it was written in 1796, during the period in which Vittorelli visited Bassano after the death of his father. The departure of the "Tedeschi" left Bassano more or less as always: "i Tedeschi sono finalmente partiti e le campagne di V.E. hanno sofferto assai poco, di che veramente sono lieto, e di che posso accertarla senza inganno. Io penso di ritornare fra due giorni o tre.[6] The return to Venice referred to was to be short-lived, and he subsequently divided his time between Padua and Bassano.

Vittorelli counted Giustina Michiel, one of the last truly great ladies fo the Venetian salon society of the "Settecento", amongst his friends. Writing from Rome Vittorelli refers to the political situation:

Sente dalle Gazzette che Napoleone non ha coraggio di far nuove leve. Come dunque resistere a un torrente di nemici? Non sarebbe strano (secondo il mio pensiero) che egli per destar un fanatismo generale nei Francesi rinunziasse furbescamente al trono, e rimettesse in piedi l'antica repubblica, signoreggiandola, come capo, per qualche tempo e aspettando il momento di farsi incoronar di bel nuovo.[7]

1814 marked the year of his final return to Bassano, where he occupied a villa at Felette, and dedicated himself to study and the simple life. His willingness during this time to read the efforts of friends and offer advice, is revealed in his letters of the period, along with his own views on poetic style. In a letter to Don Piero Martinato, in 1814, he praises in his work the qualities believed by him to constitute true poetic talent: "Ella è in possesso da lungo tempo dello stil vero, lontanissimo da qualunque gonfiezza, e da quella forestiera preziosità, che è di moda. Ciò vuol dire che non sono troppo note le regole di una sobrietà giudiziosa, e che non si vuol per guida la sempre infallibil natura nella poesia".[8]

In 1816 he was appointed Press Censor by the Austrian Government, an office which was renewed at his request. "Il Vittorelli non piegò la schiena al Vincitore. Si accontentò di chiedere, già vecchio e malato, un modesto ufficio nelle beate lagune, quando vide che per averlo bisognava salire le scale dei potenti, si accontentò di essere nella sua piccola città 'censore alle stampe', di fare della sua villa delle Felette un asilo di poesia".[9]

The year 1816, finds Vittorelli depressed and dissatisfied with his lot . . .: "io sono stucco e ristucco di abitar fra gente senza educazione, senza fede e senza gratitudine . . . la campagna non offre un asilo di sicurezza e massimo in tempo di notte".[10]

The letter to Angelo Dalmistro reveals his entire disillusionment with the world at large and his loyalty to those he still regards as his friends. In October 1816 he signs himself as Press Censor,[11] and nine years later supplies evidence of occupying the same position.[12] Vittorelli ended his days in Bassano on June 12th, 1835: "lontano dagli avvenimenti politici, nella solitudine campestre, curando le numerose edizioni delle sue poesie, ricevendo ammiratori ed amici, attendendo al giardino ed all'orto, poi — quando si fecero più gravi gli acciacchi della tarda età — si trasferì in quel modesto casino d'Angarano sulla destra del Brenta, dove il 12 Giugno, 1835, a 86 anni, chiudeva serenamente i suoi giorni".[13]

Despite his old age and general weakness, he kept in correspondence with his many friends, never failing to express openly his true feelings and physical complaints.[14] Writing in 1851, Luigi Carrer stated: "Jacopo Vittorelli era l'ultimo dei poeti che rappresentassero l'indole letteraria del secolo scorso; ora quell'antico secolo è intieramente scomparso".[15]

Vitorelli's *Il tupé* was published in 1773. Ironically it is addressed to "donne gentili", straight away bringing to mind both the sublime and the ridiculous. The poem is divided into two Canti, the first of which refers to ladies, the second to gentlemen. In this respect it attempts to embrace the cultivation of artifice by both sexes, so spanning the world of both Pope's *The Rape of the Lock* and Parini's *Il giorno*. The poet ponders on the "tupé" itself, the "toilette", fashions, the figure of the hairdresser, as well as openly referring to Pope's heroine and the fate of her lock. He opens with an address to the "donne gentili":

> Donne gentili, se vi tocco il dente
> Nel medesimo sito in cui vi duole,
> Fate il viso giulivo e sorridente.
> Mostrando d'aggradir le mie parole;
> Ch'io canterò, se Febo mel consente,
> Quella piramidal superba mole,
> Che vi formate in testa con la chioma
> E vince quasi il Culiseo di Roma.
> (Vittorelli, *Il tupé*, 1.1.)

> A voi consacro queste rime incolte,
> Dove a narrar le glorie io m'apparecchio
> Di quel caro tupé, nel qual rivolte
> La mattina spendete in su lo specchio
> Usurpando cosi molt'ore e molte
> Al primiero istituto e a l'uso vecchio
> Di dividere in due sempre il mattino,
> Parte ai capelli, e parte al damerino.
> (Vittorelli, *Il tupé*, 1.11)

Vitorelli's irony is biting from the onset. The sheer mass of the "tupé" is identified with the extensions of the ancient Roman Empire, while its comparison to objects of stone robs the ornament of any intrinsic poetic life. The concept is continued with the use of the verb "apparecchiare" with regard to narration:

> Dove a narrar le glorie io m'apparecchio
> Di quel caro tupé . . .

Just as the "tupé" is the concealer of nature, so thus is the poetic language describing it devoid of grace, lightness and spontaneous poetic life. That poetic decadence illustrates social decadence is clear with the description of the "toilette": it reveals itself as a vast artificial flower obediently opening its petals to display beauty aids, and a reflection of nature based on scientific principles which to the lady of the "bel mondo" is far more precious than natural relations. The mirror which merely produces the reflection placed in front of it, is, as a scientific achievement, and a servant of pride, rated higher than Mother Nature's own plan. It is in subtle passages such as stanza IV that Vittorelli is at his very best: he has succeeded in contrasting Nature and Art with regard to life itself and life-style, and has condensed concepts and implications, scaling all down in order that they exist within the miniature world of the dressing-table, having given free expression to space and time in the opening two stanzas:

> Già de la ricca femminil toletta
> Ubbidienti s'aprono le foglie
> Fillide avanza, e il parrucchier le assetta
> Un bianco lino su le rosee spoglie:
> Indi s'inoltra, e la gentil seggetta
> Su l'origliero morbido l'accoglie,
> Onde col fido vetro or si consigli
> Che val più del marito e più dei figli.
> (Vittorelli, *Il tupé*, 1. iv)

The theme of nature, and the correction of its defects is demonstrated as a profession: the professional hairdresser draws on scientific and philosophic principles. Vittorelli is the first to demonstrate objectively and thus ridicule self-adornment as a discipline requiring total concentration and dedication. Theories are now applied not merely to body functions and behaviour, but also to the visual aspect of being:

I. XIII

E già senza di lor non può l'altero
Piramidale altissimo edifizio
Fabbricar destramente un parrucchiero,
Che dotto e accorto sia nel proprio uffizio.
Gitene a professar altro mestiero
Kepler, Loke, Neuton, Wolfio, Leibnizio,
Boscovich, Archimede, e voi Bernulli
Che a petto di costor siete fanciulli.

XIV

I parrucchier se nol sapeste ancora
Sanno la geometria meglio di quanti
Vivono adesso, e vissero finora.
Celebri matematici prestanti:
E la loro virtute al secol d'ora
Si premia al suon di lucidi contanti:
E se a voi le accademie aperte foro,
Le borse in vece s'aprono a costoro.

XV

Ei siegue intanto, e gli esteri capricci
Ne la sua Dama di copiar procura,
Una corona di capei posticci
Tutto adempie l'error de la natura;
Poi saggiamente i veri e i compri ricci
Con ritorti ferruzzi ei rassicura
Onde scansarle ciò, che un tempo avvenne
A la cornacchia de le finte penne.
(Vittorelli, *Il tupé,* I. XIII-XV)

Once again the fusion of the sublime and the ridiculous constitutes the mock-heroic element of the lines: academic qualities are fused with attributes denoting architectural ability: the dressing of the "tupé" is seen in much the same manner as the construction of a building: "l'altero/Piramidale altissimo edifizio/Fabbricar destramente." Such an operation demands mathematical precision and mastery in workmanship.

The hairdresser is in his own field an academician. The use of the verb "professar" in relation to Kepler, "Loke", Neuton, Wolfio etc.; indirectly illustrates the fact that the art of hairdressing is seen truly as a profession demanding a knowledge of mathematical science.

128

More rewarding still is the office of hair-dresser than that of great intellect. The Academies have their doors open to the mighty of mind, but commercial success drives the architect of the hair to increasingly exotic creations. Not merely does his art entail an obscuring of nature, but also its close fusion with art, to the extent that neither one or the other is completely discernable. The "tupé" however, as the society it represents, is destined to be swept away by the French Revolution. Vittorelli identifies the "tupé" with bricks and mortar, which can be constructed and demolished as a result of a social whim. Later, the destruction of the "tupé" will be poetically demonstrated by Angelo Talassi and Lorenzo Pignotti.

One could indeed note that Vittorelli's approach to the "tupé" is entirely objective: he has taken an historical and literary approach to the object of decoration. In Canto I stanza V its use in Greek and Roman society is stressed as follows:

> Rancido è un uso tal, quindi ci narra
> La Greca storia e la Romana espressa
> Che del Tupé l'invenzion bizzarra
> Ne'secoli stantii piacque al bel sesso:
> E ce ne da bastevole caparra
> Solennemente Giovenale stesso,
> Il qual con bicro ciglio adotte adotta.
> Sì lubrici edifizi alto rimbrotta.
> (Vittorelli, *Il tupé*, 1. v)

In modern literature the most famous work built around a piece of hair is of course Pope's *The Rape of the Lock*. This has been referred to by Savioli and Duranti, but Vittorelli is the first "Settecento" poet to use the ornament itself, either natural or false as the subject of an entire poem. He also uses the reference to Pope in *Il tupé* to illustrate modern literary pre-occupation with such a topic:

> Pur sovra tutto a gli occhi mascolini
> Degno d'imitazione e di riflesso
> Parve quel mucchio d'elevati crini,
> Che la femmina avea sul fronte istesso
> E gli uomini restavan si piccini,
> Quando a le donne si facean da presso,
> Che invasero il marito ardenti voglie
> Di pareggiar la torreggiante moglie.
> (Vittorelli, *Il tupé*, 11. vi.)

Forse la Bella, che al Tamigi in riva
Inconsolabilissima si dolse,
Poi che mano sacrilega e furtiva
L'intemerata boccola le tolse,
Se tanta ferie di ricciuoli ordiva,
Quanta modernamente esiger sciolse,
Non avria forse per un solo riccio
Fatto l'occhietto timido e rossiccio.
(Vittorelli, *Il tupé*, 11. x.)

In the first Canto (vi) the dwarfing of the gentleman, brings the
poem a step further towards the grotesque, while at the same time
robs the lady of her delicate and genteel qualities, which were part of
the eighteenth-century tradition. The idea of the destruction of the
wig is also subtly introduced: all vision is blocked by the gross object, which fills time and space, and which finally demands destruction. This will be the vein in which Angelo Talassi will write his
mock-heroic poem *La piuma recisa*.

The "tupé" becomes now an object in its own right, separated
from the individual. Its original function was to adorn. It becomes itself an object of decoration, it is the subject of poetic works. Thus the
protagonist is no longer a person, but a thing, resembling life only in
the illustration of man's or woman's cult of the artificial:

E quindi nacque il barbaro costume
Di quell 'immenso orribile cuffione
Che de gli aerei ricci in sul cacumè
L'ambiziosa femmina si pone.
E quindi ancor le vario-pinte piume,
I fiori di Vinegia e di Lione
Le fettucce, i merletti ed il malanno.
Che accrescono il tupé, l'origin hanno;
(Vittorelli, *Il tupé*, 11. xiii.)

One has already witnessed the isolation of the object in the poetry of
Bondi and Colpani. The intrinsic activity of objects based on scientific
principles denotes the continuity of human invention, and the setting
in motion of systems. In the case of the "tupé", however, the object
is indeed isolated, and seen as a useless and lifeless mass. There is no
justification for its existence, it serves no useful purpose, and becomes the symbol of inutility.

130

After the dehumanisation of the "dama", at the conclusion of the poem, there is finally new life given to the "tupé". In the achievement of a final unity the poet brings together classical and eighteenth-century literature, the sublime and the ridiculous, Bernice and Belinda. When full circle is achieved: it is the triumph of the ridiculous which is celebrated.

> E quella chioma innanellata e bella.
> Che a gli altari di Venere si offerse,
> La qual in vaga luminosa stella
> Per decreto del ciel poi si converse.
> D'una tal cetra a l'armonia novella
> Udiasi lamentevole a dolerse;
> Che vorebbe esser chioma un'altra volta
> Per comparire in un tupé rivolta.
> (Vittorelli, *Il tupé*, 11. xxi.)

The lock "la qual in vaga luminosa stella", that of Berenice and Belinda, is personified, has the power of lamentation and wishful thinking. Following its transference to the spheres and its transformation from artifice to nature, it desires once again to return to earth in the form of a "tupé": that is, as a higher form of artifice. Its place of arrival would be Tuscany:

> E, se là giunto, dove il gran contrasto
> A soffrir ebbe de l'invitto Orazio,
> Ritentasse oggimai di dare il guasto
> Persenna stesso à la città del Lazio
> Un tupé col suo giro immenso e vasto
> Del ponte chiuderia l'aperto spazio.
> E diriasi al finir de la gran lutta
> Un tupé sol contro Toscana tutta.
> (Vittorelli, *Il tupé*, 11. xxvi.)

Vittorelli can be considered a follower of Parini in that he succeeds in satirising society. His poetry: "Rispondeva a un bisogno istintivo dell'anima: era – in quell'età di trapasso, in cui si sentiva che il vecchio mondo crollava sotto l'impeto furioso di nuove brame e di nuove ideali – un blando e salutare rifugio dello spirito, un oasi serena, in cui era dolce dimenticare e sognare."[17] His choice of vocabulary does indicate that he has absorbed the versions of Conti and Bonducci: "bianco lino"; "l'origliero morbido"; "fido vetro"; "ricca

131

femminil toletta". With reference to Belinda's lock, Vittorelli uses the term "boccola"; this is a significant choice since in Venetian dialect "boccola" is a rosebud, the symbol of love.[18] In this way Vittorelli offers his own interpretation of *The Rape of the Lock*:

> Forse la Bella, che al Tamigi in riva
> Inconsolabilissima si dolse
> Poi che mano sacrilega e furtiva
> L'intermerata boccola le tolse.

Vittorelli's role in this history of the Italian poetry of the "tupé" is as follows: he followed in the footsteps of Savioli and Duranti in referring to Pope's *The Rape of the Lock*. He, in his social satire *Il tupé,* follows in the school of Parini. But his most vital role from our point of view is that of one who provides a lengthy poem dealing with the social custom of wearing a "tupé", and decorating it with pearls, lace and feathers. The poem prompts the critic to look to Talassi and Pignotti. In the works of these poets the verbal attack on such social uses is poetically expressed in terms of an attack on the object of decorum itself. An attack modelled on Pope's rape, which is a source of inspiration for all above mentioned poets. Vittorelli's triumph is however the triumph of the ridiculous:

> Sarebbe difficile trovare chi agguagliasse il nostro poeta nelle frivolità di vestire con leggiadria o con magnificenza, secondo i casi le cose più minute e più dozzinali. Un meschino arredo della "toilette" femminile, una stravagante opinione scientifica, uno strumento d'arte qualunque, son ritratti sì nettamente, sì al vivo, con tanta nobilità, con tanta eleganza da rendere maravigliati i più provetti ed esperti scrittori.[19]

Giacomo Vittorelli was a man of immense literary, social and political experience, who was most at home in the salon of Giustina Michiel at San Moisè, or in the countryside surrounding Bassano del Grappa. His "rime" and social poems sought to preserve the purity and grace of both worlds, at a time when change, approaching revolution and social instability was the order of the day. He, as a personification of the dying world of Arcadia, poetically preserved the diminishing grandeur of late eighteenth-century Venice:

> Comunque, del Parini egli non ebbe nè il vigore della concezione poetica nè l'amara ironia, pago soltanto di ritrarre e di irridere nelle stanze festose, com-

poste "per sollazzo nell'ozio operoso di una tranquilla indolenza", la moda volubile, contro cui il giovane poeta lancia i suoi strali d'oro, senza volontà di far troppo male. Poemetti, quindi, "Il tupé" e "Lo specchio" tra il satirico e il burlesco, tra il *Mattino* del Parini, e il *Riccio rapito* del Pope.[20]

Vittorelli counted as friends the famous and not so famous literary figures of his day. Colpani, Duranti, the celebrated Algarotti and the Cardinal Bishop of Brescia Giovanni Molino were amongst his closest associates, as were both Pindemonte brothers and Boscovich. Pindemonte admired his work to the point of wishing he had created Vittorelli's *Maccheroni* himself. Writing to Remondini, the poet quotes Pindemonte as having written: "Intanto io vi scrivo questa lettera perchè non posso a meno di non dirvi, che prima di partir da Verona ho letto i vostri "Maccheroni" ad un crocchio letterario, che si raduna ogni Vénerdì in casa d'una veronese coltissima Dama; a che l'applauso fu tale che avrei desiderato essere autore di quei Maccheroni più che diventar Re di Francia."[21]

Our main concern is the consideration of Vittorelli as the poet of the "tupé", which he presents as both graceful and grotesque, which he cultivates and derides, and the eventual discarding of which we see as a result of the light irony with which the object is presented. It becomes identified with the "Settecento" which Vittorelli both revered and ridiculed, and invites attack as a symbol of pride, ornamentation and social superiority.

Notes to Chapter IV

1 Bib. F. Caffi, *Vita e opere di J. Vittorelli* (Venice, 1835); L. Carrer, pref. in *Poesie di J. Vittorelli* (Venice, 1851); S. Rumor, *Gli scrittori vicentini dei secoli XVIII & XIX* (Venice, 1905); B. Compostella, *Cenni storici e genealogia della famiglia Vittorelli* (Rome, 1906); A. Simioni, J. Vittorelli, *Vita, Scritti* (Rocca S. Casciano, 1907); A. Simioni, *Jacopo Vittorelli* (Bassano del Grappa, 1935); W. Binni, *Preromanticismo italiano*, op.cit., pp. 233-4; Ed. Marzorati; *Le correnti*, op.cit., pp. 43, 59, 539, 540, 556; A. Piromalli, *L'Arcadia*, (Palermo, 1975) pp. 48, 60, 88.

2 A. Piromalli, *L'Arcadia*, op.cit., p. 48.

3 R. Schippisi, in *Le correnti*, I op.cit., p. 540.

4 Forlì, Biblioteca Comunale, MS Piancastelli, Aut. 22. Doc. 2, rit. 5 letters of Jacopo Vittorelli. There are 22 autographed letters in the library. In a letter to his father in the year of his admission to the Collegio dei Nobili at Brescia, he writes:

10 Dec. 1761,
Brescia.

Carissimo Signor Padre,

Non devo lasciarla senza mia nuova. Sa quali quanto alla mia salute sono ottimo, quanto a'miei diportamenti mi rimetto al P. Superiore, non volendo io dir bene di me nè potendone dir male. La prego di riverirmi caramente la Sig.^{ra} madre, e Zia, a il Sig.^{re} Zio, e di riverirmi caramente i fratelli; e come figliolo oss.^{e} le bacio le mani,

Di suo Sig. Padre cariss.
Aff.^{mo}obed.^{mo},
Figlio Giacomo.

5 Bassano del Grappa, Biblioteca Civile, Bassano del Grappa. Epistolario Remondini, XXIII-4. The following letter conveys the confusion and lack of clear information as to the true state of affairs in the Veneto at the time, and the difficulties entailed in retiring to ones home:

16 Obre., 1796.

Io sono in una confusione grandissima e mi figuro lo scompiglio di tutti voi altri. Io non parto certamente da Venezia se io non vengo assicurato da voi di poter venire e di poter agire. Ho consultato circa l'absenza di Vittori, e circa gli oggetti da lui asportati, ed a tutto vi è pronto rimedio. Ho il consulto in iscritto, e lo porterò meco. Se avete biada di ogni sorta, vendetela per carità, o dovrete darla per forza senza danaro. Avvertitene il Can. D. Luigi per quella porzione che spetta a me. Se è necessario, acciocchè io possa venire, qualche passaporto di codesti ufficiali Tedeschi, vedete di provvedermelo, e di mandarlo. Qui si sentono mille discorsi opposti fra di loro. Chi dice che Bassano è pieno di Tedeschi che si ritirano: chi dice di no. Fatto sta che il Principe è senza danaro e che si vanno meditando nuove imposizioni da mettersi agli abitatori di Venezia. Prego la divina misericordia a non abbandonarci del tutto. Scriveta con frequenza e avvisatemi di ogni cosa. Addio. Riverisco la Sig. na Tonina, e Dio vi consoli –

Giacomo.

Vettori, secondo il parer mio, starà degli anni prima di capitare. Sul di lui ritorno non conviene far conti.
The letter is addressed:

Al Nobile Signore
Il Sig. Andrea Vittorelli
Bassano.

6 Bassano del Grappa, Biblioteca Civica, Epistolario Remondini, XXIII, 4. The letter to the State Inquisitor is written from Bassano, and provides an insight into political and social conditions and climatic conditions in Bassano.

Eccellenza,

I Tedeschi sono finalmente partiti e le campagne di V.E. hanno sofferto assai poco, di che veramente son lieto, e di che posso accertarla senza inganno. Io penso di ritormare fra due giorni o tre. Spero che L'ecc. Donà abbia fatti degli altri tentativi riguardo al affare, e dal consiglio di V.E. Non mi distaccherò comunque ita sia la faccenda. Remondini è in Venezia, nè ho potuto far seco parola alcuna riguardo alla ristampa del poema. Posso affermarle bensì che atteso l'attual disordine del Commercio, moltissimi operaj della stamperia sono stati licenziati e molti torchi soppressi. Leggerò volentieri, i versi del Marchese Tommaso, e le risposte. Qui fa un freddo diabolico, e quest'aria sopraffina, a cui sono disavvezzo, mi punge le carni, e mi penetra rabbiosamente nei pulmoni. V.E. si guardi dall'intemperie della stagione, e mi conservi la sua benefica padronanza. Bacio le mani a Lil e alla sua Dama. Riverisco l'abate e il Sig. Carlo, e pien d'ossequi mi Chiamo –

Suo dev. ^{ssimo}Servitore,
Giacomo Vittorelli.

7 Forlì Biblioteca Comunale, MS. Piancastelli aut. 22. The letter reveals much of Vittorelli's personality – his attitude to life, his depressions and his opinion of Napoleon. As a communication to Giustina Renier-Michiel, it is also of historical importance:

A Sua Eccellenza,
La Signora Giustina Michiel,
Venezia.   Roma, 27 Aprile.

Due momenti fa ebbi una cortesissima Sua in data del 22 marzo, cioè un buon mese dopo di essere stata scritta. Par che tutto congiunga a farmi più disgustosa la solitudine. Non una, ma due volte mi recai a Padova, onde terminar l'affare del mio casino, la di cui affittanza durava ancora per anni tre, e che da me fu sciolta col doloroso sacrifizio di ducati cento. Padova non mi vedrà più, io penso di terminar la mia vita fra i villani ed i cavoli, obliato e trascurato dalla fortuna, che non mi fu amica mai. Bisogna essere vili per meriter le sue grazie, e io sono fatto di altra tempera.

Sento dalle Gazzette che Napoleone non ha coraggio di far nuove leve, come dunque resistere a un torrente di nemici? Non sarebbe strano (secondo il mio pensare) che egli per destar un fanatismo generale nei Francesi rinunziasse furbescamente al trono, e rimettesse in piedi l'antica repubblica, signoreggiandola, come capo, per qualche tempo e aspettando il momento di farsi incoronar di bel nuovo.

Ma questo forse è uno di quei ghiribizzi che saltano in testa agli ipocondriaci, massimamente in certe ore buje, e in certi passeggiati da solo a sole come uso spesso di fare il suo attaccatissimo

                                            Vittorelli.
8 Bassano del Grappa, Biblioteca Civica, Epistolari Remondini XXXIII-4.

                    20 Ott. 1814

Dilettissimo Amico,

Le rinnovo quelle grazie, che altra volta le mandai sulla cortese lettera dedicatoria, e sui bellissimi idilli, che le è piaciuto di spedirmi. Io ne ebbi due copie dal nostro Gamba, e tre pochi giorni dopo dalle mani stesse dell'ottimo di Lei fratello. Ella è in possesso da lungo tempo dello stil vero, lontanissimo da qualunque gonfiezza, e da quella forestiera preziosità, che è di moda. Ciò vuol dir che non sono troppo note le regole di una sobrietà giudiziosa, e che non si vuol per guida la sempre infallibil natura nella poesia. Mi vien detto che l'osservatore lodi moltissimo il suo librettino, e io me ne compiaccio anche per quella parte, che mi riguarda in tanta onorevolezza.

Non mi resta ora che a pregarla di conservarmi gelosamente quella benevolenza, che ella mi ha giurato in faccia del pubblico, e pieno di cordial gratitudine e di sincera estimazione me le professo

                    Suo vero amico e servo,
                    Giacomo Vittorelli.

The letter is addressed: Al Reverendo Sig.
                            D. Piero Martinato,
                            Arciprete di Zimella,
                            Lonigo.

Vittorelli's correspondence also reveals a desire for perfection and precision in his own work;
An example of this is to be seen with reference to an undated letter to Francesco Quanti of Padua, contained in the Forlì Biblioteca Comunale, MS. Piancastelli, aut. 22. It reads:

Bassano 16 luglio.

Trovando io assai oscura e mal digerita la terza e quarta strofe dell'anacreontica, gliele spedisco rinovate tutte due dandole pieno arbitrio di scegliere.
Ier sera ebbi una gentil visita dal suo amabilissimo e coltissimo genero, e le ne rende grazie proposite —

Mi ami, e mi creda,
Il suo Vittorelli.

9   Attilio Simioni, *Jacopo Vittorelli*, op.cit., pp. 17-8;
10 Forlì Biblioteca Comunale, MS. Piancastelli, aut. 22.
Al chiarissimo Ab. Angelo Dalmistro.

Roman-basso, 5 Ag. 1816.

Amico Dilettiss.

Il nostro Toni fa ritorno ai patri Lari e al suo comperello per salvare possibilmente il frutto della sua industria dalle ugne della miseria e dalla rapacità. Io forse non lo avrei lasciato partire se non fossi assai dubbioso di fermarmi qui per due grandissime ragioni. La prima è che io sono stucco e ristucco di abitar fra gente senza educazione, senza fede e senza gratitudine. La seconda è che in anni così stremi o per meglio dire così perversi la campagna non offre un asilo di sicurezza e massimo in tempo di notte. Accoglietelo dunque, con bontà assicurando ciascheduno in nome mio che io me lo distacco dal fianco malvolentieri, e che io sono rimasto contentissimo de'-suoi buoni costumi, dell'opera sua e del suo totale contegno. Anzi, nell'atto del partire ho dovuto dargli un contrassegno della mia soddisfazione colla mancia di due argenti Napoleoni. Conservatemi l'amor vostro — state bene e credi vostro

Amico, Vittorelli.

11 Forlì Biblioteca Comunale, MS. Piancastelli, aut. 22.
Al Signor Podestà di Bassano.

Bassano, 19 Ottobre, 1816.

In risposta all'ossequiato di Lei foglio 18 corrente mi trovo in dovere di mandarle copia di una lettera pervenutami dal Regio Ufficio Centrale di censura e previsioni di libri e stampe in Venezia. La qual lettera, esigendo da me una intera ubbidienza dovrà servirmi di regola infallibile per l'avvenire.

E col più profondo rispetto ho l'onor di segnarmi – Il Regio Censore alle stampe,

Giacomo Vittorelli.

12 Bassano del Grappa, Biblioteca Civica, Epistolario Parolini, X. 11.

Altezza Imperiale Reale,
Piacque all'Altezza Vostro Imperiale Reale essermi
continne Largitrice negli anni scorsi di una gratificazione per l'opera, che io presto in Bassano, come Censore alle stampe. I motivi della ossequiosa mia istanza le quali trovarono benigno accoglimento nel cuore paterno del serenissimo Vicerè si rinnovano pur troppo col rinnovarsi dell'anno, ed io presento all'eccelso Benefattore altra supplica per ottenere anche adesso que'generosi tratti di munificenza, ai quali è avvezzo l'animo incomparabile dell'ottimo Principe.

Bassano 8 Dicembre, 1825.
Giacomo Vittorelli.
Censore alle stampe in Bassano.

13 Attilio Simioni, Jacopo Vittorelli, op.cit., p. 18.
14 Bassano del Grappa, Biblioteca Civica, Epistolario Remondini XXIII.4. In a letter of 1832, addressed to Monsignor Mazzarelli he states:

L'anno ottantesimo terzo è stato finora, ed è per me fatalissimo. Guai se non avessi al fianco il mio solito Acate, il mio cordiale Amatori! E ciò che mi avvilisce più di tutto è certa malinconia, ed una quasi continua vigilia. Oh! quante volte nel corso della notte vengo alla Camera di Monsignore, e piango e fo le mie discolpe, ed egli mi compatisce e mi perdona. Che dirò poi di quel grande e tenero sonetto che pochi giorni fa venne a farmi una visita così affettuosa. Ah quando mai pagherò tanti debiti? Non vorrei morire fallito.

Ella che è tanto dolce e gentile non mi dimentichi in quel suo Vaticano, dove a qualche Santo non sarò forse nè discaro nè estraneo. Con grandissima riverenza le bacio le mani –

In 1830, writing to the Central Office of Censorship, he states:

La lettera di cotesto ossequiatissimo ufficio 12 febbraio 1830. N. Primo Riservato, mi fu letta solamente questa mattina al letticciuolo, ove giaccio immobile da parecchi giorni, sorpreso da potentissimi dolori colici, che non mi lasciano trovar requie nè dì nè notte. A ciò si aggiunga la logora età mia di anni ottanta e mesi tre, che mi additano assai vicino il termine della vita. Scrivo intanto per altrui mano, e supplico la umanità di cotesto riguardevolissimo ufficio avolermi concedere un piccolo tratto di giorni, onde io possa di proprio pugno rispondere alle superiori domande col necessario inguinto dettaglio.

15 L. Carrer, *Poesie di J. Vittorelli*, op.cit., prefazione.
16 In *Poemetti e stanze di Giacomo Vittorelli* (Padua, 1773).
17 Attilio Simioni, *Jacopo Vittorelli*, op.cit., p. 19.
18 Vittorelli, a native of Bassano del Grappa in the Veneto, was consciously playing on the word.
19 L. Carrer, *Poesie di J. Vittorelli*, op.cit., pref.
20 Attilio Simioni, *Jacopo Vittorelli*, op.cit., pp. 25-6.
21 Bassano del Grappa, Biblioteca Civica, Epistolario Remondini, XXIII, 4.

Signor Conte Amatiss.

Bassano, 13 Ott.

Novelletto mi ha questa mattina del Venerdì consegnata una lettera vostra, nella quale, − una per le Grazie; ma se non viene la tarda sera io non posso darla in mano alla graziosa Crefrosine. Ora ve ne mando una della stessa Ninfa, la quale, non sapendo ciò che io m'abbi per Lei colla posta di stamattina, cioè coll'uomo vostro vi darà forse qualche dolce rimprovero.

Pindemonte mi scrive cosi − Pochi giorni prima di partir da Verona ho ricevuto una copia delle vostre bellissime poesie. Le ho rilette con piacer nuovo, ed ho pur gustato i fattivi cangiamenti con lusinga ancora del mio amor proprio, veggendo essere di qualche autorità presso a voi il mio giudizio. Intanto io vi scrivo questa lettera, perchè non posso a meno di non dirvi, che prima di partir da Verona ho letto i vostri "Maccheroni" ad un crocchio letterario, che si raduna ogni Venerdì in casa di una Veronese coltissima dama; e che l'applauso fu tale che avrei desiderato essere autore di que "Maccheroni" più che diventar re di Francia. E notate che in quel crocchio vi erano Lorenzi e Pompei, due poeti celebri, che ne son rimasti rapiti, e che pensando che a quelle ottave corrisponda anche il resto, sono ansiosissimi di leggere netto il libro. Io ne ho goduto infinitamente per la parte, che prendo alla vostra gloria letteraria, ed a tutto ciò che vi riguarda, e non ho potuto a meno di non parteciparvi tosto quest'approvazione del Veronese Parnaso ecc.. − che ve ne pare? Consultate Vicenzo se io debba credere a questi lodi. Mi diletta infinitamente la vostra gloria, e gli onori che a voi si fanno. Io sento cose belle da ogni banda, e belle le credo, perchè di tutte meritevole siete. M'inchino a vostra eccellenza,

> Addio,
> Giacomo Vittorelli.

The letter is undated, and addressed:

A Sua Eccellenza
Il Con: Giuseppe Remondini,
    Bologna.

CHAPTER V

Angelo Talassi extemporary poet "par excellence"

1 *The adventures of an extemporary poet*

The second half of the eighteenth century saw a literary revival flourish in Ferrara. Dating from the sixteenth century, a slow political and intellectual decadence had eaten into the city, and the poets and artists who had flocked there during the Renaissance had become a mere memory. Even the ancient nobility had deserted the city. The mid-eighteenth century, however, had at least five names worthy of mention. Antonio Frizzi (1736-1800), Girolamo Baruffaldi (1665-1755), who is called by Unghi "Uno dei più vasti ingegni della Ferrara settecentesca", Francesco Leopoldo Bertoldi, who corresponded with Tiraboschi, Amaduzzi and Monti, while Alfonso Varano (1705-1788) achieved fame as poet, philosopher and writer of two tragedies. He has also been referred to as a successful translator. The *Dizionario Enciclopedico della Letteratura Italiana* supplies the following entry for Angelo Talassi[1] the subject of this chapter:

> Improvvisatore del XVIII. Si sa solo che era di Mizzana nel Ferrarese, che cominciò la carriera di improvvisatore nel 1774, e che, dopo aver percorso gran parte d'Europa, si stabilì alla corte di Braganza. Non se ne hanno notizie dopo il 1796. Ebbe gran fama, e ne resta un alto elogio di C. Goldoni (*Memoirs*, Parte III, cap. XXVIII). Ne furono pubblicati rime, alcuni poemetti, interessanti per le notizie che danno sulla vita e sui tempi di Talassi. Ne restano anche lettere inedite.

In 1778, Talassi's most important work was published. Pride of place goes to *La piuma recisa*. The *Gazzetta poetica di Ferrara* appeared in the following year. In this, political observations alternated with improvised poems. In 1789, his *Poesie varie* were published in Venice by Zatta. Above all, Talassi excelled in descriptions of the fate of the traveller or wandering poet. This is seen in *La piuma recisa*, also in *Aventures singulieres d'un voyageur aejien*, (Paris, 1781) and also in his later poem *L'olmo abbattuto* (Lisbon, 1795).[2] Talassi also wrote a dramatic work, *Il trionfo della virtù*, (Lisbon, 1794). The following year he set to work on a poem entitled *Giovanni*, modelled on Tasso's *Rinaldo*. His output is interesting from the point of view of his handling of the social satire and his reference to English customs. Before embarking on a detailed consideration of the mock-heroic genre in the hands of the improvisor Talassi, some attention must be given to the circumstances and conditions in which these works were written. These can be ably illustrated with reference to Talassi's letters.

Carlo Piancastelli in *Nel centinario di un olmo* states that Talassi was sent to study law in Ferrara. He soon abandoned his course, however, to concentrate on literature. In his letter of April 3rd 1779 to Amaduzzi, he declares that he is "laureato in ambe le leggi". He began his poetic career in Parma in 1774, and from that time travelled all Europe. The first letter which I have been able to trace is to Giovanni Cristofono Amaduzzi.[3] It was written on April 3rd, 1779 in Ferrara, and contains Talassi's request to Amaduzzi to support his application for the post of librarian in the Pontifical University, a post which he failed to secure, forcing him to pursue his travels in search of permanent employment. Talassi's letter to Amaduzzi begins with a reminder of the circumstances of their meeting, before introducing the purpose of his writing. The weariness of the traveller, continually seeking permanent employment, is brought home, as well as the writer's open and explicit statement of his situation: ". . .io viaggai in differenti contrade dell'Europa ricavando ovunque un discreto profitto dalle estemporanee mie fatiche." He then proceeds to the nature of his business:

Trovasi in questa Pontifica Università vacante la carica di Bibliotecario per rinunzia del Sig. D. Barotti. Io mi crederei in qualche maniera abile a cuoprirla per avere la richiesta età di anni 35, per esser laureato in ambe le Leggi, aver avuto esercizio della lingua Latina, e cognizione degli autori che hanno scritto in essa. Quanto agl'idiomi oltremontani io parlo, e scrivo correntemente il Francese ed intendo passabilmente lo Spagnuolo, il Portoghese,, e l'Inglese. Il prelodato Mons. Riminaldi Presidente della Università stessa è l'unico da cui dipende la scelta, mentre i Riformatori Eligenti non attendono che vostro senno ed il suo consiglio. A me non è ignoto quanto V.S. Illmo possa sull'animo del sapientissimo Prelato, a perciò la supplico voler appoggiare le mie richieste colla sua validissima raccomandazione, e ciò unicamente in vigore della nostra antica amicizia.

It seems to me that the letter reveals traits in Talassi's character which will be confirmed in later correspondence, and which have not been referred to by previous critics: a willingness to use any means at his disposal to secure a position, and a miserliness which will grow with the passing years: "A negozio fatto subito che avesse ottenuto l'intento vorrei in qualche modo ricompensare i passi di chi mi avesse favorito con una cinquantina di Zecchini."[4]

Amaduzzi's reply dated 10 April assures Talassi that he indeed remembers him, as a result of a strong impression he created at this first meeting: "Tutto mi è presente, ed Ella è stato più, e più volte l'oggetto della mia più vantaggiosa commemorazione." Amaduzzi makes it clear, however, that he could not be involved in any compromising situation which would by unworthy of both subjects: "Si guardi però, fuori del più confidenziale comando, di adoperare altro argomento, onde muovermi ad agire per lei. Diverrei l'uomo il più odioso a me stesso, ed il più inconseguente co'miei principi, se l'interesse giammai giungesse ad esser la molla delle mie operazioni."[5]

While Amaduzzi is unwilling to stoop to any dishonest means, one cannot doubt his sincere admiration for Talassi the artist: one believes the latter must have been an impressive figure. Carlo Goldoni, meeting him in Paris, was immediately taken with his inventive ability:

C'est dans une de ces assemblées que j'ai vu et admirè M. Talassi, de la ville de Ferrare; c'est un de ces talents suprenants debitants à l'impromptu et en chantant cent vers ou cent couplets sans jamais manquer ni a la rime, ni a la raison.

Les poètes improvvisatori ne sont pas rares en Italie, mais il en est de bons e de mauvais, et de tous ceux qui sont venus a Paris de mon temps, M. Talassi est certainment le meilleur.[6]

Between 1780 and 1795, Talassi's life proved an endless series of journeys, sojourns, visits, academies, punctuated with hopes, despair and sadness because of the frequent separations from his family. The two hundred autographed letters in the Biblioteca Ariostea, Ferrara[7] are as much a valid record of his time as are the already mentioned *Memoirs* of Goldoni, or those of Casanova. They follow his journey through Italy in 1780-1, cover a period spent in Germany between June and September 1781, nine months in Russia — from October 1781 to July 1782, followed by a spell in Vienna, where he would have liked to have settled, had it not been that his wife Santina Solimani, daughter of Leopoldo Solimani, of Ferrara, wished to return home. There follow painful spells from his wife and children, periods of exile in Paris in 1784-5 and 1787, in London and Madrid in 1790, before he finally settled in Lisbon.

The correspondence is marked by efforts to secure employment, to make contacts and to compile lists of guarantors for publishing houses, to ensure that the publication of his works provide a worthwhile venture. In a letter from Vicenza, dated June 24th, 1780, he refers to the selection of poems he is compiling for publication with the stamp of Zatta of Venice, and of the necessity to assure the publisher of financial support.[8]

> Se avessi potuto ottenere la sorte d'inchinarla personalmente quando mi sono presentato alla abitazione di V.S. ill. mo in Venezia tra altre cose le avrei parlato di alcune mie poesie, che mi sono accinto a pubblicare per mezzo delle stampe del Sig. Zatta. Contengono queste due drammi, una cantata, e molti altri componimenti, che formeranno il primo volume. Il secondo sarà riempito da altre cantate a diversi sovrani d'Europa fatte per la loro nascita. E vi sono in oltre cento ottave che formano un canto sulle principali epoche del Regno di Maria Teresa, altre ottave inviate al rè di Polonia presentate p. mano di Monsig. Archetti, con Canzoni, Giocolieri, Sonetti, e.c.

The writer goes on to name the literary figures he would wish to be associated with his work: "Fra i nomi rispettabili, che onorano quest'associazione bramerei vi fossero ancora quelli di V.S. ill. mo, del Sig. Conte Antonio, del Sig. Jacopo Vittorelli, e del Sig. Ab. Caffo giacchè quest'ultimo ci troverà nominate molte persone di sua conoscenza per il lungo domicilio che ha fatto in Ferrara."[9] The poems were eventually published in Venice in 1789, and Talassi will make further efforts in the course of his correspondence to assure financial support. Talassi's letters contain accounts of his meetings and friendships with leading personalities and literary figures of his time. An ardent opera-goer, he made friends with the male soprano Pacchierotti,[10] early in his career and followed his progress across Europe. In a letter to Tieghi, dated February 24th 1781, from

Venice, he states: "Lunedî sera fui a sentire Pacchierotti, per grazia ebbi uno scanno in mezzo in fila. Nel primo atto non c'è cosa da stordire. Una scena nel secondo, e l'Aria è qualche cosa di grande. . . Ma ci sono dei pezzi belli e seguiti maestosamente dal novello Orfeo tanto valente quanto brutto."[11]

Talassi's first meeting with the singer in May, 1781 is recalled in a letter to Tieghi of May 10th, from Mantua. At the same time, he was striving to establish himself as an extemporary poet, seeking to perform at social gatherings and to set up an "accademia". A letter of May 10th, 1781, to Tieghi reveals his efforts in this direction, and also the fact that his attention was steadfastly directed towards financial gain: "Dite al Sig. Ronchi, che ho fatto i suoi saluti al gentilissimo Sig. Romanati, che forse mi assisterà nel fare la mia accademia, se succederà in Teatro come vorebbe Berti. Il Vice-Pres.e Mr. de St. Laurent, che mi vuole domenica suo commensale vorebbe ch'io la facesse in una sala, ma il profitto sarebbe assai minore."[12] Fourteen days later Talassi reports on the proceedings in a letter dated May 24th 1781: "La mia accademia fu nella sera prefissa nel teatro Nuovo . . . i biglietti venduti sono stati 189. Le persone ed altri ebbero l'ingresso gratis."[13]

Talassi's travels were soon again to take him out of Italy to Munich, Dresden, Berlin, St. Petersburg and finally to Vienna, before re-entering Italy in March 1783. From Prague, July 7th, 1781, one of many references is made to Corilla Olimpica (1727-1800), teacher, mentor and friend of Talassi: "In Firenze passai dieci giorni coll'amica Corilla. Essa che dovera passare in Russia, invitata da quella Sovrana ha ricusato d'andarvi così persuasa da Ginori e Nardini."[14]

From Dresden on July 16th, comes news of his success as an extemporary poet, while from Berlin, on August 25th, evidence of further trials and humiliations. From Dresden he writes: "Nel sabato 23 l'Elettrice vedova mi fece andare alla sua dimora di Forseneid, ove pur cantai due argomenti, il primo fra pochi dato dalla stessa Elettrice sulla tranquillità della vita campestre, venuto poi colà il sovrano me ne diede un altro da me eseguito in ottave, cioè un paragone fra Pietro il Grande, e Fernando Cortez."[15] The visit to Berlin at first appeared disappointing. Many attempted to interest the King in Talassi's talents, but all in vain: "Tutti i tentativi furono inutili perchè Federigo disse aver già idea del canto improvviso mentre aveva udito negli anni scorsi l'Abbe Tancini, che essere assai lento gli aveva fatto sudar sangue."[16]

However, all was not as hopeless as it appeared, and a letter of October 23rd, reveals a certain success in Berlin. He succeeded in holding an "accademia" attended by ministers of State, and financial reward was encouraging, and he succeeded in rubbing shoulders with the high society of Berlin. Vienna proved the capital in which Talassi was most happy, and which he believed offered the greatest opportunity for the permanent establishment of his reputation. There he met Da Ponte[17] and Salieri,[18] taught Italian to foreign students and visited the homes of the nobility. As soon as he arrived in Vienna, he set about securing teaching hours. His pupils appear to have been rich, prominent members of society, with the exception of "un garbato giovane irlandese a cui spiego tre volte la settimana il *Pastor Fido* . . .[19]. In the same letter of November 23rd, he refers to his first meeting with the Abate Da Ponte:

> Qui c'è un abate D. Lorenzo da Ponte, Veneziano, che vedo molto spesso. Egli improvvisa assai bene. Noi abbiamo spesso volte per divertimento cantato a vicende in ottavo. Ha avuto ultimamente la fortuna d'esser poeta del teatro con la mediazion del Gran Ciamberlano Rosenberg, e dal Maestro di Capella Salieri. A primavera verrà qui una compagnia fatta in Venezia dal Durazzo per rappresentare opere buffe alla corte. Al detto abate è stato promesso uno stipendio annuo di fiorini 800, o di 400 dei nostri scudi.

Six weeks later in a letter dated January 12th, 1783, he informs Tieghi: "Mi trovo unicamente spesso in compagnia dello Abate da Ponte. Non poche volte abbiamo alternate insieme le ottave estemporanee per farci udire a poca brigata. Due volte vi si è trovato il Sig. Salieri di Legnano Maestro della Capella Imperiale, che avete udito nominare."[20] The following five months will find Talassi once more in Italy – in Verona and Venice where he meets Giovanni Pindemonte and Angelo Mazza, and later in Bologna and Genoa. Then he will spend nine months in France. In a letter from Venice dated April 25th, 1783, Talassi states his age, providing evidence that he was born in 1745. He also refers to a meeting with Mazza:

> Il nuovo parocco della Boara è il Signor D. Carlo Zitti il quale fu bibliotecario in Casa Pisani. La sua età è forse eguale alla mia, cioè di 38 anni . . . Rivi-

di al suo albergo il Mazza nel giovedi 24. Esso era obbligato di non dividersi mai da due sposi S. Vitali, perchè lo sposo, antico medaglione geloso come una bestia ha dato di sè scene orribili, che l'hanno reso sommamente ridicolo.[21]

Talassi's sojourn in France during 1783-4 proved dismal in the extreme. Having disembarked at Marseilles, he made his way to Avignon, where he was obliged to teach Italian to make a living. Then he proceeded to Paris where he met Goldoni, dined with Piccini,[22] but found it extremely difficult to make ends meet. His letters to Tieghi (Jan. 26th, 1784, February 22nd, 1784) are full of regret at having abandoned Vienna,[23] while those to his wife Santina urge strict economy. That of December 19th, 1783 illustrates clearly his wretched condition: "Non ti scrivo più d'una volta al mese perchè le lettere costano, ed io non sono in istato di spendere. Quali cose poss'io narrarvi, mia cara Santina se non che calamità, e miserie."[24] The poetic works referred to in the letter of June 24th, 1780, from Vicenza, were still unpublished in 1786, and in fact did not appear until 1789. On May 13th, 1786, Talassi wrote to his friend Tieghi from Venice, explaining the position regarding his work:

Quello che ho potuto ottenere è che il Zatta, il quale è forse il più accredito tra i veneti stampatori, dopo aver veduto il Primo Tomo delle cose mie si è offerto di stampare mille copie colla spesa di cinquanta zecchini con che io ne sborsai la metà e così avessi 50 copie da esitare come più mi piacesse ... siamo convenuti che io procuri un numero considerabile di firme, o sia associazioni 14 lire veneto al Tomo, mentre quando avrò un numero certo di sottoscriventi senza denaro anticipato, manderà loro il manifesto, e un mese dopo farà uscire il Primo Tomo.[25]

On May 20th, again writing to Tieghi, Talassi gives evidence of having been to London the previous year. This was his second visit, having already been to the English capital in 1777. We are aware of his first visit from a letter to Tieghi, dated Madrid, March 16th, 1790. In a reference to a certain Sig. Bologna, he states: "Esso fu presente alla mia accademia data nel sabato 27 febbraio anniversario di quella che diedi in Londra nel 1777."[26] The relevant quote from the letter of May 20th reads: "A Padova doveva cantar un certo Crescentini da me conosciuto l'anno scorso a Londra. . ."[27]

During 1787, Talassi once again spent a period in France. In the selection of letters in the Biblioteca Ariostea, in Ferrara, there are three from Paris dated Jan. 20th, 1787, March 11th, 1787 and May 6th of the same year. In the Summer of 1787 he again returned to Italy. Letters indicate his presence there from August 1787 to June 1789. They reveal endless travel and fruitless efforts to secure appointments and academic positions. His letters of the period reveal activity mainly in Northern Italy, no further south than Romagna, and come from Genoa (August 11th and September 7th 1787); Florence (October 1787 and May 17th, 24th and June 7th, 1788), Padua (June 14th, 16th, 28th, 1788), Imola (July 12th 1788), Faenza (July 22nd '88), Venice (Nov. 15th, December 13th), Castelfranco (Jan. 6th, '89), Milan (May 9th 1789), Turin (June 24th, July 15th, 17th, 18th, '89). The end of '89 marks his departure for Spain, and he will later move to Portugal, where he is eventually offered a position at the Court of Braganza.

In her husband's eternal absences from home, Santina Talassi had become the subject of local gossip. By July 1789 even her closest friends had refused to associate with her, and she was no longer on speaking terms with Talassi's dearest friend Tieghi. In a letter dated July 18th, 1789 from Turin, Talassi implores his friend not to desert Santina: "Scordatevi dunque tutto il male che vi è stato detto contro di lei: Vedetela, ascoltatela, assisterla, consigliatela nè la scacciare dal vostro fianco con una fredda indifferenza perchè una cattive lingua vi ha parlato male contro di lei."[28] Talassi also urges his wife to avoid public scandal and to behave as an honourable wife and mother.[29]

The possibility of Talassi entering into permanent employment at court was suggested early in March 1791. He at once informed Tieghi, pointing out that no less than 600 scudi a year would be sufficient to support his family: "Mi è stato parlato di restare al Real Servizio, ma io non accetterò senza un assegnamento decente, e senz'aver la permissione di venire a prendere la mia famiglia. Di ciò non ne parlate altro che con Santina, e non con alcun altro."[30] On March 17th, he has already accepted the position and apologises to his wife for not having consulted her in advance: "Perdonate Santina dilettissima se ho accettato senz'aspettare il vostro consenso perchè il tempo e la distanza de'luoghi non permettevano ch'io potessi consultarvi mi persuado per altro che ringrazierete la providenza (error in original) che mi manda un pezzo di pane stabile e decoroso."[31]

However, his family did not follow him to Lisbon at this point. In 1793 there are letters written to Santina in Ferrara, and a lengthy epistle to Giovanni Battista Costbili Containi of Ferrara dated Lisbona 6 February 1794 explains some of Talassi's domestic problems, which may explain why his family did not join him in Lisbon: "Pur troppo quello che previdi due anni fa, e che vi scrissi nella prima mia lettera è succeduto, e varie confidenzioni mi hanno indotto a ricondurre la mia famiglia a Ferrara."[32]

On his return to Lisbon, Talassi set to work on a mock-heroic work *L'olmo abbattuto*, to which he will refer frequently in letters to Santina and Tieghi. L.N. Cittadella in his biographical note on Talassi, states that in 1796 he called his family to join him in Lisbon: "Ma non si potrebbe dire se avenisse in fatto che la famiglia già partitasi da Ferrara in detto anno 1796, e giunta a Livorno s'imbarcasse poi per Lisbona; giacchè dopo quest'epoca nulla più si conosce nè della medesima, nè di lui, sebbene l'Ughi nel suo Dizionario degli illustri ferraresi lo ponga vivente nel 1804, in cui stampava questo suo libro.[33]

Talassi's two hundred autographed letters, in the Biblioteca Ariostea, Ferrara, provide a fascinating insight to the character of the man who excelled in the field of extemporary poetry and in the realm of the mock-heroic. They offer a fascinating glimpse of eighteenth-century intellectual life in Venice, Vienna, Paris. They also contribute to a new awareness on the part of the reader, of the nature and the contribution to the "poeta improvvisatore". Momo Franceschini correctly comments: "la sua vita è infatti rappresentative delle condizioni dell'improvvisatore settecentesco di mestiere. . . L'imperio intellettuale italiano, che aveva dominato assoluto l'Europa del XVIII secolo fino ai primi bagliori dell'incendio francese, doveva essere annientato dalla più grande rivoluzione dei tempi moderni."[34]

La piuma recisa

The poem most often referred to by critics as being Talassi's best known work is *La piuma recisa*, a mock-heroic satire in ten Canti, published in Venice in 1778. It has been called a free imitation of Pope. Cittadella refers to it as a poem: "lodato da Minzoni, che lo dice fatto a simiglianze del *Riccio rapito* di Pope, e pieno di erudite note intorno a cose vedute ne suoi viaggi, attribuendogli anche 'bei tratti di una vena facile e feconda' ".[35] Franceschini sees it as a mock-heroic attack on feminine pride: "*La piuma recisa* va riguardato come una satira contro eterno femminismo che amava adornarsi di piume costose e rare, moda che partita da Parigi, emporio ricco di strane pellegrine mode che doveva spandersi per tutta l'Europa."[36] With regard to the role of *The Rape of the Lock* in Italian literature, and the diffusion of English customs in eighteenth-century Italy, *La piuma recisa* is an important document. In fact the work can be said to fall clearly into two sections, one comprising the first three Canti in which Talassi decries female pride, and attacks the object which has become symbolic of such vanity — namely the feather. The rest of the poem has little direct connection with the main theme; it describes travels through England, English customs and concludes on a note of praise for British liberty. The poem is dedicated "Alla illustrissima Signora Teresa Testori Scaccerni, Cittadina Ferrarese". The lady in question had acted as hostess to the Duke of Gloucester during his sojourn in Ferrara: "S.A.R. Guglielmo Enrico Duca di Glocester, Fratello del Monarca Britannico, alloggiò in casa del Sig. Francesco Scaccerni degnis. consorte della Sig. Teresa in Ferrara, nel suo passaggio per essa città."

Talassi's opening resembles Conti's Ariostean rendering of Pope:

> Canto la pugna memoranda, e fiera
> Un giorno accesa della Senna in riva
> Per vago crine, a cui di Piuma altera
> A torre il fregio audace destra arriva.
> (Talassi, *La piuma recisa* I (i))

> Canto l'offesa, la vittoria e'l pianto,
> Lo sdegno, la battaglia e la sconfitta,

> Pel riccio tronco, che diè tanta briga
> A'Silfi, a'Gnomi, al'Ipocondria, al cielo
> Onde al fin risplendette astro novello.
>> (Conti, *Il riccio rapito.*)

In stanza vii of Canto I, Talassi's lines continue the spirit of the opening:

> Ma se talora i Spettator poteo
> Empir di maraviglia, e di diletto
> Cagion funesta diventò una volta
> Di battaglia, di pianto, e d'ira stolta.
>> (Talassi, *La piuma recisa,* Canto I. vii)

The first Canto of the poem could be defined as the celebration of beauty, colour and ornamentation. The society, with which the reading public was already familiar by Talassi's time, is sketched by the hand of a fluent humourist, as opposed to one effecting mere caricature. The biting sarcasm of Parini is missing, as is his gift for creating the crystal cameo; nor is there the grotesque imagery of Vittorelli: it is as though Talassi were painting a make-believe world of colour and feathers which evaporates with the cutting of the feather of the title. The influence of Conti and Pope is further apparent with regard to the references to the dressing-table, the hairdresser and the mirror. Talassi reproduces the "bel mondo" of Pope, Parini, Vittorelli and Bondi with Goldonian humour and wit. In his description of decorative feathers, he does so in the manner of the librettist of "opera buffa":

> Gode la fronte coronar di queste
> Ogni grave matrona, ogni donzella,
> E fan per loro le femminee teste
> Grata comparsa più superba, e bella.
> Cedon le cuffie, e l'elevate creste
> Alla donnesca bizzaria novella,
> Di cui gli esempi con stupor ritrovi
> In mille foggie ovunque il piè tu muovi.
>> (Talassi, *La piuma recisa,* Canto I. v)

> Fra quanti di beltà rari prodigi
> Vantò giammai l'avventurosa Francia,
> Fu l'ornamento della gran Parigi
> D'Aurisa il crine, e la fiorita guancia.

Ben mille cori ella si rese ligi
Coi strali accesi, che dagli occhi lancia,
E per formar più lacci ai doni, ch'ebbe
Dal Ciel nascendo, quei dell'arte accrebbe.
(Talassi, *La piuma recisa*, Canto I, viii)

The above lines reveal a facility of poetic inspiration: one is aware of Talassi's creative gifts: there is lacking, however, a precision with regard to detail and imagery. Pomp and colour seem to be what Talassi aims at creating. In the following passage depicting the "cicisbeo", the poet succeeds in drawing a convincing type, rather than attempting to pinpoint any individual characteristics:

Fu Celidauro quel mortal felice
Scelto d'Aurisa Cicisbeo compagno:
Fortuna non gli fu molto fautrice,
E il padre gli lasciò poco guadagno.
Ma sì leggiadro a lui vantarsi lice,
Che dal paragonarlo non rimango
Con Ciparisso, O Ganimede, O Adone,
O qual altro si vuol più bel garzone.
(Talassi, *La piuma recisa*, Canto I, xiv)

I do not believe that the poetry of Talassi can be considered in the same light as that of the "poeti didascalici" of the eighteenth century. The extemporary poet relies on rhyme, colour and fluency. In the section containing the list of articles of adornment, Talassi seems in command of an endless supply of vocabulary depicting decorative objects:

Quivi tu puoi mirar ritratti, e specchi,
Cuffie, ventagli, e nastri a più colori;
Manti per li due sessi e nuovi, e vecchi,
Gomme, pastiglie, quintessenze, odori,
Pietre per adornar collo, ed orecchie,
Scattole, anelli, e pizzi, e finti fiori,
Con fibbie, astucci, e ricche mostre d'oro
Del più moderno soprafin lavoro.
(Talassi, *La piuma recisa*, Canto I, xxi)

The effect of the various colours momentarily dazzles the reader. There is no poetic subtlety such as that found in Pope's description of the sylphs, merely a blinding display of colour:

152

O qual comparsa degli Amanti al ciglio
Fan tante piume di color diverso!
Non sol ci vedi il nero, ed il vermiglio,
Il bianco, il giallo, il violetto, il perso.
(Talassi, La piuma recisa, Canto I. xxiii)

Clarity of expression ranks high amongst Talassi's poetic attributes. The poet possesses the ability to introduce a specific object or individual, convey its visual image, and state its function, often within the space of four lines. This is the case in the presentation of the dressing-table, the hairdresser and the mirror. The description is shorter than those of many of his contemporaries, but no less clear. In fact in the case of Talassi's poetry, the lack of descriptive detail and precision renders the object more rounded, if rather less refined. The following three passages, I believe illustrate this point:

Ma tempo è omai, che la gentil toletta
S'alzi d'amor per rallumar il foco;
Quest'e della beltà l'eccelso trono,
D'onde rifulge con più chiaro dono.
(Talassi, La piuma recisa, Canto I. xxxv)

Venga colui, che nell'esperta destra
L'avorio tiene a inanellar le chiome,
E come gli additò l'arte maestra
Impogna al capo le ricciute some.
(Talassi, La piuma recisa, Canto I. xxxvi)

La bella intanto tien siffato il guardo
A quel cristallo, che le sta rimpetto,
Che per strana magia non è mai tardo
A raddoppiar il presentato obietto.
(Talassi, La piuma recisa, Canto I. xlii)

In each case, Talassi relies on a principal verb which conveys both the function of the object in question and at the same time a visual image, which remains identified with the entire scene. In the case of the "toletta", the verb is "rallumar", the hairdresser's duty is to "inanellar le chiome", while "raddoppiar" is the principal verb in the lines on the mirror.

Canto I is largely devoted to the illustration of feminine frivolity. Canto II contains the cutting of the feather along with a detailed

153

description of the scissors and the slow yielding of the object of decorum. There are also references to Pope's sylphs and their inability to defend the lady from the barbarous attack. Pope's *Rape of the Lock* takes place at a tea-party at Hampton Court. Talassi's cutting of the feather takes place in the theatre, where it proves an obstruction to spectators taking note of activity on and off the stage. Stanza XXVIII contains a warning. The action begins at stanza XXXI:

> Femmina altera, se dal Crin non levi
> Quest'importuno abbigliamento a un tratto
> Un qualche gioco qui aspettar ti devi,
> Ch'alli tuoi giorni non ti fu mai fatto.
> (Talassi, *La piuma recisa,* Canto II. xxviii)

While it can be said that Pope, for the most part, achieves his effect by juxtaposing the sublime and the ridiculous, Talassi achieves his by contrasting refinement and vulgarity: the scissors, an object which is best suited to manicures within the boudoir, becomes useful within the theatre. It is interesting to compare the following lines to those of *The Rape of the Lock*. III 1. 125-32.

> Un pajo avea di forbici taglienti
> Delle più fine, che levò di tasca.
> Prima mi par, che accorciar l'unghie tenti,
> Nè d'averle ad altri uso idea gli nasca;
> Riflette poi che sono armi possenti
> Per vendicarlo appien di quella frasca,
> Col far il taglio sulla vana testa
> Di quelle piuma, che gli fu molesta.
> (Talassi, *La piuma recisa,* Canto II, xxxiii)

Several efforts are necessary before the object of pride is finally severed. It is likened to the oak tree and the head at the block, natural grandeur is combined with horrific effect:

> Al primo colpo di feral bipenne
> Come non è la quercia al pian distesa,
> Ma cento replicati urti sostenne
> Colle radici, che le fan difesa;
> Quella crudel percossa alfin le venne,
> Per cui piegando da un sol lato pera;
> Da quella parte chi rimane al basso
> Affretta altrove il timoroso passo.
> (Talassi, *La piuma recisa,* Canto II, xxxix)

La man di nuovo ardimentoso spinse
Verso la penna, che più stava in alto,
Colli due ferri uniti insiem la strinse
Sinchè cedette all'ostinato assalto.
Ben quattro volte sostenersi finse,
Ma poi fu d'uopo fare a terra un salto,
Lasciando in fronte l'altra parte mozza
Con vista ahi troppo obbrobriosa, e sozza.
(Talassi, *La piuma recisa,* Canto II, xlii)

That the incident is directly based on the subject of Pope's poem is
clear from the reference to the absent sylphs, whose presence offered
little protection to Belinda, the protagonist of *The Rape of the Lock.*

E Voi, maligni Silfi, ah dove foste?
Quand'un fregio sî bel colui recise!
Nè alcun di Voi coll'arti sue nascoste
Contro il ferro crudel la man frammise.
Eppur dovean piacervi in fronte poste
D'una sî amabil Dea quelle divise:
Così mostraste aver valor posticcio
Quando tagliossi di Belinda il riccio!
(Talassi, La piuma recisa, Canto II, xlv)

Aurisa's wrath is no less self-contained than Belinda's; but while that
of the latter retains dignity of expression, Talassi portrays his lady
as the spoiled darling of a pampering society: the mock-heroic humour of Pope is replaced by a witty portrait of bad temper:

La scaltra donna, che il marito vede
Facile a secondar li suoi deliri,
Del finto duol ne'strani segni eccede
Con tronchi accenti, e lagrime e sospiri.
Batter il suol con dispettoso piede,
Far onta al crine, e al bianco sen la miri,
Gettar lungi da se monili, e vezzi,
E pizzi, e nastri, e vel mettere in pezzi.[37]
(Talassi, *La piuma recisa,* Canto III, xvi)

A battle then ensues between Celidauro, the protector or "cicisbeo",
and the thief of honour. When Moreno believes that he has killed
Aurisa's "cavalier servente" he at once panics, and decides to flee to
England. It is at this point that the work takes on a new dimension,

155

and becomes relevant as an historical documentation of eighteenth-century knowledge of English life and customs.

That Talassi himself had travelled from France to Dover and on to London is apparent from his description of Moreno's journey. The references to England begin with an account of Moreno's financial problems and the currency difference:

> I miei Luigi fineranno in breve,
> E se dovrà cambiarli alli confini,
> Ov'Anglica moneta si riceve
> Composta di ghinee, soldi, e scellini,
> La tasca mia sarà ridotta lieve,
> Talchè finiti sieno i miei quattrini
> Nei primi dì, che stamperò i vestigi
> Nella Città Reina del Tamigi.
>
> (Talassi, *La piuma recisa,* Canto IV, xxx)

There follows a reference to his first night in England and the journey to London:

> Ora il tempo mi par della partenza,
> Poichè una notte sola in Dovre stette,
> Pochi scellin pagò la Diligenza
> Per star sull'imperiale ove si mette
> Quattro rossi destrier, pieni d'ardenza
> Nel divorar la via pajon **saette**,
> Nè merto inferior credo si trovi
> Ad ogni posta ne'più freschi, e nuovi.
>
> (Talassi, *La piuma recisa,* Canto V, xxvi)

> Giungon seguendo la gran via maestra
> A Cantoberia, che a fermarsi invoglia,
> Acciò prepari mano esperta, e destra
> Il grato umor della Cinese **foglia**.
> Si tarderà a pranzar fino a Rochestra
> Città mediocre, e d'ornamenti spoglia.
> Il miglior pasto è l'arrostito bue,
> Che l'Anglo noma le delizie sue.
>
> (Talassi, *La piuma recisa,* Canto X, xxvii)

It is indeed true that Talassi brought to Italy first-hand information on English life, in a way his poetic contemporaries never succeeded in doing. The Ferrarese poet does not merely concentrate on life within the "bel mondo" of colour and coquettishness, but, as can be said of Goldoni, provides life itself with its basic necessities, such as food, transport, money. The term used in description of tea "Il grato vapor della Cinese foglia" is much similar to Bonducci's terms in his translation of the "party" episode in *The Rape of the Lock*. The coffee is called by Bonducci "i grati umori", the cups are "la Chinese terra".[38] In addition to such references to English life, Talassi immortalises one of England's foremost beauties in *La piuma recisa*, and by way of a foot-note pays tribute to her family; on her recovery from illness, wisdom is combined with beauty:

> Tu pur vi fosti dopo il morbo reo,
> In cui ti minacciò Parca maligna
> Granby immortal, che la natura feo
> Sì bella, onde sei l'Anglia Ciprigna.
> Tu non sol di beltade ergi trofeo,
> Ma ti dimostri ognor saggia e benigna,
> Come quando l'onor ti piacque darmi
> D'udir miei rozzi estemporanei carmi.
> (Talassi, *La piuma recisa*, Canto VI, Lxiii).

Talassi's note reads as follows: "Sua Ecc. Lady Marchesa di Granby, Nuora del Duca di Rutland, e sorella del Duca di Beaufort, Dama di una sorprendente bellezza, chiamata da i suoi isolani stessi la Venere Britannica. Essa è dotata inoltre delle più pregevoli qualità dello spirito, e fu coll'eccelsa sua Genitrice ad onorare il mio Benefizio, dato ai 27 Febbraio 1777 in Londra all'Hicksford Room, Brewer Street, coll'assistenze del celeberrimo violinista Sig. Giardini."[39]

British political institutions are also represented in *La piuma recisa*, and two stanzas are dedicated to Halifax, who forbade conscription within the city of London.

> Perchè conosca bene il mio Lettore
> L'indole altera, e il genio di costui,
> Dirò, che forse in Anglia alcun Signore
> Non fu mai generoso al par di lui;
> Ma lo prendea talor il nero umore
> D'andar prima del tempo ai Regni bui
> Con volontario colpo di pistola,
> La qual senz'agonia la vita invola.
> (Talassi, *La piuma recisa*, Canto VI, Lviii).

> Mostrossi al Ministero ognor contrario
> Nel gran Senato, emulator di Roma,
> Oppositor al Regio Segretario,
> Che dal gelato Settentrion si noma.
> Credea vano disegno, e temerario
> L'America voler per forza doma,
> Dicea l'ingiusta Pressa alto tiranno
> E biasmava il comprar sangue Alemanno.
>
> (Talassi, *La piuma recisa*, Canto VI, Lvix)

A footnote to the term "Pressa" reads as follows: "La pressa è un atto del Parlamento d'Inghilterra con cui si da facoltà all'ammiragliato d'ingaggiar per forza i marinari in tempo di guerra. Ciò si oppone alla tanto decantata immaginaria Libertà inglese. Trovandomi io in Londra, il Lord Mayor Hallifax proibì quest'ingiusta oppressione nel ricinto della Città. Ma si eseguiva tutto giorno nelle parti di Westminster."

La piuma recisa does not conclude without some moralising on the part of Talassi. Travelling has broadened his outlook and he derived some advantages from disaster. Knowledge and wisdom have replaced pride. In Talassi's work the gentlemen learn wisdom from dealing with life and its basic necessities, as a result of contact with pride and fastidiousness — Pope's Belinda, too, learns wisdom as a final result of the cutting of her hair:

> Pur da'disastri suoi può trar vantaggio
> Senza troppo avvilirsi il miser'Uomo,
> Col divenir più moderato, e saggio,
> Col porre in bando il primo orgoglio domo.
> Tale nel cominciar del suo viaggio
> Fu il nuovo Camerier, ch'io qui vi nomo,
> Poi per le piume, che gli davan pena
> D'Erasto in magazzin fece una scena.
>
> (Talassi, *La piuma recisa*, Canto VII, iii)

La piuma recisa plays however an extremely important role in the poetry of the lock, or the "tupé". In it is contained a lenghty account of the destruction of the object of decoration, an assault on an object of decorum which has assumed various roles in the course of the poem. It symbolises the exaggeration of the artificial, which renders it a bore and a nuisance. Not only does it have no practical function, but it obscures the view of social activity within the theatre, as well as blotting out totally the most important action — that taking place on stage.

It must also be borne in mind that the "piuma recisa" is not the "tupé" itself, which within certain conventions could be regarded as a necessary addition to fashionable dress, but that it brings us to yet another dimension, within the world of the lock, that is, further object, adding to the glitter and glory of the "grande dame". The decadentism of the entire social scene is thus symbolically conveyed. From the grotesque identification with time and space, amphitheatres and pyramids in Vittorelli's work, one passes to a more decorative dimension of decadentism, with the description of the assault on the object decorating an object of ornamentation. Talassi's work thus carries us a step further from nature. From the poetic point of view, Talassi's feather brings us into contact with the celebration of beauty and colour and the make-believe world of feathers, tassles, and vivid silks. The poet from Ferrara appears in command of an endless supply of vocabulary, which is identified with the world of the feather, and which evaporates with the destruction of the symbol of this world. *La piuma recisa* illustrates human delight in the colourful, providing a further escape from the rigidity of every-day social life and conventions. In addition to providing a light-hearted illustration of "society at play" and a symbolic rejection of, and attack on the disintegrating "bel mondo" at large, *La piuma recisa* is also a souvenir of Talassi's first visit to England in 1777. It demonstrates his reading of Pope, and his acquaintance with translations of *The Rape of the Lock* by both Conti and Bonducci. It provides evidence of Pope's influence in yet another field of poetry — that of improvisation.

In addition to providing a criticism of the frivolity and fashion of his time, Talassi contrasts two societies; that of the "bel mondo" and that of the world of natural responses and spontaneity of expression. One finds that in the end it is simplicity and natural wisdom which conquers. Finally *La piuma recisa* illustrates a wealth of knowledge with regard to English customs, eating habits, and life in general. With the experience of one wo has frequented the society salons of London, he names a well-known beauty, politician and musician. He pays tribute to England's democratic institution, while creating a poetic association between British liberty and the new-found wisdom of his gentlemen protagonists.[40]

Talassi proved one of the most fluent eighteenth-century writers professing an interest in England in general and in Pope in particular. In addition to the title of poet, traveller, socialiser, he also can be considered a writer of the mock-heroic genre, having written two mock-heroic, full-length poems. The last poet of the eighteenth-century to profess a similar interest in England and English literature, and who wrote a full-length mock-heroic poem modelled on *The Rape of the Lock* was Lorenzo Pignotti, whose work *La treccia donata* was published in Florence in 1808.

Notes to Chapter V

1 Bib. C. Goldoni, *Memoirs*, 111, xxviii; C. Piancastelli, *Nel centenario di un olmo* (Bologna, 1923); C. Zaghi, "Angelo Talassi, poeta aulico della Regina Maria di Portogallo, in *Corriere Padana*, 29 Marzo, 1928; C. Zaghi "Angelo Talassi poeta vagabondo", in *Stir*, Marzo, 1932; M. Franceschini, *Un poeta estemporaneo del settecento: Il ferrarese Angelo Talassi* (Codogno, 1938); G. Natali, *Il settecento*, op.cit., p. 92; B. Croce, *La letteratura italiana del settecento* (Bari, 1949), p. 306.

2 The date of the first publication of *L'olmo abbattuto* is erroneously stated in *Dizionario Enciclopedico della Letteratura Italiana* as being 1789.

3 Giovanni Cristofano Amaduzzi, born Savignano di Romagna, 18th August, 1740. Studied at the Cathedral School at Rimini, and having taken minor orders left for Rome in 1762. He remained in this city until his death. Dedicated himself to the study of oriental languages. In 1769, his protector Cardinal Ganganelli was elected Pope, with the title of Clement XIV. In June 1769 he was appointed Professor of Greek language at the Archiginnasio della Sapienza in Rome. In 1770 he became press supervisor for the Congregazione di Propoganda. Until 1775 was a member of Arcadia, with the name Biante Didimeo.

4 Savignano di Romagna, Biblioteca Comunale, MS. 16.

5 Ibid. Both letters are included in Appendix.

6 C. Goldoni, *Memoirs*, III, XXVIII, ed. Du Verger (Paris, 1946), p. 198.

7 Biblioteca Comunale Ariostea, Ferrara, MS. I, 501. Most of the letters are addressed to the Ab. Tieghi, Secretary to the Marchese Bevilacqua Cantelli, Ferrara.

8 Bassano del Grappa, Biblioteca Civile, Autografi Remondini XXI. 18. For complete letter see Appendix.

9 Ibid.

10 Gasparo Pacchierotti, Fabriano 1740 – Padua 1821. Italian male soprano. Successful in principle roles from 1769. Triumphed in London in 1778. Sang Venice, Vienna, Milan. Retired in 1792, reappearing only for the benefit of Napoleon 1796. The performance referred to by Talassi was of *Giulio Sabino*.

11 Ferrara Biblioteca Comunale Ariostea MS. I. 501. Full text to be found in Appendix.

12 Ibid.

13 Ibid.

14 Bassano del Grappa, Biblioteca Civica Autografi Gamba XII, E.2.

15 Ferrara Biblioteca Comunale Ariostea, MS. I, 501.

16 Ibid.

17 Lorenzo da Ponte (originally Emanuele Conegliano), born Ceneda 1749, died New York, 1838. Italian poet and librettist. Settled in Vienna as court poet to Joseph II. Wrote three operatic librettos for Mozart: *Le nozze di Figaro, Don Giovanni,* and *Così fan tutte.* From 1793 to 1805 he worked at Drury Lane Theatre in London; left England secretly and arrived in America in 1805. From 1826-37 he held the Chair of Italian at Columbia University. Wrote an entertaining autobiography. In 1825, with Manuel Garcia, he first presented Italian opera in the United States. In 1833 was responsible for the establishment of the Italian Opera House in New York.

18 Antonio Salieri, born Legnano 1750; died Vienna 1825. Italian composer of some 40 operas. At one time believed responsible for the death of Mozart. Teacher of Beethoven, Schubert and Liszt, his music was enthusiastically received in Paris and Vienna where he settled. His most famous opera is *Tarare* (1787), written to a text by Beaumarchais.

19 Ferrara Biblioteca Comunale Ariostea, MS. I, 501. Letter of November 23, 1782.

20 Ferrara Bib. Comunale Ariostea, MS. I, 501.

21 Ibid.

22 Niccolò Piccini, born Bari 1728; died Passy 1800. Italian composer whose most famous work is *La buona figliuola* (1760). *L'Olimpiade* (1768) followed up this triumph. Was Gluck's most famous rival. On the French Revolution in 1789, he returned to Naples. Was feted on his return to Paris in 1798.

23 See appendix.

24 Ferrara Biblioteca Comunale Ariostea, MS. I, 501.

25 Ibid.

26 Ibid.

27 Ibid.

28 Ibid.

29 Ibid.

30 Ibid.

31 Ibid.

32 Forlì Biblioteca Comunale. MS Plancastelli Aut. Azzolini.

33 Nota biografica di L.N. Cittadella, in *Nozze Maffei-Mazzoni* (Ferrara, 1869).

34 M. Franceschini, *Un poeta estemporaneo del settecento il ferrarese* Angelo Talassi, op.cit., p. 121.

35 L.N. Cittadella in *Nozze Maffei-Mazzoni,* op.cit.

36 M. Franceschini, *Un poeta estemporaneo del settecento, il ferrarese* Angelo Talassi, op.cit., p. 119.

37 Pope. *The Rape of the Lock* III, 1.155-160, describes Belinda's rage in the following terms:

"Then falsh'd the living lightening from her eyes,
And screams of horror rend th'affrightened skies.
Not louder shrieks to pitying Heaven are cast,
When husbands or when lap-dogs breathe their last;
Or when rich China vessels, fall'n from high,
In glitt'ring dust and painted fragments lie!"

38 "I focosi del vin spirti fiammeggiano,
Dagli argentei beccucci i grati umori
Scorrono, e intanto la Chinese terra
Riceve nel suo sen l'onda fumante."
(A. Bonducci, *Il riccio rapito*)

39 Felice di Giardini, born 1716, died 1796. Virtuoso Italian violinist.

40 All quoted passages from *La piuma recisa* are taken from: *La Piuma Recisa di Angelo Talassi* (Venice, 1778).

CHAPTER VI

The social satire and Lorenzo Pignotti

With the work of Angelo Talassi, the absorption of Pope's fantasy world into the oral tradition is established. It is also to be believed that the fate of Belinda and other frivolous females was carried further afield than Italy, and excited the attention and interest of more than the intellectually-oriented reading public. Another writer who demonstrated a deep affection for the mock-heroic genre, and revealed an extraordinary knowledge of English letters, was Lorenzo Pignotti. A doctor by profession, academic by occupation and poet and historian by inclination, Pignotti belongs exclusively to the cultural world of the second half of the eighteenth century. With both scientific and literary preparation, Pignotti proves exponent and critic of the Tuscany of Peter Leopold.

Lorenzo Pignotti, the son of Santi Pignotti and Margherita Curlandi, was born at Figline, Val d'Arno, on August 9th, 1739. As a small child he moved with his family to Arezzo, where he entered its Seminary and pursued an extended period of study. On completion of his course he abandoned the ecclesiastic life, and set about the pursuit of science at the University of Pisa. He was in later life to hold the Professorship of Physics at that University and to become its President.

A number of biographical inaccuracies are to be found in factual accounts of the writer's life. The first of these forms part of the introduction to his *Storia della Toscana*, (Pisa, 1813) in which the anonymous biographer states: "Nel Seminario di Arezzo non era ancora escito dalla classe degli studenti che fu reputato degno di esser maestro. La celebrità che distingueva il Pignotti ancora giovane, impegnò Mons. Filippo Incontri, che allora copriva la sede Vescovile di Arezzo . . . a proporgli di occupare il posto del Landi, allorchè questi fu chiamato dalla Cattedra alla cura della anime."[1]

Four years later, Aldobrando Paolini, in his *Elogio storico filoso-fico di Lorenzo Pignotti*, with slight variation, supports the theory that Pignotti's brilliance resulted in his appointment to a teaching post by the age of eighteen:

> La fama di questo fenomeno nell'ordine degli ingegni, pervenne dalla scuola alla corte del prelato Inghirami, che si consolò seco stesso dei frutti raccolti nel suo seminario, e deliberò di incardinarvi il Pignotti, nominandolo professore di Belle Lettere nella sua età di soli 18 anni per rimpiazzare la celebrità del Landi, di lui maestro, che avendo provvisoriamente insegnata la Rettorica, dovette restituirsi alla sua pieve di San Giovanni a Capolona nella diocesi aretina.[2]

Oreste Brizi, in 1842, also states that Pignotti gained a Chair at the age of eighteen.[3] Such belief, that Pignotti taught at the Seminario d'Arezzo, was widely held during the nineteenth century,[4] and it was not until Ugo Viviani set about checking the authenticity of such facts that the correct details of Pignotti's early life emerged in 1932. Viviani had expressed an interest in the poet from Figline ten years earlier in 1922. Then he had considered his satirical reproduction of doctors and medicines in his poetry and fables.[5] On consideration of three accounts of Pignotti's life in Arezzo, he concluded that all three, that is to say the anonymous writer of 1813, Paolini and Brizi, stressed that he taught at the Seminary there; the latter two stated that his appointment dated from the time he was eighteen; the anonymous writer stated that it was Incontri who promoted him to Landi's post, Paolini declares that it was Inghirami. Viviani in an article entitled "Grossolani errori nelle biografie del medico e poeta Lorenzo Pignotti", considers the careers of Landi, Incontri and Inghirami. His discoveries include the fact that Landi was ordained priest in 1735, and five years later in 1740 was transferred by Mons. Incontri to San Giovanni a Capolona. At this point Pignotti would have been scarcely one year old! The bishop Inghirami was elected to the diocese of Arezzo in 1755, and died in 1774. It was he who directed the Seminary at Arezzo, when Pignotti was in his eighteenth year. The Archivio di Murello contains only one reference to Landi, in which it names him as Professor of Rhetoric for the months of May, June and July, 1759. His place was then taken by Don Giovanni Battista Tognaccini of Florence. In checking Pignotti's activity at the Seminary in

Arezzo, Viviani finds a record of his entry, in the Archivio di Murello, Codice n. 178, 15, Giugno 1750. It reads: "In questo giorno et anno fece il primo ingresso in questo Seminario Aretino il chierico Lorenzo, figlio di Santi Pignotti di Figline, e nipote di Lorenzino Pignotti, abitante in Arezzo, con pagare lire 25 come diocesano, ed ogni sei mesi la rata anticipata."[6] Underneath there are entries for the years 1750, 1751, 1752 and 1753.

Codice N. 167 containing the names of extern students contains the following entry: "Il Sig. Lorenzo, figlio del già Santi Pignotti principiò a venire alla scuola di questo Seminario all'apertura della medesima nel mese di novembre 1753 con pagare ogni anno le solite lire 12." Underneath is recorded the payment of six lire in half-year instalments from Nov. 3rd 1753 to April 3rd 1756.

In Codice N. 178, in the list of boarders there is the following entry for the date 2 November 1756: "In questo suddetto giorno et anno fece il suo primo ingresso in questo Seminario Aretino il chierico Sig. Lorenzo, nipote di Lorenzo P., abitante in Arezzo, con pagare scudi 31 come diocesano ed ogni sei mesi rata anticipata." There follows record of payment for years 1757, 1758 and up to August 31st, 1759. That is the final entry for Lorenzo Pignotti in the records of the Seminario di Arezzo.

From the above information, Viviani deducts that Pignotti entered the Seminary as a boarder in 1750, and that he remained there until 1753. From 1753 to 1756 he attended courses as an extern student, and from 1756 to 1759 he returned as a boarder. The significant point which Viviani establishes is: "Che ai 31 di agosto 1759 il Pignotti avesse lasciato il Seminario e non fosse ivi rimasto come maestro di Rettorica o Prefetto, lo dimostra poi il fatto che in nessun elenco dei professori o dei Prefetti del Seminario ho potuto ritrovare il suo nome."[7] In other words it is false to assume that Pignotti occupied the teaching position left vacant by Landi. Viviani declares that on leaving the Seminary he pursued his scientific studies at the University of Pisa: "Andò a Pisa agli studi, ma a spese di suo zio: frequentò i corsi dell'anno scolastico 1759-66 laureandosi in medicina e filosofia nel 1763."[8] Viviani also establishes that it was in 1763, the same year in which he graduated in medicine, that Pignotti was admitted to the Accademia degli Arcadi Forzati.

In 1769, Pignotti was appointed as a teacher of physics at the Accademia della Nobilità di Firenze, where he remained until 1774, when he was given the position of Professor of Physics at the University of Pisa. Both the *Dizionario critico della letteratura italiana*, and the biographical note compiled by Mario Fubini in *Lirici del Settecento*[9] states the date of his appointment to Pisa as 1775. I have however consulted the University archives. In Sec. C.I. 2, Pignotti is listed as early as 1774 as Professor of Physics:

> Exc. D. Laurentius Pignotti Arretinus
> aget de natura et affectionibus
> corporum. Hora 2 pomerid.[10]

Pignotti remained in Pisa to the end of his days, and from 1809, was President of the University.

The aforementioned facts provide biographical details of Lorenzo Pignotti, and with the exception of Paolini's study, make no attempt to come to terms with his literary achievement.[11] Gaetano Burgada, in an article entitled "Un imitatore del Parini" in *La gazzetta letteria*, 15 Sett. 1894, comments on the influence of Parini's *Il giorno* on *La treccia donata*. Ugo Frittelli, in *Lorenzo Pignotti favolista*, treats of Pignotti the imitator of Gay, La Fontaine and Moore, and comments on the social interest of the fables, while Luigi Rossi provides a short comparative study in *La treccia donata, poema eroi-comico di Lorenzo Pignotti* (Padua, 1906). It was not until 1931, with Giovanni Lenta's *Pope in Italia*[12] that further attention was paid to *La treccia donata*. There is no attempt however to arrive at a critical assessment of the work, although Lenta is in no doubt as to the influence of Pope on Pignotti. With regard to modern critics, references to Pignotti can be found in Binni's *Preromanticismo italiano*[13] and in Moloney's *Florence and England: Essays on Cultural Relations in the Second Half of the Eighteenth Century.*[14] In both Giuseppe Savoca's contribution to *Il Settecento* (Bari, 1973)[15] and Mario Fubini's note in *Lirici del Settecento,*[16] the title of Pignotti's mock-heroic epic, a free imitation of Pope's *The Rape of the Lock* is given erroneously as *La treccia rubata*.

What then is the extent of Pignotti's popularity today? Little original research has been carried out; there is confusion with regard to dates and titles; no extensive work has been done on his satire, or *Storia della Toscana*. Today he is principally remembered as a writer of fables.

Pignotti's interest in English literature, and the influence of Alexander Pope on his thought and poetic execution is of much importance to this study. While working at the Accademia dei Nobili, Pignotti found himself in Florence at a time when the cultivation of English literature, taste and fashions proved extremely popular. Landini's *Tempio della filosofia* (1752) is dedicated to Mann; it was written in praise of Newton. Fashions were anglicised, Antonio Cocchi kept part of his diary in English. Pignotti's demonstration of his interest in English literature belongs to the period of his work at Pisa. *La tomba di Shakespear* (1779), *L'ombra di Pope* (1781) in addition to *Agli autori della raccolta d'Inglesi poesia intitolata, The Florence Miscellany; Lettere sopra i classici* (1808) and *Imitazioni di satire di Giovenale e d'Orazio* (1808), all reveal a profound admiration for English literature. Pignotti was admired by and admired some of England's most cultured and elegant women of his day. *La tomba di Shakespear* is dedicated to the celebrated Mrs. Montagu. "La Duchessa di Rutland nata Somerset, la principessa di Cowper, Ladi Elisabetta Compton, e la celebre donna M. Montagu furono tra le coltissime Dame d'Inghilterra le principali ammiratrici del poeta toscano."[17]

In his dedication of *"La tomba di Shakespear"*, Pignotti refers to the literary activity of Mary Wortley Montagu, he addresses it "alla celebre donna Mrs. Montagu in occasione della di lei applauditissima opera in difesa di quel poeta". The poem, conforming to the vision genre abounds with references to English literature which includes Milton's *Paradise Lost*, Dryden's "Alexander's Feast", Gray, the actor Garrick, and Pope. It is to *The Rape of the Lock* which Pignotti refers in connection with Pope:

> E quei che il furto della chioma bionda
> Seppe cantare in sì soavi tempre. (1.473-74).[18]

Pignotti followed on this reference to the English poet with his "Ombra di Pope", written in 1781. In this vision poem he paid tribute to Pope as translator of the Illiad, and writer of *Essay on Man*,

Eloisa to Abelard and *The Rape of the Lock*. Further acknowledgment of Pope is to be seen in his *Lettere sopra i classici*, (Florence, 1800) and in *Imitazioni di satire di Giovenale e d'Orazio* (Florence, 1808).

The influence of English literature is undeniable on Pignotti's poetic output. Full measure of this will be seen in consideration of his satirical writing: "Ma il Pignotti, studiosissimo anche della letteratura inglese, oltre il Parini ha avuto dinanzi agli occhi Il *Riccio rapito* del Pope che allora correva trionfante da un capo all.altro d'Italia e aveva incontrato una singolare fortuna."[19] The poet from Figline who displayed a depth of admiration for classical and philosophic writing succeeded in reproducing, indulging in and criticising the frivolous society of the late eighteenth century. As one with both scientific and literary training, his moralising is subtly conveyed in *La treccia donata*. It is the English influence in general, and the influence of Alexander Pope in particular, which occupies a major part of this study.

Pignotti's social criticism finds its expression in the reproduction of a society in tireless pursuit of fashion, and which has established its own laws and rituals directed by Love. In this presentation Pignotti succeeds in capturing the sugar-coated world of the fairy-tale where magic castles, subterranean caves and tinsel-like glitter are the order of the day. The "bel mondo" is transformed to a fairy-land in which caricature has no real place: one finds instead the unreal described in terms of the real. One finds some larger than life figures alongside the highly coloured or over-decorative. Pignotti's "bel mondo" is in no way similar to the miniature elegance of Conti or Savioli, or to the grotesque, implying decadence in some of Vittorelli's works. His social satire is not biting, as is Parini's. Instead, Pignotti's work maintains a freshness and a spontaneity rarely encountered in the work of eighteenth-century poets. The subject is love, the object symbolising love and infidelity is the "treccia donata" and the plot progresses by means of a series of social intrigues.

Of prime importance is the presentation of the highly coloured world of the society lady, the manner of description of the hair, the symptoms and effects of "Noia" corresponding to the Spleen in *The Rape of the Lock* and the "tempio della sciocchezza" with its inhabitants corresponding to those of the world of Pope's *Dunciad*. Thus it is Pope, read both in translation and in the original, who is the source of, and the inspiration behind *La treccia donata*. It is my belief that with some condensation, *La treccia donata* would prove a favourite children's tale; all the essential ingredients are there and the concept of space expressed within the world provides a fantastic escape hideout where life is seen as a series of charms and colours. The home of such dreams is the moon:

> Su nel vuoto paese della Luna,
> Che fra loro gli Astronomi han partito,
> Qual di Polonia il regno, ove' s'aduna
> Ciòcche guaggiù dagli uomini è smarrito,
> Le speranze di Corte, i sogni lieti
> De'Progettisti, e i plausi de'Poeti;
> (Pignotti, *La treccia donata*, Canto I, vi)

The entire concept of a coloured far-away land gives the imagination free play, Pignotti sets this atmosphere early in the poem, in order that is provide a background to the story. The vocabulary is well chosen — the "vuoto paese della luna" is empty since it contains nebulous hopes and day-dreams which evaporate on the first contact with reality. It is the territory in which all and nothing meet and become identified. It is the last refuge of the young and not so young, and the permanent residence of the Goddess of fashion. Just as dreams are seen as abstract personifications, so the Goddess of fashion is a coloured personification of the child-like conception of beauty. The fickleness of fashion is expressed in terms of the changing colour of her dress, reminiscent of Tasso's description of Fortuna in *La gerusalemme liberata;* her eternal movement conveys a larger than life quality, while the changing colour of the dress, in addition to its symbolic significance also succeeds in blinding the eye of the imagination:

> Non siede in trono, anzi non ha mai posa;
> L'agili scote tremolanti piume;
> Le muove il vento ognor la rugiadosa
> Veste, che in color varj in faccia al lume
> Si cangia sî, che varia ognor la vedi,
> Quantunque volte a rimirarla riedi.
> (Pignotti, *La treccia donata*, Canto I, xi)

In keeping with Pope's filmy projection of the sylphs, Pignotti creates an impression, half-way between nature and art, but on a gigantic scale. The Goddess of fashion is at once a feathered bird and a lady wearing a dewy dress. Her gestures are expansive and her influence is seen with regard to the face, which, whether smiling or serious, is mesmorised:

> Le gravi faccie e le ridenti rende
> Sue schiave; or le parrucche intesse, or ella
> Le immense toghe ai Senator distende.
> (Pignotti, *La treccia donata*, Canto I, x)

This is a poetic world of exaggeration, where outlines are dimmed and basic qualities stressed, akin to the world of the "land of sweets" later given life in Tchaikovsky's ballet *The Nutcracker*. The crystal walls adorned with figures create the impression of tinsel decorations on a huge decorated Christmas cake: this is illustrated with reference to Canto I stanza xii:

> Sulle pareti simili ai cristalli
> Pinte si stan vaghe figure ornate
> Di varj drappi e rossi e persi e gialli,

In many respects this is the miniature world of Savioli and Parini in the reverse. While in the case of the mentioned poets the reader appears to hover over the artistic world, Pignotti dwarfs his reader with the limitless stretch of his imagination. Yet his message is clear: fantasy and frivolity directed towards fashion can blind, dazzle until the beholder becomes lost in a world in which taste, shade and measurement dictate every move. In Pignotti's world, not only are objects larger and more brilliantly coloured than in everyday life, but they are also mirrored in their surroundings, creating an almost overpowering effect:

> Dell'auree stanze entro il purpureo lume
> Di colorate liste e l'ali e il tergo
> Pinte, vaghe farfalle apron le piume,
> Che or giù, or su nell'incantato albergo
> Vengono e vanno, e istabili, inquieti
> Si specchian nella lucida parete.
> (Pignotti, *La treccia donata*, Canto I, xvii)

In the above lines, the purple and gold of ceremonial regalia is combined with the effect created by individuals resembling giant butterflies, and both are finally reflected in the glittering walls.

If the illustration of the splashes of colour launched by Pignotti may lead the reader to suspect a certain lack of finesse in the work, let me at once assure him of the contrary. The ballroom scene reveals the poet at his most refined, controlled, yet succeeding in portraying the dancers, their glances and movement in a variety of poses. Here Pignotti achieves the visual creation of the world of the ballet, combining order and wantonness, leaving the impression of the moving heads, decorated with jewels and feathers:

> Cresce la vaga folla, e in tutti i canti
> Fra bel tumulto vedi a cento a cento
> Affollate ondeggiar teste galanti, –
> Come le spiche allo spirar del vento,
> E tremolar brillando in faccia al lume
> E fiori e gemme e nastri e veli e piume.
>
> (Pignotti, *La treccia donata*, Canto IV, vi)

The measured paces of the dance is conveyed in the first three lines of the passage, building to a central "crescendo" while concluding on the same note as the opening.

The above discussed ambience provides the setting for *La treccia donata*, a social milieu which we know exists only in the imagination, yet which we can conceivably build for ourselves on the contemplation of a colourful object. It is the interchange between the fanciful and fantastic which allows the reader to indule in Pignotti's colourful escapism while keeping in mind the moral of the piece.

The exact date of the poem is not known. It was published in Florence in 1808, and was dedicated: "Alla Sua Eccellenza, il Sig. Melzi d'Eril, Duca di Lodi, Gran Cancellier Guarda – Sigilli del Regno d'Italia, Gran Cordone della Legione d'Onore e Gran Dignitario del Real Ordine della Corona di Ferro." We do know, however, that it was written many years before its publication, as Pignotti's "avviso al lettore" indicates. Pignotti also states his moral intentions in writing a poem which appears merely to deal with feminine frivolity:

Sì; io vi do nel mio Poemetto uno sguarcio di antiquaria galante: nè questo è tutto: avvezzo a cercar sempre la moralità nel racconto delle mie favole, non ho obliato che un gran principio morale potean trarre dalla lettura di esso tanto le Giovani quanto le Vecchie. Le prime, sorridendo alla narrazioni delle follie di quelle che con tanta amarezza or le condannano, impareranno ad esser caute ed indulgenti per la generazione avvenire; le seconde, divenute ora savie e ritirate per disperazione, riconoscendo nel mio quadro la pittura dei capricci, e delle avventure, che sì famose un giorno le resero, cesseranno una volta dal garrire contro le vezzose imitatrici de'loro amabili delirj . . .

Pope's *The Rape of the Lock* is the source of inspiration for the poem, though in fact many passages of Pignotti's work are direct parodies of the English poem. The title of the former, concerns not a stolen lock, but one presented by a lady as a love token, and later bestowed on her rival. The plot of the poem is condensed by Luigi Rossi in his work published in 1906:

Eurilla e Silvia, rivali in amore, si contendono Daliso, specie di Giovin Signnore che attratto prima dalle artificiali bellezze dell'una e ricevutone, singolare dono, una bionda treccia, s'innamora poi della seconda assai più giovane e più bella. Ma questa esige da lui tutti i pegni de'suoi passate amori e, fra essi, anche la famosa treccia. Si accontenta costei? Neanche per sogno, per arrecar maggio dispetto alla rivale appende la treccia ad un lungo bastone che, Silvia camuffata da Circassa e Daliso da Bassà, portano ad una festa da ballo ov'ella faceva bella mostra di sè . . .[20]

The opening Canto, entitled "Il Tempio Della Moda" contains much colour and movement, with many lines recalling Pope's *The Rape of the Lock*, and a direct reference to "Il furto delle chiome bionde" on the banks of the Thames:

> Donne, so quanto ben da voi s'adopre
> Il tempo, onde rapirvelo non oso;
> Pur se vi resta dopo le bell'opre
> Della toeletta alcun momento ozioso,
> Fra la noja e i sbadigli un fuggitivo
> Sguardo volgete a quel ch'io, canto e scrivo.
> (Pignotti, *La treccia donata,* Canto I. iii)

> Dimme le cause, tu, che sulle sponde
> Cantasti del Tamigi in dolci note,
> O Musa, il furto delle chiome bionde;
> Le vaghe risse a te non sono ignote,

> E i soavi puntigli femminili
> Son d'ogni clima le follie simili.
> (Pignotti, *La treccia donata*, Canto I. v)

The above is the first of many references to the lock of hair of the title which changes hands as quickly as fashion and is symbolic of fickleness and infidelity. The world of make-believe is quickly introduced with a description of the temple of fashion, which is placed above vapourous clouds, which create the impression of giant candy-floss:

> Sorge un Tempio magnifico, di quella
> Lieve sostanza lucida formato
> Onde il manto si tesse Iride bella,
> Di strana architettura: ei sta posato
> Sopra le nubi, e a ogn'aura, che si muove,
> Cade, e tosto risorge in forme nuove.
> (Pignotti, *La treccia donata*, Canto I. vii)

Pope's sylphs are represented in Pignotti's poem by the "folletti" or pixies whose duties and commitments include guardianship of the dressing-table, and the adornment of the nymph. They are:

> Spirti che già informaro umani petti
> Di giovani galanti, e di vezzose
> Dame per fino gusto un dì famose.
> (Pignotti, *La treccia donata*, Canto I. xix)

This resembles the following lines in Pope:

> As now your own, our beings were of old,
> And once inclosed in woman's beauteous mould;
> Thence, by a soft transition, we repair
> From earthy vehicles to these of air.
> (Pope, *The Rape of the Lock*, Canto I. 47-50)

Their transition to earth is poetically conveyed by Pignotti:

> Piene sol dell'idee del gentil mondo,
> Come fiamma che al ciel vola leggiera,
> Riedon pur esse alla nativa sfera.
> (Pignotti, *La treccia donata*, Canto I. xx)

Their precision in the enactment of their duties is expressed in I.xxii, the final two lines of which come directly from Pope:

Quando con si leggiadra simetria
Composto il crin, la veste, il vel vedete
D'Eurilla, questa voi, di Giammaria
O di Lisetta, industre opre credete,
Ciechi mortali! di più alto viene
L'influsso, e non son questa opre terrene.
(Pignotti, *La treccia donata,* Canto I. xxii)

The busy sylphs surround their darling care,
These set the head, and those divide the hair,
Some fold the sleeve, while others plait the gown:
And Betty's praised for labours not her own.
(Pope, *The Rape of the Lock,* Canto I, 145-8)

Both Conti's and Bonducci's versions correspond closely to the original:

Stannole intorno affacendati i Silfi:
Chi adorna il capo, chi comparte il crine,
Chi la manica piega e chi la veste;
E per opra non sua Lisca si loda.
(Conti, *Il riccio rapito,* Canto I. 206-9)

Conti's version provides a list of abstractions identified with feminine behaviour, on the other hand Bonducci employs a more conversational tone:

Alla manica quei, questi alla gonna
Fanno pieghe ingegnose, e Silvia intanto
Per lavori non suoi lode riporta.
(Bonducci, *Il riccio rapito*, Canto I.
(conclusion.)

In stanza xxiii of the same Canto, Pignotti gives a more detailed account of the pixies activity:

Chi de'ricci le polvi, e chi le rare
Essenze custodisce; all'aureo manto
Le pieghe altri conserva, altri distende
L'ali, e dall'aura un vago crin difende.
(Pignotti, *La treccia donata*, Canto I. xxiii)

The ordered articles on the dressing-table reproduced so often by Italian poets of the "bel mondo" form part of *"La trasmigrazione dell'anima*. Pignotti combines in humorous fashion both science and elegance:

Sulla Toletta misti erano acciso
E polvi e libri e telescopi, e un neo
Nel saggiator caduto era rimasto
Attaccato sul viso a Galileo,
E un ago da una bussola staccato
Era tramezzo alle forcine entrato.[21]

Pignotti's protagonist resembles Pope's Belinda in that her adornment, hairstyle, disposition and some articles worn are obviously taken from Pope. Belinda wears a cross on her neck, "on her white breast a sparkling cross she wore,/Which Jews might kiss, and infidels adore". (*The Rape of the Lock*, II, 1. 7-8). Eurilla too is similarly adorned:

Indi in argenteo carcere ristretto
Forma splendida croce, che già gode.
Di dover ondeggiar su bianco petto.
(Pignotti, *La treccia donata*, Canto I. xxv)

Giovanni Lenta, with reference to Canto VI of the poem entitled "Il Casinò, E La Sfida" points out a close resemblance between Pignotti's "casinò" and Pope's Hampton Court: "Il casinò del Pignotti corrisponde mirabilmente al Hampton di Pope."[22] Rather than an imitation of Pope's lines, I believe the description of the "casinò" constitutes a parody on Pope. Let us compare them:

Close by those meads, for ever crowned with flowers,
Where Thames with pride surveys his rising towers,
There stands a structure of majestic frame,
Which from the neighb'ring Hampton takes its name.
(Pope, *The Rape of the Lock*, Canto III, 1-4)

The building is majestic and inspires awe. Pignotti's edifice, also situated on a river, and crowned by Flora, is by no means imposing. In terms of contrast we have passed from the sublime to the ridiculous:

Dell'Arno in riva, ove nell'onda pura
Tremolar Flora i suoi palagi scorge,
Per fama illustre più che par struttura
Sacro alla Vanitade Ostello sorge,
E l'edificio suo poco sublime
Colla modestia del suo nome esprime.
(Pignotti, *La treccia donata*, Canto VI, i)

177

The temple of pride is not eye-catching, it serves amongst other things, as a centre of gossip:

Quest'almo Tempio, che de'Cavalieri
All'ozio mattutin pur si disserra,
Perchè communicarsi i bei pensieri
Possono e i scandoletti della Terra.
(Pignotti, *La treccia donata*, Canto VI, xvii).

Gossip is the principle pastime also at Pope's miniature Hampton Court:

One speaks the glory of the British Queen,
And one describes a charming Indian screen;
A third interprets motions, looks and eyes;
At every word a reputation dies.
(Pope, *The Rape of the Lock*, Canto III, 13-16)

Up to this point the similarities between the two works are as follows: they are mock-heroic epics, set in a centre of historical fame and elegance. The protagonist, a member of high society, goes through the ritual of self-beautification, is served by unearthly creatures, who in the case of Pope's work, evolve from a higher order of spirits. In the case of Pignotti's poem the "folletti" or pixies return to earth by means of flame, to attend the beautiful. Pope's world touches on the spiritual, where earthly form dissolves and becomes identified with the elements. Eurilla's servants have returned after death in the form of "little people", not dissimilar to those of the germanic fairy tale. The central theme common to both poems concerns the cultivation of the lock of hair, its symbolism and final fate. However, the point must be stressed that Pignotti's world is more imaginative and of broader horizons than Pope's. The latter's "little world of Hampton Court" is created according to the same scale as the figures and their social activity. Pignotti, I believe, operates on two diverse scales. The world of the moon, the temple of fashion, and the temple of stupidity together with their royal over-seers, are larger than life. The "casinò", however, represents a return to a smaller scale surroundings in which the characters are free to operate without fear of being dwarfed. In this stylistic respect it can be argued that there is a resemblance to the miniature world of Pope. The element of parody is seen clearly in Pope, the structure of the palace forms the object central to the lines quoted on the previous page. Pignotti points out clearly that his building is neither of noble proportions, nor does it give its name to a district or locality. Its name is pride and to this it owes its fame. True historical fame and grandeur is thus placed alongside presumed self-importance and stupidity: it is the replacement of the sublime by the ridiculous.

As in the case of Pope, Pignotti introduces the lock in Canto II, and underlines its identification with fidelity. The rituals of love are followed. It can indeed be said that the poem is one of amourous intrigue centred round the object which symbolises fidelity – the lock. It is first referred to in Canto II, xiii:

> Fra i pregi, onde costei gisse più altera,
> Lunga vedeasi ed ampia chioma bionda,
> Che a'rai del Sol s'assomigliava, ed era
> Fina, e qual oro lustra; e in lucid'onda
> Quando ell'era disciolta (ed era spesso)
> Scendeva in auree fila al piede appresso.
> (Pignotti, *La treccia donata*, Canto II. xiii)

> Del sacro crine il nuovo amante avea
> Leggiadra cifra in un gemmato anello,
> E in esso un cor piagato si vedea
> intesto in mezzo ai cari nomi, e quello
> Per patto, in segno del suo cor ferito,
> Portar dovea perpetuamente in dito.
> (Pignotti, *La treccia donata*, Canto II, xvi).

Pope identifies Belinda's eyes, rather than her locks, with the light of the sun. He then immediately follows with the description of the locks:

> This nymph, to the destruction of mankind,
> Nourish'd two locks, which graceful hung behind
> In equal curls, and well conspired to deck
> With shining ringlets the smooth ivory neck.
> (Pope, *The Rape of the Lock*, Canto II, 19-22)

Eurilla's fashion was to provide each lover with a lock of her hair:

> Ella donar solea di sì vezzoso
> Crine piccola ciocca ad ogni amante.
> (Pignotti, *La treccia donata*, Canto II, xiv)

179

She had favoured Daliso with a particularly large portion:

> Un'ampia Treccia avea donata ancora;
> Splendido dono, e insolito finora.
> (Pignotti, *La treccia donata,* Canto II, xvii)

The ritual performed by Daliso indicates Pignotti's intention of reproducing a society governed by the respect accorded to Love, which becomes a social and personal religion:

> Questo soave pegno, riverente
> Tre volte il dì scoprir dovea Daliso
> Soletto, e venerar devotamente
> E star su quel cogli occhi intento e fiso,
> E sospirando meditarvi cose
> Tenere, soavissime, amorose.
> (Pignotti, *La treccia donata,* Canto II, xviii)

> A sì bella custode, a sì cortese
> Mastro Daliso fu dunque concesso
> Con invidia dell'altre, ed ella prese.
> Poi formalmente sì gentil possesso:
> Il contratto si strinse, e furon fatti
> In buona forma e legalmente i patti.
> (Pignotti, *La treccia donata,* Canto II, xix)

The Baron's ritual to love in Pope's work is not exactly similar, but no less amusing:

> But chiefly Love, — to love an altar built,
> Of twelve vast French romances, neatly gilt.
> There lay three garters, half a pair of gloves;
> And all the trophies of his former loves:
> With tender billet-doux he lights the pyre,
> And breathes three amorous sights to raise the fire.
> (Pope, *The Rape of the Lock,* Canto II, 37-41)

The attraction of Eurilla's rival Silvia is seen in terms of her more youthful locks. Once again here the influence of Pope's lines is clear: the locks in the case of the English poem decorate the neck of Belinda; Silvia's curls adorn her youthful bosom:

> Il crin bruno ma fino e delicato
> Sulla fronte in un gruppo era raccolto,
> Cinto da un roseo nastro e mal frenato,

Che in qualche ciocca pendulo e disciolto,
Sul sen scherzando tremulo e lascivo,
Il nativo candor facea più vivo.
(Pignotti, *La treccia donata,* Canto III. xlii)

Scherzando ella gli chiede ove nasconde
La celebrata Treccia, e se adorata
L'abbia quel giorno, e ride egli risponde
Con un languido sguardo: ogni dorata
Chioma s'ecclissa di quel nero a fronte,
Che di coprir superbo è la tua fronte.
(Pignotti, *La treccia donata,* Canto III, xlviii)

Within Pignotti's poem lies the contrast between yough and age, beauty and decay. This is symbolised by the artificial aids adopted by Eurilla, and the natural freshness of Silvia. Both poems contain however a warning of approaching old age in terms of greying hair:

But since, alas! frail beauty must decay,
Curl'd or uncurl'd, since locks will turn to grey;
Since painted, or not painted, all shall fade,
And she who scorns a man must die a maid.
(Pope, *The Rape of the Lock,* Canto V, 25-28)

Tempo verrà quando canute e rare
Avrà le chiome, che scemato il fasto.
Sarà la prima al tuo divino altare
A porger voti; ed oh qual bel contrasto
Faran le tue divise pellegrine
Colla grinzosa faccia e il bianco crine!
(Pignotti, *La treccia donata,* Canto VII, xxx)

In the final Canto Eurilla is further reminded of approaching age in startingly realistic terms:

A Eurilla, pria che a te, di morir tocca,
C'ha più di te quattordici anni almeno:
Il Tempo già l'arco fatale scocca.
Al bel mondo già muore ella e vien meno,
Pasci gli sguardi tuoi sulle nascenti
Rughe, sul crin canuto e i negri denti.
(Pignetti, *La treccia donata,* Canto X, xxiii)

Pignotti's work lacks the classical refinement of Pope; it also lacks his subtlety and pointed wit. Pignotti is colourful and inventive; his world contains the magical elements of the fairy-tale, and the brightness and variety of the picture book. While aspects of *La treccia donata* can be regarded as parody on the English poem, they never descend to the level of skit, or the figures to the world of caricature. The final fate of the lock illustrates what I mean in making the above statement. After much debate and deliberation, it is finally decided that the lock must be burned:

> Stride l'aurata Chioma, e in lievi e torte
> Nubi il vapor per l'aria si distende,
> E nello stesso tempo, o dura sorte!
> Tutto d'Eurilla il credito si perde;
> E pari appunto a quel fumoso nembo
> Cade d'oblio nel tenebroso grembo.
>> (Pignotti, *La treccia donata*, Canto X, lxxxxix)

> Sorte stabil non v'è: Sparta ed Atene
> Giaccion sepolte sotto i sassi e l'erba:
> Rotta vacilla per l'Egizie arene
> Ogni mole più eccelsa e più superba
> Convien pertanto aver pazienza, O Belle,
> Se muor bellezza, e aggrinzasi la pelle.
>> (Pignotti, *La treccia donata*, Canto X, xc)

Belinda's lock mounted to the lunar sphere. In keeping with the lock of Bernice it mounted on high, a shining light in the heavens, and an immortal reminder of Belinda's beauty. Pope supplies a final reminder that the Muse will finally ascribe Belinda's name amongst the stars.

Eurilla's lock creates a light of a different nature. It creates merely clouds of smoke, which soon become extinguished, leaving in their wake the blackness of oblivion. The poem ends on a mock-heroic note, with Pignotti's ironic exclusion of the reminder that the Muse has conveyed further life and fame to "La treccia donata."

Pignotti did not solely adapt the central object of Pope's poem *The Rape of the Lock* to his needs in writing his mock-heroic poem. One finds that the "Noia" which exists in Pignotti's make-believe world corresponds to Belinda's "spleen", and that the canto containing the detailed descriptions of the "tempio della sciocchezza" and its inhabitants is derived directly from Pope's *Dunciad*. It is worth noting that there was no Italian translation made of *The Dunciad* during the eighteenth century. There was a French version published in London in 1781. This could have been studied by Pignotti. I am more inclined to believe, however, that he read the work in the original English. One finds in the case of passages influenced by *The Rape of the Lock* that Pignotti is nearer to Pope than to either Conti or Bonducci.

In Canto II of *La treccia donata,* entitled "Il Cavalier Servente", there is supplied the origin of the "ciscisbeo", his social function, and his pastime:

> Di scandoli sottil comentatore
> Assertor franco, e le più volte autore.
> (Pignotti, *La treccia donata,* Canto II, iv)

There are also, in the same Canto, some descriptions of "la noia", which as already stated, conforms to Belinda's spleen. "Noia" is contained in an impressive palace, decorated with rich style and pomp: love in order to locate "la noia", takes wings, and finally arrives at a lordly establishment

> Sapendo ove trovarla; ecco che move,
> Rapidamente Amor l'aurate penne,
> Fende leggier gli aerei campi, e dove
> Sorgea nobil palazzo alfin sen venne –
> V'entra, e la Noja tosto egli ravvisa
> In mezzo al fasto, ed alle pompe assisa.
> (Pignotti, *La treccia donata*, Canto II. XL).

The personification of "Noia" conveys inactivity and intensive boredom:

> Su morbido guancial giace e sbadiglia
> Con occhio sonnolento, e or s'alza, or siede
> Sui ricchi arredi ora girar le ciglia.
> (Pignotti, *La treccia donata,* Canto II, xlii)

> Ali nere ella veste, ond'e che invano
> I martir suoi da lei fuggono lunge;
> (Pignotti, *La treccia donata,* Canto II, xliii)

It appears that Pignotti drew the greater part of his inspiration for "la Noia" and "Il Tempio Della Sciocchezza" from *The Dunciad* by Pope, one can nevertheless note some similarities between the fol-

lowing quotation from *The Rape of the Lock* and lines-quoted
on the previous page:

> Swift on his sooty pinions flits the gnome,
> And in a vapour reach'd the dismal dome.
> No cheerful breeze this sullen region knows,
> The dreaded east is all the wind that blows.
> Here in a grotto, shelter'd close from air,
> And screen'd in shades from days' detested glare,
> She sighs forever on her pensive bed,
> Pain at her side, and Megrim at her head.
>
> (Pope, *The Rape of the Lock,* Canto IV, 18-25)

Daliso, speeded by love, and rendered proud as a result of his precious
love-token, dominates the scene. Thus within the dominion of boredom and apathy, a love-token assumes disproportionate significance:

> Ma cedono tutti quando appar Daliso
> Conscio di sua importanza, egli severo
> Passa, e i rivali appena guarda in viso
> Che la donata treccia il rende altero.
> Dono caro, e fatal, Treccia funesta
> Che nel bel mondo orride guerre appresta.
>
> (Pignotti, *La treccia donata,* Canto II, lxx)

"La sede della fantasia in Pignotti e la grotta della Ipocondria in Pope
sono due descrizioni gemelle. . ."[23] This statement is to a certain
degree correct, but it could be more accurate to regard Pignotti's
poetry in Canto V, entitled "Il Consulto Medico" a fusion of both
the world of the "Cave of Spleen" and *The Dunciad.* In *The Rape of
the Lock*, the inhabitants of the cave of spleen suffer merely from social ills, i.e. ill nature, affectation, pride, while the inhabitants of the
cave of Fantasy suffer from bodily ills, in addition to the more significant literary and intellectual shortcomings. "Il Consulto Medico"
can also be regarded as a light-hearted attack on the medical profession.[24] The cave of Fantasia is in:

> Un solitario dirupato monte
> Cinto di densa nebbia. . .(V.I.)
>
> (Pignotti, *La treccia donata*, Canto V, i)

The monster, dullness, is the son of madness:

Ma quel mostro, che all'egro ed all'insano
E allo stolto poeta i sogni invia,
Mostro che nacque già dalla Follia. . .
(Pignotti, *La treccia donata,* Canto V, ii)

Qui corpo aereo, e senza peso, il dorso
A una chimera preme, e per le vuote
Regioni del nulla affretta il corso
L'oscura Metafisica, che scuote
Ed agita per l'aria ogni momento
Vane vessiche pregne sol di vento. . .
(Pignotti, *La treccia donata,* Canto V, iv)

The genealogy of the figure resembles Dullness:

Dulness o'er all possess'd her ancient right,
Daughter of chaos and eternal Night:
(Pope, *The Dunciad,* I, 11-12)

At l. 29, she is equated with Folly. The attendants on the central figure in the cave of Fantasy of Pignotti resemble the Goddesses' servants in the cave of spleen in *The Rape of the Lock.*

In veste femminil l'Ombra è ravvolta
Con pompa negligente, e su dorato
Sedil protesa giace; erra disciolta
La chioma all'aure; ora un tremor gelato
Tutte le scote le convulse membra,
Ora da calda febbre arder rassembra.
(Pignotti, *La treccia donata,* Canto V, viii)

L'Astio, il Capriccio, la mancata Speme
Le Pretension svenevoli, le Lezie
Di Vanità con larga dose insieme.
(Pignotti, *La treccia donata,* Canto V, xiii)

Here stood ill-nature like an ancient maid,
Her wrinkled form in black and white array'd;

There Affectation, with a sickly mien,
Shows in her cheeks the roses of eighteen,
Practised to lisp, and hang the head aside,
Faints into airs, and languishes with pride.
(Pope, *The Rape of the Lock,* Canto IV, 27-28, 31-34)

The section of the poem, however, which shows most influence of *The Dunciad* on Pignotti is Canto VII entitled "Il Tempio della

Sciocchezza". In keeping with the procedure in Pope's poem, the Goddess surveys dominions and subjects. There is a lengthy description of their activity and its effect. Pignotti's Goddess verges on the comical, while Pope's is more sophisticatedly ironical:

> In goffa maestà d'impertenenza
> Siede la Diva, e nel paffuto e tondo
> Viso dipinta sta la compiacenza
> Di veder quanti sudditi ha nel mondo;
> Che quai dall'Austro spinti al lido i flutti
> Con benda agli occhi e lei sen corron tutti.
>
> (Pignotti, *La treccia donata,* Canto VII, ix)

> All these, and more, the cloud compelling queen,
> Beholds through fogs, that magnify the scene.
> She, tinsell'd o'er in robes of varying hues,
> With self-applause her wild creation views;
> Sees momentary monsters rise and fall,
> And with her own fools – colours guilds them all.
>
> (Pope, *The Dunciad*, I. 79-84).

Pignotti's Goddesses' subjects are divided into two groups: one, the members of which through silence gain the reputation of great intellects, the other through pedantry:

> Ma stuol sì vario d'abiti e di viso
> In due schiere grandissime e diviso.
>
> (Pignotti, *La treccia donata,* Canto VII, xi)

> Contien la prima il gregge numeroso
> Di quei ch'esister conoscendo appena,
> Dormon la vita in torpido riposo,
> Poco al piacer sensibili, o alla pena;
> Che del silenzio col favor sovente
> Passan per saggi ancor, gregge innocente.
>
> (Pignotti, *La treccia donata,* Canto VII, xii)

Pignotti's ability to give life and movement to his lines, and to provide a separate rhythm for each figure of speech mentioned in the following sestina, illustrates well his power over words: it reveals an ability to convey life and personality to every animate object:

> In pompa oriental di quà s'avanza
> La Metafora sulle ali di vento;
> Le Antitesi in grottesca contraddanza

Fanno fra lor comico abbattimento;
E con distorti piè, slocate braccia,
Van gli Anagrammi, e con mentita faccia.
(Pignotti, *La treccia donata*, Canto VII, xv)

These above lines originate in *The Dunciad*, but one can clearly observe how Pignotti has made the material his own; how by means of contrast and variation a variety of images emerge: "pompa oriental", "grottesca contraddanza", "mentita faccia". Pope's lines represent an orderly confusion, Pignotti's have an element of wantonness:

She sees a mob of metaphors advance,
Pleased with the madness of the mazy dance!
How tragedy and comedy enbrace;
How farce and epic get a jumbled race;
(Pope, *The Dunciad*, I, 67-70);

The further changing of form and union of opposites sees Pignotti giving life to books, which change form and content under the very eye:

Non così folte leva Austro le arene
Sul mauro lido quanto numerosa
Folla di libri in ogni dì qua viene;
Prosa fornita in versi, e versi in prosa,
Libri agronomi, economi, morali,
Novelle, elogi, prediche e giornali.
(Pignotti, *La treccia donata*, Canto VII, xix)

Once again some lines from Pope can be indicated as the source of the above lines. Both poets excel in providing balance and contrast, and ability to provide opposites within the same line:

Here to her chosen all her works she shows;
Prose swelled to verse, verse loitring into prose:
How random thoughts now meaning chance to find,
Now leave all memory of sense behind;
How prologues into prefaces decay,
And these to notes are frittered quite away.
(Pope, *The Dunciad*, 273-78)

Pignotti's Goddess is the personification of animal studipity. The entire portrait is lacking in sarcasm or ironic sophistication:

> Sta questa Larva pettoruta e trionfia,
> La faccia ha grave, e appunto al bue conforme,
> La testa grande e lieve, e d'aura gonfia,
> D'asin le lunghe orecchie, e il ventre enorme.
> L'ali ha di struzzo, e per levarsi a volo
> Le batte ognor, nè s'erge mai dal suolo.
>   (VII, xliv).

Pope diversely paints a picture of refined stupidity:

> Her ample presence fills up all the place;
> A veil of fog dilates her awful face:
> Great in her charms! as when on shrieves and may'rs
> She looks, and breathes herself into their airs.
>   (Pope, *The Dunciad*, I, 261-64).

Vile insects in the world of *The Dunciad*, take poetic feet, while Pignotti uses the same terms to describe the activity of the critic: the spirit which pervades the following lines is very much that demonstrated in Pope's *Essay on Criticism*, but the vocabulary is obviously influenced by that of the world of *The Dunciad*:

> Questo i più vili insetti di permesso
> Erge in critici; e già dalle lor sedi
> Caccian Marone, Omero, Apollo istesso:
> Questo ai quinqua genarj Ganimedi
> Di meritar nutrisce la speranza
> Da Belle di tre lustri amor, costanza.
>   (Pignotti, *La treccia donata*, Canto VII, xlv.)

> Here she beholds the chaos dark and deep,
> Where nameless somethings in their causes sleep,
> Till genial Jacob, on a warm third day,
> Call forth each mass, a poem or a play:
> How hints, like spawn, scarce quick in embryo lie,
> How new-born nonsense first is taught to cry,
> Maggots half-formed in rhyme exactly meet,
> And learn to crawl upon poetic feet.
>   (Pope, *The Dunciad*, I, 55-62).

It is clear that Pignotti's *La treccia donata* leans heavily on both Pope's satires, *The Rape of the Lock* and *The Dunciad*. Both English poems, so diverse in ambience and spirit, provide the dual theme and complexity of Pignotti's poem. It can be argued that *La treccia donata* represents a series of contrasts and contradictions embracing light and darkness, reality and fantasy, the sublime and the ridiculous. Its moralising touches the artificial and artistic world, with the final illustration that ardour and artifice finally go up in smoke.

Pignotti has taken his point of departure from an imaginary world and within this world has incorporated the customs and fashionable rituals of the "bel mondo". One thus witnesses the fusion of the real, the imaginative and decorative. The over-riding impression is, in the early part of *La treccia donata*, of the fantastic. For this reason the irony, wit and mild sarcasm can never appear cruel or biting; all is both possible and permissible in the world of the moon, and the temple of fashion. From the theme of fashionable dress, and its colourful imagery, Pignotti proceeds to reproduce fashionable behaviour, manners and intellectual and academic practices.

With the shifting from the vivid descriptions of colour, and its impressionistic effect within the social salon, Pignotti brings his work literally down to earth until it becomes identified with Pope's "bel mondo". The scale becomes more minute and the lock, ladies and perfect "cavalier servente" are introduced. What is more, the world of the "casinò" is identified with that of Hampton Court, except for the fact that pride and stupidity in Pignotti's poem determine even the appearance and frame of the structure. Instead of one lady, Pignotti introduces two, representing contrasts and opposites: youth and age, nature and artifice, the eternal rivals within eighteenth-century poetry. The lock itself, originally symbolising fidelity in love, becomes an object of ridicule demonstrating Daliso's infidelity.

Belinda and Eurilla have much in common; each wear a cross, are served by supernatural creatures at the elaborate dressing-table, and perform rituals to beauty, fashion and artifice. Daliso's grandeur is on a more refined scale – he has much in common with Parini's "Giovin Signore". Pignotti's message is one of tolerance communicated by means of the projection of a colourful world of charm and playful wit. It is a world where all is coated in sweetness, and the "belletto" or artificial beauty aids resemble "blancmange". This is by no means the whole story, however. Pignotti conveys his message in a second key, where the light and colour yields to the blackness of murky mists and vapours. The moralising is directed towards the world of the intellect, as opposed to that of the fantasy, and the personae represented are no more life-like than those of a morality play.

Pignotti's imagery serves his sarcasm with regard to his view of those who allow themselves to stray from the path of reality. The pedant, poor critic and would-be intellectual, is as far removed from reality as the foolish lady, the social butterfly who allows her thoughts to carry her to enchanted castles and glittering balls. It would appear, however, that Pignotti considers the former, the pedant, more objectionable and deplorable than the "grande-dame". Both are seen in action, one escaping to the higher elements, the other descending to the subterranean caves; one identified with butterflies, the other with maggots and insects. It is ironically the group identified with the intellect that descends lowest, and is described in the darkest forms. In the end, the over-indulgent in fantasy is seen as foolish, but harmless.

It is true then that Pignotti in his poem has fused the world of *The Rape of the Lock* and *The Dunciad*. He provides a two-toned satire contrasting light and darkness, sophistication and vulgarity and offers a two-fold message of social and academic tolerance. In addition, he provides two ladies, contrasting Nature and Art, and he addressed the poem to young and old, urging each to learn tolerance and maturity. Of consequence, his is a literary style of sharp contrast, and it could be argued that an easy link is not created between the two contrasting elements in the poem. It could also be said that the work lacks structural unity, but I feel that the central theme is pretentiousness, and that Pignotti uses every device to illustrate the contrasting elements of stupidity in a light and serious vein: "Chi conosce l'inglese bene preferisce certo i cinque canti di Pope ai dieci del Pignotti. Quelli sono più concisi, più succosi, a più armoniosi, più brillanti, questi più diffusi e meno interessanti, perchè l'argomento è tutto fantastico, senza legame, con veri fatti della vita, se non generali."[25]

That Pope is the greater poet there can be no doubt, that Pignotti's works merit more critical attention than they have been hitherto accorded, is a fact beyond dispute. His contribution to the mock-heroic genre is significant, his fables poke gentle fun at society in a style appealing to children and adults alike. As a lyric poet, Pignotti provided many lines worthy of inclusion in poetic anthologies. Three short examples I believe, serve to illustrate the poet's ability by means of variation of light and shade, sound and silence, and by harmony of sound and movement, to provide vignettes or rural and social life:

> Sorgea la notte, e il velo umido ed atro
> Alla faccia del suol stendeva intorno;
> Co'tardi buoi, col rovesciato arato
> Già dai campi il villan facea ritorno;
> E colla lieta famigliuola al fianco
> Sedeva a parca mensa il fabbro stanco.
> (Pignotti, *La treccia donata,* Canto IV, i.)

> Cresce la vaga folla, e in tutti i canti
> Fra bel tumulto vedi a cento a cento
> Affollate ondeggiar teste galanti,
> Come le spiche allo spirar del vento,
> E tremolar brillando in faccia al lume
> E fiori e gemme e nastri e veli e piume.
> (Pignotti, *La treccia donata,* Canto IV, vi).

> E già le coppie in armonia concorde,
> Ai dolci atti accoppiando i dolci sguardi,
> Seguono il suon delle canore corde,
> Coi pronti passi or frettolosi, or tardi,
> Già ferve, si moltiplica, e s'avanza,
> In lungo ordin la vaga contraddanza.
> (Pignotti, *La treccia donata,* Canto IV, xi).

In Alexander Pope, Lorenzo Pignotti found a kindred spirit. One whose classical training and imaginative creativity enabled him to parody the classical epic and provide the most popular poem in eighteenth-century Italy by a foreign writer. With the advent of the Neo-Classic period, Pope's Italian popularity began to wane. The theoretical approach to being and behaviour yielded to a preoccupation with the individual within his society, and its political implications. The cultivation of the rococo miniature gave way to a life-sized and politically orientated Neo-Classicism. Pope's poetry, and consequently the output of his imitators was doctrinal to an age, and remains a record and commentary on the many aspects of the eighteenth century.

191

Notes to Chapter VI

1 "Biografia d'anonimo di Lorenzo Pignotti" in *Storia della Toscana sino al principato* (Pisa, 1813).

2 A. Paolini, *Elogio storico – filosofico di Lorenzo Pignotti*, (Pisa, 1817).

3 Oreste Brizi, "Biografia del Dottor Lorenzo Pignotti" in *Almanacco Aretino per gli anni 1841 e 1842*, (Arezzo, 1842).

4 See also Angiolo Tavanti, *Lorenzo Pignotti*, 2nd ed. (1846); F. Rodriguez, *Vita di Lorenzo Pignotti* (Florence, 1896); R. Rugani, *Vita di Lorenzo Pignotti e cenni storici sulla favola* (Siena, 1922).

5 Ugo Viviani, "Il medico Pignotti contro i medici" in *Curiosità storiche e letterarie aretine* (Arezzo, 1922), pp. 250-4.

6 U. Viviani, "Grossolani errori nelle biografie del medico e poeta Lorenzo Pignotti" in *Atti e memorie dell'accademia Petrarca di Scienze, lettere ed arti di Arezzo,* nuova serie, a, X1, (1932), p. 4.

7 Ibid., p. 5.

8 Ibid.

9 *Lirici del Settecento* (Milan, 1959), p. 629.

10 There appears to be some misunderstanding regarding the birth-place of Pignotti. The *Dizionario della letteratura italiana* states his birthplace as being Florence, while he is referred to as "aretino" in the Milanese edition of the *Favole e novelle*, 1826, and the edition of his poetry published in Florence in 1833. The same is the case in the edition *Favole e novelle e poesie varie di L. Pignotti, aretino* (Turin, 1852).

11 Aldobrando Paolini in his "Elogio storico-filosofico di Lorenzo Pignotti" provides some interesting comments on the mock-heroic and Pignotti's contribution.

12 Op.cit., pp. 53-8.

13 Op.cit., pp. 229-232.

14 Op.cit., pp. 54, 84, 151.

15 G. Savoca, "L'arcadia erotica e favolista dal rococò al neoclassicismo" in *Il Settecento*, op.cit., p. 398.

16 *Lirici del settecento*, op.cit., X1, p. 629.

17 Aldobrando Paolini "Elogio storico – filosofico di Lorenzo Pignotti" op. cit., p. 85.

18 L. Pignotti, *Favole, novelle e poesie* (Turin, 1852).

19 Luigi Rossi, *La treccia donata, poemetto eroicomico di Lorenzo Pignotti, Raffronti ed osservazioni* (Padua, 1906), p. 14.

20 Luigi Rossi, *La treccia donata, poemetto eroicomico di Lorenzo Pignotti, raffronti ed osservazioni*, op.cit., p. 6.

21 *La trasmigrazione dell'anima*, in *Lorenzo Pignotti, Favole e Novelle inedite* (Bologna, 1887), novella 1.25.

22 Giovanni Lenta, *Pope in Italia*, op.cit., p. 56.

23 Giovanni Lenta, *Pope in Italia*, op.cit., p. 55. Lenta, however, sees *The Rape of the Lock* as Pignotti's source of inspiration for *La treccia donata*. He totally ignores the significance of *The Dunciad*.

24 Pignotti frequently ridiculed the medical profession in his poems and fables. See Favola X111 — *La morte e il medico* in *Poesi di Lorenzo Pignotti Aretino*, Firenze, MDCCCXX111, p. 52 and Favola XV1, *La Sanità e la medicina*, p. 80.

25 Giovanni Lenta, *Pope in Italia*, op.cit., p. 50.

APPENDIX I

MS letters of Angelo Talassi

BASSANO del GRAPPA – BIBLIOTECA CIVICA, MS Autografi Remondini XXI – 18.

Illmo Sig.^e Sig. Tron Colmo

Se avessi potuto ottenere la sorte d'inchinarla personalmente quando mi sono presentato all'abitazione di V.S. Illma in Venezia tra le altre cose le avrei parlato di alcune mie poesie, che mi sono accinto a pubblicare per mezzo delle stampe del Sig.^e Zatta. Contengono queste due drammi, una cantata, e molti altri componimenti, che formeranno il primo volume. Il secondo sarà riempito da altre cantate a diversi sovrani d'Europa fatte per la loro nascita. E vi sono inoltre cento ottave che formano un canto sulle principali epoche del Regno di Maria Teresa, altre ottave inviate al re di Prussia da Berlino a Sans Souci, altre al re di Polonia presentate p. mano di Mgr. Archetti, con Canzoni, giocolieri, sonetti ec. Il Sig. Zatta vorebbe ch'io gli procurassi un numero sufficiente di sottoscriventi, e già a quest'ora ve n'è una sessanta circa. Fra i nomi rispettabili, che onorano quest'associazione bramerei vi fossero ancora quelli di V.S. Illma del Sig. Conte Antonio, del Sig. Jacopo Vittorelli, e del Sig.^e Ab^e Caffo, giacchè quest'ultimo ci troverà nominate molte persone di sua conoscenza per il lungo domicilio, che ha fatto in Ferrara. V.S. Illmo è stato mio principalissimo Protettore in Bassano come non manco qui di dirle e al Sig. Arnaldo Tormieri uno dei miei associati, ed a quant'altri mi accade parlare della sua persona. Pregola volermi conservare quest'istesso Padroncino ovunque io mi sia, e quando le riesca di far riempire queste quattro firme come avverrà infallibilmente se si degna impegnarsi a quest'effetto, favorisca farle passare a Venezia nelle mani del Sig.^e Antonio Zatta al Traghetto di S. Barnabà e il quale a suo tempo le farà avere il manifesto e poco dopo il primo Tomo, che sarà seguitato un po' più tardi dal secondo. Scusi V.S. Illma la libertà che mi prendo affidato alla sua solita gentilezza, e in capo voglia favorirmi di qualche riscontro può rispondermi a Milano mettendo la lettera *Ferma in Posta*. Di Milano passerò poi a Torino, indi a Parigi per restarvi lungo tempo e se colà potrò ubbidirla graditissimi mi saranno i suoi comandi, pregola di portare i miei ossequi alla gentilissima Dama sua consorte, ed alli mentovati Sig. Conte Antonio Sig. Vittorelli, e Sig.e Ab.e Caffo favorendomi inoltre di riverire in mio nome il Sig. Francesco Parolini, e l'amabilissima Sig.a Bettina. Resto perfine in attenzione de'suoi favori colla maggior riconoscenza e stima.

D.V.S. Illma

Vicenza 24 Giugno 1780.
Dev.mo obb.mo Serv. V.
Angelo Talassi.

Savignano di Romagna, Biblioteca Comunale, MS 16' 98-99'
Letter to Giovanni Cristofano Amaduzzi, with the latter's reply.

Illmo. Sig. Colmo.

È da tanto tempo, che V.S. Illmo non avrà avuto occasione di sentirsi ricordare il nome mio, che forse la sarà intieramente uscito dalla memoria. Io ebbi l'onore di sua conoscenza costì nell'Anno Santo mentre improvvisavo a vicenda nell'Arcadia colla celebre Corilla e mi sovviene, che fui appunto da lei introdotto per la prima volta presso Monsig.e Riminaldi. Dopo quel tempo io viaggiai in differenti contrade dell'Europa ricavando ovunque un discreto profitto dalle estemporare mie fatiche. Sono ora venti mesi circa ch'io mi sono restituito alla Patria, dove ho inteso più volte le di lei nuove e dal P. Lett. Federici Benedettini, e dal Sig.e Lett. Ferri. Io, però non avrei mai ardito incommodarla, se non fosse il presente incontro. Trovasi in questa Pontificia Università vacante la carica di Bibliotecario p. rinunzia del Sig.e D. Barotti. Io mi crederei in qualche maniera abile a cuoprirla per avere la richiesta età di anni 35, per esser laureato in ambe le leggi, aver avuto esercizio della lingua latina, e cognizione degli autori che hanno scritto in essa quanto agl'idiomi oltremontani io parlo, e scrivo correntemente in Francese, ed intendo passabilmente lo Spagnuolo, il Portoghese, e l'Inglese. Il prelodato Monsig.e Riminaldi Presidente dell'Università stessa è l'unico da cui dipenda la scelta, mentre i Riformatori Eligenti non attendono che il suo cenno ed il suo consiglio. A me non è ignoto quanto V.S. Illma possa sull'animo del sapientissimo prelato, e perciò la supplico voler appoggiare le mie richieste colla sua validissima raccomandazione, e ciò unicamente in vigore della nostra antica amicizia. Se io non credessi di offendere la sua delicatezza ardirei spiegarle con tutta ingenuità, che a negozio fatto subito che avessi ottenuto l'intento vorrei in qualche modo ricompensare i passi di chi mi avesse favorito con una cinquantina di Zecchini. Di tanto io m'impegno con qualunque voglia efficacemente assistermi presso Monsig.e in caso che V.S. Illma non volesse tale incarico, o non fosse frequentemente seco, come in passato. Io vorrei vedere in qualche guisa di assicurarmi un po' di pane nella mia Patria p. non esser costretto a ricorrere un'altra volta alla pietà di stranieri. Di tanto sono ad incommodarla p. ora mentre sieno di perfetta stima in attenzione delle sue grazie passo immutabilmente a dirmi.

> Di V.S. Illmo.
>
> Ferrara 3 Aprile 1779.
> Dev.ssmo oblig.mo Serv.e
> Angelo Talassi.

Amaduzzi's reply is as follows:

Monsieur

Mi seppe Ella imprimere troppo viva idea di sè, e del suo valore in tempo della sua dimora in Roma, perchè io non possa nè ora, nè mai perderne la memoria. Tutto mi è presente, ed Ella è stato più e più volte l'oggetto della mia più vantaggiosa commemorazione. Può pertanto da se stessa Ella comprendere, con quanto piacere io assuma l'incarico di coadiuvare le di lei brame. Si guardi però, fuori del più confidenziale comando, di adoperare altro argomento, onde muovermi ad agire per lei. Diverrei l'uomo il più odioso a me stesso, ed il più inconseguente co'miei principi, se l'interesse giammai giugnesse ad esser la molla delle mie operazioni. Restino dunque come non fatte in conto alcuno le pecuniarie sue esibizioni, che fanno torto a lei, ed a me, ciò è al di lei merito, ed alla mia delicatezza. Parlai pertanto ieri mattina a Monsig.e Riminaldi, il quale non ha mai lasciato di riguardarmi con occhio di parzialità, sul particolare di codesta Libreria, che ora forma un giusto di lei intento. Mi disse di aver ricevuto anche una di lei lettera e mi comunicò il tenore della risposta. Mi soggiunse di aver ricevuto premure anche per parte del Sig.e Baruffaldi, che però manca del requisito della laurea; e mi palesò anche una certa sua propensione per il Sig.e Don Lorenzo Barotti, sebbene anch'esso destituto dello accennato requisito. Tutta volta riconobbe in lei un pieno merito per conseguire quest'impiego, mostrò piacere, che Ella ne potesse riuscire con buon esito, e mi promise di raccomandarla con premura, e con lode ai Signori Riformatori colla lettera, che ai medesimi scriveva questa sera medesima. Questo è quel poco, che dopo molte insinuazioni io ho potuto implorare in di lei favore. Io veggio, che le insinuazioni dell'Abate Righini Seg.rio dell'Università, che ha un continuo carteggio confidenziale col prelato, sono le più efficaci per movere a risoluzione l'animo del medesimo; perciò Ella si valga di questo lume per rendersi in quest affare di miglior condizione sopra degli altri. Se in altro son buono a servirla mi comandi con libertà sicuro di trovare in me uno, che non ha un animo dissimile da quella sincera dichiarazione di stima, e d'affezione, che lo qualifica,

Roma 10 Aprile, 1779.
Suo Dev.mo ed Obbligato Serv.e ed Amico
Giovanni Cristofano Amaduzzi.

Praga 7 Luglio 1781.

Sig. Ab.^e Gentiliss.^{mo}

Benché sia più di un anno ch'io son partito da Vienna non ho mancato di ricercare, e d'avere le di lei nuove. Prima me ne parlò in una sua lettera il degnissimo Sig.^{re} Segretario Verdi. Poi più ampiamente nello scorso Carnevale mi diedero di lei ragguaglio i due suoi fratelli in Venezia, ove mi portai colla mia Santina. Io vedevo quasi ogni giorno il Dottore, col quale ho amicizia da otto anni. Mi fu detto il di lei viaggio in Italia, l'educazione al di lei senno commessa del Giovine Foscarini, ed altre cose, che tutte mi fecero piacere, perchè le recarono onore, e vantaggio. Nella scorsa estate io fui a Roma e Napoli, tornando per la Toscana. In Firenze passai dieci giorni coll'amica Corilla. Essa che doveva passare in Russia, invitata da quella sovrana, ha ricusato d'andarvi così persuasa da Ginore e Nardini. A me è nato il pensiero d'intraprendere un così gran viaggio alla sorte. Mia moglie, che in Dicembre mi ha fatto padre di un fanciulletto tutt'ora vivente in mano della nudrice ha voluto seguirmi, ed esser meco a parte in tutti gli incontri. Essa attualmente quà ritrovasi, e m'impone di farle mille, non un saluto. Siccome io mi fermerò venti e più giorni in Berlino ardisco chiedere a lei la finezza d'una commendatizia per il Sig. Marchese Lucchesini, che so essere suo concittadino, ed amico. Il detto cavaliere è in istato di potermi giovare quando lo voglia, e ciò sarà quando io gli sia raccomandato con calore. Ardisco sperar questo dalla bontà ed amicizia, che il nostro Sig. Ab.^e Lena ha sempre per noi dimostrato. Quando sia in grado di favorirmi mandi la lettera richiesta con sopracoperta a me diretta *ferma in posta* a Berlino, ov'io mi troverò ai primi d'agosto. Conservi memoria di un cattivo improvvisatore. Mi riverisca la Sig.^a Caterina Putton, l'accennato Segret'Regio, se più costì si trova, e più di tutti il sempre grande ed immortale Metastasio onor premiero delle Tosche muse, credendomi perfine nella maggior gratitudine, e stima di lei. Sig. Ab.^e Preg.^{mo}.

Dresda 9 Luglio 1781.

La presente fu da me scritta in Ratisbona, mentre contavo passare per Praga, ma ho poi dovuto fare una strada diversa p. Norimborga, Bayreuth ed io porgo nuove suppliche p. la commendatizia in mio favore al Sig. Marchese Lucchesini, pregandole farmela avere a Berlino più presto che le verrà permesso dalle sue occupazioni col rinnovarle insieme colla mia Santina come sopra.

Obbl. Serv.^e ed Amico
Angelo Talassi.

Ferrara, Biblioteca Comunale Ariostea, MS I. 501.

VI

A Monsieur l'abbé Jacques Tieghi
Secretaire de M. le Marquis Bevilacqua Cantelli a Ferrara.

Venezia, 22 Febbraio 1781.

Amico Carissimo.

Lunedì sera fui a sentire Pacchierotti per grazia ebbi uno scanno in mezzo in fila. Nel primo atto non c'è cosa da stordire. Una scena nel secondo, e l'aria è qualche cosa di grande. Non ci ho trovato da ammirare quanto in quella di Padova, ma ci sono dei pezzi belli eseguiti maestosamente dal novello Orfeo, tanto valente quanto brutto.

1X   Mantova 3 Maggio, 1781.

Amico Colmo,

Dite al Sig. Ronchi, che ho fatto i suoi saluti al gentilissimo Sig. Romanati, che forse m'assisterà nel fare la mia accademia, se succederà in teatro come vorebbe Berti. Il Vice Presid.^e M. de St. Laurent, che mi vuole domenica suo commensale vorebbe ch'io la facesse in una sala, ma il profitto sarebbe assai minore. Il Sig. Romanasi ha promesso di darmi in libertà la sera dei 21, Berti promette di assistermi nelle spese d'illuminazione, orchestra ecetera. Quest'altro giovedì ve ne saprò dire di più. Domenica a sera è la prima recita. L'Olimpiade è orribilmente castrata, e ridotta in due atti.

XIII   Dresda 16 Luglio, 1781.

Dopo avervi scritto l'ultima volta ebbi altre due chiamate dall'Elettor Palatino. Due volte io cantai in sua presenza alla sua deliziosa villeggiatura di Nymphenburgo. La prima ebbi un paragone fra la caccia e l'amore, e la definizione della favola d'Io con Argo centocchiuto addormentato. La seconda cantai un tema del nunzio Bellisoni sul tenuto di Cagli in sdruccioli, ed un paragone fra la pittura, e la musica. Nel sabato 23 l'Elettrice vedova mi fece andare alla sua dimora di Forseneid ove pure cantai due argomenti, il primo fra pochi dato dalls stessa Elettrice sulla tranquillità della vita campestre, venuto poi colà il sovrano me ne diede un altro da me eseguito in ottave, cioè un paragone fra Pietro il Grande, e Fernando Cortez. Io partii nel Lunedì 25 da Monaco, cioè nello stesso giorno, in cui mi scrivevaste da Ferrara.

XIV   Berlino 25 Agosto 1781.

Amico Caro,

Nel mercoledì 1 agosto mi posi nella carozza giornaliera al fianco della mia Santina, e giunsi in Forzdam dopo le sei della sera. Ommetto le perquisizioni, che si fanno alle porte, e negli alberghi per sapere d'onde e a che si venga. Nella stessa feci presentare tue lettere che avevo p. il Marchese Lucchesini Ciamberlano di confidenza di S.M. o sia del vostro eroe. La mattina dopo il Marchese cui io ero cognito senza saperlo perchè mi aveva udito a Roma l'Anno Santo, mi colmì di finezze. Esso non ardî mai di proporre al Re se mi volesse sentire. Solamente più volte fece cadere sopra di me il discorso perchè il re aveva letto il mio nome nel rapporto e aveva chiesto chi mi fosse. Fu in ciò aiutato dal Principe d'Hohenloe, canonico di Colonia, che mi conosceva di nome e che pranzava sovente col monarca. Tutti i tentativi furono inutili perchè Federico disse aver già idea del canto improvviso mentre aveva udito negli anni scorsi l'Abbé Tancini, che essere assai lento gli aveva fatto sudar sangue. Vedendo che nulla si poteva ottenere dal re il Marchese mi fece improvvisar in sua casa nel sabato 4, e da un ufficiale che mi aveva udito fece parlare al Principe Ereditario. Promise S.A.R. di sentirmi ma la cosa non ebbe effetto per un motivo a me incognito. . .

XV   S. Pietroburgo. 23 Ottobre 1781.

Amico Caro,

Nello stesso giorno in cui vi scrissi da Berlino come il 25 agosto pranzai col Marchese Lucchesini, col segretario di Sardegna e col bravo filosofo M. La Grange. Io ebbi dal Marchese un nuovo regalo per le mie rime estemporanee. Il Segret. Santo Sig. Richieri concorse più di ogni altro a farmi fare un'accademia nel Martedî 28. Fu questa onorata da ministeri esteri, ministeri di stato ed altri personaggi di distinzione. Il guadagno che ne rimborsai passò la mia aspettazione e ne rimasi contento. Nel mercoledî pranzai in casa del Barone Borch fra molta nobiltà.

Questa mattina sono chiamato dall'inviato di Portogallo, ma non so cosa voglia da me. Ho conosciuto questo Signore in Lisbona, in Londra e all'aja. Qui mi ha ascoltato con molta cortesia.

XXIII   Venezia, 10 Aprile, 1783.

Amico Caro,

Sabato pranzai in casa Mocenigo ove cantai due temi. In detta casa
cenai e cantai nuovamente la Domenica. Nel Martedî pranzai col Sig.
Pietro Zaguri. Più tardi fui assistente al pranzo Mocenigo senz'aver
voglia di mangiare di nuovo. In quel giorno era tornato da Padova il
Sig. Cav. Giovanni, e poco dopo era giunta l'unica sua figlia Sig.ª
Pisanetta Moglie del Giovane Sig. Francesco Pisani da S. Stefano della
cospicua famiglia tante volte da voi nominatami. Anche questa volta
ci furono nuove canzoni estemporanee, come pure ieri, giorno in cui
pranzai nuovamente in casa Mocenigo.

XXV   Venezia, 25 Aprile, 1783.

Il nuovo parocco della Boara è il Signor D. Carlo Zitti, il quale fu
bibliotecario in casa Pisani. La sua età è forse eguale alla mia, cioè
di 38 anni. Mi vien detto che sia nomo sciolto, apregiudicato, adatto
alla società, e fornito di egregie doti.
    Rividi al suo albergo il Mazza nel Giovedî 24. Esso era obbligato
di non dividersi mai da due sposi S. Vitali, perchè lo sposo, antico
medaglione, geloso come una bestia ha dato di sé scene orribili, che
l'hanno reso sommamente ridicolo. Questa non è gente da viaggiare,
ma da star chiusi nella loro tana. Mazza mi tratenne più di due ore
per recitarmi le sue ottave sdrucciole di rime indiavolate delle quali
mostra avere tanta compiacenza.

XL111
Letter to: Santina Solimani Talassi, Ferrara.

Parigi, 19 Dicembre 1783.

Carissima Consorte,

Non ti scrivo più d'una volta al mese perchè le lettere costano, ed io
non sono in istato di spendere. Quali cose poss'io narrarvi mia cara
Santina se non che calamità, e miserie. Vi scrissi che avevo trovato
tutti gli ambasciatori fuori di Parigi. Il loro ritorno non mi è stato
sin'ora di alcun vantaggio. Il nunzio sopra cui confidavo alquanto
non mi ha dato il minimo aiuto e mi ha consigliato a partire. L'ambas.
veneto Dolfin ha detto volermi far cantare in sua casa ma sinora nulla
ha concluso. Quello di Portogallo è ancora in campagna, non l'ho
veduto. Nel lunedì 17 Nov. giunto a casa presso di strada di Bocage
ci trovai il Margravio d'Auspach nipote del re di Prussia e ci cantai un
argomento. Ho stentato dopo di presentare alcuni sonetti al detto
principe, che non ho più veduto. Ma ha fatto darmi 2 Luigi, misero
dono niente principesco, ieri l'altro pranzai coll'Ambasciatore di
Napoli, ch'io conoscevo un tempo in Inghilterra. Egli è il solo fra gli
ambasciatori di cui vedo di poter sperare qualche assistenza in un
meschinissimo benefizio che darò prima della metà di gennaio.
    Misero in capo di pregarvi al risparmio, e alla economia questa
dilettissima moglie. Quest'è purtroppo è il temp calamitoso, in cui
debbo scongiurarvi a vivere colle maggiori misure, perchè veggo affatto impossibile di porvi mandare quelle mensilità che mi lusingavo
essere in istato di potervi fornire. Vi assicuro che mi levo il pane dalla
bocca e ringrazio affatto colla borsa vuota nel mandarvi quel poco
che posso.

Dev.ssmo Consorte
Angelo Talassi.

LVlll
Letter to: Abate Tieghi, Venezia, 1º Maggio, 1786.

Amico Colmo,

Circa alla stampa delle mie poesie vi dirò che Venezia non è Parigi dove si possono vendere i manoscritti a denaro costante. Quello che ho potuto ottenere è che il Zatta, il quale è forse il più accreditato tra i veneti stampatori dopo aver veduto il primo tomo delle cose mie si è offerto di stampare mille copie colla spesa di cinquanta zecchini con che io ne sborsai la metà e così avessi 50 copie da esitare come più mi piacesse. Non essendomi piaciuto questo progetto e non aver io tal somma da sborsare e quand'anche l'avessi non volendo io azzardarla siamo convenuti che io procuri un numero considerabile di firme, o sia associazioni 14 lire venete al Tomo, mentre quando avrà un numero certo di sottoscriventi senza denaro anticipato manderà loro il manifesto, e un mese dopo farà uscire il primo Tomo. Non è stato possibile indurlo a dar fuori subito il manifesto, e così bisognerà che preghi ad uno ad uno i presenti e i lontanti dai quali spero di esser favorito.

Dev.ssmo Serv. ed Amico,
Angelo Talassi.

LXlV
Letter to Tieghi,
Mantova, 1º luglio, 1785.

Carissimo Amico,

Io vi ho detto sinceramente in qual maniera abbia meco agito il Sig. Marchi Strozzi, di cui ho veduto il letterino pieno di bugie. Esso non è stato alla mia accademia, ne credo abbia mandato alcuno in sua vece. Il Sig. Marchese Bianchi non è stato nemmeno esso all'accademia ma ha mandato un zecchino Romano per il suo biglietto. Si è qui detto da alcuni, che quando sarà per andar in scena la prima opera per l'apertura il Sig. Card.^e abbia intenzione d'impiegarvi alcuni Ferraresi. Si dice che Pati scriverà la musica, che Gambuzzi metterà su i balli, e che io avrò l'altissimo onore di scrivere il Libretto. Nugae, nugae, á Paris, á Paris, né cattedre né incombenze di effimero poeta drammatico.

Suo, Talassi.

LXV1 Letter to Tieghi,
Milano, 18 Agosto, 1786.

Amico,

La mia accademia numerosa di sole 60, 70 persone ebbe luogo venerdì corrente. Il prezzo alla porta era arbitrario onde non si raccolse molto. La mattina seguente mi presentai all'anticamera dell'E. Sig.^e Conte di Castelbarco per ringraziarlo. Esso mi invitò per quel giorno a pranzo dopo avermi fatti passare due zecchini per il suo biglietto. Durante la tavola e dopo ancora mi colmò delle maggiori finezze.

Il residente veneto mi ha condotto una sera alla commedia Francese et voilà tout. Il Sig. Marchese Castiglione cui ero raccomandato mi ha dato due volte da pranzo e con altri pochi è stato uno de'miei associati. Nemmeno Milano mi sedurrà più in avvenire a ritornarci. Benché Venezia non dia gran cose è sempre assai migliore. Sono stato un pajo d'ore col degnissimo Sig.^e Abate Parini autore delle due versi scioltaggini, ch'io preferisco alle altre, cioè *Il mattino* e *Il mezzogiorno*. Esso è tornato dal lago di Como, più infermo che sano. . .

LXVIll Letter to Tieghi.

Amico Carissimo,

Vorrei in tale occasione dimostrare il mio giubilo con più felici rime
— sarà in vostra libertà il dire o il non dire ch'io ne sia l'autore — non
sperando gloria letteraria da si misera produzione, di cui non tengo
copia ma vi mando l'originale in anima, e in corpo.

> Le mura e i campi, che i Sforzeschi diero
> Ai tuoi gran avi qual mercè ben degna
> D'opre onorate, e di valor guerriero
> A torti invan l'altrui livor s'impegna.
> Di Cesar prode sotto il giusto impero.
> Nell'insubre terren, Temide regna.
>
> E te ripon nel dritto tuo primiero
> Mentre de'tuoi rivali e voti sdegna.
> Signor del tuo trionfo il tempo è questo.
> Vanne sull'Adda, e fra i vassalli tuoi
> Il magnanimo cor fa manifesto
> Così ciascun di lor godendo poi
> Sarà del lieto evento a cantar destro
> Il nuovo onor de'Bevilacqui Eroi.

Correggere, cancellare, fare quello che vi pare. Lo rilascio in vostra
mano. Sarebbe bene se lo fate stampare che ciò fosse a Rovigo — o
altrove, non costì, non solo per evitare le severe discussioni di codesti
ignoranti barbassori, ma anche per i titoli convenienti al vostro Pa-
drone. . .

CIII Letter to Ab. Tieghi, Ferrara.

Amico,

Purtroppo vedo che voi ci date ascolto mentre voi ricusate di più
vedere la mia povera moglie. Ah no! caro mio amico, non l'abbando-

nare così a causa di una lingua infernale. Voi mi avete professato in mille incontri la vostra eterna amicizia. Fare dunque che questa si estenda ancora alla mia infelice compagna calpestata. e infamata a torto perchè la mia cattiva fortuna non vuol ch'io possa essere al suo fianco. Scordatevi dunque tutto il male che vi è stato detto contro di lei. Vedetela, ascoltatela, assisterla, consigliatela nè la scacciare dal vostro fianco con una fredda indifferenza, perchè una cattive lingua vi ha parlato male contro di lei. Purtroppo vedo che avete vergogna parlare con mia moglie e ciò mi confessate nella seconda vostra segnata di 7 corrente.

Torino, 18 Luglio, 1789.

CXXXIV Letter to Ab. Tieghi, Ferrara.

Salvaterra, 5 Marzo, 1791.

Amico,

Mi è stato parlato di restare al Real servizio, ma io non accetterò senza un assegnamento decente, e senz'aver la permissione di venire a prendere la mia famiglia. Di ciò non ne parlate altro che con Santina, e non con alcun altro. Mi è stato supposto che mi vogliono offrire 500 scudi l'anno ma i viveri e l'affitto di casa essendo altissimo vi vorebbero almeno 600.

CIXXXII

Eccellenza,

Spero che dentro quest'anno uscirà in luce un mio poema eroicomico L'Olmo Abbattuto del quali il Real Principe del Brasile ha già accettato la dedica. Questo fu già da me compito l'anno scorso, e sarebbe già stampato in gran parte a quest'ora se in dicembre non accadeva la soppressione della mensa censoria, tribunale che esisteva per la Revisione dei Libri. Ora sto scrivendo un poema serio di diciotto corti canti, che avrà per titolo *Il Giovanni*, e sarà da me presentato alla principessa di Brasile, figlia primogenita del Re Cattolico.

Lisbona, 1795.

Forlì, Biblioteca Comunale, Autografi Azzolini, T.
Letter to Sig.ᵉ Giovanni Battista Costabili Containi, Ferrara.

Lisbona 6 Febbrajo 1794.

Amico Carissimo,

Purtroppo quello che previdi due anni fa, e che vi scrissi nella prima mia lettera è succeduto, e varie considerazioni mi hanno indotto a ricondurre la mia famiglia a Ferrara. Era dapprima intenzione della mia Santina di stabilirsi in Bologna ma essendo noi colà giunti non potemmo trovare una casuccia o appartamento conveniente in quattordici giorni che vi restammo. Dal piccolo Reno vi scrissi subito pregandovi di pronta risposta, e restai meravigliato di non vedere vostri caratteri. In fine di luglio passammo costî ed allora seppi che voi non eravate in paese, essendomi stato detto che voi eravate ai Bagni di Pisa in compagnia di Sig. Luigi Massario. Rimasi in patria sino ai 12 di Agosto giorno *Quem semper acerbum* (sic di voluistis) habebo. Non imprenderò a dirvi quanto siamo costata questa fatal divisone da tre oggetti estremamente cari al cuor mio. Se dovrò più mai aver il piacere di rivederti quest'è quello che non saprei dire, e niun mortale può darmi una tal sicurezza. Il motivo per cui mia moglie voleva fissare il suo soggiorno in Bologna era per ischivar l'occasione di aver più d'avanti gli occhi il Battani. Ella dice che negli ultimi anni ne'quali costui ha frequentato la di lei casa, l'ha compromessa più di una volta servendosi del suo nome in varj suoi raggiri, che meglio potrebbesi chiamar trufferie. Ella ha avuto torto d'impiegare due volte l'opera vostra nel mandar lettere a un tal soggetto, e nel pregarvi di riceverne le risposte.Quando Santina ciò ha fatto credeva di non più vedere Ferrara, e così credevo anch'io perciò un rifugio d'amicizia per una persona, che le aveva prestato varj servizi nel corso di otto anni la indusse a voler saperne le nuove. Quando ha preso la risoluzione di nuovamente abitare in patria si è determinata a non voler più alcun commercio e relazione col Battani. Non avendo noi costî domicilio, e non volendo incommodare alcuna delle nostre conoscenze entrando in Ferrara andammo a smontare al Leon Bianco ove restammo un giorno. Il Battani corse subito a quell'albergo, ma il Cameriere gli disse che non ci eravamo. Nel giorno seguente comparve egli in casa di certe Sig.^{e} Bonamici ove la mia famiglia era passata per restarci provisionalmente. Mia moglie essendosi subito ritirata in altra stanza tenni al detto Battani un discorso adattato alle circostanze. Prima della mia partenza mi raccomandai tanto a Mosig.^{e} Vicelegato quanto al Sig.^{e} Marchese Gualengo, acciò il Battani fosse seriamente ammonito a non dare alcuna molestia a mia moglie. Così mi giova credere che avvenga, e colui essendo già passato alle seconde nozze farà bene a badare a casa sua senza turbar l'altrui quiete. Non mi dilungo a farvi una descrizione del mio viaggio nel ridurmi nuovamente alla foce del Tago. Avendo voluto riveder alla sfuggita la bella Etruria, mi tratenni cinque giorni in Firenze, e quindici in Livorno. In quest'ultima città ebbi qualche traccia di voi in casa dei Signori Nardi, ove parmi aver udito che voi siate stato a conversazione. In sole sedici ore feci il tragitto marittimo da Livorno a Genova. Venti giorni mi arrestai ozioso sulle sponde Ligustiche, indi partii con un inco che portava due Corrieri a Barcellona. Nel primo d'ottobre dopo 7 giorni di marce posi piede a terranella capitale della Catalogna ove alloggiai otto giorni in casa del Sig. Gregory Console Britannico. Ad onta degli spauracchi, che mi si volevano fare partii alla volta di Madrid in una buona carrozza in compagnia di due Ginevrini, e senz'incontro di ladri o d'altre molestia vi giunse in tredici giorni e mezzo. Dopo aver ivi riposato per alcuni giorni passai all'Esedriale, ove fui ospite di Mgr. Nunzio Vincenti. Tornato a Madrid alloggiai quattro giorni col Conte Giuseppe Bernardi, stato per dieci anni console di Venezia qui in Lisbona. Partii soletto in un calessetto a due mucchi che mi portò in otto giorni a Badajoz. Fui obbligato di far nove leghe a cavallo per non aver trovato vetture. In estremos trovai un buon Calesse, col quale venni sino ad Aldengallega, tre leghe di quà distante. Rividi il mio abbandonato ritiro ai 25 di Novembre dopo mia lontananza di cinque mesi e 22 giorni dal mio congedo d'un semestre. Spirava il giorno di S. Andrea, e così ebbi la soddisfazione di ritornare alcuni giorni prima del termine prefissomi. Qui rimango nella solita inazione perchè il Teatro di Corte è ancora chiuso e quand'anche forse aperto il Sig.e Martinelli poeta che da moltissimi anni dimora al Real servizio avrebbe sempre la precedenza. Io me la passo nella stessa guisa, che vi ho detto in altre mie lettere case che frequento con assiduità sono quelle del Nunzio Bellisoni, a cui le attuali circostanze ritardano l'ostro Latino, e dell'Ambasciatore di Spagna di cui v'ho già parlato in altre lettere. Presso quest'ultimo viene spesso il Commendator Ruffo Siciliano, nuovo ministro del re di Napoli col quale si hanno spesso questioni di letteratura e di poesia. Quanto alle nuove politiche essendo noi in un'estremità dell'Europa passano molte settimane talvolta senza che ne sappiamo nulla, e solamente i P — Inglesi vengono da Falmouth a di quando in quando. Se scrivo non di rado certe filostrocche poetiche è per impiegare il tempo, non per averne guadagno. Qui v'è ora un Teatro d'Opera Italiana ch'è stato fabbricato di nuovo in pochi mesi, ed a cui è stato dato il nome di S. Carlo in onore della Principessa Carlotta. È un edifizio assai grande, mancante però di prospetto esteriore. Si pensa di farlo ma non con magnificenza che corrisponda al resto perchè il zelo di chi ha fatto una si gran spesa pare alquanto intiepidito. Benchè vi sia per la Corte un Palco smisurato niuna dette. Persone Reali sinora ci è stata, ed il mio interesse vorebbe che non mai vi andassero. Io ci sono stato una sola volta in Dicembre, ed ho veduto che questo Teatro è assai frequentato. Già avete udito dire, che qui non cantano donne, e sono castroni in abito donnesco quelli che ne fanno le veci. Il primo di questi effeminati eunuchi è un certo Caporaline, che ha molto incontro. È stato scritturato ultimamente Rovedino, e si vorebbe avere ancora il bravo buffo Morelli, ma gli hanno fatto proposizioni troppo tenui. Qui v'e dall'anno scorse la famosa cantante Todi, ch'è una portoghese moglie d'un violinista Napolitano. Essa tornerà a mettersi in giro per andar a cantare in diversi Teatri giacché il marito mi dice aver Ella perduto cinquanta mila scudi Rom. circa, che aveva nelle mani Mr. la Borde, già celebre millionario Banchiere della Corte di Francia. Comincia essa il suo giro da Madrid, ove le sei mila pezzi duri, abitazione e carrozza. Quando sono passato pochi mesi sono per quella Città il Teatro Italiano era pochissimo frequentato non ostante il merito di due acerrime rivali la Morichelli e la Banti. Nella sera del 20 gennaio sono stato a vedere l'Assemblea Inglese detta Longroom ov'era Ballo e cena. I francesi che qui si trovano non vi comparvero per esser l'anniversario della morte del loro Re. Il Conte di Chalon, noto in codeste parti perchè fece abbruciare una barca di Zatti quando stava in Venezia è qui ancora considerato come Ambasciatore di Francia, ed ha alla porta del suo Palazzo lo Stemma degli oppressi gigli circondato da un nero velo. Si crede che questa corte gli passi per generosità io mila crusadi, o sia cinque mila scudi Rom. Quanto all'assemblea Inglese essa è aperta per molti mesi dell'anno in tutti i Venerdî, e da due cene con Ballo in ogni anno, una cioè in gennaio per il compleanno della Regina d'Inghilterra. L'altro in Decembre per quello della Regina di Portogallo. È aperto qui ancora un Teatro di Commedia Portoghese detto del *Salitre*, ove posi piede tre anni sono, nè più sono stato in appresso. Tali sono i divertimenti della fangosa Lisbona, de'quali poco sono a parte. Il Lucchese Lunardi che fu il primo Votator. . . in Inghilterra, e riuscî bene ne'suoi viaggi tanto in Napoli che in Madrid e altrove avendo avuto poca fortuna solo in Roma, e in Lucca trovasi qua da otto o nove mesi. Ha fatto un circondario di tavole, ed ha esposto in un alto casotto il suo pallone, che fa vedere ai curiosi al prezzo di un testone Portoghese, o sia di 12 bajocchi e mezzo a testa. Egli dice che farà un volo ma non so quando. Vorrebbe aver presente alla sua assensione la Corte, ma parve difficile, che ciò succeda. Un giorno che ne abbiate tempo passeggiando per Città vi prego a darvi l'incomodo di andar a trovar mia moglie, che vi vedrà volentieri. Essa abita in casa del Sig. Dott. Fabiano Bianchini non molto lontano dallo Spirito Santo in una strada che ha un nome poco grazioso. Credo, però per quanto mi scrive che non continuerà ad abitar a casa sua perchè il Dott. è divenuto importuno con certe pretese che vi potrà dire ella stessa. Ho raccomandato a mia moglie e a D. Tieghi di trovare un maestro di lingua francese per la mia Cattina. In caso che non l'avessero trovato favorite indicarle alcuno che crediate a proposito, e possa aversi a prezzo discreto. Vi prego pure dirmi con schiettezza. in quale stato di salute avete trovato la mia famigliuola, e quanto ad essa appartiene, che possa interessarmi. Nel rispondermi vi prego di fare il seguente indirizzo: *Al Sig.*[e] *Teodosio Scarpelli Recapito al Sig.*[e] *Giacomo Albertazzi di Pietro, Lisbona,* mi farete il favore di presentare i miei complimenti alli Sig.[e] Massari, siccome mi avete fatto il piacere di fare altre volte. Scrivetemi le nuove del paese, che crediate possono essermi grate o anche indifferenti. Datemi sempre buone notizie del vostro stato, che auguro sempre il più invidiabile che possa darsi. Conservatemi la pregiata vostra amicizia, e credetemi quale sarò in ogni tempo.

Di voi carissimo amico
Dev.[mo] Serv. ed Amico Vero,
Angelo Talassi.

APPENDIX II

MS letters of Lorenzo Pignotti

*Bassano del Grappa, Biblioteca Civica, Autografi
Remondini XVIII – 7.*
Letter addressed Al Nobil Uomo
Il Sig.^e Giuseppe Remondini, Bassano.

Firenze, 28 luglio, 1800.

Illmo Sig.^{re} Suo Colmo,

Non prima della scorsa settimana mi è pervenuta una gentilissima sua
segnata dal dì 20 giugno, nè so sì straordinario ritardo che collo scon-
certo attuale delle cose d'Italia: e mi fa meraviglia come appunto fra
i rumori di Marte si pensi alle muse. Ma giacché ella che tante volte si
è degnato di ristampare le mie poetiche bagatelle, vuole anche in
questi tempi sì poco opportuni, nuovamente occuparsi di esse, le dirò
che l'ultima edizione delle mie favole è stata fatta in Pisa dalla società Tipografica meno di due anni sono: questa è la più compita
giacché venne voglia allo stampatore di raccoglierne tutto ciò che si
trovava di mia perla toscana, e gonfiò edizione fino a tre tomi.
Questa edizione però è quasi tutta esitata, e non ne resteranno che
una cinquantina di copie in mano all'editore. Proverò che le sia in-
viata una copia di questa edizione: ella poi penserà se le convenga
stampare le sole favole ovvero le altre poesie: ma osservi bene: un
altra volta ch'ella si degnò interrogarmi le mandai un'edizione di Livorno la più compita in cui però le aggiunte non erano tutte sulla
fine, ma alcune sparse nel corpo di due tometti, ed i suoi revisioni ne
lasciarono parecchie e non aggiunsero che quelle poche che si trova-
vano in fondo, allor quando ella porrà mano a questa edizione gra-
dirò saperlo perchè se avessi qualche correzione o altro gle la possa
inviare, e desideroso che comandi ho il piacere di dirmi

di V.S. Illma
Dev.^{mo} e obb^{mo} serv.^e
Lorenzo Pignotti.
Firenze 28 luglio.

Bassano del Grappa, Biblioteca Civica, autografi
Gamba X11, C.6.
Undated letter addressed:
A Sua Eccellenza
Il Sig.^{re} Generale March.^e
Manfredini Maggiordomo Mag.^e
di S.A.R.

Poggio a Caiano.

Eccellenza,

Carletti ha veduto una lettera scritta dal ministro degl'affari esteri di Francia M^{r.} le Brun A M^{r.} La Flotte nella quali gli dice presso a poco queste parole: *procurate di coltivare cotesta corte*, che ci ha mostrato *ottime disposizioni ed in* specie l'amicizia del *March.^e Manfredini* essendo nostra intenzione di *conservare colla Toscana* una perfetta neutralità: Carletti mi ha detto ciò spontaneamente al primo tasto che gli ho dato. La sua critica che in genere di novità è molto buona trova falsa la nuova dell'uccisione della famiglia reale combinando la data della Gazzetta di Cleves in cui è riportato con altre nuove sicure. Mi ponga ai piedi delle L.A.A.A.

e mi creda V.E.
Um. Dev.^{mo} e Obb^{mo} servitore, Domenica Sera.
Lorenzo Pignotti.

Florence, Biblioteca Nazionale, MS Gonelli, 30° No. 228-229.
Pisa 1790.
Letter addressed to: Monsieur Joseph Rome a Florence.

Monsieur,

Ieri per mezzo del Sig. Fenzi mi fu pagata la somma di scudi ottanta, lire 615 per estinguere il debito della Religione di Malta al Collegio della Sapienza, e non ho mancato invito questa mattina di portarmi alla Cancelleria dello studio ov'è questo affare per estinguere il 1º debito. Il Cancelliere non à potuto ricevere il denaro, perchè ancora non aveva i necessari documenti del computista. Io però avendogli detto di voler fare una protesta e depositare il denaro prima della scadenza del tempo limitato. Mi à assicurato esser cosa inutile perchè vi sarà tempo ancora qualche mese prima di cader nelle pene. Nondimeno per non lasciare alcuna cautela sono stato a trovare il computista Sig.ᵉ Pennari all'ufficio, il quale mi ha detto che per oggi non era possibile di avere li pronto la dimostrazione e il computo esatto del debito, ma che per mercoledî lo avrebbe dato, e ancor esso mi à assicurato che vi saranno ancora tre mesi prima d'incorrere nelle pene e spero pertanto mercoledî renderla servita, e mercoledî sera spedirle per la posta le opportune ricevuta. Intanto col desiderio di nuovi suoi comandi ho il piacere di dirmi.

Suo dev.ᵐᵒ e obb.ᵐ servitore,
Lorenzo Pignotti.

Letter addressed to:
Abbé Ciampi, Professore di lungua greca all'università di Pisa.

Ill.ᵐᵒ Sig.ᵉ Ciampi,

Mi rallegro del suo stabilimento nel nostro corpo, e del suo arrivo in cotesta città: ebbi notizie del suo passaggio per Firenze dal Sig.ᵉ Zannoni e sono obbligato alla sua bontà.

Intanto desidero sapere da lei se ella sia nella disposizione (come mi parve) di tenere dei giovani nel suo collegio. Quand' ciò sia avrei un giovinetto di S. Casciano di assai buona indole ch'è il nipote del Professor Corbellacci. Suo padre non volendo dare incomodo al fratello cerca un posto ove collocarlo quando ella sia in disposizione di

riceverlo abbia la bontà di avvisarmi il prezzo della dozzina, e quella
biancheria o altro che bisogni. La prego a perdonarmi l'incomodo e a
credermi.

Firenze 1. Ott.re.   Suo dev.^{mo} e obb. servitore,
                                      Lorenzo Pignotti.

Forlì, Biblioteca Comunale, MS Piancastelli, P. A12.

Illmo Sig.^e Suo Colmo,

Mi ànno fatto sommo piacere le sue nuove e le rendo infinite grazie
delle gentilezze da lei usate al Sig.^e Cav.^e Payne. Mi rallegro delle
replicate edizioni della sua bell'opera: questo è il segno sicuro del
loro merito. Il Sig.^e D. Tommaso Corsini le fa i suoi complimenti.
Non mancherà di farle avere una copia dell'ultima edizione delle mie
favole che si fa adesso in Livorno.
   Bramerei una notizia da V.S. ch'è tanto versato nell'istoria della
bella letteratura. Ella conosce il celebre avvenimento della disfida e
pugna de'tredici Italiani, e tredici Francesi seguita sotto Barletta.
Leggo nel Giovio nella vita di Consalvo come il Vida celebrò in versi
questo avvenimento glorioso al nome italiano. Non m'è venuto fatto
però di trovare finora questa poesia. Le sarei obbligato s'ella me la
potesse indicare.
   La nostra deputazione p. fare le giunte al Dizionario della Crusca
le si raccomanda. Io providerò occasione di servirla, e colla più p.
fetta stima ho l'onore di dirmi.

Di V. Illmo   Dev.^{mo} e obb.^{mo} servitore,
Firenze 10 Maggio 1788.   Lorenzo Pignotti.

Letter of 14 August 1790.

Illmo Sig.^e Suo Colmo,

Mi trovo gentilmente favorito d'una stima sua la quale mi da il piacere di potere obedire uno benché leggerissimo suo comando. Quei che coltivano i medesimi studi si debbono riguardar come amici, benché non si conoscono personalmente, e quasi confratelli sono in obbligo di prestarsi scambievolmente la loro opera ove le circostanze lo richieggano. Il piacere ch'ella m'a procurato più volte colle sue elegantissime latine elegie mi viene raddoppiato adesso nel vedere ch'ella à ugualmente caro alle Latine che alle Italiane muse. Ho letto con sommo piacere le sue belle ed energiche traduzioni, e mi darò ogni cura p. chè sieno impresse colla maggior nitidezza di cui sien capaci i Fiorentini stampatori, che ànno molto degenerato da i Piumbi e da i Torrentini. Abbiamo poi sentito tanto il Sig.^e D. Tommaso Corsini che io con sommo piacere la sua prossima venuta in Firenze, dove e in qualunque altro luogo e tempo mi troverà qual sinceramente mi dico.

Di V.S. Illmo.

Firenze 14 Agosto 1790.
Dev.^{mo} e obb.^{mo} Servitore,
Lorenzo Pignotti.

Letter of 12 March, 1794.
Addressed to: Ill. Sig.^e Suo Colmo,
Il Sig.^e Cav.^e Pietro Gualtieri, Arezzo.

Illmo Sig.^e e A.C.

La ringrazio della memoria che conserva della nostra antica amicizia, e del dono poetico che mi à inviato, che ho letto con piacere e dove trovo della facilità di stile e delle imagini nuove ed elegantemente espresse. Ella mi annunzia sei copie, ma devo dirle p. sua regola che ne ò ricevuta una sola. Mi conservi la sua amicizia; faccia i miei ossequi al nostro comune amico D.^e Presciani, ed alla Sig.^a Lucrezia, e a chi si ricorda di me, e mi creda.

Suo dev.^{mo} Servitore ed Amico,
Lorenzo Pignotti.

Pisa, 1 Obre 1795.

A'C'

Il giovane di cui mi parlai meritamente con moltissima lode è il Dottore Antonio Mencarelli che non ha finora contratto alcuno impegno, e sta attualmente in Firenze studiando la legge pratica ma più la bella letteratura. Senza esagerarvi vi dico che pochi giovani credo sieno esciti dall'università col corredo di cognizioni che ha' acquistato questo giovine. Ha studiato molto bene le fisiche e le mattematiche a segno da poterle insegnare a de i giovinetti: è dottorato in legge, ed è versatissimo nel dritto pubblico: a tutto ciò aggiunge la cognizione delle lingue Greca, Latina, francese, inglese e spagnola, è stimato moltissimo dal Granduca che gli da di quando in quando de i soccorsi de i quali vive e di un ajuto di sei scudi al mese che gli da il Principe D. Tommaso Corsini P. le lezioni che gli da di lingua inglese e di Fisica. Queste son tutte cose precarie onde accetterà sicuramente qualunque stabilimento fisse anche piccolo che gli progettiate. Vi avverto che la prima vista di lui non ve ne darà grande idea giacché non assuafatto alla gran compagnia si confonde un poco p. soggezzione: ma fatelo parlare a lungo, ne sarete contento: io lo raccomandai p. le cose legali all'auditor Lessi onde anch'ei lo conosce. In somma voi farete un'opera di carità se trovate qualche stabilimento a questo giovane e nello stesso tempo vi farete molto onore colla vostra proposizione giacché attualmente sarebbe assai difficile trovare un giovine della sua età così corredato di cognizioni così volonteroso di faticare e nello stesso tempo così savio e modesto.

Addio, state bene e comandatemi: Io
sono

V. aff.^{mo} Amico,
Lorenzo Pignotti.

Pisa, 2 Giugno, 1806.

A.C.

Vi scrivo poche linee P. accusar la ricevuta della vostra L. Mi rallegro
sempre più con voi. Io conoscevo bene i vostri talenti, e che non vi
mancava che un Teatro ove spiegarli. Vedo dalle lettera di Saliceti
quanto son conosciuti e il conto che si fa di voi, ne sono sommamente contento. Ho risposto in questo corso la posta a Saliceti. O
prima o poi conto di venire, ma conviene ch'io prenda bene le mie
misure, e faccia il viaggio come posso; ma veggo che p. questa estate
non mi sarà possibile. Ho fatto i vostri saluti a i comuni amici, e gli
farò anche alle fornari(?) a cui scrivevo nella settimana. Spero che la
Savviezza dell'Imper.^e de Francesi che *tanto oprò* col senno e *colla
mano* farà finalmente chiudere il Tempio di Giano. La persona di cui
mi domandate potrà avere sicuramente sei in settemila scudi fiorin-
tini di rendita: ma molto più in seguito dovendosi in lui ch'è solo
rinnirsi ciocchè sparso e diviso in tre. Più viventi addio.

V. Amico,
Pignotti.

Letter addressed: A Monsieur Pierre Torrigiani a Florence.

Signore,

Riflettendo a ciò che ha avuto la bontà di comunicarmi, tanti, e si
recenti oggetti sulla riforma dell'università di Pisa mi si stavano
avanti, che non è facile il comprenderli in un piccolo spazio.

Mi limito però a poche cose, il numero dei Professori è troppo copioso; converebbe che le Cattedre fossero in minor numero, e di materie più utili: fra queste specialmente anderebbero riguardare con special favore La Chimica, l'Istoria naturale, le Fisica sperimentale, l'Astronomia, l'Anatomia: queste scienze per bene esercitar si hanno bisogno di spese non piccole: la data delle suddette è assai piccola, e non possono con essa essere esercitate molto lodevelmente: le dati si contengono nel Libretto manoscritto intitolato – Stato dell'università di Pisa – che ebbi l'onore di darle: Ella può vederlo, e farci quelle aggiunte se crederci necessarie.

L'antico metodo delle Pubbliche Lezioni è assai difettoso onde convien mutarlo, e bandire quelle brevi lezioni, che solo per formalità si facevano, e accrescere il numero delle private: Qualche altra Cattedra utile si potrebbe aggiungere, come di medicina legale, e forse di mascalcia, o sia veterinaria. Questi sono gli oggetti che mi si stavano improvvisamente d'avanti: Intanto ho l'onore di dirmi.

Pisa 27 Marzo 1809. Dev.mo Obb.mo servitore,
Lorenzo Pignotti.

Undated letter without address.

Firenze, 4 Agosto.

A.C.

La Casa Corsini vi ringrazia delle gentili vostre espressioni. Il Principe vi vedrà volentieri nella sua venuta costa colla corte, e farà tutto quel che può p. servirvi. Io non ho potuto a meno benché co i capelli canuti di scrivere quattro versacci ve gli mando, prendeteli ma come frutti d'inverno come nespole o sorbe. State bene, comandatemi.

Addio. Aff. A.
L. Pignotti.

Undated letter addressed to Mons. L'Abbe Ciampi, Venise.

Firenze 5 Obre.

Illmo Sig.^e Ciampi,

Oltre il primo fattomi p. venire dal Sig.^e Matteini, ricevei un altro esemplare del suo dotto ed elegante opuscolo in cui si veggono quasi rari ritratti de i classici Greci Latini e Italiani: io h'o letto con sommo piacere giacché è una della migliori scuole l'osservare come si sono fra loro imitabili, e con quanta varietà ed eleganza lo stesso sentimento è stato espresso dagli uomini grandi. Quando ella lo ristamperà, che veramente lo merita, la consiglio ad impugnare questa parte giacché si può così bene con passi specialmente di Dante e dell'Ariosto che ànno nelle smodazioni e quasi traduzioni spesso on eguagliati o superati gl'originali: mi permetta di riportarle una breve similitudine di Virgilio tradotto dall'Ariosto.

Non attenermi in questo tempo è il segno più certo quanto io riceva p. tanto le mie congratulazioni. Si è molto parlato di lei con qualche persona autorevole che può giovarle, e disidero e spero rivederla fra noi. Mi comandi e mi creda.

Suo dev.^{mo} Servitore,

Lorenzo Pignotti.

Communication addressed to:
Il Sig.^e Vittorio Forromtroni(?) Arezzo.

A.C.

Siete restato servito. La Casa sta a vostra disposizione. Non abbiamo novità veruna, solamente è morto il povero Marchese. Il Gran Priore vi fa i suoi saluti come fanno tutti gl'amici e anziché.

Addio,

Aff. A.
Pignotti.

Undated letter addressed to:
Mr. Joseph Morosi, Professeur de Mecanique a Milan.

Pisa, 17 Febb.º

Mi rallegro del vostro felice ritorno e come i saggi viaggiatori siate or tornato ricco di utili scoperte: queste sono quelle che dovevano specialmente da voi osservarsi, o non vi paiono piccoli oggetti le spille gl'aghi, la lana i cotoni, giacché da quest'oggetti moltiplicati si forma la ricchezza nazionale: voi siete in obbligo di communicargli specialmente a cotesto paese che vi à fornito i mezzi di potere acquistare le cognizioni: e se mai volete scriverne (che vi consiglio a farlo parcamente) astenetevi dalle riflessioni politiche che possono dispiacere e produrvi dei disgusti, applicate in pratica le scoperte alla arti e fate che cittadini di cotesto regno v'applaudiscono e conoscano in pratica che siete stato loro utile coi vostri viaggi. State bene. Fatemi spesso delle vostre nuove e credetemi.

V. Amico,

L. Pignotti.

Firenze 6 Febb. 1776.

Amico,

Ieri finalmente dopo un lunghissimo intervallo di tempo il consiglier
Tavanti ricevè lettere da Fontana il quale era giunto in Parigi e si
trovava incomodato da qualche piccolo assalto di Colica. Egli ha
scritto una lunga lettera nella quale rileva la leggerezza del Cassini e
l'avidità di quella famiglia che ha guadagnato essa sola sovra due
milioni di lire nell'esecuzione delle carte di Francia. La lettera è
passata in mano di S.A.R. È stato interrogato anche Boschovich che
ha detto lo stesso appunto, ed ha soggiunto che in Toscana vi sono
quattro o cinque più capaci del Cassini, fra i quali nomina voi.
   Credo che la deputazione Maremmana tornerà presto. Quà abbiamo grand'umido dopo un orrido freddo. Fate i miei auguri alla
Sig.ª Bettina ed alle Sig.ª Cipî.

Addio.

Pignotti.

Firenze 12 Marzo, 1793.

Car.mo Amico,

Fate fare a vostro figlio il memoriale chiedendo alla clemenza di
S.A.R. le scadute terzerie(?) e mandatemelo a posta corrente. Il Gran
Priore vi saluta. Fate i miei ossequi alla vostra vasa.

Addio,

Aff.º A.
Lorenzo Pignotti.

Firenze 7 Aprile, 1793.

A.C.

Il memoriale verrà per informazione a Mr. Fabbroni, onde procurate officiarlo affinché faccia una favorevole informazione. Io ho detto tutto quello che ho potuto in favore di vostro figlio – Martini e Fiaschi sono ben disposti. Avrete sentito le buone nuove dell'armata Austriaca e la rotta di Dumarier (?) Salutatemi tutti di vostra casa.

Addio.

Aff. A.
L. Pignotti.

Firenze 12 Giugno, 1793.

A.C.

Non ho replicato finora alla gentilissima vostra perchè l'ho trovata jeri al mio ritorno di campagna. Mi rallegro della ristabilita salute di vostro figlio. Il Sig.^{e} Marchese Manfredini verrà costà martedì o mercoledì: siccome abiterà in Pisa andrà solo a i Bagni per tornare ogni giorno, così avrete opportunità di vederlo e frequentarlo prima ch'egli parta potete almeno p. una volta raccomandargli vostro figlio: mi pare che il cielo a rischiararsi io stasera o dimani gli mostrerò la vostra prefazione, e ve ne dirò qualche cosa nel p. ordinario. Fate i miei saluti alla vostra casa. Fonambroni il Pr. P.^{re} a D. Neri vi restituiscono cordialmente i vostri. Fate poi i miei più distinti ossequi al Sig.^{e} Conte e Contessa di Windis-graetz: avrei scritto al Sig. Conte ma p. ora non ò avuto soggetto.

Addio.

Aff. A.
Pignotti.

Firenze, 15 luglio, 1793.

Car.^{mo} Amico,

Credo conforme vi scrissi altra volta che le cose di vostro figlio, per quanto ho' potuto congetturare andranno bene. Per la prefazione non ebbi mai luogo negl'ultimi giorni di trovarmi solo col Sig.^e Marchese onde non potei fargliela leggere. Ma il Fiaschi non vi trova niente di male: prima ch'egli parta (se volete) potete fargliela leggere addirittura. Vi scrivo questi due versi in fretta.

Addio.

Aff. A.
Pignotti.

Undated letter to Professor Slop.

A.C.

Ho il piacere di darvi notizia come S.A.R. ha accordato che vi si paghino le terzerie (?) arretrate di vostro figlio. Questo è intanto qualche cosa. Spero che alla fine tutto andrà bene.

Addio.

Aff. A.
Pignotti.

Undated letter.

Ho molto piacere che il Sig.^e Mechain sia partito contento del nostro governo e della nostra università.

Il Sig.^e Marchese indugierà forse ancora qualche giorno prima d'andare a i Bagni, come torno a Firenze gli farò i vostri saluti a Tito e ditegli che gli scriverò nella futura settimana.

Non è che un caso il potermi venir l'occasione di dire una parola in favor d'un giovane ch'io conosco: in questo azzardo voi vedete che non si può molto contare. State bene salutatemi tutta la vostra casa.

Addio.

Aff. A.
Pignotti.

Firenze, 29 Giugno.

A.C.

Vi sarà resa la presente da i due giovani Principi Tarberini a i quali vi prego mostrare la specula e se potete in mancanza di Santi l'orto botanico. Sono due giovani colti ed istruiti come vi accorgerete dalla loro conversazione.

Comandatemi.

Addio.
V.A.
Pignotti.

PART II

CHAPTER I

An Essay on Man in eighteenth-century Italy.
Trends and tendencies in translation

I

While the *Essay on Man* was not the first of Pope's works to appear in translation in Italy, it was the work which proved of most academic interest during the eighteenth century. Although it cannot be said to have given birth to a new genre in Italian literature, it stirred the interest of no less than eight known translators, and various attempts have been made at imitation. The first translation to appear was that of Celestino Petracchi, which was published by Moscheri, Naples, in 1742. This was followed by the version of Antonio Filippo Adami,[2] first published with the stamp of Arezzo in 1756, and reprinted no less than six times before the close of the century: — in Venice in 1757, 1758, 1761, 1773 and 1790; it was also published in Naples in 1768. This was the most widely read version, and of consequence the most influential rendering; in fact it was generally, and falsely, believed to have been the first attempt at translating the work. The third version to appear was that of Giammaria Ortes,[3] Venice 1757, with reprints in Bologna and Florence 1776. Around the same time, Pillori also translated the work, while Giovanni Salvenini (also called Castiglione) published a version in 1760, with the stamp of Berne. Before the close of the century, three more translators attempted to reproduce Pope's thoughts. The first of these was one Graziosi of London, who dedicated the work to T.B., hence the ambiguity created with regard to the name of the author; the next was G.M. Ferrero, who published in 1768, in Turin, and finally came the translation by Gian Vicenzo Benini (Creofilo Sminteo). The latter owes his fame to his translations of the works of Pope, and whose *Saggio sull'uomo* proved infinitely more successful than either his *Lettera d'Eloisa ad Abelardo* or his *Riccio rapito*. The above quoted names and dates indicate that from the end of the first half of the eighteenth century, the subject of Pope's philosophic essay proved immensely popular, attracted a variety of translators from the principal centres of culture and was widely read by the educated class. The number of editions published in Venice and Naples bears testimony to the interest shown in Pope's work in particular, and to philosophy in general in these centres. The presence of a British Ambassador in both cities goes a long way towards explaining the popularity of English matter.

By far the most influential of the translations was, as has already been stated, the version of A.F. Adami, which does not however represent a direct link with England and the English language, as it was taken from the French version by the Abbé du Resnel. The 1757 edition published in Venice by Gian Battista Novelli is entitled: "*I principi della morale o sia Saggio Sopra L'Uomo*, poema inglese di Alessandro Pope tradotto in versi sciolti italiani dal cavaliere Anton-Filippo Adami con la giunta di Critiche e Filosofiche Annotazioni, e di varj egregi componimenti dello stesso traduttore, come può vedersi nella prefazione che segue." The "critiche e filosofiche annotazioni" consisted of an ode entitled "Riflessioni sulla religione e sulla morale contenute in un'ode responsiva ad una lettera poetica anonima indirizzata ad Urania scritta nell'idioma francese; Le prove dimostrative della verità della religione cristiana dedotte dai lumi della ragione", "In lode della traduzione del poema di Pope fatta dall'illustriss Sig. Cav. Anton-Filippo Adami"; and a series of sonnets. In the editor's preface, it is erroneously stated that Adami's translation is the first of its kind: "Questa traduzione in versi italiani a me vien supposto, che non sia stata finora eseguita da veruno altro dei nostri."[4] Reference is made to praise received from A.M. Card. Quirini, Battista Richeri, Scipione Maffei and Pietro Metastasio. In a letter from Verona, dated 29 luglio 1753, Scipione Maffei states: "Ho ricevuto i nobilissimi Componimenti, dai quali non meno ricavo il suo ingegno, e la sua dottrina, che la pietà. Ho però motivo di doppiamente rallegrarmi con Lei: continui pure ad esercitare con tanto frutto l'ingegno, e ad acquistarsi gloria per questo Mondo, e per l'altro."

232

That Adami has studied and contemplated the theories of Boling-broke set to verse by Pope and rendered into French by Du Resnel, there can be little doubt. The influence of Pope is most obvious in his consideration of happiness, the relationship between God and Man and the plea for enlightened or illuminated reason expressed in the poema "Riflessioni sulla religione e sulla morale". His considera-tion of the role of man, and his ability to bring about universal peace is expressed in the following lines in Stanza viii of the poem:

> Quindi nel petto/Sentiamo verso di lui, verso noi stessi,
> Verso i simili a noi teneri moti
> Sorger di puro affetto,
> E se l'Uom di lui ben'usi
> E già saggio a bastanza; e questa sola
> Scienza, potria render d'Eroi fecondo,
> E in bel nodo di pace unire il Mondo.
> Non vi è lido sì inospito, e selvaggio,
> In cui questo non scenda
> Di benefica luce amico raggio:
> L'American feroce
> Il nudo Peguano,
> Il gelido Lappon portano anch'essi
> Della regolatrice
> Legge i dettami entro del seno impressi.[5]

One cannot state that the above lines are exact reproductions of Pope, but his influence cannot be denied here, or in the following lines in stanza x:—

> Sotto la scorza di un Saper fastoso,
> Più grandi ancor, che d'umil Genio in seno,
> Si annidano sovente
> I difetti del cuore, e della mente.
> Questa è quella Ragion, su cui disegni,
> Che l'uom con fiero passo,
> Senza che Iddio lo regga, e lo rinfranchi,
> Le Vie del Cielo a misurar s'impegni,[6]

Stanza xii is concerned with pride, jealousy and betrayal, man's turning from man when no longer guided by affection:

> Sorgono le Cittadi in ogni lato
> Figlie più, che di affetto,

Di timor, d'impotenza, e di sospetto,
E l'Uom dell'Uom nemico
Col suo stesso rival per sua salvezza
Si stringe in lega, e finge un volto amico,[7]

On the above evidence, can one define Adami as a successful poet. One is aware of balance and clarity throughout; in stanza viii however, the structure of the sentence is obvious and the manner in which the balance is achieved, when repeated, creates the impression of a shallow technique, i.e. "Sentiamo verso di Lui, verso noi stessi... sorger di puro affetto." Clarity is achieved by means of explanation, as opposed to a reproduction of the factual precision of the poetry of Pope. Adami introduces conditions and alternatives showing that he has above all a theory or concept to convey, and for him the poetic form is merely a framework for such concepts. This judgment is, I believe, reinforced when one considers his translation of the *Essay of Man*.

It would be wrong to consider Adami's version in the light of pure translation, since inspiration does not spring from the original English: as a work of art it cannot be regarded as valid since it provides neither great poetry nor convincing philosophy. Neither can it be said to represent a completely faithful reproduction of Pope's ideas. Criticism of this translation is provided in the preface to the version dedicated to T.B. and published in London by Graziosi, in 1765: "Il Cavaliere Adami, cui è dovuto il pregio di valorosa poeta, s'è lasciato trasportare dalla sua fantasia, Onde ha fatto parlare il Pope, com'egli si figurò che dovesse parlare".[8] Indeed it could be said that Adami is fascinated by abstract ideas, to which he gives full play in his work, with the result that the English poet's irony is completely lost.

It must also be pointed out that Adami would have found it extremely difficult to convey anything of Pope's epic style, apt word choice or precision, given that he was working from a translation, the writer of which agreed, that the metaphysical content of the original was all important: "In the *Essay on Man*, he (the reader) will meet with all that metaphysics teach, with any great degree of certainty, relating to the knowledge of ourselves, and all the necessary Rules which Morality lays down for the practice of our Duty to God and Man."[9] Du Resnel goes on to describe the style, in his opinion, most suitable for the rendering of the *Essay* into French:. . ."Brevity was, in my opinion, to be most successfully imitated by a close stile, not weakened by scrupulous Regard to Connection, or a rigid adherence to the Niceties of construction – The French are not satisfied with Sentiments however beautiful, unless they are methodically disposed."[10] Du Resnel above all views Pope as a didactic writer, one who appeals to the Reason, as opposed to the Imagination. It is therefore as a poet of ideas that he is communicated to the French, and of consequence, to the Italians:

> With regard to my Stile, I suppose it is not necessary to inform the Reader, that he is not to expect here the Pomp and Elevation of the Epic language or of those poems of which the diction is adapted to marvellous events and great actions. Instruction, not imagery, is the Business of the Didactic writer, and the excellencies of his stile are simplicity, accuracy and perspicuity. The poets of this class, if they can claim that title, apply to the Reason, not the Imagination, and are therefore not at Liberty to give full play to the efforts of Genius.

So Du Resnel translated into French an essay of ideas, governed by reason, and expressed in the briefest fashion. This was Adami's point of departure.

The force of the original I.112-122 is missing in the translation. It lacks precision and conciseness. Pope's ten lines are rendered by fifteen in Italian, and the rhetorical power is missing, as a result of each imperative verb not falling on the first word in the line, as is the case in the English:

> Volgi, rovescia a tuo vantaggio solo
> L'ordine di Natura, e le costanti
> Sue leggi, a genio tuo, cangia e disponi:
> Arbitro d'ogni grazia, e d'ogni bene.
> Moderna l'Universo a tua talento:
> Accusa il Ciel, se in grembo a te non versa
> Tutti i suoi doni, e tutte in te non spende
> E le sue tenerezze, e le sue cure;
> E se alle doti, onde già sei ricolmo,
> La miglior non aggiunge, e la più grande
> Di renderti impassibile, e immortale.
> Siegui le oblique vie de i tuoi delirj;
> Fatti Dio del tuo Dio; ponti in sua vece

Sul trono, ov'Ei già siede, e senza tema
Giudica ancor la sua giustizia istessa.[12]

Go wiser thou! and in thy scale of sense,
Weigh thy opinion against providence;
Call imperfection what thou fanciest such.
Say, here gives too little, there too much:
Destroy all creatures for they sport or gust,
Yet cry, if man's unhappy, God's unjust;
If man alone engross not Heaven's high care,
Alone made perfect here, immortal there.
Snatch from his hand the balance and the rod,
Re-judge His justice, be the God of God.
(Pope, *An Essay on Man*, I. 113-122)

It can be argued that the sense of the original is conveyed, but a mere reproduction of Pope's general idea is not enough. Such is also the opinion of Giovanni Lenta in *Pope in Italia*.[13] His assessment of the value of Adami's works is as follows: "Assai piccolo; perché non è una traduzione ma un'ampia parafrasi che soffoca l'epigrammatico di Pope, che si allontana spesso, che sopprime spesso dei versi, che fraintende. Per ogni verso di Pope l'Adami scrive almeno tre endecasillabi, i pensieri più semplici sono affogati in un mare di parole." In dealing with the biting ironic lines regarding Newton, explanation takes the place of Pope's spontaneous sarcasm:

De' puri Spirti il penetrante ingegno
Il corto nostro intendimento mira
Con occhio di pietà, quello che tanto
In noi desta stupor, Nevvton l'illustre,
Il gran Nevvton, non è forse per loro,
Che quanto sembra astuta scimmia a noi.[14]

Superior beings, when of late they saw
A mortal man unfold all Nature's law,
Admired such wisdom in an earthly shape
And show'd a Newton as we show an ape.
(Pope, *An Essay on Man*, II. 31-4)

Adami's version replaces Pope's condescension and scorn with pity – "con occhio di pietà", and avoids the repetition of the word "showed" in line 34 which conveys balance and uniformity. The two Italian lines:

Il gran Nevvton, non è forse per loro,
Che quanto sembra astuta scimmia a noi.

are merely a prose statement. There is the attempt to imply an intellectual vision of the universe with the choice of term "penetrante ingegno", while the limited human vision is conveyed with "corto nostro intendimento", conferring an element of space and spatial measurement on the entire poetic creation. The effect is, however, spoiled by the next lines referring to Newton. Authority of expression is not a strong element in Adami's technique. For this reason the rhetorical passages do not come off, as they are lacking in expressive power and exaltation of tone. This can of course be accounted for by the fact that Adami is proceeding from Du Resnel. Rhetoric and effect is sacrificed in the French version to logic, and explanatory passages. The following two passages, I believe, illustrate this point:

i   l'Uomo in tal guisa
Per me de i suoi doveri instrutto appieno,
De i suoi voti indiscreti abbia rossore,
E i suoi pregij, e i suoi vizj al fin conprenda;
E sbandito l'error, tolte, e depresse
Le capricciose idee, contro il fallace
Ragionar de i mortali, in salvo poste,
E vendicate restino, e difese
Le sante Leggi del Fattore Eterno.[15]

The latent tracts, the giddy heights explore
Of all who blindly creep, or sightless soar;
Eye Nature's walks, shoot folly as it flies
And catch the manners living as they rise:
Laugh where we must, be candid where we can,
But vindicate the ways of God to Man.
    (Pope, *An Essay on Man*, I. 11-16)

ii   Temerario mortal! la tua ragione
Pace non ha se a risaper non giugne
Per qual cagion, per qual disegno ascoso
Sì piccolo, sì fiacco, e sì ristretto
Nelle tue viste ti formò Natura.
Ma prima insegna a me, donde addiviene,
Che più imperfetto ancora nato non sei.[16]

Presumptuous man! the reason wouldst thou find,
Why form'd so weak, so little and so blind,
First, if thou canst, the harder reason guess,
Why form'd no weaker, blinder, and no less,
(Pope, *An Essay on Man,* I. 35-38)

The first passage quoted bears little resemblance to the original, and as a result of the confusion obviously existing in the writer's mind, the Italian sense is not at first sight clear. In fact one positively only recognises the last two Italian lines quoted as belonging to Pope. The second passage is rendered in simplistic fashion. Here there is no effort to reproduce Pope's juxtaposition of reason and weakness, or his subtle exercise in repetition. The above examples (I believe) provide sufficient evidence of Adami's incapability of producing Pope's philosophy through the poetic medium. Balance and subtly yield to the conversational and explanatory. It would not be completely accurate however, to regard the poem a total disaster or imply that Adami is not representative of an age. Epistle II dealing with human behaviour obviously carried a great appeal for the Italian writer, and here one finds that Adami reproduces clearly and poetically human reactions:

Appena agli occhi nostri ci si presenta,
Qual'odioso mostro il vizio appare!
Ma questo primo orror col tempo scema,
E la sua vista ci sconvolge meno;
Indi sedotto il cor con lui fa lega:
L'Uomo allor del vizio a suo talento
Fissa i confini, e dal capriccio retto,
Non più dalla ragion, biasma, e loda;
Nè mai volto a se stesso, in sè non vede
Quegli eccessi, che in altri egli condanna,[17]

Vice is a monster of so frightful mien,
As to be hated, needs but to be seen;
Yet seen too oft, familiar with her face,
We first endure, then pity, then embrace.
But where the extreme of vice, was ne'er agreed:
Ask where's the north, at York, 'tis on the Tweed;
In Scotland, at the Orcades, and there,
At Greenland, Zembla, or the Lord knows where –

No creature owns it in the first degree,
But thinks his neighbour farther gone than he.
                    (Pope, *An Essay on Man*, II. 217-226).

The personification and active force of vice is successfully conveyed, and the pact between man and vice is more obvious than in Pope's work in which mankind is expressed in terms of "we" and "creature". The progressive building up of a relationship between vice and man is conveyed in terms of verbs. Adami, having created the immediate effect with "odioso mostro", "primo orrore", allows the verbs convey the entire relationship. "Scema", "sconvolge meno", "fa lega", "fissa i confini" illustrate the diminishing will-power and the domination of vice. The point to point regression is administered with a lightness of touch and careful word choice. The same movement and lightness is also achieved in the lines describing the innocent lamb licking the hand raised to shed his blood:

Quell'innocente agnel, che al fin del giorno
A perir condannò tua fame ingorda,
Se avesse la ragion, che a te fa scorta,
Se del colpo fatal fosse presago,
Forse che in calma attenderia la morte?
Fino al momento estremo ei sta scherzando
Le fresche erbette a pascolar su i prati
Scevro d'ogni timor, d'ogni sospetto,
In mezzo dell'orribile periglio,
E accarezza giulivo il braccio istesso,
Che di ferirlo in atto è già disteso,
Fortunata ignoranza, error felice,
Che al nostro inquieto cor vela il futuro.[18]

The lamb thy riot dooms to bleed today
Had he thy reason, would he skip and play?
Pleased to the last, he crops the flowery food,
And licks the hand just raised to shed his blood.
Oh blindness to the future! kindly given,
That each may fill the circle mark'd by Heaven.
                    (Pope, *An Essay on Man*, I. 81-86)

Adami provides thirteen lines for Pope's six; this is one occasion in which the extra lines do not appear incumbent. The skipping movement, the lamb's lack of fear and the final stroke of the slayer are magnified, almost presented in slow motion so that they become symbolic of destiny and fate.

Though it has been made abundantly clear that Adami's translation is not a literary success, consideration must be given to the significance of Adami with relation to this work. The edition in question reveals Adami as a philosophical thinker, who wishes to create his own poetic works based on the philosophy divulged by the popular interest in Pope. He reveals himself as one with a general, as opposed to a particular interest in metaphysics, the result of which is a rather simplistic approach to essence and being. As a translator, his approach is that of one aiming at an approximate rendering, as opposed to a precise one. In neglecting precision and exact statement, one is faced with a softer, milder, less ironic poem, which without doubt provided plenty of food for thought for the pre-Romantic and Romantic poets obsessed with the role of Nature and Destiny. The influence however of Adami's work cannot be disregarded, when one considers the number of editions published, and the fact that it appeared in the principle centres of philosophic and scientific speculation of the "Settecento". His achievement, however trite, marks the first solid evidence of public interest in Alexander Pope's *Essay on Man*.

II

The third translation to appear during the eighteenth century was that of Giammaria Ortes. It can be defined as "poesia filosofica", in that it recaptures the rhetoric of Pope at almost all times and it can be regarded as poetry in its own right, demonstrating "sensismo settecentesco". It first appeared in Venice in 1757, and the anonymous version that appeared in Florence in 1776, is in fact that of Ortes[19], as is also that of Bologna of the same date. In his preface entitled "Il traduttore a chi legge", Ortes pays tribute to the English poet, but makes it very clear that although he has translated the work as it is written, he does not hold the views of Pope with regard to final causes, fatalism and religious tolerance.

Ortes declares that his translation was indeed completed in or around 1746. In the preface to the 1776 edition entitled *Saggio sopra l'uomo, diviso in quattro lettere d'Alessandro Pope, trasportato dalla poesia inglese nell'italiana*. MDCCLXXVI, he states:

La presente traduzione fu da me fatta trent'anni innanzi, per compiacere un soggetto rispettabile, che io stimava moltissimo, e che perfin ch'ei visse è sempre riguardato come il mio Bolimbroche, con quale certamente ei poteva paragonarsi per qualità d'animo, e per elevatezza di spirito. Essendomi essa ora capitata alla mano, l'o voluto trascrivere per migliorarla, con intenzione di tirarne alcune copie in stampa.[20]

It is Pope's spiritual qualities and exalted mind which most appeal to Ortes, and this is apparent when one considers his style in translation. However, Ortes disassociates himself from many of Pope's more personal convictions:

In essa v'an molte massime di ottime morale, quali io approvo molto volentieri, ed abbraccio. Ma ve ne anno alcun'altre intorno alle cause finali, al fatalismo, alla tolleranza delle Religioni, e simili, alle quali io non potrei assolutamente adattarmi. De'Sovrani altresì, e d'e loro Ministri, parla l'Autore con ariditezza, e talvolta con certa acerbità, che è fuor di ragione; ma che può a lui perdonarsi come aquello nato in Inghilterra, d'un partito contrario alla Corte, non potea parlarne favorevolmente, massime a quei tempi, ne'quali i partiti in quel regno erano assai animosi. Io però nel tradurre la sua opera, avendo dovuto anco in questo conservare i suoi sentimenti, e le sue espressioni; ognun vede ch'io potea ciò fare, senza prendere parte alcuna dal canto mio in que'sentimenti, e in quelle espressioni medesime, quali in effetto io lascio tutte al suo Autore; dichiararando di rispettare i Sovrani, e i loro Ministri, e di non riconoscere in essi alcuno di quei difetti, che, immagina la fantasia riscaldata d'un Poeta Inglese.[21]

One notes here Ortes' attitude towards the work of the translator, and his desire to reproduce exactly the content of the original. He is complemented on this precision by his friend Alberto Rimbotti, who, having requested a copy of the translation, writes acknowledging it and conveying his congratulations.[22] That Ortes' work merits the title of philosophical poetry is borne out when one studies the following passage from Epistle II. A flexibility of movement is added to Pope's original with reference to the constancy of activity, the contrast brought out strongly between active and passive, and between reason and passion when viewed as two opposite poles. Ortes uses no rhyme, opting for the "verso sciolto" with usually thirteen syllables per line:

> Nell'indolenza sua lo stoico inerte,
> Mal sî lusinga di virtù costante.
> Cotal costanza inoperosa e lenta
> Somiglia quell'ardor contratto al petto,
> Per cui tutto il restante delle membra
> Gelido ne riman, grave e abbattuto
> Nell'azion sta di costanza il vanto,
> Non nel riposo, e appar nelle burrasche
> Dell'alma interne, allorachè sovente
> Per preservare il più, naufraga il meno.
> Or di quest'azion nell'ampio mare
> Di vita, son le passioni i venti,
> E è ragion la carra direttrice.
> Alla sua mèta ognun drizza la prora,
> E nella ferma calma il Dio dell'onde
> Non si trattiene, Ei spesso incalza i venti
> E preme il dorso ai nembi e alle procelle.[23]

> In lazy apathy let Stoics boast
> Then virtue fix'd; 'tis fix'd as in a frost;
> Contracted all, retiring to the breast,
> But strength of mind is exercise, not rest.
> The rising tempest puts in act the soul,
> Parts it may ravage, but preserves the whole.
> On life's vast ocean diversity we sail,
> Reason the card, but passion is the gale;
> Nor God alone in the still calm we find,
> He mounts the storm, and walks upon the wind.
> (Pope, *An Essay on Man,* II. 101-110.)

The quoted lines reveal a real attempt to convey the complexity and dualism of Pope's work, although it cannot be denied that the general effect is one of flatness. Ortes, dispensing with rhyme, allows for a greater freedom of expression, but it could also be argued that such a choice reveals an inability to accurately render Pope's thoughts and cope at the same time with the poetic medium. From the poetic viewpoint, effectiveness is achieved with the repetition of the word "costanza" indicating in turn both activity and inactivity, and bringing to mind the role of the word in the eighteenth-century melodrama — its identification with romantic passion and ardour,

242

and at the same time with resolute steadfastness. However, a rhyme-scheme would have rendered Ortes' poetic associations more pointed, and more in keeping with the spirit of arcadian poetry. The term "ardore" is identified with "azione" and finally with "costanza". And so we find a "costanza", "inoperosa e lenta" and that in turn identified with the "burrasche dell'alma interne". Such identifications confer an activity and lightness of touch associated with the works of Metastasio, but within a work of the philosophic nature of the *Essay on Man*, the device does not quite come off.

The translation is more successful in the precise clear-cut poetry of statement. Though the following lines cannot be regarded as a literal account of the original, the sense of the passage is communicated without recourse to the more decorative devices seen in the first extract under consideration:

> È ver, che il forte al debole sovrasta
> E che l'Uomo si reputa il bel genio
> Fra tutti gli animali, ai quali impera
> E le cui debolezze ei più conosce.[24]

> Grant that the powerful still the weak control;
> Be man the wit and tyrant of the whole:
> Nature that tyrant checks; he only knows
> And helps, another creature's wants and woes.
> (Pope, *An Essay on Man,* III. 49-52)

I believe that the translation of Ortes represents an attempt to create a poetry of ideas, a taste for which was developing during the mid-Settecento. The passages dealing with the origin of art, of passion, and of ideas are quite successfully rendered:

> Le passion quai semi onde risulta
> Ogni creata intelligente essenza,
> Ancorché destinate a contrastarsi
> Con quel contrasto regolato, all'opre
> Dan miglior forma. E in ver se mal s'adopra
> Ciascun per estirpar quegli elementi
> Dai quai risulta; e basta che per l'orme
> Segnate da natura, e gl'incammini
> Dove sorge ragione, e che il soverchio
> Empito loro altrui nocivo estingua.

Amor, speme, letizia, alma e ridente
Famiglia di piaceri; Odio, spavento,
Tristezza, e di dolor treno lugubre
Temperati con arte, all'intelletto
Donan l'equilibrio, e qual in tela
Sentimento di lumi, ad ombre misti,
Danno all'opre miglior grazia e risalto.[25]

Passions, like elements, though born to fight
Yet, mix'd and soften'd, in this work unite:
And tis enough to temper and employ;
But what composes man, can man destroy?
Suffice that reason keep to Nature's road,
Subject, compound them, follow her and God.
Love, hope, and joy, fair pleasure's smiling train,
Hate, fear, and grief the family of pain.
These mix'd with art, and to due bounds confined,
Make and maintain the balance of the mind:
The lights and shades, whose well accorded strife
Gives all the strength and colour of our life.
(Pope, *An Essay on Man*, II. 11-122).

Ortes in his translation of the above lines reveals himself a true disciple of the enlightment, in that he poetically fuses Pope's contrasts and opposites in terms of light and shade, illumination and ignorance, i.e.

Odio, spavento,
Tristezza, di dolor treno lugubre
Temperati con arte, all'intelletto
Donan l'equilibrio, e qual in tela
Sentimento di lumi ad ombre misti,
Danno all'opra miglior grazia e risalto.

This fusion of "lumi" and "ombre" represents a "contrasto regolato" constituting thus a more perfect form. The concept of passions being as seeds which produce created intelligence, belongs to Ortes, rather than to Pope, and provides an identification of the various forms of nature, of the concrete with the abstract. Thus Ortes' poetry becomes one of essence and form, harmony and disorder reconciled in a "contrasto regolato". In the poetry of Pope, the conflict is highlighted and appears more in evidence. Ortes creates instead a poetry of abstractions at all times projecting an idealogical and poetic unity.

244

The enormousness of creation is expressed in terms of time and space and visually conveyed by the use of nouns expressing a circle, either static or in motion — i.e. the use of nouns: — "punto", "catena", "giri", "anello":

> Ma di sî vasta immensità, l'umana
> Virtù visiva ora non và che ad un punto,
> E della gran catena interminata,
> Che tiene il tutto in consonanza, e piega
> Per vari piani in ampi, o in brevi giri
> Attaccata a un anello, il comun moto
> Degli altri che la tragge e la conduce,
> Seguita, e il come, e lo perchè n'ignora.[26]

> But of this frame the bearings and the ties,
> The strong connections, nice dependencies.
> Gradations just, has thy pervading soul
> Look'd through? or can a part contain the whole?
> Is the great chain, that draws all to agree,
> And drawn, supports, upheld by God or thee?
> (I. 1. 29-34).

In the lines on Man's becoming familiar with vice, by providing a series of verbs, Ortes builds to a climax in two lines. Pope supplies three verbs in one line, presenting the situation in a matter-of-fact manner; the translation, while departing slightly from the spirit of the original, succeeds in bringing home the horror of such familiarity in melodramatic tones; the use of the term "deformità" to convey Pope's "monster" once again demonstrates Ortes' preoccupation with form and man's deviation from it:

> Orrido in vista è il vizio, e pur se spesso
> Sta sotto gli occhi, il guardo assuefatto
> La sua deformità più non rileva.
> S'incomincia a soffrir, si compatisce.
> Si scusa, si difende, si ricerca,
> Alfin s'abbraccia, e a gradi più lontani
> Se ne trasporta l'odioso nome.[27]

> Vice is a monster of so frightful mien,
> As, to be hated, needs but to be seen;
> Yet seen too oft, familiar with her face,
> We first endure, then pity, then embrace.
> (Pope, *An Essay on Man*, II. 217-220).

Ortes then, in his translation *Saggio sull'uomo,* shows himself as one deeply interested in the philosophic content of the work; he also aims at capturing arcadian lightness and precision, as illustrated in the quotation of the translation of Epistle II, 1. 101-110. It cannot be said that he is totally successful in this respect since the projection of "costanza" and "ardore" as active forces demands a less prosaic style. Donald B. Clark, in his article "The Italian Fame of Alexander Pope", refers to the version as "an interesting anonymous translation of 1776, which disclaims sympathy with Pope's "fatalism".[28] He goes on to describe the work as "a compressed translation which, though hardly poetic and unusually cacophonous for the liquid Italian tongue, caught something of Pope's economy of words."[29] For this reason, the version is clear cut, and successful in passages of direct statement. It represents an attempt to fuse philosophy and arcadian gracefullness, the result being that the lightness of touch is weighted by the philosophic ponderings, which do after all constitute the subject of the work. Perhaps it can be said that Ortes' translation can be considered yet another example of a work in which philosophical pondering killed poetry. The original work, however, does not suffer the same fate, since Pope's brilliance of poetic expression serves to imprint the basic moral truths on the memory, and provides a refinement of the universal vision.

While Ortes' version is successful as regards translation, and is representative of an age, the prose translation published in London in 1765 by Antonio Graziosi, and dedicated to T.B. is of little value. The work is not divided into sections, and its continual use of the first person plural renders it extremely boring. The literal translation often does not convey the sense of the original and is, as a result of the translator's non-comprehension of his subject, expressed in un-idiomatic Italian. The publisher, in an attempt to boost the present version, provides criticism of previous translators, praises his own, and adds a brief summary of the content of the work. He begins by stating:

> Benché la versione sia in prosa, conserva tutta la vivacità e il brio del poeta inglese, Pope non è autore tanto facile a tradursi. Il Petracchi, che primo volle provarsi in questa impresa, ci ha data una Traduzione, non so se io dico Italiana, o Malabarica, in cui ha mostrato di non intendere il suo origi-

nale. Il cav. Adami, cui è dovuto il pregio di valoroso poeta, s'è lasciato trasportare dalla sua fantasia, onde ha fatto parlare, come si figurò che dovesse parlare. Degli altri traduttori nulla dirò, ma credo che la miglior traduzione di questa non siasi ancor fatta, e che servirete al comune piacere col pubblicarla.[30]

With reference to the content of the *Essay on Man*, the publisher states:

Il tutto tende alla cognizione nell'uomo, rapporto a sè stesso, e alla cognizione di Dio. Senza avvilirlo sa conoscere l'uomo a se stesso, fa trionfare i diritti della ragione, ne insulta che la rea superbia di coloro, che si solevano contro Dio, e penetra vogliono nei disegni e nelle opere dell'infinito.[31]

The first point which strikes the reader, on a close examination of what I call for convenience the Grazioso translation, is the lack of variety of tone. The translator plods ahead, and in the process obscures the meaning of his subject. A notable example of this lack of variety occurs in the opening section of the essay, where the first person plural imperative is used no less than nine times. Pope avoids repetition by variation of the second person singular imperative with the first person plural. The Italian translator achieves no such variety, as this passage illustrates:

Penetriamo le vie più segrete; trasportiamoci nei luoghi più elevati, e scopriamo ugualmente ciò che si asconde fra le tenebre e ciò che al sublime s'inalza.
Esaminiamo i passeggi della natura; arrestiamo la follia nella sua carriera, ed afferriamo i costumi nella lor nascita. Ridiamo quando si deve; mostriamo candore quando si può; ma **soprattutto** giustifichiamo presso gli uomini la condotta di Dio.[32]

> Together let us beat this ample field,
> Try what the open, what the covert yeild!
> The latent tracts, the giddy heights explore
> Of all who blindly creep, or sightless soar;
> Eye Nature's walks, shoot folly as it flies,
> And catch the manners living as they rise:
> Laugh where we must, be candid where we can,
> But vindicate the ways of God to man.
> (Pope, *An Essay on Man*, I. 9-16).

Where a literal translation is attempted, the result is often flat. Repetition used in the original, in order to achieve effect, in this version is usually unsuccessful, i.e.: Homo presentuoso, giacchè pretendi scoprir la ragione perché sei stato formato sì debole, piccolo, e cieco; dimmi prima di ogni altra cosa, perché non sei stato formato più debole, più piccolo più cieco di quello sei.[33] In Pope the same sense and repetition achieves a totally different effect by virtue of word order, verse and subtle irony:

> Presumptuous man! the reason wouldst thou find,
> Why form'd so weak, so little, and so blind?
> First, if thou canst, the harder reason guess,
> Why form'd no weaker, blinder, and no less?
> (Pope, *An Essay on Man*, I, 35-38)

On another occasion, the literal translation over simplifies the wit and imagination of Pope. There is no attempt at all to come to terms with alliteration, a problem which was successfully surmounted by Conti in his translation of *The Rape of the Lock*. In the following passage, the static images of cobbler, parson, friar and monarch fail to capture the reader's attention or imagination:

> L'onore e la vergogna non nascono dalla nostra condizione. Fate bene ciò che dovete fare; Ecco in che consiste l'onore. La fortuna ha posto qualche piccola differenza fra gli uomini: uno sta bene colli suoi cenci l'altro ne'suoi brocati: il ciabattino nel suo grembiule di pelle, il prete nella sua veste talare: il monaco col suo capuccio, il re colla sua corona.[34]

> Honour and shame from no condition rise:
> Act well your part: there all the honour lies.
> Fortune in men has some small difference made,
> One flaunts in rags, one flutters in brocade;
> The cobbler apron'd, and the parson gown'd,
> The friar hooded, and the monarch crown'd.
> (Pope, *An Essay on Man*, IV. 193-198)

There are many more examples which could be provided, but my purpose is merely to illustrate that this prose translation has little to contribute in terms of literary merit. It could nevertheless be helpful to the student of English in providing a basic, non stylised resumé of the essay. Had it not been published so late (1765), twenty-three years after that of Petracchi, nine years after that of Adami, and eight years after Ortes' version, it might have assumed an historical importance on the grounds that it attempted to transfer to Italian. the thoughts of the foremost English poet of the day.

III

Hitherto, in consideration of some of the translations of Pope's *Essay on Man*, I have attempted to ascribe to each, qualities for which the work was memorable, culturally successful, or at least useful to the interested reader. It became apparent that Adami's work was the most influential, Ortes' a genuine effort at poetic expression springing from the original English, and Graziosi's the least successful. Ortes' work rose above the level of sheer translation, and Adami's frequently fell below it. The other translators mentioned vary, but for the most part are adequate, with some moments of true inspiration. If one were to seek in translation a mere transference of thought, without pretentions towards the creation of a new work in its own right, perhaps the work of Gian-Vincenzo Benini would prove most satisfying. However, such a desire eliminates all idealism from the part of the reader, and the translator, and so deprives one of the pleasure of hoping to find a work comparable to Conti's *Il riccio rapito*. The work of Benini can be classified as a successful translation, less exalted in tone than the original and by far more valid than his versions of *Eloisa to Abelard* and *The Rape of the Lock*. Lenta describes his approach as follows: "Si serba in generale abbastanza fedele al testo, sì che la sua versione può servire di buon aiuto a capire l'originale per chi non è ancora perfettamente versato nella lingua Inglese."[35] Lenta also makes the point that "L'Epistola di Eloisa ed *Il riccio rapito* sono più malmenati e manomessi".[36]

Benini's translation appeared in 1788, and is reprinted in *Capi d'Opera di Alessandro Pope, dedicati al Cavalier Lampel* (Venice, 1825). The introductory note refers to previous translations — Adami's and Ferrero's. He comments unfavourably on the anonymous version, and quotes its first five lines. The criticism is based on the belief that the verse is in the style of Salvini[37] and that the expression of English verse in an Italian literary style is an anachronism:

La sua traduzione del Saggio Sull'Uomo benché tratta dal testo inglese, com'ei dice e noi non dubitiamo, è dessa or troppo fedele o troppo libera, e sempre fuor di ragione e di tempo. I pensieri inglesi sotto la penna dell'innominato traduttore vi sono si travolti ed inviluppati e l'eleganza vi è sì perenne che rendono questa traduzione altrettanto oscura quanto disaggradevole. I suoi versi, quanto pur son versi, sono del gusto Salviniano, ed eccone un saggio nella traduzione de' due sopra segnati versi del poema.[38]

Surprisingly Benini regards a work by the Venetian poet Pietro Chiari a translation rather than an imitation. I have not included it in this assessment since I believe it to be an imitation of Pope, in no way resembling a translation. Benini's comments on Ferrero's work is complimentary: "Molto caso all'incontro dovrebbesi far della quarta, dettata in nobile stile e fornita di dotte e giudiziose osservazioni, se traduzione e rima non fossero due cose eterogenee che un felice accidente, più che il sapere e l'ingegno ci fa qualche rara volta soltanto veder insieme."[39]

A thought which must strike readers of translators or publishers introductions to these versions, is that the translations were not as well known or widely circulated as one would have imagined! It is surprising that Benini in 1788 is aware of only four other versions besides his own, one of which was an imitation. There appears to have been a complete ignorance of the work of Petracchi, Salvenini, Pillori, Graziosi and Ortes, since the latter's version which appeared in Venice in 1757 does not appear to have been known to either the translator or the publisher. Adami's translation was generally considered the first to appear, while the publisher of Graziosi's translation in 1765 refers only to the work of Petracchi and of Adami.

The opening of Benini's version is clear-cut and commands our attention, though it lacks the authority of the original:

> Svegliati amico e al cortigiano orgoglio
> Lascia i piccol omai fallaci oggetti
> Perchè la vita il sol poter ci lascia
> Di riguardar ciò che sta a noi d'intorno
> E di morir, esaminiamo almeno
> Dell'uomo la scena: labirinto insieme
> Confuso e regolar.[40]

> Awake, my St. John! leave all meaner things
> To low ambition and the pride of kings.
> Let us since life can little more supply

Than just to look about us, and to die
Expatiate free o'er all this scene of man;
A mighty maze, but not without a plan.
(Pope, *An Essay on Man*, I. 1-6).

Benini's gift lies in his ability to capture the precision and lightness of touch of Pope — this is clearly demonstrated in his translation of the passage dealing with the spider's touch:

Quanto nel tatto è mai squisito il ragno!
Sensibile in — estremo alla più fina
E leggera impression del più sottile
Filo della sua tela, ei sembra nato
Per viver sol nell'opra che à tessuto.
E quant'è alfine delicato il gusto
Dell'ape industre che sa trar col labbro
Dall'erbe stesse velenose e amare
La più dolce e benefica rugiada![41]

The spider's touch, how exquisitely fine!
Feels at each thread, and lives along the line:
In the nice bee, what sense so subtly true
From poisonous herbs extract the healing dew?
(Pope, *An Essay on Man*, I. 217-220)

One is aware of the recurrance of the letter "S" in the Italian which conveys an atmosphere of quietness and industry to the passage. The words "fina", "leggera", "sottile filo" convey a delicacy of execution calling to mind the miniature in art, dear to the late eighteenth century. There are occasions when however, Pope's clear straightforward statement, which speaks for itself, in the hands of Benini becomes an involved explanation:

Son figli dell'orgoglio
Questi vani lamenti; e sino a dove
Spinge l'orgoglio i suoi delirj? l'uomo
Esser angel vorria, l'angelo Dio;
E se di questo il temerario ardire
Di ribellion colpevole lo rese
E fu dal ciel precipitato all'imo,
Sulle perfide tracce de'ribelli
S'avvia per quel, mentre le leggi e i dritti
Di natura e del ciel turba e confonde.[42]

In pride, in reas'ning pride, our error lies,
All quit their sphere, and rush into the skies.
Pride still is aiming at the blest abodes.
Men would be angels, angels would be gods.
Aspiring to be gods, if angels fell,
Aspiring to be angels, men rebel.
And who but wishes to invert the laws
Of order, sins against the Eternal Cause.
(Pope, *An Essay on Man*, I, 123-130)

Benini does not succeed as does Pope in juxtaposing "angels" and "gods", heaven and earth. Here the passage borders on the explanatory and loses the pithiness and flexibility of tone of the original. While I believe Benini's work can be classified as a most successful translation, there are some passages which do stand out in their own right. This is particularly so with regard to demonstrative lists, where the translator takes a free hand in supplying appropriate adjectives to accompany abstract nouns:

Siccome pianta sterile ed ingrata
Alle cure e ai sudor del buon villano,
Se ad un tronco selvaggio avvien s'innesti,
La sua, debile in – pria, radice tosto
Da quell'estrano vigoroso succo
Nuova forza riceve e nuova vita,
Cresce s'alza si abbella e di più verdi
Foglie pompeggia e di più ricche frutta;
Così dalle passion più basse ancora
Le più belle virtù nascon talvolta:
L'umiliante tristezza, il vil timore,
La dura ostinazion, l'ira, perfino
Quai non son di virtù ricche sorgenti!
Può lo sdegno produrre un puro zelo,
Un magnanimo ardir, l'accidia nutre
Della filosofia l'amor; l'invidia
Delle anime vulgar vile tiranna,
Nobile emulazion divien de'dotti
E ne'guerrier; la voluttà ristretta
In fra certi confin, eccita e crea
I più dolci del cor nobili affetti.[43]

As fruits, ungrateful to the planters care,
On savage stocks inserted learn to bear;

> The surest virtues thus from passions shoot
> Wild Nature's vigor working at the root.
> What crops of wit and honesty appear
> From spleen, from obstinacy, hates, or fear!
> See anger, zeal and fortitude supply,
> Even av'rice, prudence, sloth, philosophy,
> Lust, through some certain strainers well refined,
> Is gentle love, and charms all womankind;
> Envy, to which the ignoble minds a slave,
> Is emulation in the learned or brave.
> (Pope, *An Essay on Man*, II. 181-192)

Benini's first eight lines transform the wit of Pope to a passage of genuine nature poetry. The process of growth rises to a climax in the lines:

> Cresce, s'alza si abbella e di più verdi
> Fogli pompeggia, e di più ricche frutta.

The wit of the passage is lost in the explanatory lines:

> Così dalle passioni più basse ancora
> Le più belle virtù nascon talvolta.

This is, however, compensated for, I believe, by the addition of adjectives to the abstract nouns, resulting in "l'umiliante tristezza" – "il vil timore", "dura ostinazion". However, one must bear in mind that the more individual and poetic the work tends to be in its own right, the less faithful it rates as translation. Benini's work proves most successful both as a version of Pope's, and as a poem communicating universal truths, the functions of nature, and the activities of its smaller products. It combines precision and lightness with the poetry of clear statement found in Pope; it successfully brings to life the poetic miniatures found in *An Essay on Man*. Although at times descending to the explanatory, its expression can never be defined as awkward or clumsy, and there is no style variation within passages dealing with a singly subject, which conveys a uniformity on the poem as a whole.

Most important, of the four translators discussed, Benini's is the only one which can be regarded as a successful rendering of Pope, taking its point of departure from English. Adami, as already discussed, was following the French of Du Resnel; Ortes, whose work proves interesting, does not quite master the poetic medium, while the translation T.B. edited by Graziosi, being in prose serves the purpose of, in my opinion, informing the reader, but not of delighting him. Pope had of course attempted and is generally accepted to have achieved both functions, in *An Essay on Man*.

It is also to be noted that Benini, from the outset, aimed at brevity and precision in his rendering of the poem. In this respect he demonstrates a true understanding of the English poet's intentions and technique. Having considered a prose rendering, he chose verse and rhyme for two reasons:

> l'uno non è nuovo, cioè che le massime ed i precetti scritti in tal modo colpiscono il lettore più fortemente alla prima, e son da lui ritenuti più facilmente dappoi; l'altro all'incontro comparirà altrettanto strano quant'esso è pur vero, ed e ch'io mi trovai in grado di poterli esprimere più brevemente in questa maniera che nella prosa stessa, nè v'ha niente di più certo, che la forza e la grazia degli argomenti delle istruzioni dipendono in gran parte dalla brevità.[44]

Benini's choice of the nouns "forza" and "grazia" in relation to the discourses of the work reveal a clear understanding of the dual quality of the poem, and of Pope's success in both the field of the didactic and delightful.

Pope's *Essay on Man* proved the English poet's most translated work in Italy during the eighteenth century. In England it received critical acclaim until the appearance of translations in Europe. It was with the publication of some versions in French, both in verse and in prose, and that of Du Resnel, which was more a paraphrase than a translation, that a discordant note was sounded. It must be stated that Pope's convictions are neither clearcut, nor developed, and never proceed beyond generalisation. Yet inexplicably his Italian translators appear more drawn to Pope the "philosopher" than Pope the poet. With reference to the four translations discussed, it is my opinion that only Gian-Vincenzo Benini possessed a true appreciation of Pope the poet, his ability to condense concepts and to reproduce the miniature. By virtue of their Italian reproductions of the English poet, it cannot be argued that Adami, Ortes or the writer of the Graziosi translation show any deep poetic appreciation, and their introductory notes imply that they were drawn to the work as a result of idealogical content.

The inability to reproduce Pope's poetry in such a manner as to create a valid poetic composition in its own right does not necessarily admit a lack of recognition of the poet's ability. The demands presented by a work such as the *Essay on Man* were enormous, and those drawn to the subject of Man and his behaviour evidently did not possess the ability to do justice to Pope's verse. The genre of the philosophic poem appealed in eighteenth-century Italy as did the classical tradition on which it was based. There was also a general acceptance of his poetic ability. Evidence demonstrates that the inability to produce Pope's expressions adequately in the Italian tongue did not dissuade his admirers from translating him. Some obviously believed that what he had to say merited a hearing, even in prose.

Notes to Chapter I

1 Both the Bonducci and Conti translations of *The Rape of the Lock* were written before Petracchi's version of the *Essay on Man* appeared. Bonducci's was published in Florence in 1739. Conti's did not appear in Italy in print until 1756 in *Prose e poesie* (Venice, 1756).

2 Anton Filippo Adami, b. Florence 1720 – d. 1761. Poet and translator. Translated *Il Brittanico* by Racine (Florence, 1752), edited *Poesie scelte filosofiche ed eroiche* (Florence, 1753), Pope, *Saggio Sull'Uomo* (Arezzo, 1756), also wrote *Dissertazioni critiche* (Pisa, 1756); *Raccolta di leggi e statuti sui possessi ed acquisti dalle manimorte, con varie dissertazioni di celebri autori* (Venice, 1767).

3 Giammaria Ortes, b. Venice 1713, d. 1790. Member of the Camaldolesi order. Studied in Pisa between 1734 and 1738. In 1743 he left the religious order and returned to Venice in 1756.
Errori popolari intorno all'economia nazionale (1771); *Dell'economia nazionale* (1774): *Dei fide commessi a famiglie* (1784); *Riflessione su la popolazione delle nazioni per rapporto all'economia nazionale* (1790); *Opere* (Padua, 1830).
Bib. A. Meneghelli, *Elogio di Giammaria Ortes* (Venice, 1814); F. Lampertico, *Giammaria Ortes e la scienza economica a suo tempo* (Venice, 1865); L. Barioni, "Un economista poeta del Settecento" in *Miscellanea in onore di Vittorio Cian* (Pisa, 1909); M. Petrocchi, *Razionalismo architettonico e razionalismo storiografico* (Rome, 1947).

4 A.F. Adami, *I principi della morale o sia Saggio Sopra l'Uomo, poema inglese di Alessandro Pope, tradotto in versi sciolti italiani dal Cavaliere Anton-Filippo Adami con la giunta di critiche e filosofiche annotazioni, e di varj egregi componimenti dallo stesso traduttore, come può vedersi nella prefazione che segue* (Venice, 1757).

5 Ibid. p. 134

6 Ibid. p. 137

7 Ibid. pp. 139-40

8 *Saggio sopra l'Uomo,* diretto a T.B. (London, 1765) p. 4.

9 Du Resnel "Discours preliminaire du traducteur, *Les principes de la morale et du gout,* en deux poemes traduits de l'Anglois" (Paris, 1736). Translation by Dr. Johnson, in *Pope, The Critical Heritage,* edited by John Barnard, op. cit., pp. 286-7.

10 Pope, *The Critical Heritage,* edited by John Barnard, op.cit., p. 291.

11 Ibid. p. 294

12 A.F. Adami, *I Principi della morale o sia Saggio Sopra l'Uomo,* op.cit., pp.

13-14; p. 13 1. 9, p. 14, 1. 1-10.
There are no line references in this edition. For the convenience of the reader line references per page are supplied.

13 G. Lenta, *Pope in Italia*, op.cit., pp. 84-5.
14 A.F. Adami, *I principi della morale o sia Saggio Sopra l'Uomo*, op.cit., p. 31, 1. 12-7.
15 Ibid. p. 6, 1. 16-24.
16 Ibid. p. 8, 1. 15-21.
17 Ibid. p. 44, 1. 1-10
18 Ibid. pp. 10-11, p. 10, 1. 27-34; p. 11, 1-5.
19 Giammaria Ortes, *Saggio sopra l'Uomo, diviso in quattro lettere d'Alessandro Pope, trasportato dalla poesia inglese nell'italiana* (Venice, 1776).
20 Ibid. p. (iii).
21 Ibid. pp. (iii-iv).
22 Venice, Biblioteca Museo Correr, MS R. 5. The first letter from Florence is dated 17 April 1781. The relevant section reads:

"Grandissimo contento mi farebbe l'acquisto della traduzione fatta da V.S. Illma del poema di Pope che ho con massimo piacere letto che desidero avere in proprietà onde quando discardo non le sia di favorirmela, che le sarò sempre grato per questo favore quando me lo conceda".

The letter of appreciation is dated 3 July 1781 and the appropriate section reads:

"mi pervenne la traduzione del *Saggio sull'uomo* del Sig. Pope, libro che fino dalla gioventù ha fatto la mia occupazione e che poi lo leggerò in una lingua – non proprio al trattare in poesia materie alte e gravi. Sono stato molto contento nel leggerlo in Lingua Toscana, e con la precisione propria della sua maestà e della sua scienza. Le sono obligatissimo di un dono il maggiore che potesse farmi. Le ne sarò grato fino al mio termine della vita. Un dono ne richiede un altro e potrà sempre domandarmi cosa che le possa far piacere, ed io sarò in dovere in contentarla, come la sua traduzione mi ha soddisfatto grandemente, e mi sarà di una sempre forte ricordanza, mentre con tutto il maggiore ossequio sono.

Di. V. Illima,
Devotissimo Servo
Alberto Rimbotti".

23 Giammaria Ortes, *Saggio sopra l'uomo*, p. 20, 1. 11-27. There are no line references in this edition. Line ref. per page is supplied.
24 Ibid. p. 33, 1. 9-12.
25 Ibid. pp. 20-1; p. 20.1. 38-31, p. 21, 1. 1-13.
26 Ibid. p. 3, 1. 3-10.
27 Ibid. p. 26, 1. 3-9.
28 Donald B. Clark, "The Italian Fame of Alexander Pope", art.cit., p. 360.

29 Ibid. p. 361.
30 *Saggio sopra l'uomo*, A.T.B. (London, 1765) pp. 4-5.
31 Ibid. p. 5.
32 Ibid. p. 8.
33 Ibid. p. 10.
34 Ibid. p. 79
35 Giovanni Lenta, *Pope in Italia*, op.cit., p. 85.
36 Ibid.
37 Anton-Maria Salvini, b. 1653, d. 1729. Florentine poet and translator.
38 Gian-Vincenzo Benini, *L'uomo del Pope* (Venice, 1788) p. 25.
39 Ibid. p. 26.
40 Ibid. pp. 33-4. The edition does not contain line references. For the convenience of the reader line reference per page are supplied; p. 33, 1. 1-3; p. 34, 1. 15.
41 Ibid. pp. 49-50; p. 49. 1. 24-5; p. 50. 1. 1-7.
42 Ibid. pp. 42-3; p. 42. 1. 19-25; p. 43. 1. 1-3.
43 Ibid. pp. 72-3; p. 72. 1. 19-25; p. 73. 1. 1-14.
44 Gian Vincenzo Benini, *Capi d'Opera di Alessandro Pope* 1. (Venice, 1825). pp. 56-57.

CHAPTER II

Chiari, Cerretti, Rezzonico and *An Essay on Man*

Reference has already been made to the fact that the influence of Pope's *Essay on Man* was most reflected in the work of translators who wished to communicate his philosophical idealogy. Works which rank as imitations of Pope can be said to be lacking in originality and poetic inspiration. Two of them, however, demand our attention as they are of historical interest: one by Pietro Chiari and the other by Luigi Cerretti. Chiari's poem was published by Giuseppe Bettinelli with the title: *L'Uomo, Lettere Filosofiche in versi martelliani dell' Abate Pietro Chiari poeta di suo Altissimo Signore, il Sig. Duca di Modana, sull'idea di quelle di M. Pope intitolate: The proper study of Mankind is Man.* The work is addressed to "Sua eccellenza il Sig. Marco Foscarini, Cavaliere e Procuratore di S. Marco", and the note to the reader is preceded by lines stating the writer's claim to the title of philosopher: "Filosofo mi vanto, e la mia Stella è questa, senza rispondere nulla a chicchessia rispondo: E delle mie risposte giudice voglio il Mondo."[1] Judgement appeared in the form of a vicious attack by Giuseppe Baretti, which appeared in the *Frusta Letteraria No. XXI*. Donald B. Clark sums up Baretti's displeasure in the following words:

> The attack is vitriolic: Chiari does not understand the English use of the letter h; he mistakes a line from Pope for a title; he bases his translation on the French prose paraphrase made by Du Resnel, and his translation, though one of the few Italian ones in rhymed couplets, does not limit itself to ten syllable lines as does the original of Pope.[2]

Both Baretti and Clark commit the error of believing that Chiari's work is intended as a translation rather than an imitation based on Pope. Natali in *Il settecento*[3] refers to it as an imitation. One needs just to read the note "L'autore a chi legge" to understand that Chiari stresses that his work should not be regarded as mere translation:

Queste mie Lettere Filosofiche non si prendano da chi le legge per una semplice traduzione di quelle del M. Pope sullo stesso Argomento; perocchè non poteano esser tali; nè tali a me piacque di farle; perocchè il sistema filosofico dell'eruditissimo scrittor Inglese, attribuendo alla materia un po' troppo, non ben si accorda agli occhi di chi ne sa colle massime più cattoliche dell'Evangelo alle quali, nelle più poetiche espressioni medesime mi protesto religiosamente attaccato. Dico in secondo loco, che tali a me non piacque di farle; perocchè dovendomi dipartir ne'principj dalla filosofia Inglese, m'è parso bene d'allontanarmene ancora nel resto, per inserire nell'Opera mia quanto di meglio hanno scritto su questo proposito Orazio, Seneca e Cicerone medesimo.[4]

The poet then goes on to defend himself against attackers who might accuse him of mere borrowing:

Non mancherà per tutto questo chi voglia onorarmi col titolo di rubatore, e Plagiario: quasi che pompa io faccia de' ritrovamenti degli altri. Neppur questi tali nell'onorarmi si prodighi aspettino da me altra giustificazione, o risposta, senonchè queste Lettere son opera mia, dichiarandole tali il Proverbio latino assai trito: "Nihil sub Sole novum", e i replicati precetti di Tullio, di Aristotele e di Quintiliano da quali si raccomanda e si celebra la buona imitazione de'vecchi scrittori come strada infallibile per arrivare prestamente a saper qualche cosa nel Mondo.[5]

Chiari demonstrates a critical attitude to Pope's work and reveals his intention of returning more closely to the world of classical culture. In common with Pope, however, the Venetian poet stresses the pride of man, the perfection of Nature as a system, and the conflict between one, and many. Stanzas XL, and LX resemble Epistle I l. 35-43:

Umanità superba, dell'esser tuo che pensi?
Del mondo inter che fai, se tu non fai da sensi
Di lui quel Sol ti parla di luce tal fecondo
Che cento volte, e cento pinge in un anno il Mondo.[6]
(Chiari, *L'Uomo*, I. XL.)

Nulla di ciò sai dirmi, e tutto dî non temi
Dal Caos della tua mente produr nuovi sistemi
Archimede novello osi col tuo sapere
Forse ne'giri loro di migliorar le sfere.
Folle ragione umana, cerca alla Quercia Annosa
Perch'ella sia più grande del Giglio, e della rosa,
(Chiari, *L'Uomo*, I. LX)

Presumptuous man! the reason wouldst thou find,
Why form'd so weak, so little, and so blind?
First, if thou canst, the harder reason guess,
Why form'd no weaker, blinder and no less?
Ask of they mother Earth, why oaks are made
Taller and stronger than the weeds they shade?
Or ask of yonder argent fields above,
Why Jove's satellites are less than Jove?
(Pope, *An Essay on Man*, I, 35-42)

The Venetian poet, in keeping with eighteenth-century philosophical doctrine, sees man's awareness in relation to external influences on the senses, but he applies a totally religious significance to sensations. He combines free composition with lines closely modelled on Pope. Stanza C. could be regarded an approximate reproduction of the English poets thoughts; stanza CX qualifies for the term translation:

Se sapesser le bestie, qual sia dell'uom la sorte,
Non amerian la vita, che per bramar la morte.
Se de'celesti spiriti l'uomo sapesse a fondo
Avria di sè rossore, in odio avrebbe il mondo.
Agnellino innocente, la gola mia vorace
Te condanna alla morte, e tu la soffri in pace.[8]
(Chiari, *L 'Uomo*, C).

Heaven from all creatures hides the book of Fate,
All but the page prescribed, their present state;
From brutes what men, from men what spirits know:
Or who could suffer being here below.
(Pope, *An Essay on Man*, 1. 77-80).

The following passage is a precise rendering of Pope, based on Du Resnel's paraphrase. It must be borne in mind that Chiari's attempt to reproduce Pope's heroic couplets cannot be regarded as unsuccessful. This passage, I believe, proves this point:

Perchè 'l cor suo non vedi, il tuo pastor ti coglie
A saltellar nel Prato, a ruminar le foglie.
S'egli t'annoda i piedi, e poi ti leva in spalla
Tu belando il ringrazj d'ir seco lui alla stalla.
Se là giungendo, il tuo carnefice villano
Snuda l'acciar tagliente, tu baci a lui la mano.
Tieni alla gola il ferro, e pur lambendo il vai

Sol perchè 'l tuo destino, misero agnel non sai
O! ignoranza profonda dell'avvenire oscuro
Tremerà l'uom di tutto, se tu nol sai sicuro.[9]
(Chiari, *L 'Uomo*, I, CX)

Chiari's poem provides more detail than that of the original, and relies on imagery in the creation of pathos. Throughout the passage the effect is built up in terms of contrast, between innocence and contrivance, delicacy and violence, and between the lightness of poetic touch in the early part of the stanza and the rhetorical note on which it concludes. This use of variation of tone and style removes Chiari's work from the realm of that of mere borrower or slavish imitator, and confers a certain individuality on the work as a whole. In his lines on hope, Chiari once again takes his inspiration from Pope, but orders his thoughts according to his own fashion. Indeed it can be said that Chiari's work conforms to that of Pope in that it treats of the same subject, themes and order of ideas. But the expression of these belongs to Chiari alone. Often the tone of the original is altered, replacing Pope's clearcut statement with melodrammatic outbursts. Such is the case with regard to the following stanza:

Ah speranza, speranza, che in tutti noi predomini!
Per l'armonia del Mondo quanto ti deggion gli uomini!
Tanto l'ajuto tuo dall'uom non si ricusa,
Che di te stessa ancora l'uomo superbo abusa.[10]
(Chiari, *L 'Uomo*, I. CL.)

Hope springs eternal in the human breast.
Man never Is, but always To be blest.
The soul uneasy, and confined from home,
Rests and expatiates in a life to come.
Lo, the poor Indian! whose untutor'd mind
Sees God in clouds, or hears Him in the wind.
(Pope, *An Essay on Man*, I. 95-100).

As can be observed, Pope's is the poetry of statement, Chiari's is an address to hope, which he identifies with the harmony of the world. His world shifts from the particular to the abstract, his best lines so deal with references to existence in the abstract and the perfectly ordered Scale of Being:

Scala maravigliosa, che dall'umile ortica
Ti fa salir per gradi sino alla Quercia antica!
Catena indissolubile, che unisce strettamente
Per mille, e mille anella all'infinito il niente!
Qual distanza al di sotto tra un verme, e l'esser mio?
Qual distanza al di sopra passa dall'uomo a Dio!
E l'uno spazio, e l'altro empion di mano in mano
Mille viventi, e mille, privi di corpo umano.
E l'uno spazio, e l'altro esser potrebbe empito
D'altri viventi incogniti da un numero infinito.[11]
      (Chiari, *L 'Uomo*, I. CCXL)

See, through this air, this ocean and this earth,
All matter quick, and bursting into birth.
Above, how high, progressive life may go!
Around, how wide! how deep extend below!
Vast chain of being! which from God began,
Natures ethereal, human, angel, man.
Beast, bird, fish, insect, what no eye can see,
No glass can reach; from infinate to thee,
From thee to nothing.
(Pope, *An Essay on Man*, I. 233-241).

While Pope embraces a variety of beings to illustrate the degrees of
existence, Chiari names and juxtaposes Man and the worm:

    Qual distanza al di sotto fra un verme, e l'esser mio?

One notes a touch of the pessimism which will later be associated
with Leopardi. The greatness of the universe and the concept of
space between man and God, between man and the lower creatures is
stated, but the poetic juxtaposition of man and the worm allows for
the consideration of the lowliness of all creatures. This is further
developed in Stanza L. Epistle II, where Chiari clearly reproduces
Pope's concept:

    Invece di dar legge alla Sapienza eterna,
    Dentro se stesso accenda la cinica lanterna.
    Qual sia, che si ritrovi, per sua fatal vergogna,
    Un, che dormendo parla, un, che vegliando sogna!
    Quando usciti a'dî nostri dal sen dell'Inghilterra
    Nevvton inarrivabile, a far stupir la terra,
    Te guardò Europa tutta, maravigliata, e lieta,

> Quasi non più veduta fatidica Cometa,
> Quasi fratel gemello di Castore, e Polluce
> Trar dall'ombra ti vide la variopinta luce.[12]
>
> (Chiari, *L'Uomo*, II. L.)

The achievement of Newton is emphasised by Chiari in terms of light imagery "fatidica cometa", "Castor e Polluce", "vario pintaluce"; the same light imagery prevails in the lines contrasting passion and reason:

> La passion ci sprona; ma lo fa spesso in vano;
> Ragion sta sempre in trono colle bilancie in mano.
> L'uomo senza passioni fora ozioso, e lento;
> Senza ragion sarebbe il moto suo violento.
> Sarebbe un fior campestre infra mill'altri nato
> Per verdeggiar, per crescere, e infracidir sul prato.
> Saria un vapor notturno, che striscia in cielo, e splende;
> E da se stesso ammorzasi come da se si accende.[13]
>
> (Chiari, *L'Uomo*, II. LXXX).

The subject is that of Pope's original, yet the emphasis here is on light and personification. Chiari appears however to lean poetically in the direction of passion, allowing the man to be dominated by emotional poetic expression in terms of a flower and a nocturnal vapour capable of self-annihilation. Reason is allocated one dignified line in which Chiari succeeds in capturing her traditional personification:

> Ragion sta sempre in trono colle bilancie in mano.

The necessary combination of reason and emotion is forcefully brought out, with man struggling in a sea of emotion guided by reason, the compass:

> L'uomo è sempre un Nocchiero nel veleggiar più lento,
> Quando portar non lasciasi a discrezion del vento.
> La ragione è la bussola, ma la ragion può solo
> Gir in balia del vento, senza smarrire il polo.
> Combattean gl'elementi nel primo Caos profondo
> E pur da 'lor contrasti ha sussistenza il Mondo.
> Colla ragion combattono le passioni ancora,
> Ma senza'il lor contrasto l'uom non sussiste un'ora.[14]
>
> (Chiari, *L'Uomo*, II. CL.)

Pope's forcefullness is the result of brevity in such passages: Chiari succeeds in conveying sustained movement with expressions such as "veleggiar più lento", "gir in balia del vento", "senza smarrire il polo". Stability in terms of contrast is provided by the juxtaposition of the verb "sussistere" and the concept of contrast indicated in turn by "contrasti," "combattono" and "contrasto". It is in passages such as this that the Venetian writer reveals an ability to present a familiar passage in such a manner that the reader both recognises it, and finds in it a new appeal to the imagination, as a result of the development of Pope's imagery.

Often Pope's English appears almost dull in comparison to Chiari's lines which evoke the world of nature.

> Sarebbe un fior campestre infra mill'altri nato
> Per verdeggiar, per crescere e infracidir sul prato.

Pope's touch at this point is heavier:

> Fix'd like a plant on his peculiar spot,
> To draw nutrition, propagate and rot.
> (Pope, *An Essay on Man,* II. 63-64).

It cannot be claimed that Chiari translates Pope, neither however does he distort him. It would appear that he enjoyed giving poetic life to the English poet's views on Man and indeed, often with a shift of emphasis. An interesting example of this are Chiari's lines on vice and humanity. In Pope's *Essay on Man* Vice itself is the subject, while in the Italian under consideration it is towards man and humanity that attention is directed:

> Misera umanità! alla ragione ne chiedi,
> Che tocca a lei distinguere ciò, che da te non vedi;
> Un mostro tale è il vizio, che s'egli agli occhi tui
> Si tragga il vel soltanto, deve tremar di lui.
> Pur lo guardi sì spesso, e sì vicin gli stai
> Che pria non ti dispiace, indi ti piace assai.[15]
> (Chiari, *L'Uomo,* II, CC.L).

> Vice is a monster of so frightful mien,
> As to be hated, needs but to be seen,
> Yet seen too oft, familiar with her face,
> We first endure, then pity, then embrace.
> (Pope, *An Essay on Man,* II. 217-220).

It can be observed that at this point, as in the case of the passage
beginning "Ah speranza, speranza" (I.CL.), Chiari cannot avoid an expression of self-involvement with the cares of humanity, and avoids
the air of superiority assumed by Pope in his attitude to Man and
Mankind, resulting in the English poet's self-distancing from the
other members of the human race.

Sufficient examples have been given, I believe, to demonstrate
that Chiari's work takes its inspiration from Pope, that he follows the
order and structure of the *Essay on Man*, that he writes in the heroic
couplet, and that he relies on his own imaginative creativity in order
to give a further poetic dimension to Pope's works. One basic difference between the two, however, is that Chiari stresses Man, Mankind
and humanity throughout, as is seen for example in the passage
dealing with vice. I therefore disagree with Giuseppe Baretti in his
statement that the Venetian poet mistakes a line from Pope for a
title. I believe Chiari intended the line "The proper study of mankind
is man", as the subject of his own work, illustrating at the same time
his own interpretation of the Epistle.

A reader can, however, I believe, be pardoned for believing
L'Uomo to be a translation of Pope, particularly when one bears in
mind the fact that Chiari, without competent English, was obliged to
read Pope in translation. One must also agree that Chiari sets out to
claim that a work of the nature of *L'Uomo*, in imitation of classical
writers, provides the greatest attempt to instruct about the world. He
takes a critical and corrective view of Pope, yet uses his work as the
foundation of his own. He dispenses with the English poet's theory
of matter, and claims the addition of Horatian and Ciceronian concepts. It is true to say that Chiari inserts some classical references;
this can be seen with reference to the following passage on happiness:

> Lieto si chiama il ricco, c'ha d'un millione il fondo.
> Lieto si chiama il povero, che non ha nulla al mondo.
> Canta in istrada il Cieco, per mendicar il pane;
> Va saltellando il zoppo, per far, che balli un cane,
> Fa da Eroe l'ubbriaco, il Pazzo da Catone:
> Nel suo cervello al Chimico par oro anche il carbone
> L'ignorante Arcifanfano decide al tavogliero
> Dell'Edipo di Sofocle, dell'Odissea d'Omero

266

Contro l'Opera altrui s'alza declama e scrive,
Perchè buone le dicono, egli le vuol cattive.[16]

The rich is happy in the plenty given,
The poor contents him with the care of Heaven.
See the blind beggar dance, the cripple sing,
The sot a hero, lunatic a king;
The starving chemist in his golden views
Supremely blest, the poet in his Muse.
(Pope, *An Essay on Man*, II. 1. 265-70).

Pietro Chiari, however, can in no way be regarded as original. Taking Pope's poem, he confers on it his own style, taste and approach. At times he verges on the melodramatic, demonstrating less control and discipline than Pope, but more personal involvement. Chiari directs his attention towards the individual with whom he closely identifies. Pope treats of beings, from whom he creates the impression of dissociation. Yet notwithstanding these minor differences, one is never under the impression that the Venetian writer has made the poem his own, it is the imitated which is constantly before our eyes rather than the imitator. In his next philosophic essay, which contains several references both to Pope's *Essay on Criticism* and *Essay on Man*, Chiari states that he no longer takes his point of departure from a single source, but from all philosophers. This, it can be gathered, does not make for coherence, or the disciplined development of thoughts, supplying further proof of a developing Italian fashion for a poetry of "ideas", without regard to sources, schools, or logical development. It once again proves the point that the "philosophic poem" could not be regarded as "pure philosophy", when deprived of its original forcefulness, precision and mastery of technique. In both translation and imitation, it merely bore witness to the absorption of Pope's poetry in an attempt to come to terms with being, behaviour, and the origin of ideas. In the introduction to *La filosofia per tutti* (Venice, 1956) Chiari states:

Altro motivo non ebbi di scrivere queste Lettere Scientifiche sopra il Buon Uso della Ragione, fuorché quello di ben impiegare le ore mie meno occupate del giorno, e dare agli amici miei, cui sono dirette delle nuove testimonianze di gratitudine, che sempre più degno mi rendano dalla loro benevolenza. Se nelle altre mie Lettere Filosofiche sopra l'Uomo ho voluto cammi-

267

nare sull'orme di M. Pope, in queste m'è parso meglio di profittare dei Filosofi tutti, senza seguitarne nessuno. Tanto non mi vergogno d'imitare, e ricopiare il buono dove lo trovo, che ho preso l'espediente di aggiungere a queste mie Lettere annotazioni copiose, che palesi facessero anche alle persone meno versate gli eruditi miei latrocinj.[17]

The second work referred to as an imitation of the *Essay on Man* is Cerretti's poem *La filosofia morale*. Both Graf and Natali refer to it as an imitation of Pope. Viglione[18] identifies Cerretti's poem with Epistle II of the *Essay on Man*:

A noi importa l'epistola – quella che tratta della natura e dello stato dell'uomo considerato in sè stesso, come individuo del quale si esaminano le forze e le debolezze, il senso e la ragione, i vizi e le virtù, le passioni e i fini relativi distribuiti utilmente alle varie classi sociali a tutti gli individui nelle diverse età della loro vita.[19]

Viglione declares that Part II of Cerretti's poem is so closely modelled on the English poet's work that unnecessary explanations are not called for: "Quindi comincia la seconda parte dell'ode, dove si legge un passo che è aperta imitazione di quello su riferito del Pope, così aperta che non c'e bisogno di inframezzar i bei versi con note e osservazioni inopportune."[20] Cerretti's poem is in fact short, composed of a mere eighty-six lines, the first forty of which are directed to his friend Auronte, inviting him to breathe the fresh air of nature:

Dal facil colle ove innalzò Fiorano
A la vergin di Iesse are votive,
Mesto sol perché troppo a te lontano,
Candido Auronte, il tuo fedel ti scrive.[21]
(I. 1-4).

The concluding lines of the poem are also addressed to Auronte, providing a structural unity and allowing the philosophic discourse to occupy the central section:

Tu stesso, Auronte, allor perdona al pianto,
Tributo estremo de l'affetto antico:
Assai sarà che di viola e acanto
L'ossa tu sparga de l'estinto amico.[22]
(1. 83-86).

Consideration of the opening and closing passage indicates a work of classical proportions, depicting the harmony and beauty of nature, and its ability to effect a periphering force on thoughts. Nature inspires philosophic pondering and stimulates an outcry against pride which is personified by science:

> Altri studi, altre cure, altro diletto
> Grave filosofia qui al core infonde,
> Non quella che, sprezzando umano affetto,
> Superba il capo oltre le nubi asconde.[23]
>   (1. 41-44).

Man aspires to imitate the deity, and demonstrate his own ignorance in comparison to the all wise:

> Emulo de gli Dei l'arduo intelletto
> Contempli pur dietro i suoi voli ardito
> A l'infallibil calcolo soggetto
> L'ampio giro de'mondi e l'infinito.
> Ma poi che pro? squarci il suo vel natura,
> Vincasi del destin l'ordine immoto;
> Ricco d'inutil lume, in nebbia oscura
> Sarò poi sempre a me medesmo ignoro.[24]
>   (1. 49-56).

The above lines are obviously inspired by Pope. Viglione underlines an essential difference: "L'intonazione ironica delle prime quartine è l'eco fedelissimo di quella del *Saggio sull'uomo*, con la sola differenza che mentre il Pope mira a fiaccar la superbia dell'uomo che in se incarna la scienza, il Cerretti punge l'orgoglio della scienza stessa.[25] This fact accounts for Cerretti's emphasis on the abstract. Pope is concerned with movement and action. In the Italian poet's lines the following terms predominate: "arduo intelletto", "l'infallibil calcolo", "l'ampio giro", "l'infinito", "l'ordine immoto". Pope's passage is made up of a series of imperatives denoting physical gestures:

> Go, wondrous creature! mount where Science guides,
> Go measure earth, weigh air, and state the tides,
> Instruct the planets in what orbs to run,
> Correct old Time, and regulate the Sun;
> Go soar with Plato to th'empyreal sphere,
> To the first good, first perfect and first fair;
> Or tread the mazy round his followers trod,

And quitting sense call imitating God;
As Eastern priests in giddy circles run
And turn their heads to imitate the Sun,
Go, teach Eternal Wisdom how to rule —
Then drop into thyself, and be a fool!
(Pope, *An Essay on Man*, II. 1. 19-30).

Cerretti's address to the Goddess corresponds to Pope's lines referring to action stimulated by modesty; unlike Pope, however, the Italian poet states the importance of service to the fatherland, and has recourse to classical reference in order to demonstrate virtue:

Te dunque seguo, o dea, te che comprendi
Tutte de l'uom le passioni ascose,
E a la patria e a se stesso utile il rendi
Ne'vari offici ove la sorte il pose.[26]
      (1. 57-60).

Ma, se a me stesso e a le tue leggi infido,
Dando al sentier de la virtù le spalle,
Levar di me dovessi infame grido
Del vizio seduttor battendo il calle;[27]
      (1. 81-84).

Pope emphasises the smallness and poverty of man's ability, the power of passion and vice in the form of self-love. Behind his lines there is greater force of expression since he relies on imperatives, as he demonstrates the exposure of human weakness:

Trace Science then, with modesty thy guide;
First strip off all her equipage of pride;
Deduct but what is vanity or dress,
Or learning's luxury, or idleness;
Or tricks to show the stretch of human brain,
Mere curious pleasure, or ingenious pain;
Expurge the whole or lop the excrescent parts
Of all our vices have created arts;
Then see how little the remaining sum,
Which served the past, and must the time to come!
(Pope, *An Essay on Man*, II, 43-52).

It is my belief that Pope's influence is here apparent but cannot be over-rated. On account of its brevity, it does not qualify for the description of "imitation" of Pope. One must merely state that it is

based on Pope's philosophy as expressed in the *Essay on Man*, Epistle
II. It would be true to say that Cerretti has condensed Pope's
thoughts, Viglione's conclusion is as follows: "Il Cerretti finisce per
rivolgersi a meditare sui problemi di filosofia morale, sui principi,
della natura umana, sulle passioni ascose, sul vizio e sulla virtù, sui
destini assegnati alle umane creature nelle varie loro condizioni".[28]
Though a philosophical piece, it is clothed in Neo-Classic devices
providing a heaviness of style not identified with the quoted passages.

As Epistle II has been seen as the source of inspiration for Cerretti's *La filosofia morale*, so it can be argued is Epistle III the guiding light behind Rezzonico's *Origine delle idee*, in which the role of Nature, Time and Matter, in the creation of the universe is demonstrated: "Nell'incompiuta *Origine delle idee* (1778) secondo la sua stessa dichiarzione, il Rezzonico "epilogò" la dottrina di Bonnet, Condillac e Robinet, dimostrando, attraverso la rappresentazione della famosa statua condillachiana che tutte le idee hanno origine dei sensi".[29] The following passage, I believe, bears a close resemblance to Epistle III, 1. 7-25 of the *Essay on Man*:

> Da che spiegò l'eterno Fabbro in enti
> Le nude forme, che in bell'ordin poste
> Ridean in cima al creator pensiero,
> Ei delle cose le materie prime
> Alla Natura vigile commise
> Segretamente, e per compagno il Tempo,
> Re delle ore volanti, a lei fu dato
> A far palese la bell'arte e il mondo
> Del pensoso silenzio in sen cresciuto.
> L'antica delle cose arbitra e madre
> Al gran lavor di multiformi obbietti,
> Tacita intende, e di si fine trame
> Empiendo va la variata tela,
> Che invan lincea pupilla immobilmente
> Sul finissimo ordito esplora, e segue
> Il lieve striscio della spola artefice.[30]
>   (1. 70-85).

The creation of the world by the Deity, following a precise order and
aided by Nature, Time and Matter, is the subject of the above lines,

as is the intellectualisation of the act. Thus, from the subject point of view it can be said to resemble the following:

> Look round our world; behold the chain of love,
> Combining all below and all above.
> See plastic Nature working to this end,
> The single atoms each to other tend.
> Attract, attracted to, the next in place
> Form'd and impell'd its neighbour to embrace.
> See Matter next, with various life endured,
> Press to one centre still the general good.
> (Pope *An Essay on Man*
> III, 7-14).

This is the poetry of ideas and contemplation which flourished during the mid-eighteenth century. If one were to ponder on the extent of the influence of Pope's *An Essay on Man* solely on actual creative writing, the impression would be negative. However, considering his popularity, and the esteem in which he was held during that period, and regarding the translations of the *Essay on Man* as both works directed towards the enrichment of Italian literature, and the diffusion of the fame and philosophic poetry of the man, one can regard the few imitations as further proof of his recognition in the field of poetic philosophic writing.

In Italy, unlike Germany, the incongruity of poetry and philosophy was not probed or realised to any great extent by critics of Pope, whose approach to his philosophical reasoning does not advance beyond generalisation. In 1755 in Germany, Moses Mendelssohn and Gotthold Lessing published an ironic brochure *Pope ein Metaphysiker*. They argued that the poet and philosopher had both distinct functions to perform; that they ordered thought differently, and that the poet could borrow his philosophy from any system without reference to the rigorous consistency of a metaphysical system. The same concept, that a poet does not offend seriously when he uses language less precise than that appropriate to theology had already been put forward by the Abbe Prevost. "On lui pardonne ensuite quelques dereglemens d'imagination, avec d'autant plus d'indulgence, qu'il n'en est souvent que plus admirable lorsquil semble perdre ainsi le pouvoir de la regler. Bonne ou mauvaise, cette excuse a plus de force pour Mr. Pope, que pour un autre."[31] It is not surprising that Pope's *Essay on Man* should have aroused such interest on the continent. It is surprising that his work, however, be the subject of such philosophical discussion and disputes in France, Germany and Switzerland. There is no evidence that such involved analysis of the content of the *Essay* took place in eighteenth-century Italy. In the world of arcadian detachment, and enlightened reflection, he remained the most perfect of poets, the diffuser of rhymed ideas, whose work, to quote Lorenzo Pignotti, would have been even more acceptable if it leaned less heavily on metaphysics.

Notes to Chapter II

1 Pietro Chiari, *L 'Uomo* (Venice, 1758) p. vi.
2 Donald B. Clark, "The Italian Fame of Alexander Pope", art. cit., p. 359.
3 G. Natali, *Il Settecento*, op.cit., pp. 588-93.
4 Pietro Chiari, *L 'Uomo*, op.cit., p. xi.
5 Ibid.
6 Ibid. p. 3.
7 Ibid. p. 4.
8 Ibid. p. 5.
9 Ibid. p. 6.
10 Ibid. p. 7.
11 Ibid. p. 11.
12 Ibid. p. 17-18.
13 Ibid. p. 19.
14 Ibid. p. 22.
15 Ibid. p. 26.
16 Ibid. p. 27.
17 Pietro Chiari, *La filosofia per tutti, Lettere Scientifiche in versi martelliani sopra il buon uso della ragione* (Venice, 1956). It is noted that while *L 'Uomo* was written in 1755, the Venetian edition did not appear until 1758. Donald B. Clark in his article "The Italian Fame of Alexander Pope", p. 359 states the date of *La filosofia per tutti* as 1763. The edition which I consulted in the Biblioteca Marciana, Venice was published in Venice in 1756.
18 Viglione, "Una nota all'influsso di A. Pope sulla letteratura italiana", in *A. Vittoria Cian, i suoi scolari dell'università di Pisa*, op.cit., pp. 134-9.
19 Ibid. p. 135.
20 Ibid. p. 138.
21 Luigi Cerretti, *La filosofia morale*, in *Lirici del secolo XVIII* (Milan, 1877), p. 178.
22 Ibid. pp. 179-80.
23 Ibid. p. 178.
24 Ibid. p. 179.
25 Viglione, "Una nota all'influsso di A. Pope sulla letteratura italiana", op.cit., pp. 138-9.
26 Luigi Cerretti, *La filosofia morale*, in *Lirici del Secolo XVIII*, op.cit., p. 179.
27 Ibid.
28 Viglione, "Una nota all'influsso di A. Pope sulla letteratura italiana", op.cit., p. 139.
29 Giuseppe Savoca, "I poemetti di C. Castone della Torre di Rezzonico", in

Il Settecento, op.cit., p. 617.

30 C. Castone della Torre di Rezzonico (1778).

31 *Le pour et contre*, 16 (1738), 238-9.

CHAPTER III

The eighteenth-century Italian poetry of "monacazione"

It can be argued that Pope's *Eloisa to Abelard* represents a portrait of individual unhappiness, and a philosophic assessment of the plight of a protagonist in a given situation. It is a dramatic and yet an organised illustration of contrasts, and provides historical evidence of attitudes to reason, as the sole dominating force. In eighteenth-century Italy it represented the approaching pre-Romantic era, and demonstrated the significance of the emotions as a superhuman force.

By the beginning of the nineteenth century the work had been translated by Antonio Conti, the Abate Greatti, Pietro Chiari and Gian-Vincenzo Benini. That the creative imagination of Italian poets was kindled is borne out by the works of Giuseppe Ceroni – *Lettere di sei donne ai loro sposi ed amanti* (Milan, 1808), Francesco Gianni, *Eloisa ed Abelardo*, argomento con metro obbligato proposto dal Chiari, S.P. Prof. D. Antonio Lambertenghi in *Poesie di Francesco Gianni* (Florence, 1827); and Ippolito Pindemonte *Lettera di una monaca a Federico IV re di Danimarca*. However, most relevant to this discussion is the contribution of Antonio Conti, who demonstrates a vast knowledge of English life and letters. His treatment of the epistolary genre is extremely relevant to a study of eighteenth-century Italian literature and an understanding of Conti the poet and priest.

The figure of Eloisa, is derived from the medieval heroine, and the entire poem derives from the correspondence of Eloisa and Abelard. "Deriving as it does from the letters of Eloisa and Abelard it is almost inevitably bound up with the epistolary tradition."[1] But as Henry Pettit continues to point out "it may be that Eloisa is neither pure epistle nor pure drama."[2] In other words, the work is marked by conflict, ambiguity and dualism with regard to structure, tone and themes. It is therefore not a totally medieval projection of a twelfth century dilemma. Eloisa in the hands of Pope is "a highly intelligent

277

English woman of the early eighteenth century, devoted to love at a time when the God of love was being materialised into a mere physical passion."[3] Such a fusion of themes naturally demands a high degree of technical ability. The rigid outlines and often rhetorical tone can have a stifling effect on the pathos within the poem. Such pathos, I believe, becomes the point of departure for translators and Italian readers, who see the subject of the poem as one of inner conflict.

With regard to a philosophical interpretation of the principle themes of the work, *Eloisa to Abelard* could be at first consideration a conflict between the active and contemplative way of life, but one must stress that for Eloisa the active life has been ruled out for all time, and the entire struggle is within the realm of the contemplative life. This comes to light in the contrast between suppression and expression, reason and passion, stone and sentiment, and poetically these opposites are expressed in terms of light and shade. One finds heat, light, emotion and colour as expressive of one metaphorical group, and cold, darkness and death representative of the other. We witness, then, an "emotionally liberated" figure, whose expressions are indicative of both fulfilment and frustration.

It is my belief that Pope's *Eloisa to Abelard* brings together religion and poetry at a time when both were recovering from the seventeenth-century dismissal of both as mere frivolities: "Bacon, Locke and Newton, while wishing to preserve religion (though inevitably it was trimmed to natural theology and deism), had no use and little respect for poetry."[4] Thomas Sprat, of the Royal Society, believed that science should supply the subject matter and inspiration of poetry, while reason be its ruling force, and Locke, in his "Essay Concerning Human Understanding", had advocated the application of a scientific method to the study of the human mind. While Locke and Newton were to dominate eighteenth-century thought, there came about a reaction on the part of the man of letters who set out to oppose science. The style of the philosophic transactions of the Royal Society left much to be desired: "In attempting a factual plainness and conciseness, many writers had avoided the old sins of eloquence only to fall into the opposite errors of a stilted barrenness, a conventional phraseology, and a low poverty of expression".[5]

Pope's *Dunciad* is in fact an attack on the all-time low level of expression of would-be letterati of the time, whom he identifies with the crawling creatures on which they carried out experiments. Swift's *Gulliver's Travels* demonstrates how closely its author followed the scientific treatises of his day. The Academy of Lagado in his novel, represents the ridicule of the aspirations and achievements of what were considered at the time great intellects. Swift and Pope, in keeping with the trends and theories of their time, applied a rational study to the mind of man and his entire being. *An Essay on Man* is an illustration of the study of man in the abstract. Pope, here, as has been seen, identifies with Newton's evidence for an orderly universal system. Yet Pope represents the triumphant revitalisation of poetry. This is particularly the case in *Eloisa to Abelard,* where reason vies with emotion, the passions are rationalised, calmed but not quenched, all within the poetic medium. In *Eloisa to Abelard* then, Pope combines and attempts to identify the Newtonian cultivation of order with Locke's scientific examination of human experience. In theory the final conclusion of the poem sees the logical and rationalistic acceptance by the protagonist of her situation, while in practice the emotional dimension has been given free play.

It cannot pass unnoticed that eighteenth-century critics of Pope were aware of the conflict between religion and love contained in the Epistle. It was, however, its pathos, tenderness and passionate outpouring of the self which appealed to most. It is clear that the "poetry of the senses" was both welcome and wallowed in, after a time of non-cultivation of the emotional. Writing in 1745, William Ayre with reference to *Eloisa to Abelard* stated: "There is a spirit of Tenderness, and a Delicacy of sentiment runs all through the letter; but the prodigious conflict, the War within, the difficulty of making Love give up to religious vows, and Impossibility of forgetting a first real Passion shine above all the rest." Joseph Warton, considered the Letter, along with *Windsor Forest* and *The Rape of the Lock*, the poems by which Pope would be most remembered, they, he felt, touched nature, and the heart: "This Epistle is, on the whole, one of the most highly finished and certainly the most interesting of the pieces of our author; and together with the *Elegy to the Memory of an Unfortunate Lady* is the only insistance of the pathetic Pope has given us." Goldsmith was not merely aware of the face value of the poem, but had followed its success in other European countries. "It may be considered as superior to any thing in the epistolary way; and the many translations which have been made of it into the modern languages, are in some measure, a proof of this." Dr. Johnson was drawn to the poem as a result of its ability to strike the imagination and its confrontration of hope and resignation conferred a dignity to the atmosphere: "The mixture of religious hope and resignation gives an elevation and dignity to disappointed love, which images merely natural cannot bestow. The gloom of a convent strikes the imagination with far greater force than the solitude of a grove."

From the above quotations it would appear that pathos, delicacy of expression, emotional upheaval, and appeal to the imagination were the most outstanding features of Pope's *Eloisa to Abelard* for the eighteenth-century critical reader. Such themes however bring into question the entire nature and role of the emotions. Is the individual controlled entirely by reason, or in fact can the emotions take control of the individual? What is the extent of their control, and what is their relationship to the conscience in general, and to guilt feelings in particular? Is then *Eloisa to Abelard* an academic treatise in dramatic form, or love poetry of the highest quality. Perhaps Ada Prospero has such questions and possibilities in mind when she states: "Eloisa è veramente una grande poesia d'amore, ma l'amore che l'ha inspirata è l'amore della letteratura."[10] *Eloisa to Abelard* appeared in 1717, before the dilemma therein presented became a romantic theme "par excellence." Yet the poetic, and dramatic representation of the contemplative life was not something new to the Italian "letterato" of the time. The taking of final vows, and the withdrawal of the virgin from secular life had by this time become an occasion for poetic celebration. In the period of Arcadia the poetry of the cloister had become an accepted genre, a genre which with the passing of time becomes laden with artifice, containing elements of Petrarchism and Neo-Platonism, touches of wit and rococo refinement. Towards the end of the century, consideration is also given to the psychological battle raging within the mind of the individual, with the result that the entire tone and mood of the poetry verges on the Romantic. In other words, the excesses, refinements and contradictory aspects of the eighteenth century are reflected stylistically and thematically in this poetry, and the theological, philosophical and psychological aspect of the taking of vows is considered. Along with compositions to celebrate births, marriages and deaths, the sonnet or ode in praise of "Monacazione" is one of the most representative and popular themes of the day.

Eloisa to Abelard then represented a new dimension of this theme. It dramatically illustrates the combination of ardour and guilt, consummated and sublimated love. To the Italian reader it, I believe, must have appeared both touching and daring. Most important, however, it represented a genre known to Italy at the time, and with which Italians identified. It serves to illustrate how Alexander Pope was identified with eighteenth-century thought. Concepts regarding behaviour, good taste, and monastic life were all of prime consideration at the time, and came to life in "razionalismo-empiristico", "la poesia del buon gusto" and "poesia per monacazione". Therefore in studying, translating, and imitating Pope, Italian poets were merely probing, perfecting and developing germs of poetry and thought which had been undergoing significant changes in the course of the century. Poets known for their celebrations of religious professions include Eustachio Manfredi, Gianpietro Zanotti, Ferinand' Antonio Ghedini, Saverio Bettinelli, Onofrio Minzoni, Luigi Cerretti, Angelo Mazza and Giovanni Paradisi. Their poetry ranges from that of profound religious feeling, to that of wit and cynicism, from sincerity and spontaneity of approach to mere uninspired imitations, as will be seen in the following analysis of their work.[11]

One of the earliest and most sincere poets demanding our attention is Eustachio Manfredi (1674-1738). In his youth he studied law, letters and mathematics, and in 1699 was appointed Professor of Mathematics at the University of Bologna. A member of the Royal Academy of Paris, he was highly praised by Fontenelle. His "poesia di monacazione" is particularly deeply felt since his celebration of woman becomes an expression of his own feelings. In 1700, the lady loved by Manfredi entered a convent, and was immortalised in the canzone "Per la monaca Giulia Caterina Vanda": "È il tema di monacazione che, poi logorato da una consuetudine tutta esteriore, appare nel Manfredi fresco e nuovo, reso poetico da un sospiro di nostalgia per una fuga dal mondo di dolci figure giovanili, unito ad una sincera nota di ammirazione e di interesse per la vita spirituale che si svolgeva in quelle candide anime femminili."[12]

Another limpid composition in the same vein is "Per una monaca di casa Davia." One finds in these works a prime example of arcadian Petrarchism combined with the evocation of the world of the "Dolce stil nuovo". The role of light symbolism combined with Neo-Platonism is central to the entire canzone, and sight, light and truth are here poetically identified, and combine to convey the concept of immortal woman, who is yet ambiguously of this world. This is clearly perceived in the following lines from the canzone to Giulia Vanda:

> Donna, negli occhi vostri
> Tanto e sì chiara ardea
> Maravigliosa, altera luce onesta,
> Che agevolmente uom ravvisar potea
> Quanta parte di cielo in voi si chiude,
> E seco dir: non mortal cosa è questa.
> Ora si manifesta
> Quell'eccelsa virtude
> Nel bel consiglio che vi guida ai chiostri;
> Ma perchè i sensi nostri
> Son ciechi incontro al vero,
> Non lesse uman pensiero
> Ciò che dicean que'santi lumi accesi.
> Io gli vidi e gl'intesi,
> Mercè di chi innalzommi, e dirò cose
> Note a me solo, e al vulgo ignaro ascose.[13]
>
> (1. 1-16)

Here, one gathers that the philosophy of love of the "silnovisti" has been transformed to a totally personal experience in the case of Manfredi. The poem is: "Uno dei documenti poetici più notevoli, un'alta prova di stile animata da un sottile ma sincera ispirazione in una condizione di Arcadia più originalmente fedele al modello petrarchesco, più interiormente attenta all'analisi e all'espressione di sentimenti raffinati e sinceri".[14] The poem also contains a description of a debate between Nature and Love, as to how fitting garment can be designed for the ceremony. Manfredi then makes use of the late medieval Neo-Platonic concept in order to convey the immortality of the figure:

Tosto che vide il mondo
L'angelica sembianza
Ch'avea l'anima bella entro il bel velo:
Ecco, gridò, la gloria e la speranza
Dell'età nostra: ecco la bella imago
Sì lungamente meditata in cielo.[15]

(1. 33-8).

Qual io mi fessi allora,
Quando il leggiadro aspetto
Pien di sua luce agli occhi miei s'offrio,
Amor, tu'l sai, che il debile intelletto
Al piacer confortando, in lei mi festi
Veder ciò che vedem tu solo ed io,
E additasti al cor mio
In quai modi celesti
Costei l'alme solleva e le innamora:
Ma più d'Amore ancora
Ben voi stesse il sapete,
Luci beate e liete,
Ch'io vidi or sovra me volgendo altere
Guardar vostro potere,
Or di pietate in dolce atto far mostra,
Senza discender dalla gloria vostra.[16]

(1. 65-80).

The eyes and the veil are of course objects on which attention will be concentrated, but we find that in this poetry, the hair, scattered to the wind, will assume great importance. Its function is two-fold; the ceremony of the cutting of the hair is described in order to add pomp to the occasion: symbolically it presents the breaking with worldly preoccupations. Poetically however it performs various functions in that it allows the poet to vary from the sensual to the spiritual, and provides an object on which attention can be concentrated, as will be seen in the poem "Per monaca" by Giampietro Zanotti. Another work of importance, Pope's *The Rape of the Lock* will demonstrate the cutting of hair for a different purpose, while the lock itself will become symbolic of an entire society, civilisation, and later, in the near grotesque terms of Vittorelli, an entire world. In his sonnet IX, Manfredi refers briefly to the hair, symbolic of a life renounced: "Su la soglia d'un chiostro ogni ornamento/Sparso, e gli ostri, e le gemme al suol vedrai/ E il bel crin d'oro se ne porta il vento". It is written for a nun, and reveals a fusion of Dantesque and Petrarchan influence. The entire mood of the poem is reminiscent of Dante in the *Vita nuova*: ladies move pensively with slow steps, their faces full of compassion, and eyes full of tears. The personification of beauty and honesty does not accompany them any longer. *Her* light is extinguished:

> Vergini, che pensose a lenti passi
> Da grande ufficio e pio tornar mostrate,
> Dipinta avendo in volto la pietade
> E più ne gli occhi lagrimosi e bassi,
> Dov'è colei, che fra tutt'altre stassi
> Quasi sol di bellezza e d'onestate,
> Al cui chiaro splendor l'alme ben nate
> Tutte scopron le vie d'onde al ciel vassi?
> Rispondon quelle; Ah non sperar più mai
> Fra noi vederla! Oggi il bel lume è spento
> Al mondo, che per lei fu lieto assai.
> Su la soglia d'un chiostro ogni ornamento
> Sparso, e gli ostri e le gemme al suol vedrai;
> E il bel crin d'oro se ne porta il vento.[17]

The influence of Dante *Vita nuova* XX11 is obvious.[18] Manfredi's lady is identified with light, which is extinguished with her renunciation of the world. Despite the many borrowings from both Dante and Petrarch,[19] Manfredi's poem bears a touch of originality: the lady has not been the victim of physical death, but has withdrawn from the world. She has carried her light within, and left the symbols of wealth and artificial light on the threshold of the convent. Thus Manfredi succeeds in combining the visual and atmospheric aura of death and lamentation, with the concept of a new life symbolised by a pure light, as opposed to that created by the glitter of social ornamentation. This "poesia di monacazione" represents the survival of Beatrice and Laura in the eighteenth century, not by way of mere imitations of the sonnets of Dante and Petrarch, but by conferring on the symbolic creature a new function. As a symbol of a new life she enters the social conventions of the eighteenth century.

Giampietro Zanotti (1674-1765) was defined by Bettinelli as one of the "celebri bolognesi." Others included Ghedini, the Marchese Orsi, Ferdinando Antonio Campeggi and Pier Jacopo Martelli. Though

284

born in Paris, he spent a great part of his life in Bologna, where he died in 1765. His poem "Per monaca" reveals a lightness of touch and witty disposition, but there is little religious feeling in the work, and when he returns to the medieval concept of the nun as the bride of Christ, the lack of both sincerity and inspiration is apparent. The poem opens with the following lines:

> Venticel dall'ali aurate,
> Saldo tienlo quel bel crine;
> Guarda ben dalle rapine
> Quelle fila sî pregiate.
> Là t'ascondi fra quei tanti
> Rami, e taci.
> Sai che i venti tutti quanti
> Son rapaci.[20]
>
> (1. 1-8).

The visual aspect of the hair occupies the main section of the poem. Its movement, sound within leaves, and light generated from the object dominates. One is aware of poetic life being transferred from the individual to the object, and the poetry verges on the decadent. The lock becomes symbolic of the relationship between Heaven and Earth, and there is the allustion to the lock of Berenice:

> Gonfi e accesi nelle gote,
> Ecco poi venirne mille;
> E dai vanni escon faville,
> Mentre il sole li percote.
> Chi gli ha persi e chi gli ha azzurri,
> Altri biondi,
> E fan mille bei susurri
> Tra le frondi.
> E la chioma va dispersa,
> Che d'ogni altra portò il vanto;
> Nè fu vaga quella tanto,
> Ch'ora in begli astri è conversa;
> Della sua non fa l'Aurora
> Paragone, Che si piacque e piace ancora
> A Titone.[21]
>
> (1. 25-40)

The remaining lines, while representing a crystallised classicism, display lifelessness, and detachment of emotions:

E vorran saper qual bella
Ninfa ornar sî belle chiome;
Chiederanno quale è il nome
Dell'ignota Verginella:[22]

(1. 65-8)

Ha un amante, ha un suo diletto
A cui vive intatta e pura,
Ch'è ben tal che l'assecura
Dall'altrui lascivo affetto.[23]

(1. 105-8)

At this stage in its development, the poetry of "monacazione" contains little emotional involvement, love is referred to without the slightest hint of sensuality, and sensitivity and finesse are directed towards technique, as opposed to the feelings of a girl in question. Later in the poetry of Mazza and Cerretti the personal and individual reactions of the protagonist will be displayed. Nevertheless the poetry contains a refinement and a delicacy which reveal Zanotti's poetic gifts. Although the line "venticel dall'ali aurate" conveys frivolity and lightness, the tone becomes personal in the following lines and verges on the conversational: "Guarda ben dalle rapine;" "La t'ascondi fra quei tanti/Rami". The further description of the hair involves piling on of imagery: Zanotti's fluency as a poet is apparent with the use of "Gonfi", "mille", "faville"; the latter term introduces light imagery and variation of colour, while sight is then transformed to sound: "E fan mille bei susurri tra le frondi." With mythological allusion the poetic contrivance is complete.

It can be said that the poem begins on a personal note where the movement of the hair and wind convey lightness. The tone then becomes more stilted with the introduction of sight, colour sound and classical mythology. It enters the world of contrived classicism with the poetic miniature of the nymph wishing to adorn herself with the lock. "Ha un amante, ha un suo diletto" appears to take the form of the naturalness of the opening, but it serves to introduce the concept of the bride of Christ. Thus there is the fusion of lightness and seriousness of concept, while the over-riding impression is one of a poetic game.

If religious fervour is completely absent in Zanotti's poem, the same cannot be said for the work of Ferdinand'Antonio Ghedini (1784-1767). A close friend of Eustachio Manfredi: "che ne conosceva profondamente le belle qualità morali e intellettuali, procacciò che fosse nominato professore di umane lettere nel collegio Sinibaldi, e in questo ufficio durò fino al 1767 che morì."[24] His sonnet "Alla signora Maria Riva che nell'anno 1719 vestì l'abito religioso de'Santi Bernardino e Marta in Bologna" is a deeply felt piece of religious expression which takes the form of a dialogue in which the words of the nun are of the most basic simplicity, and without the slightest trace of an assumed poetic diction. Their placement within the sonnet further highlights the poet's message:

> Ferma: ove vai? Di questo chiuso esiglio
> Ahi quante indarno penitenza vinse!
> Fiero, chi verginella a tal costrinse,
> O gliel permise, o ne le diè consiglio!—
> Taci: al fuggir, come al miglior m'appiglio
> Io per me stessa; a ciò nissun m'astrinse;
> O se a qui rinserrarmi altri mi spinse,
> Fu Gesù, con cui solo io mi consiglio.—
> Ah dentro tane ognora i rei serpenti
> Stien chiusi, e in celle fiere belve e crude,
> Non le cose leggiadre ed innocenti.
> Dunque il vizio perchè non si rinchiude?
> Cessi o d'errar tal mostro infra le genti,
> O da lui fugga e ne scampi virtude.[25]

The sonnet is noteworthy for, in addition to its simplicity, the contrasting themes of freedom and compulsion, free choice of vocation, and enforced imprisonment. This is brought out by the choice of verbs placed in the mouth of the interrogator: "costrinse", "permise", "diè consiglio". One notes a softening of the tone, with the firmest verb coming first. The nun's discourse is also developed by means of verbs denoting strength of will, and action: "fuggir", "astrinse"; "rinserrarmi", "spinse". The final climax of her words is achieved with "Fu Gesù, con cui solo io mi consiglio." Further contrast is achieved by the evocation of the "enclosed" world, and the "world outside", and the consideration of the isolation of virtue.

Contrasts of a different nature are apparent in "Per Monaca Cappuccina in Venezia" of the "anti-arcadico" Saverio Bettinelli, (1718-1808). Bettinelli, who had written of Pope as the most perfect of poets, without defects, provides a poem with a detached opening after the manner of sixteenth-century Classicism:

> Muse, l'altera e bella
> Città che 'l mar circonda,
> Oggi a cantar m'appella
> Una leggiadra e bionda,
> Vergin, ma cruda tanto,
> Che d'ognun sorda è al pianto.[26]
> (1. 1-6)

The contrast between the life rejected, and that embraced is referred to in terms of dress and sound:

> Gli splendidi ornamenti,
> Le ricche vesti aurate,
> I coturni lucenti
> In Parnaso lasciate,
> E i giochi, i risi, i vezzi,
> Troppo a garrire avvezzi.
> In umil gonnellette
> Venitevi raccolte;
> Delle vostre selvette
> Più solitarie e folte
> L'abitator soltanto
> Silenzio abbiate a canto.[27]
> (1. 13-24)

The City of Venice is visually presented, and also seen as an active force calling on the poet to celebrate the "monacazione". The vocabulary conveys an individual resembling the icy Renaissance nymph, for example, Silvia in Tasso's *Aminta*: she is "altera e bella"; "leggiadra e bionda", but "cruda tanto". Bettinelli, later employs his gift of evocation to illustrate the glitter of social life: "splendidi ornamenti", "ricche vesti aurate"; "coturni lucenti", are chosen to dazzle while the climax of social activity conveys a medieval atmosphere: "E i giochi, i risi, i vezzi/Troppo a garire avvezzi." Humility is conveyed by diminutives such as "gonnellete", "selvette".

The artificiality yields however to sensitivity with the reference to love, and the girl's family. Here is indicated a side of the girl's personality, ignored up to this time. Here one witnesses an understanding on the part of the Jesuit poet, of the human sensations and emotions of the individual, which are not eliminated with the taking of vows:

> Non rammentate mai
> Amor dinanzi a lei,
> Se non volete i rai
> Turbar degli occhi bei,
> E il viso a poco a poco
> Vederla far di foco.[28]
>
> (1. 25-30)

> Non le lodate il viso,
> Le guance porporine,
> Il cenno, il guardo, il riso;
> Non le lodate il crine.
> Ahi! lo vedrete in breve
> Preda d'un aura lieve.[29]
>
> (1. 37-42)

To this point our demonstrations of style and quotations of the "poesia di monacazione" reveal a world deeply seated in Classicism, with Greek and Roman models, as well as heavy leaning on Dante and Petrarch. Classicism, Petrarchism and, Neo-Platonism are the guiding forces of this genre, which at times yield chiselled images of refined beauty, but which are seldom a sincere expression of the occasion. In fact one could state that this poetry is particularly representative of Arcadia, described in *La frusta letteraria:* 'fantasia parte di piombo parte di legno' del Crescimbeni, gli 'smascolinati sonettini', dello Zappi 'pargoletti piccinini, tutti pieni di amorini'.[30]

Manfredi, as has been seen, uses the eyes as symbols of light and virtue, and also as a mode of conveying lamentation and pathos. The nun is Beatrice, not leaving the world through physical death, but by the identification of her will with that of the Creator. He leans heavily on medieval philosophy, bringing a seriousness of intention to his poetry. Zanotti sees the same scene in a much lighter vein, while Ghedini, by means of a clearer adoperation of verbs, brings out the renunciation aspect of the choice of the religious life. Interesting from our point of view is the fact that even within the cult of the "poesia di monacazione" the symbolism of the lock, and of the hair, is all important. As regards symbolic significance, and, as an object of decorum, it is central to the poetry.

The poem "Il chiostro" by Luigi Cerretti, (1738-1808)[31] is, however, of primary significance as it represents a new depth of feeling and understanding. Cerretti, who in "La filosofia morale" imitated Pope's *Essay on Man*, is the first to recognise an internal battle raging within the protagonist, and refers also to the subjugation of her will to the will of a superior being. Historically this poem marks an important step on the path towards the evocation of the figure of Eloisa, and the internal drama later reproduced by Conti, Ceroni, and Pindemonte. Cerretti dares ask if the girl really knows where she is going, thereby introducing the concept of knowledge of destiny, and control of the passions:

> Or, poi che il fato a la crostumia riva
> Ch'oggi i tuoi fasti onora
> Guida i miei versi ancora,
> Dimmi, o diletta al ciel vergin, che schiva
> Tanto le umane affezioni aborri,
> Sai tu ben quel che lasci e dove corri?[32]
>
> (1. 37-42)

Cerretti, in his poem, distinguishes between the usual veiled language used on such occasions, and the reality of the individual choice. In his reference to truth, he also indicates the theological concept of religious vows: the identification of the will of the person in question with the will of God, the free sacrifice of the will, made with the will itself:

> Ah! pria che quel tuo crin preda de'venti
> Cada reciso al suolo,
> Odi un momento solo,
> Odi i non lusinghier liberi accenti,
> Che provocato al suon de l'aurea lira
> Insolit'estro a le mie labbra inspira.
> Io non t'adombro il ver. Scabra inaccessa
> È la via che tu imprendi;
> E se poggiar contendi.
> Pugnar ti converrà contro te stessa;
> Nè basterà, per far tuo spirto invitto,

Una vittoria sola, un sol conflitto.[33]
(1. 42-53)

Cerretti stresses that the life will be made up of battles against the senses, and a continual need to dominate the self. The intellectual aspect is conveyed by the use of the words "voglie", "comando", "mente", "domar". Here the nun is seen as actively subduing the raging passions and emotions, and she emerges, for the first time, as one voluntarily following her chosen course in life:

Negar tue voglie, ed a l'altrui comando
Serva far la tua mente;
A la stagione algente
Nel silenzio comun vegliar pregando;
E dopo molte aver preghiere sparte
Impallidir su meditate carte;
Frenar l'ire rubelli; attorte funi
Cingar sott'aspre lane,
E le voglie profane
Con frequenti domar pianti e digiuni:
Fuggir lievi piacer, scherzi innocenti;
A le labbra talor negar gli accenti:[34]
(1. 55-66)

This modern approach yields in the second half of the poem to a more typically arcadian contrast between the simple and sophisticated life, between nature and artifice, and the life-style of Fille and the protagonist of the poem. The message of the work is contained in the fact that Fille is not at peace with herself, nor is she mistress of her own destiny. At this point a covert reference to freedom, and the importance of being the arbitor of one's own destiny is touched upon:

Pur crederai? Fille, che par sì lieta,
Da le sue pompe è oppressa:
Arbitra di sè stessa
Non è, sè il vuol: tiranno uso lo vieta:
Prepotente ei la segue in ogni loco,
E vegliar la condanna al ballo, al gioco.[35]
(1. 103-8)

Cerretti has succeeded in combining within a traditional form, truth and reality with regard to the religious life, a theological aspect of vow-taking expressed in lines of a refined rococo style. The poem ends on a note of peace, with the traditional reference to the embrace of the eternal bridegroom. More important, however, is the fact that the psychological implications of choice are touched upon, and that the individual and her mind are placed to the fore. The concept of self-sacrifice is all important in the consideration of the development of the poetry of the individual. Cerretti's nun is "vittima volontaria", one who willingly puts her will at the service of the will of another: "Negar tue voglie ed a l'altrui comando/Serva far la tua mente." The result is a form of self-torment and self-realisation taking the form of a battle of the wits: "Pugna ti converrà contro te stessa" — there will be a conflict and victory. The concept of domination of the emotions, by the self or by the collective views of others is also touched upon. The society lady is dominated by society and its usages. She is forced to take part in social life: "Arbitra di se stessa/Non è, se il vuole, tiranno uso lo vieta." Cerretti's poem then, is primarily an exposition of the human will, the concept of freedom, and the portrayal of a being who in keeping with Dante's Piccarda, in *Paradiso III* has chosen to serve. Cerretti, given his cultural background,[36] must have been conscious of the impact of this work since it represents an artistic fusion of "l'Arcadia razionalistica e sensista".

Another poet noteworthy for his consideration of the mind and intellect of the nun, is Angelo Mazza, better known for his translations of the St. Cecilia Odes by Dryden and Pope, and his cultivation of beauty, order and harmony in poetic compositions such as "La musica e Santa Cecilia"; "L'aura armonica"; "Bellezza armonica ideale"; "Musica direttrice del costume"; "Musica ministra della religione"; "La melodia". He is, in the words of Benini: "insofferente di argomenti volgari e contrasanti con la sua tematica dell'armonia.[37] Mazza (1741-1817) points towards the Neo-Classicism of Monti and Foscolo, in that the pursuit of harmony reveals itself as the principle theme of the majority of his works. The intrinsic order of the universe is verbally expressed with reference to the musical form. He can thus be regarded as one soaked in the spirit of the early "Settecento", singing the praises of systematic order, yet harmoniously uniting this ordered world to that of new Classicism, freely and joyously expressed. Perhaps he is best defined as one who, along with Rezzonico, was capable of uniting the various stylistic and thematic elements of the century.

The celebration of the taking of the veil however, together with the cutting of the hair, occupied much of Mazza's attention, as can be seen when one turns one's attention to the sonnets "Per monaca"; "Per monaca il cui padre passava a seconde nozze"; "Uso dei sensi"; "Estasi religiosa"; "Le recision dei capelli". In consideration of these poems, one becomes aware that Mazza's gift lies in musically reproducing themes, concepts and lines of other poets, and identifying them with the central message of his own poem. One is aware of the direct borrowing from Dante in "Per monaca", and from Petrarch in "Estasi religiosa". As in *Inferno* V where the word "Amor" and its repetition carries the poetry to an emotional crescendo, so also is the case in "Per monaca", where it becomes the poet's source of inspiration:

> Te colser le infallibili saette
> Onde sue prove il divo amar corona;
> Amor che a nullo amato amor perdona
> Una te volle de le sue dilette.
> Per ricovrarti fra le poche elette,
> Con voce che ne l'anima risuona,
> Amor, che non divide amor, ti sprona
> Dal padre, che pensoso in sè ristette.
> Misero padre! Vedovato e solo
> Ultima del tuo sangue unica speme
> Costei ti lascia, e te'n disdice il duolo:
> Sacra colomba che sospira e geme
> L'aerea torre, e le fuggenti 'l suolo
> Penne distende per le vie supreme.[38]

Mazza succeeds in creating harmony of expression by giving movement to thoughts and aspirations. It is largely a poem of abstractions, which are fused so skillfully as to avoid the creation of an effect of emptiness or hollowness. "Amor", the protagonist, creates the "infallibil saette" which take the form of thoughts in the mind of the young girl: "Con voce che ne l'anima risuona/Amor, che non divide amor, ti sprona." The effect of such thoughts in turn cause her father to withdraw into himself — "pensoso in sè ristette". The final image is of the dove of peace spreading his wings towards the upper sphere, symbolic of a higher state — "le vie supreme".

One has the impression that Mazza is more interested in the linguistic possibilities offered by a subject than in the subject itself. "La recision dei capelli" is most striking for its light imagery and symbolism, hair representing sensual passion and sacrifice, introducing classical mythology, and ending on a religious note, on which the return of the hair represents the resurrection of the body. In other words, emotional experience, mythology and Christian doctrine are brought together by means of the symbols and images evoked by the hair of the title. Religious fervour, one feels, is not the guiding force behind the poem:

> Il bel tuo crine, ove legato ed arso
> Molti cuor giovinetti Amore avrebbe,
> Spirto divin poi che 'l raccolse e l'ebbe
> Mostro là sua già tronco e a i venti sparso;
> Da lui che di mercè non fu mai scarso
> A quanti 'l mondo e sue mal'arti increbbe,
> Nel balen d'un sorriso un fulgor bebbe,
> Che sembrò novell'astro in cielo apparso.
> Ed or, vergin, più vivo arde che il trino
> Giuramento ti annoda al tuo desio,
> Augure stella del tuo bel destino:
> E 'l vedrai, rivestita il vel natio,
> Colà nel giorno che non ha mattino
> Tornarti in fronte e sfavillar di Dio.[39]

Here Mazza focuses on the hair, and identifies it with linguistic brilliance and splendour. The hair identified with light, a purveyor of love, once shorn becomes a star — the virgin's guiding star which symbolises her ardour and religious devotion. The light symbolism in the sonnet exists on three levels — firstly as a natural crowning glory "legato ed arso"; secondly as a "novell'astro in cielo apparso", where the reader's imagination succeeds in visualising the image, and finally transcending time, it will more shine on the forehead of the virgin for all eternity. Through the object — the hair and its symbolic conversion to light, Mazza succeeds in uniting Heaven and earth, converting space to time, closing with a reference to eternity. Here he proves his ability as also in the case of "Per monaca" to convert abstractions to musical images. He possesses "vigoria di pensiero unita a corto fervore di fantasia, e che sappia, specialmente nelle molte sue odi intorno alle cause, alle varie manifestazioni e agli effetti dell'armonia musicale, dar forma poetica ai concetti astratti del platonismo".[40] It is my belief that this comment can be applied to the two poems already discussed. Entirely successful when focusing on a poetic object, Mazza is equally in control when creating a poetry taking its point of departure from an abstraction. The contemplative mind of the nun is the subject of "Estasi religiosa, which takes its opening line from Canzone XVII of Petrarch: "Di pensier in pensier la mente suole/Ratta levarsi da'cognati obbietti/Al sommo, ond'ella è imago, eterno sole,/Che di sè le fa specchio, uno in tre aspetti". A definition of Mazza's poetry is not easy to effect, given that many elements of "Settecento" civilisation go to constitute his style. In *Preromanticismo italiano* Binni refers to his: "Strano platonismo sensistico" and states that: "Suoi temi di poesia non più puramente scientifica si avvertirà anzitutto un atteggiamento di meditazione complessa, non riducibile all'illuministica descrizione di congegni anche mentali".[41] In consideration of Binni's view of Mazza's "platonismo sensistico", I believe that the definition is apt, although he does not provide examples. I believe that the poet takes his point of departure from a subject which strongly appeals to the senses — for example music, the effect of which he attempts to objectively assess in abstract terms. In the case of the poetry of "monacazione", the subject is religious ardour carried to its final conclusion, and expressed in terms of meditation and contemplation. His topics and themes could indeed be referred to generally, as the effect of beauty and love on the mind. His role in the history of the poetry of the cloister is interesting, in that he at once distances himself from his subject, in order to provide its abstraction rather than its detailed projection.

The poetry of "monacazione" of both Onofrio Minzoni and Giovanni Paradisi conforms to "poetry of occasion", revealing exalted tone, classical references and little personal involvement, but once again it serves to illustrate both the solemnity of the occasion and the literary genre of which it constituted a part. The sonnet "Per monaca" by Onofrio Minzoni (1735-1817) is set in a totally artificial framework provided by a cloud, which parts in order to reveal a dramatisation of a religious reception. Honesty and Beauty, in the role of hand-maidens, richly adorned, perform symbolic gestures. The former cuts the hair, so establishing a break with the past; the latter places the veil on the virgin's head, so pointing to her future way of life. The poetic contrivance is clear at the opening and conclusion of the poem. The cloud performs the function of a theatrical curtain, which parts and departs, having exposed the scene. The sonnet can be divided into three parts; the invocation to the cloud, itself threefold; the symbolic reception ceremony; the kiss of union, and departure of the cloud. The central section of the sonnet provides the vision of three women, and one bears in mind that the entire scene represents the taking of three vows.

The invocation to the cloud opens the sonnet and prepares for the splendour of the temple alongside the secrecy of the ceremony taking place therein:

> Apriti, o nube, che lambendo vai
> Del sacro tempio le superbe volte;
> Tu, che gran cose tieni in grembo accolte;
> Candidissima nube, apriti omai.
> (1. 1-4)

The rhetorical address to the cloud is followed by the dramatic revelation of two creatures, at once active and contemplative. Their actions are both light and majestic. "Onestade" can be interpreted as purity, it combines with "Beltà" to personify love and grace, which are symbolised by roses and celestial light. It is divine love which is indicated, the roses having been gathered in heaven. Their appearance is made possible by the parting of the cloud:

> S'apre: e con atti maestosi e gai
> N'escon due donne in ricchi manti avvolte:
> Ambe di rose in paradiso colte,
> Ambe son cinte di celesti rai.
> (1. 5-8)

The first two lines above quoted convey movement and activity. Each begins with a verb, the second of which introduces adjectives "maestosi" and "gai", which indicate both lightness and grandeur. Colour and splendour are indirectly suggested, and the action continues with the descent of Onestate in order to perform the ritual of the cutting of the hair. It is noteworthy that only at this point in the sonnet is the nun of the title referred to:

> Scende Onestate, ed a colei sen vola,
> Che appiè dell'ara innamorata geme,
> E con forbice d'oro il crin le invola.
> Beltà le coglie in un purpureo velo:

While the role of virgin is passive, her short expression of choice is stated in words bordering on the sensual: "colei" — "Che appiè dell'ara innamorata geme". Her entire disposition is made clear in a single line: — humility, adoration and, uncontained emotion. The contract is sealed with a kiss, and the visual and poetic unity of the sonnet is complete with the departure of the cloud.

> Indi si bacia l'una e l'altra insieme;
> Torna alla nube, e colla nube al cielo.

This sonnet, dedicated to a nun, reveals yet another aspect of the "poesia per monacazione". Here the entire reception ceremony and emotion governing the girl's choice of life is presented in terms of a poetic tableau, not unlike that of a vision poem. Yet here all is silence, and the theatrical effect is achieved by the poetic evocation of dramatic, symbolic gestures. The role of the poet is here noteworthy, as the total effect is obtained by his imaginative, and poetic evocation of the scene in terms of dramatic narrative. On the other hand "Per monaca" by Giovanni Paradisi is devoid of all inventiveness and originality. Poetic contrivance obscures the subject matter of the material.

The social and literary importance of this poetry is clear. It was practiced by "Arcadia" and "anti-Arcadia" alike, and it is true to say that the many literary conventions of the movement were represented: ". . .anche il Petrarchismo fu piuttosto un atteggiamento esteriore, una presa di posizione polemica ed anche un modo di mettersi al sicuro rifugiandosi dietro la bandiera del poeta più raffinato, più corretto, più elegante e, soprattutto moralmente ineccepibile".[42] All of the above mentioned adjectives can be applied to this poetry of the cloister. It is not surprising therefore that Pope's *Eloisa to Abelard* could have been regarded as a work opening a new dimension of a subject which had for the most part lacked the stamp of individual emotions. Both Cerretti and Mazza represent an important aspect of the genre as they reveal themselves, as Neo-Classic poets.

For an understanding of Pope's work, Pietro Chiari relied heavily on French translations, and his version of *Eloisa to Abelard* is from Colardeau. His attitude to the ceremony of the cutting of the hair is lighthearted as is that of Zanotti. One can detect in Chiari's poem "Per una monaca" a fusion of the mock-heroic spirit of *The Rape of the Lock* and the serious approach more in keeping with the world of the cloister. For Chiari the hair is seen as a symbol of society, frivolity and worldly passions. But the lock is not merely a static lifeless object. Even the shorn hair will grow again, and develop as do thoughts and emotions. In the hands of Chiari[43] the emotions are seen as forces capable of being suppressed but not extinguished. The battle of the emotions is referred to early in the poem:

> Deh, non ti faccia pallida
> Di quell'acciaro il lampo:
> Deh, abbandonar non facciati
> Di tue vittorie il campo.
> Quel taglio sol ti annunzia
> Il fin della tua guerra
> E ti da il ciel ricovero
> Mentre lo cerchi in terra.[44]
> (1. 9-16)

> Ma 'l rubello esercito
> Si dissipa, si strugge:
> Vittorioso è Davide,
> Perde Assalon, e fugge.[45]
> (1. 21-41)

The importance of choice and will, symbolised by the stroke sheering the locks is underlined, and the description and significance of the act is followed up by the reference to the vows such a choice embodies:

> Che fai meschino? adopera
> L'acciar, che in man ti splende:
> Tronca quel crin: da un taglio
> La vita tua dipende:

Fuggi, che già ti seguono
Quel crin non vale il sangue. . .
Ma non m'ascolta ed eccolo
Sotto a tre lance esangue.[46]

(1. 33-40)

Lance, da cui difenderti
Ubbidienza or tenta,
E castità inviolabile,
E povertà contenta.[47]

(1. 45-8)

Continuity is conveyed with the reference to the growth of the hair and the recurrence of passion:

Ma un guardo, ah! non ti rubino
Quelle troncate chiome:
Un guardo sol può toglierti
Di libertà anche il nome.
Purtroppo al sol rinascere
D'un crespo crine, e biondo
Forza, e vigor ripigliando
Le passion del mondo.[48]

(1. 57-64)

Ah colle chiome celebri
Di cui tu giri altero.
Lasciasti in sen di Dalila
Tutto il vigor premiero.[49]

(1. 69-72)

Un guardo adesso, O vergine
A quelle alte rovine:
Un altro guardo intrepido
Al tuo reciso crine.
Guai se con lui rinascono
Del mondo i rei pensieri!
Trovar la morte io veggioti
Dove la vita or speri.[50]

(1. 89-96)

With reference to the poetry discussed, it is clear that religious vows, withdrawal from the world and the cutting of the hair provided a favourite subject for poetic celebration. The manner in which it was celebrated varied from the Petrarchism of Manfredi, the wittiness of

Zanotti, the detached classicism of Bettinelli, to the pre-Romanticism of Cerretti and Mazza. Minzoni's "Per monaca" deserves special attention, as it provides a memorable tableau depicting the religious reception. I have considered the "Per una monaca" by Chiari last because I believe it embodies the spirit of two of Pope's poems, *Eloisa to Abelard* and *The Rape of the Lock*. This also serves to illustrate that hair, with its religious, social, and romantic significance was becoming a more and more popular poetic subject, which as a result of the influence of Pope's *The Rape of the Lock*, finds its most colourful mock-heroic expression in the works of Vittorelli and Pignotti.

In Alexander Pope's *Eloisa to Abelard*, there was revealed a dramatisation of the world of the cloister, a world dear to the poets of Arcadia. The popularity of Pope, and the translations of his work, serve as a stimulus to the Italians to arrive at a higher level of refinement within the genre already their own, but which stood to gain in profundity of theme and stylistic presentation, as a result of Pope's work, read in the original and in translation, and in its imitation.

Notes to Chapter III

1 Henry Pettit, "Pope's Eloisa to Abelard – an Interpretation" in *Essential Articles for the Study of Alexander Pope* (Connecticut, 1968), p. 324.
2 Ibid.
3 Ibid. p. 323-4.
4 C.J. Horne "Literature and Science" in *From Dryden to Johnson* edited by Boris Ford. (Middlesex, 1957), Penguin ed. p. 189.
5 Ibid. p. 196.
6 William Ayre, *Memoirs of the Life and Writings of Alexander Pope Esg.* (1745) 2 Vols. 1. p. 71.
7 Joseph Warton, "An Essay on the Writings and Genius of Pope" (1756).
8 Oliver Goldsmith, *The Beauties of English poetry* (1767). See *Collected Works of Oliver Goldsmith*, ed. A. Friedman (1966). V. 319 1. 321-3.
9 Samuel Johnson, from the "Life of Pope" in *Lives of the most eminent English poets.* (2nd ed.) (1783) pp. 28-9.
10 A. Prospero, *Il poeta del razioncismo settecentesco, Alessandro Pope* (Bari, 1943) p. 27.
11 For a selection of the works of the poets in question see: *Lirici del Secolo XVIII* (Milan, 1877); *Lirici del settecento* (Milan, 1959).
12 *Storia della letteratura italiana*, VI *Il Settecento* (Milan, 1970), p. 378. See also in the same volume "Il petrarchismo arcadico e la poesia del Manfredi", pp. 375-82.
13 Eustachio Manfredi, "Canzone a Giulia Vanda", in *Lirici del Secolo XVIII* (Milan, 1877), p. 13-14.
14 *Storia della letteratura italiana* VI, *Il Settecento*, op.cit., p. 382. For a further consideration of Arcadian Petrarchism See W. Binni, *L'Arcadia e il Metastasio*, (Florence, 1963).
15 *Lirico del Secolo XVIII*, op.cit., p. 14.
16 Ibid. p. 15.
17 *Lirici del Settecento*, op.cit., pp. 85-6.
18 Dante, *Vita Nuova*, xxii,

"Voi che portate la sembianza umile
con gli occhi bassi mostrando dolore
onde venite che'il vostro colore
par divenuto de pietà simile
Vedeste voi nostra donna gentile?" (1. 1-5).

19 Petrarca, Rime, CCXXII, 1-4.

Liete e pensose, accompagnate e sole,
donne, che ragionando, ite per via
ove è la vita, ove la morte mia?
Perchè non è con voi com'ella sole?

20 *Lirici del Secolo XVIII*, op.cit., p. 21.
21 Ibid. pp. 21-22.
22 Ibid. p. 22
23 Ibid. p. 23.
24 *Lirici del secolo XVIII*, op.cit., p. 25.
25 Ibid. p. 29.
26 Ibid. p. 77.
27 Ibid.
28 Ibid.
29 Ibid. p. 78.
30 Mario Fubini, *Dal Muratori al Baretti* (Bari, 1968), p. 273.
31 See Francesco Solario, *Studio critico su Luigi Cerretti e le sue opere* (Florence, 1902).
32 *Lirici del Secolo XVIII*, op.cit., p. 175.
33 Ibid.
34 Ibid. pp. 175-6.
35 Ibid. pp. 176-7.
36 Luigi Cerretti, see note 2 to section 11 chapter V.
37 Walter Binni, *Classicismo e Neoclassicismo* (Florence, 1963), p. 180.
38 *Lirici del Secolo XVIII*, op.cit., p. 227.
39 Ibid. p. 229.
40 V. Rossi, *Storia della letteratura italiana* (Milan, 1930), III, p. 173.
41 W. Binni, *Preromanticismo italiano* (Rome, 1974) p. 235.
42 E. Sala di Felice in *Petrarca in arcadia* (Palermo, 1959). p. 125.
43 See *Saggio di varie poesie del Sig. Abate Pietro Chiari* (Venice, 1758).
44 Ibid. p. 88.
45 Ibid. pp. 88-9.
46 Ibid. p. 89.
47 Ibid.
48 Ibid. p. 90.
49 Ibid.
50 Ibid.

CHAPTER IV

The contribution of Antonio Conti
to the poetry of the cloister

Although Antonio Conti translated Pope's *Eloisa to Abelard* as early as 1717, it did not appear in print until 1760, when it was published along with Andrea Bonducci's translations of *The Rape of the Lock* and Thomson's poem in praise of Newton. The translation of "Eloisa" came during his second stay in England, at a time when he was consolidating his literary interests. Previously he had been occupied with scientific and philosophical studies and had been acquainted with Malebranche, Fontenelle and Leibnitz. I believe that the subject of Pope's poem appealed to him on various counts. From the philosophical point of view Eloisa, or Elisa as he calls her, must have appeared a free thinker, one rejecting limitations and all institutions imposing personal restrictions. She is also one living in a state of "pious fraud" who questions not only her emotions but also her motives, one who is determined to reject sin and embrace sensual pleasure.

Conti must also have been drawn to the poem as a result of personal experience.[1] Born in 1677, he became a priest about 1699, but he retired from active service in order to devote himself to science. George Dorris believed that the translation of *Eloisa to Abelard* followed that of *The Rape of the Lock*, for here Conti is in far greater control of his material. Of course the subject may have been more congenial to his talents, and certainly to the Italian tradition, for the genre of heroic epistles stems from Ovid.[2] This, added to the fact that the "poesia di monacazione" was part of the Italian eighteenth-century tradition, can certainly serve as an explanation for Conti's being drawn to the subject to such an extent as to compose a letter from Abelard, which follows the same linguistic style as his translation of Pope's original.

There remains to consider if Conti felt drawn to this poem as a result of its subject, or as a result of the opportunity it offered him to refine Italian poetic language. Giovanna Gronda is convinced that the answer lies in the second option — though content cannot be separated from form, the work of translation stimulates him: "A precisare il suo gusto poetico, a ricercare nell'ambito della lingua letteraria italiana i mezzi stilistici atti ad esprimere la pateticità del linguaggio popiano.[3] Thus Gronda believes that Conti is drawn to this work as a result of its linguistic possibilities, a fact which she feels is borne out by the similarities of style between the translation and Conti's own poetic composition *Lettera di Abelardo ad Elisa*. This theory is in fact supported by the fact that on his arrival in London, in 1715, he immediately set to work on translating the *Essay on Poetry* by the Duke of Buckingham. That he attempted forming his own objective assessment of poetry is clear when one refers to Conti's translation of the opening lines:

> Poesia non è, se dritto miro,
> Che musica, pittura ed eloquenza
> Leggiadramente temperate, in guisa
> Che accoppiano col nuovo il grande e 'l bello.
> Le imagini e i color dàlle pittura,
> Eloquenza gl'affetti e le ragioni,
> Musica il chiaro e dolce suon del metro:
> Tutte e tre d'imitar con grazia e forza
> Di non finta natura i parti santi.[4]

His desire to reform literature was the subject of his letters from England to Muratori, and in his preface to *The Rape of the Lock* he reveals his admiration for poets of other nations who search for new inspiration: "Io spero ch'egli vi procurerà un'ora di lettura piacevole e vi scoprirà nel tempo stesso che, mentre alcuni de'nostri poeti impiegano gli studi loro a far centoni del Petrarca, le altre nazioni aspirano a meritar il nome di poeta, ciò è d'artefice di cose nuove." With regard then to *Eloisa to Abelard*, Conti found a work based on the heroic epistle, which presented a philosophical exposition of a human problem, versed in language of untold precision and subtlety. Surprisingly, Conti in his translation plays down the philosophical element of the original; duplicity of emotion and the subtlety of Pope in his presentation of the subject is avoided. Instead we find that he provides a series of dramatic outbursts. The poem becomes a demonstration of free expression as willed by the protagonist, who reacts rather than contemplates. We have then a pre-Romantic heroine who even in 1760 represented a new breed of protagonist. The achievement is even more remarkable when one considers that such a figure was conceived as early as 1717. At that time Conti was by means of translation creating poetry which dealt with themes, and expressed imagery which later in the second half of the "Settecento" came to be associated with Cerreti and Mazza. When the "poesia di monacazione" was amongst the favourite themes of poets such as Eustachio Manfredi, Giampietro Zanotti and Ferdinand'Antonio Ghedini, Conti was producing lines straight from the heart of a convincing human being. The fact however that Conti plays down on duplicity with regard to the love theme leaves the letter without the basic contrast and conflict stressed by Pope. The latter's work is of such complexity and profundity, that it can be analysed on various levels. Not so in the case of Conti's, which becomes an expression of the individual. "Conti emphasises the romantic element, while underplaying the "gothic", softening the outlines, and stressing the pathos. The effect is more pathetic, but perhaps less moving because weaker in contrast.[5]

In excluding the first eight lines of Pope's poem, Conti in his translation dispenses with the dreary, medieval atmosphere, and also the woman's search for her motives for indulging in sensual pleasures. So the contrast between contemplation and self-gratification is not made, and the first lines take the form of a dramatic outburst tempered with emotional restraint:

> Abelardo, Abelardo, oh quanto amore
> Al tuo nome dolcissimo e diletto
> Sento svegliarsi e intenerirmi il core![6]

Since Conti did not translate the three interrogatives at lines 4, 5, 6, further emotional and dramatic weight is added at lines 10, 11, 14 of the translation:

> Arrestati mia man, ma come? Ah come!
> Ecco già scritto? Cancellate in fretta,
> Cancellate o miei pianti il caro nome.
> Povera Elisa! e qual follia t'alletta,
> A che val tu pianga e che sospiri?
> La mano scrive ciò che il cor le detta.[7]

O write it not, my hand – the name appears
Already written – wash it out, my tears!
In vain lost Eloisa weeps and prays,
Her heart still dictates, and her hand obeys.
(Pope, *Eloisa to Abelard*, 1. 13-16)

In the first sixteen lines of the translation, Conti's riorientation of the work is established. Rather than an examination of the motives and nature of the woman's emotions, the tone assumes the qualities of the dramatic theatre. One witnesses his first attempts at reformation of Italian literature, the fruit of his long sojourns out of Italy.[8] He wished to restore to poetry both immediacy, spontaneity and dramatic credibility. At a time when poets and translators sought to introduce into Italy and perfect metaphysical poetry, Conti was seeking to project beauty of sound and image, and above all demonstrate something of the human condition as it appears to the individual, as opposed to the philosopher. Therefore Conti, drawn to the *Eloisa to Abelard* for philosophical, personal and linguistic motives, creates in translation a dramatic "tour-de-force", which, it must also be remembered, is no mean linguistic achievement. It could also be argued that Conti, at a time when Metastasio was combining Cartesian philosophy and elegance of expression, was laying the foundations for the operatic libretti of the nineteenth century, in particular those of Cammerano and Romani.[9]

Conti's attitude to literature, and poetry in particular, had been greatly influenced by his stay in France and Italy. He soon abandoned Cartesian philosophy in its most absolute form, and identified more and more with the dualism of Bayle. His approach to poetry is well illustrated in the following words:

qual flagello della poesia è un geometra. . .
pareva altresì strano, che si volesse ridur la poesia,
che tutta dipende dal senso e dalle immaginazioni,
all'idee della metafisica; e si giudicasse de'versi,
come il Cartesio aveva giudicato dall'estensione
spogliata delle qualità sensibili de'corpi, cioè a dire
nulla badando alle relazioni de'sensi. . .
(*Giulio Cesare*, Faenza, 1726, p. 60)

The creation of human qualities and beautiful images are placed before all else in this translation. Eloisa is portrayed in terms of dramatic reaction. In the Italian version there is an outright rejection of God, and as the emotion heightens, Conti is inclined to give way to exaggeration.

Elisa's attitude to her own emotions is expressed in terms of dramatic opposites:

> Mi lagno del mio cor vile e codardo,
> Cangio voti ed affetti in un istante,
> Ora ardisco, or dispero or gelo, or ardo.[10]

> Now warm in love, now with'ring in my bloom
> Lost in a convent's solitary gloom.
> (Pope, *Eloisa to Abelard*, 1. 36-37)

It is interesting to compare Conti's lines published in 1760, to Da Ponte's in *Le nozze di Figaro* for Mozart 1786. Cherubino in the aria "Voi che sapete" asks for an explanation of the emotions which he feels, but fails to understand:

> Sento un affetto pien di desir
> Ch'ora è diletto, ch'ora è martir,
> Gelo, e poi sento l'alma avvampar,
> E in un momento torno a gelar.
> (Nozze di Figaro)

Despite suffering, Cherubino, like Elisa, takes pleasure in languish. While Elisa is very much a personification of the emotions and emotional conflict, one is not aware of the juxtaposition of active and passive within her character, but of the woman who totally identifies with her passion, and who proclaims ardour to be the expression of her will:

> Ah scrivi, scrivi tutto; i miei martiri
> Si congiungano a'tuoi: Pace non voglio,[11]

> Yet write, oh write me all, that I may join
> Griefs to thy grief, and echo sighs to thine.
> Nor foes nor fortune take this power away;
> And is my Abelard less kind than they?
> (Pope, *Eloisa to Abelard*, 1. 41-44)

The emphasis on the will is entirely Conti's. The verb "volere" is identified entirely with the emotions, thus illuminating any preconceived contrast between the mind and the flesh, the expressed and non-expressed. Dramatic tension is added with the use of possessives, and from the ideological point of view this following passage can be regarded as an anti-Cartesian plea in favour of emotional expression:

> Miei li spasimi son, miei son gli affanni,
> Mie le lagrime, mie: le chiede amore,
> E le chiede in vigor de'nostri danni.[12]

> Tears still are mine, and those I need not spare,
> Love but demands what else were shed in prayer;
> (Pope, *Eloisa to Abelard*, 1. 45-46)

> Amore è di se stesso il premio e il merto:
> Io non cercai che il titolo d'amata,
> O s'altro v'ha in amor nome più certo.[13]

> No! make me mistress to the man I love;
> If there be yet another name more free,
> More fond than mistress, make me that to thee!
> (Pope, *Eloisa to Abelard*, 1. 88-90)

Conti yields to exaggeration with the description of the bleeding lover:

> Come cangiossi! io veggio ancora il sangue
> Ch'esce spumando dalla piaga atroce;
> Ti veggio, sposo mio, pallido, esangue.[14]

> O barbaro, ti ferma, ed al mio seno
> Rivolgi il ferro; fu commun l'errore,
> Communi ancora le ferite sieno.
> Io vengo men; vergogna, ira, dolore,
> L'amara istoria eternamente taccia
> E il restante lo dica il mio rossore.[15]

> Alas, how changed! what sudden honours rise!
> A naked lover bound and bleeding lies!
> (Pope, *Eloisa to Abelard*, 1. 99-100)

> Barbarian, stay! that bloody stroke restrain!
> The crime was common, common be the pain.

> I can no more, by shame, by rage suppressed,
> Let tears, and burning blushes speak the rest.
> (Pope, *Eloisa to Abelard,* 1. 103-106)

Movement and action are above all conveyed in Conti's version; the blood spilled is given a dramatic action of its own; (il sangue/ch'esce spumando dalla piaga atroce;) the terms in which Elisa demands to share her lover's suffering are also delivered with authority (ti ferma, ed al mio seno/Rivolgi il ferro). Conti, under the weight of cares and suffering (Vergogna, ira, dolore) makes his heroine take faint (io vengo men.) The abstract nouns "shame" and "rage" of the original appear as contradictory emotions, conveying a complexity of feeling and disposition. These in Conti's version are replaced by "Vergogna", "ira", "dolore". The addition of the third noun "dolore" renders the expression far more free, and the result of a spontaneous outburst rather than that of a pre-conceived exposition of the state of mind of the protagonist. In fact the mind of the individual is relatively unimportant in this version. Conti is more concerned with the expression of her state rather than with the state itself.

The nun's profession and vow-taking is seen by Conti as the sacrifice of a victim on the altar. Pope uses the plural:

> Canst thou forget that sad, that solemn day,
> When victims at yon altar's foot we lay?
> (Pope, *Eloisa to Abelard,* 1. 108-9)

Conti uses the singular, making the isolation and dramatic significance of the occasion complete:

> Puoi tu scordar, quando agli altari in faccia
> Vittima fui condotta, e come avea
> Senza color la giovinetta faccia?[16]

The reaction of Heaven is in Pope expressed:

> Heaven scarce believed the conquest it survey'd,
> And saints with wonder heard the vows I made.
> (Pope, *Eloisa to Abelard,* 1. 113-114)

Conti's version is far more melodramatic:

> Il cielo ricusava il proprio acquisto,
> E con orrore udiano in Paradiso
> I voti miei gli Angioli, i Santi e Cristo.[17]

As has been made clear, Conti has concentrated on the forcefulness and authority of the protagonist, and her surroundings become a reflection of her own spirit. The "rugged rocks" become "marmi insanguinati" and the continued use of the letter "s" evokes lamentations and suffering in the silence:

> O marmi insanguinati, antri sonanti
> Di gemiti e flagelli, oh grotta algente,
> Oh sacri altari, oh simulacri santi.[18]

> Ye rugged rocks! which holy knees have worn;
> Ye grots and caverns shagg'd with horrid thorn!
> (Pope, *Eloisa to Abelard*, 1. 19-20)

Once again it must be stressed that in creating Elisa, Conti has given Italian literature its first romantic heroine. Little of the version *Elisa ad Abelardo* reflects the Italian literary climate of Conti's day — the forced Petrarchism, and the contrived elegance present in some of the poetry already discussed. Nevertheless one does find one example of the poet's attempt to recapture the delicacy and refinement of the "stilnovisti" with recourse to light imagery and symbolism:

> Un ti credeva dei beati Cori,
> Disceso in terra a rischiarar le menti
> Col lume degli angelici splendori.
> Come stella i tuoi guardi eran ridenti,
> Pien di celeste melodia il tuo canto,
> Pieni di sacra autorità gli accenti.[19]

> Thou know'st how guiltless first I met they flame,
> When love approach'd me under friendships name;
> My fancy foun'd thee of angelic kind,
> Some emanation of the'all-beauteous mind.
> Those smiling eyes, attemp'ring every ray,
> Shone sweetly lambent with celestial day.
> (Pope, *Eloisa to Abelard*, 1. 59-64)

In common with the "stilnovisti", Conti describes the lover in terms of one spreading intellectual light, come on earth in order to communicate beauty and truth in the form of love. At a further point in the poem there is another passage of light symbolism, not found in the original:

Ed io sposa di Dio. . .deh un raggio, un raggio,
Divino Spirto, del tuo lume infondi,
E raddirizza il mio torto viaggio.[20]

Ah, wretch! believed the spouse of God in vain,
confess'd within, the slave of love and man.
Assist me, Heaven!
(Pope, *Eloisa to Abelard*, 1. 177-79)

The above quoted Italian lines, together with the more contrived
references to monastic life, serve as a balance within the poem, and
slightly temper the high-powered effect created by the poetry of
ardour, heat, passion, symbolically represented by imagery of fire
and blood:

Per fuggire del mondo ogni periglio
Le verginelle in questo chiostro angusto
Per te incontraro voluntario esiglio.[21]

È semplice ma santo ogni lavoro,
E cantano al Signore inni di lode
Vergini caste in armonioso coro.[22]

From the false world in early youth they fled,
By thee to mountains, wilds, and deserts led.
(Pope, *Eloisa to Abelard*, 1. 131-2)

But such plain roofs as Piety could raise,
And only vocal with the Maker's praise.
(Pope, *Eloisa to Abelard*, 1. 139-40)

A perfect miniature of precision and taste is achieved in the lines
referring to the life of the nun. At this point Conti is nearest the
Italian poetry of "monacazione". Indeed it could be argued that the
basic conflict which comes to the fore in *Elisa ad Abelardo* is a stylistic rather than emotional one. The woman Elisa should have been,
and could have been, is expressed in conventional poetic language,
while the rebellious spirit explodes in a style which is a complete
break-away from the ordered and systematic approach to poetry of
Conti's own day. The following I believe to be a good example of
Conti's leaning on the detached classicism of Arcadia:

O felice la vergine innocente
Che cangia il mondo in solitaria cella,
E non altri che Dio respira e sente.
Ad ogni cenno ubbidiente ancella
A Dio si volge, e tutta in Lui si sface
Per soave desio l'anima bella.
Quando risplende la notturna face,
Con aurei sogni spiriti celesti
Crescon le sue delizie e la sua pace.
A lei l'anello, a lei le bianche vesti,
A lei le rose e le fragranze: a lei,
Divino Sposo. la corona appresti.
Cantan gli Angeli e i Santi i suoi trofei
Mentre la stringi all'impiagato seno,
E celebri castissimi imenei.
Per languore dolcissimo vien meno,
Là vagheggiando nell'eterno die —
Le tue bellezze e i tuoi secreti appieno.[23]

How happy is the blameless Vestal's lot!
The world forgetting, by the world forgot:
Eternal sunshine of the spotless mind!
Each prayer accepted, and each wish resign'd;
Labour and rest that equal periods keep;
"Obedient slumbers that can wake and weep";
Desires composed, affections ever even;
Tears that delight, and sighs that waft to Heaven.
Grace shines around her with serenest beams,
And whisp'ring angels prompt her golden dreams.
For her th'unfading Rose of Eden blooms,
And wings of Seraphs shed divine perfumes;
For her the spouse prepares the bridal ring,
For her white virgins hymeneals sing;
(Pope, *Eloisa to Abelard*, 1. 207-220)

Conti's translation of the passage appears a complete cameo in its own right, ranging from the quietness of the opening to a triumphant crescendo, before closing on a note of light languor. Conti's vocabulary conveys a world built of artifice (vergine innocente, solitaria cella, ubbidiente ancella). The simplicity and exaggerated humility of those lines contrasts with the blazing power of nature (quando risplende la notturna face), while the ceremony is described in terms of detached splendour.

312

Historically *Elisa ad Abelardo* must occupy an important position on account of its forcefulness of expression, and its linguistic emphasis on emotion and expressiveness. Most of all it takes its place as documentary evidence of Conti's desire to reform Italian poetry, to free it from all pre-conceived and lifeless conventions and convey a new truth, expressed in terms of beauty and harmony. Quite apart from its philosophic, linguistic and literary significance, however, "the *Lettera d'Eloisa ad Abelardo* is able to stand as a poem in its own right, and not just as a reflection of a greater work".[24]

That Antonio Conti had made the subject of the unhappy lovers very much his own is indeed evident, but full proof of his commitment to the poetic world of his own creation is arrived at only on reading Conti's own composition, discovered by Giovanna Gronda and reproduced in the *Versioni poetiche di Antonio Conti*.[25] "I due testi — traduzione e componimento originale — sono strettamente legati fra loro da corrispondenze testuali, formali e metriche, compongono una unità poetica e narrativa. . ."[26] Neither translation or original composition — *Lettera di Abelardo ad Elisa* is mentioned by Conti in his correspondence. It is not included in either the first or second volume of *Prose e poesie* which appeared in 1739, and 1756 respectively. It is true to say that both poems represent a departure from what came to be accepted as Conti's "usual style". It is thus not surprising that Foscolo, writing in 1812 to Jacopo Morelli, librarian of the Marciana stated: "benchè il Conti fosse poeta di merito, non mi pare tuttavia che avesse tanto calore d'anima e tanta armonia di verso; e dubito assai non quell'epistola (Elisa ad Abelardo), sia opera d'autore egregio, il quale o per iscrupolo di religione o per altro riguardo siasi tenuto celato".[27] The "calore d'anima" and "armonia di verso" is not demonstrated in Conti's translation of *The Rape of the Lock,* where the poet relies on Classicism, convention and expression in the reproduction of Pope's rococo masterpiece. Like Giovanna Gronda, I feel that the two letters, — translation and original — compliment each other.

The point has already been made that the most striking contrast within Conti's translation was a linguistic one, and that Pope's subtlety had been played down to a great extent. When one comes to consider Conti's composition in relation to his translation, one observes

313

that they constitute a contrast to each other. In the translation Conti abandoned the philosophical and replaced it with the psychological. Elisa in her emotional expression reveals a certain degree of fulfillment. Abelard, on the other hand, in the poem by Conti, demonstrates frustration. Elisa demonstrates her capacity for, and right to, self-expression. Hers is seen as a psychological fulfillment. Abelard experiences, on account of the violence to which he was subjected, frustration as a result of physical incapacity. Gronda believes that the two works represent the contrast between emotion, passion and reason: "A quanto di eccessivo era nella concitazione di Elisa, nel brusco stridore dei passaggi troppo repentini, si contrappone nei versi di Abelardo una monotona pacatezza, una irrigidita intenzionalità esortativa.[28] I do not feel, however, that it is correct to say that Abelard represents reason, as some of the emotional passages reveal a linguistic spirit very much akin to that of Elisa. The basic difference between the two protagonists is, I believe the taking of sensual pleasure in amorous memories, as opposed to the sexual frustration aroused by the mind's insistence on dwelling on such memories.

The similarities of tone in both works are striking, even on a first reading. The structural elements in common can be stressed also in that each opening passage takes the form of an address of one lover to the other, the central part of the poem is given over to the solitude of the suffering soul, and the conclusion foretells a final union of the dead lovers.

The similarities of expression and disposition are established from the opening of the poem by Conti:

> Elisa, Elisa, ahi qual tumulto e quale
> Interna agitazion l'anima amante
> In strane guise mi conturba e assale!
> (*Abelardo ad Elisa*. 1. 1-3)[29]

> Abelardo, Abelardo, oh quanto amore
> Al tuo nome dolcissimo e diletto
> Sento svegliarsi e intenerirmi il core!
> (*Elisa ad Abelardo* 1-3)

In line 2 'anima amante' replaces "dolcissimo e diletto;" in line 3 "conturba e assale" replaces "intenerirmi il core". But the spirit and

314

tone achieve the same effect: an emotional awakening brought about by the sight, sound and memory of the dear name.[30]

The first three lines are followed in both translation and poem with a reference by both protagonists to their wavering virtue:

> Virtù mia dove sei? Deh in questo istante
> Ritorna a me, ti poni in mezzo al core
> In minaccioso e rigido sembiante.[31]
> (*Abelardo ad Elisa* 1. 3-6)

> Abelardo, Abelardo, oh mia virtute
> Languida e vana, oh voglie ancor non dome,
> O dura eternitate, oh mia salute!
> (*Elisa ad Abelardo* 1. 7-9)

It is interesting to compare the reaction of each figure to its emotions and sensations, and the manner in which each expresses his desire to share the punishment for their wrongs:

> M'esce dagl'occhi d'umor caldo un fiume,
> Detesto i miei trasporti e i falli miei
> Mercé l'infuso a me divino lume.[32]
> (*Abelardo ad Elisa* 1. 43-45)

> Mi lagno del mio cuor vile e codardo,
> Cangio voti ed affetti in un istante,
> Ora ardisco, or dispero, or gelo, or ardo.
> (*Elisa ad Abelardo*. 1. 37-39)

> Se al par di me colpevole tu sei,
> T'acqueta al par di me se vuoi che un giorno
> T'acquisti in Ciel, se in terra ti perdei.
> Scordati quando teco fea soggiorno,
> Non rammentarmi le memorie corse,
> O ch'io di nuovo a vacillar io torno.
> Fiamma improvisa infino al cor mi corse
> Al sol pensarvi. . .ah! taci Elisa, taci:
> Le tua man, la tua penna assai trascorse.
> Perch'agli amplessi primi. . .ai primi baci. . .
> Cieca dalla passion tu mi richiami,
> Se di gioia per noi non son capaci?[33]
> (*Abelardo ad Elisa* 1. 46-57)

> Ah scrivi, scrivi tutto; i miei martiri
> Si congiungano a'tuoi: pace non voglio,

> Non voglio che far eco a'tuoi sospiri.
> Né la fortuna, né il nemico orgoglio
> Mi potranno rapir co'loro inganni
> O la mia tenerezza o il mio cordoglio.
> Miei li spasimi son, miei son gli affanni,
> Mie le lagrime, mie: le chiedo amore,
> E le chiedo in vigor de'nostri danni.
> Scrivere e lagrimar sino che more
> Resta solo ad Elisa, e questo fia
> L'alimento e il ristoro al suo dolore.
>
> *(Elisa ad Abelardo* 1. 43-54)

In reading and comparing the reactions of both figures, one can conclude that each despises their inability to overcome the senses, yet while Elisa finds relief in expression (Ah scrivi, scrivi tutto), Abelardo can only recall physical torment when past joys are recalled ("non rammentarmi le memorie corse"). It is, however, I believe for personal and physical motives that Abelard reacts in this way, rather than for any spiritual or religious conviction: this is revealed at the end of the passage: "ai primi baci/Cieca dalla passion tu mi richiami/ Se di gioia per noi non son capaci". This same fact was stressed early in Conti's poem:

> Vano è il desio, pur mi spaventa amore,
> Ché se la carne mia fu resa imbelle
> L'alma è capace ancor del primo ardore.[34]
>
> *(Abelardo ad Elisa* 1. 7-9)

Both translation and composition stress union in its conclusion. But while Elisa stresses a union of ashes, Abelardo strikes a more spiritual note:

> Tra tanto il cener tuo col mio sia misto
> Del Paracleto entro modesta tomba,
> E sul marmo si legga il caso tristo.
>
> *(Elisa ad Abelardo* 1. 349-51)

> Soffri, vinci te stessa, un dì felice
> Tu sarai meco, io teco in quel soggiorno
> Fra cui celeste fiamma non disdice.
>
> *(Abelardo ad Elisa* 1. 202-204)[35]

Giovanna Gronda believes that such similarities underline a "forced derivation" and a lack of spontaneous poetic inspiration on the part of Conti.[36] This is also her opinion with regard to his relying on Petrarchan convention: "Petrarcheschi sono i vagabondaggi di Abelardo per i boschi e le campagne in cerca di pace, petrarchesca l'assidua presenza del ricordo di Elisa. . . Si tratta ovviamente di un petrarchismo tutto di maniera di situazioni stereotipe più che di suggestioni poetiche." The Petrarchan passage in Conti's poem obviously takes its inspiration from lines 265-73 of the translation which evokes the image of Abelardo wandering in the company of nature, with Elisa following in his footsteps:

> Oh illusion! Affaticato e lasso
> Ti veggio errando in solitaria valle,
> Io dietro a te piangendo affretto il passo.
> Da spini e sterpi avviluppato è il calle,
> Lungi montagne eccelse e dirupate
> Offrono al sol le rovinose spalle.
> La più scoscesa ascendi e dietro guate
> S'io ti seguo, aggrappandomi alla balza;
> Io calco con orror le tue pedate.
> (*Elisa ad Abelardo* 1. 265-73)

Conti's passage reads as follows:

> Solitario tra i boschi io volgo il piede
> Per solevar tal volta il cor oppresso
> In cui dolce silenzio fa sua sede.
> Ma che non soffro? Il fier Satano appresso
> Insidioso mi viene in quell'istante
> E mi ricorda ogni amoroso eccesso.
> Se sotto l'ombra di frondose piante
> Adagio il fianco, egli tra foglia e foglia
> Mi fa vedere il tuo gentil sembiante.[37]
> (*Abelardo ad Elisa*, 1. 64-72)

In the translation, Elisa's presence is an imaginary one, while in the poem it is seen as a memory capable of creating a new reality for Abelard. For one it is the depiction of an ideal state, for the other a psychological guilt reaction. In both works it reveals adherence to poetic convention.

In comparing and contrasting both poems, one notes that the fundamental difference between the two works is the emphasis laid by Conti on the violent mutilation of Abelardo (1. 160-192). A detailed poetic account is provided in terms of sound, sight, reaction, and dramatic reconstruction of the scene. The sound of Abelard's pleas accompany the description of his being led away:

> L'empio veduto avresti accompagnato
> Da due ministri sanguinari e truci,
> Ciascun d'acciaro orribilmente armato.
> Ei si fecero a tergo, e in bieche luci
> In solitario luogo mi portaro;
> Io sclamo all'empio: "Dove mi conduci?"[38]
> (*Abelardo ad Elisa*, 1. 172-77)

There follows then a point to point description of the crime, alternating with thoughts directed towards Elisa. At this stage in the poem Conti arrives at a rare fusion of physical strength, expressing itself in violence and emotional ardour expressing love, demanding pity, and proclaiming the immortality of love. (1. 178-195). In each aspect of the above quoted variations, Conti proves highly successful. The visual element is clearly portrayed:

> Insiem l'un l'altro braccio mi legaro,
> Poi mi stesero a terra, e avidamente
> Le fredde membra a un punto denudaro.[39]
> (*Abelardo ad Elisa*, 1. 178-80)

The physical strength of the blow, together with its psychological implication is also achieved:

> Alcun le voci e il pianto mio non cura,
> Ergon le destre, e al fiero colpo e atroce
> Coprissi il volto ed arrossî Natura.[40]
> (*Abelardo ad Elisa*, 1. 184-186)

What then is the significance of the poem and translation with regard to eighteenth-century Italian literature? Both works illustrate Conti's deep interest in both figures. It can be said that Conti was drawn to the subject by personal identification with their plight, and the philosophical implications of the content of Pope's poem. He then sought to express dramatically the plight of both individuals. I use the word individuals since I believe that the poet-translator was seeking to express the feeling of Eloisa in the translation and of Abelard in the poem.

Eloisa is the free thinker, whose dramatically emotional reaction to a state of inner conflict is expressed in the translation of the poem. Her words transcend the "petrarchismo settecentesco" and her poetic surroundings are only faintly evocative of the "poesia di monacazione". Above all, Eloisa, in Conti's translation is one yearning for an ideal state, which she creates in her own imagination by recalling her ecstatic past.

The poem *Lettera d'Abelardo ad Elisa* is, as has been seen, modelled on the same lines as the translation of Pope's poem, while giving free play to Abelardo's disposition. One witnesses a man torn apart with guilt feelings, and the unfolding of the psychological reaction to such guilt. Placing translation and poem side by side, one sees Conti's projection of Eloisa and Abelard from the philosophical and dramatic viewpoint. Yet since one feels that it was the philosophical implication of the central dilemma which drew Conti to the subject, it seems only logical to view the conclusion from a philosophic point of view. Eloisa represents idealism and fulfillment, arrived at in the open expression of experience and aspiration. Abelard represents conformism, and the guilt and self torment which follows its violation. Eloisa and Abelard represent the inner struggle taking place within the mind of every individual yearning for an ideal state by way of self-expression, and yet conscious of, and abiding by, the laws and conventions of social order. By writing Abelard's reply Conti has drawn attention to conflict − not the conflict apparent in Pope's poem, which does not come across to a strong degree in the translation. Instead the poet-translator has highlighted Eloisa and Abelard as two contrasting abstract forces, personifying the elements of the intellect which, later in the century, will become the preoccupation of the Enlightenment.

Viewed separately, the poems illustrate a stylistic conflict rather than an emotional one. Viewed together they demonstrate the clash between idealism based on unbridled self-expression and conformism. Historically speaking, Conti's Elisa takes her place as the first great Romantic heroine. Viewed alongside Abelard, with reference to translation and poem, they both illustrate a plight, expressed in the first person, which will later be identified with the Romantic movement. It is left to Alessandro Manzoni to narrate, and demonstrate in the third person, such a dilemma, by creating the tormented Gertrude — the "monaca di Monza."

The poem *Lettera d'Abelardo ad Elisa,* is of course, relevant to the study of Pope's influence on Conti. It indicates his desire to portray the subtlety and duplicity of Pope's *Eloisa to Abelard*. In the translation, Conti failed to express the philosophical contrasts at the basis of the original. He also failed to preserve the naturalness of the setting and the "silvery" poetic quality associated with Pope. The second letter could be regarded as an attempt to come to terms with the poetic problem, while expressing more freely the pre-Romantic concepts contained in his translation. The poem, then, from the mere technical viewpoint, could be seen as an admission on the part of Conti, of inability to achieve all within one poetic whole. I, however, prefer to see it as something more personal, as deriving from his own innermost sensations, convictions and guilt feelings. I feel that both Eloisa and Abelard share aspects of the writer's own disposition, resulting in a spontaneity and freedom of expression never associated with Antonio Conti during the eighteenth century. This could provide an explanation for his failure to draw attention to both works, which unlike his other versions, could not be classified as mere adaptations or translations, but as the self identification with poetic characters. The final result is a "poesia di monacazione" with a difference, which transcends the structural, stylistic and social conventions of its time, but which I believe must be regarded as another aspect of the eighteenth-century poetry of the cloister.

Notes to Chapter IV

1 For some accounts of Conti's life see the *Vita* prefaced to the second volume of *Prose e poesie* (Venice, 1756) pp. 1-308; Gioachino Brognolino, "L'opera letteraria di Antonio Conti" in *Ateneo veneto*, XVII, (1893) pp. 162-79; 327-50; XVIII (1894) pp. 137-209, 260-310, 49-84; Delmac Hamm, "Conti and the English Aesthetics" in *Comparative Literature* VII (1956); Nicola Badaloni, *Antonio Conti – un abate libero pensatore tra Newton e Voltaire*, (Milan, 1968).

2 See George Dorris, *Paolo Rolli and the Italian Circle in London 1715-1744* (The Hague – Paris, 1967), pp. 221-2.

3 G. Gronda "Le versioni poetiche di Antonio Conti" in *Giornale storico della letteratura italiana*, LXXXVII (1970) pp. 297-8.

4 See G. Gronda, *Versioni poetiche* (Bari, 1966) p. 3.

5 G. Dorris, *Rolli and the Italian Circle in London 1715-1744*, op.cit. p. 222.

6 G. Gronda, *Versioni poetiche*, op.cit., p. 11, 1. 1-3.

7 Ibid. 1. 10-15.

8 For consideration of the attempted reform of poetry in the early eighteenth century see W. Binni in *Il Settecento*, pp. 510-21; W. Binni, "Sviluppo della poetica arcadica nel primo settecento" in *L'arcadia e il Metastasio* (Florence, 1963), pp. 125-9.

9 For a study of the operatic libretto as an art form see Patrick V. Smith, *The Tenth Muse, a Historical Study of the Operatic Libretto* (New York, 1970).

10 G. Gronda, *Versioni poetiche*, op.cit., p. 12, 1. 37-9.

11 Ibid. 1. 43-5.

12 Ibid. 1. 49-51.

13 Ibid. p. 14. 1. 100-102.

14 Ibid. 1. 109-111.

15 Ibid. 1. 115-20.

16 Ibid. 1. 121-3.

17 Ibid. 1. 127-9.

18 Ibid. p. 11, 1. 19-21.

19 Ibid. p. 13, 1. 70-5.

20 Ibid. p. 16, 1. 199-201.

21 Ibid. p. 15, 1. 154-6.

22 Ibid. 1. 163-5.

23 Ibid. p. 17, 1. 226-43.

24 G. Dorris, *Rolli and the Italian Circle in London, 1715-1744*, op.cit., p. 222.

25 G. Gronda, *Versioni poetiche*, op.cit., pp. 22-8.

26 Ibid. p. 599.

27 U. Foscolo, *Epistolario*, Edizione nazionale (Forence, 1954), Vol. IV. pp. 26-8.
28 G. Gronda, "Le versioni poetiche di A. Conti", art. cit., p. 302-3.
29 G. Gronda, *Versioni poetiche,* op.cit., p. 22, 1. 1-3.
30 See Francesco Maria Piave, *Rigoletto*, atto, 1. ii, for Giuseppe Verdi.
31 G. Gronda, *Versioni poetiche,* op.cit., p. 22.
32 Ibid. p. 23.
33 Ibid.
34 Ibid. p. 22.
35 Ibid. p. 27.
36 G. Gronda, "Le versioni poetiche di A. Conti", art. cit., p. 302-3.
37 G. Gronda, *Versioni poetiche,* op.cit., p. 24.
38 Ibid. p. 27.
39 Ibid.
40 Ibid.

CHAPTER V

The influence of Pope's *Eloisa to Abelardo* on Italian pre-Romantic poetry

Eloisa to Abelard appeared in 1717, before the dilemma therein presented became a romantic theme "par excellence", since it preceded Diderot's *La Religeuse*, the tormented figures of Gertrude in Manzoni's masterpiece, and Maria in Verga's *Storia di una capinera*. Yet the poetic, and dramatic representation of the contemplative life was not something new to the Italian "letterato" of the time. The taking of final vows, and the withdrawal of the virgin from secular life was an occasion for poetic celebration, and in the period af Arcadia had become an accepted genre, a genre which with the passing of time becomes laden with artifice, containing elements of Petrarchism and neo-Platonism, touches of wit and rococo refinement. Towards the end of the century, consideration is also given to the psychological battle raging within the mind of the individual, with the result that the entire tone and mood of the poetry verges on the romantic. In other words, the excesses, refinements and contradictory aspects of the eighteenth century are reflected stylistically and thematically in this poetry, and the theological, philosophical and psychological aspect of the taking of vows is considered. Along with compositions to celebrate births, marriages and deaths, the sonnet or ode in praise of "monacazione" is one of the most representative and popular themes of the day. Poets known for their celebrations of religious professions include Eustachio Manfredi,[1] Gianpietro Zanotti, Ferdinand'Antonio Ghedini, Saverio Bettinelli, Onofrio Minzoni, Luigi Cerretti,[2] Angelo Mazza and Giovanni Paradisi.[3] Their poetry ranges from that of profound religious feeling, to that of wit and cynicism, from sincerity and spontaneity of approach, to mere uninspired imitations.[4]

Alexander Pope's *Eloisa to Abelard* can be considered a work of emotional conflict. Since however the active life has been ruled out for Eloisa, the entire struggle is within the realm of the contemplative life. This comes to light in the contrast between suppression and expression, reason and passion, stone and sentiment, and poetically these opposites are expressed in terms of light and shade. One finds heat, light, emotion and colour as expressive of one metaphorical group, and cold, darkness and death representative of the other.[5] We witness then an "emotionally liberated" figure, whose expressions are indicative of both fulfillment and frustration. Reason vies with emotion, the passions are rationalised, calmed but not quenched, all within the poetic medium. In *Eloisa to Abelard* then, Pope combines and attempts to identify the Newtonian cultivation of order with Locke's scientific examination of human experience. In theory the final conclusion of the poem sees the logical and rationalistic acceptance by the protagonist of her plight, while in practice, the emotional dimension has been given free play.

Although the influence of Pope on Ippolito Pindemonte is generally accepted and the poem "Lettere di una monaca a Federico IV rè di Danimarca" has been afforded detailed criticism by Lenta,[6] Cimminio[7] and Gronda[8], the works of Ceroni[9] and Gianni[10] based on Pope's *Eloisa to Abelard* have largely been ignored, and their debt to both Pope and Conti unprobed. By the beginning of the nineteenth century, the plight of Elisa and Abelard proved a favourite Romantic theme, the English poem having been translated by Conti, Greatti, Chiari and Benini. That the creative imagination of poets was kindled is borne out by the popularity of the epistolary genre, and of the romantic struggle and conflict between human and divine love. By far the best known work is the above mentioned "Lettera di una monaca a Fecerico IV re di Danimarca". Here not only the essential contrast between the sacred and profane comes to the fore, but also the conflict between the Nordic and Mediterranean personality and their religious beliefs. Yet the ideas central to the poems by Pope and Pindemonte are similar. From the stylistic viewpoint, Pindemonte's work can be regarded as more restrained, controlled, in a word more spiritual than Conti's translation of Pope. "La lettera di Pindemonte è più castigata, più sobria; la sua monaca è meno fremente e più rassegnata che la suora del Paracleto."[11] One witnesses Romantic contrasts and conflicts in a Neo-Classic dressing. There is a clear Classical framework and restraint is conceived as one of the central themes of the poem: the nun, having expressed her romantic yearnings, is capable of identifying herself with an object — the written word on paper, the candle, conveying simultaneously emotion recoiled in tranquillity. This is not, however, to imply that the personal tone set in certain passages is any less convincing: "Il tormento della povera monaca che è innamorata del re danese e vive angosciamente il contrasto che la tormenta fra il desiderio dell amore terreno e quello dell amore celeste, è espresso con evidenza di sentimento, con trasporto, con convinzione."[12] The final prayer conveys an air of calmness and resignation to the entire poem, indicating a certain detatchment on behalf of both author and protagonist. The "confession" has expressed her desire to be freed of any guilt or sense of shame which lay on her conscience.

The influence of Pope and his translators is further witnessed in an examination of six epistolary poems by Giuseppe Ceroni entitled *Lettere di sei donne infelici ai loro sposi ed amanti*, written in 1803. These letters serve as confessions, and expressions of love and guilt, and while all six can be seen as a contribution to the love epistle, it is Letter IV which is of primary concern. Before proceeding to a detailed discussion, it is useful however to refer briefly to Letter I, entitled "Lettera atlantica". This is written by a woman to her lover in prison, a woman whose heart penetrates the prison door, and who Eloisa-like rebukes herself for being so daring as to put her feelings on paper:

> La mia man cancelli
> Le audaci note. . .e il core ohiemè le detta.[13]
> (Ceroni, *Lettera atlantica*, 1. 26-27).

It would appear that the direct source of inspiration is Antonio Conti's translation of the English poem. Both Italian writers aim at a brief condensation of the confused state of the protagonist. Immediacy is achieved as a result of the fact that the lines are written in the first person. Note the similarities between the lines of both writers:

> La mano scrive ciò che il cor le detta.
> (Conti, *Lettera di Elisa ad Abelardo* 1.15)

The original English is much more lengthy, verging on the melodramatic:

> O write it not, my hand — the name appears
> Already written — wash it out, my tears!
> In vain lost Eloisa weeps and prays,
> Her heart still dictates, and her hand obeys.
> (Pope, *Eloisa to Abelard*, 1. 13-16).

Yet, as in the case of Eloisa, the heart and the hand are seen as contrasting forces. It is in two following passages however, that Pope's influence is most apparent — the descriptions of the wounded bleeding lover, and of the solitary figure of the lady. In the first instance it seems to be the desire of the poet to evoke horror, in the second to convey a romantic nocturnal image:

> E il fianco aperto, il sen lacero, e tutto
> Una ferita, colle negre chiome
> Sul sembiante travolte. . . illanguidia
> Alla imagine cruda; sui ginocchj
> Tremanti il corpo ruinava, e l'alma
> Rifuggia da mortale orror compresa.[14]
> (Ceroni, *Lettera atlantica* 1. 76-81).

The detached expression of light and shade, night and day robs the passage of spontaneity, and nature cannot in any way be seen as a sympathetic witness. Its closeness to Pope's *Eloisa to Abelard* however cannot be denied. Eloisa's absence is stressed in Conti's version, while Ceroni describes the bloody sight at first hand:

> Io veggio ancora il sangue
> Ch'esce spumando dalla piaga atroce;
> Ti veggio, sposo mio, pallido, esangue.
> Dov'eri Elisa, allor? La man, la voce,
> La spada, i pianti opposti avresti almeno
> Agli empi colpi e al vindice atroce.
> (Conti, *Lettera di Elisa ad Abelardo*, 1. 109-15).

Pope had stressed the complexity of Eloisa's emotions in terms of horror, shame and rage and devoted a mere two lines to the bleeding image:

Alas, how changed! What sudden horrors rise!
A naked lover bound and bleeding lies!
(Pope, *Elisa to Abelard*, 1. 99-100).

Although the following passage cannot be regarded a literal translation of passage, the spirit is very much that of Pope's work:

Or nella stanza in cui romita siedo,
Di te favello sospirando ai nudi
Marmi, or'agli astri che l'azzurra curva
Smaltan di Olimpo, e con tremola fiamma
Tentano audaci la diurna luce
Dar'alla notte, che di brune cinse
Ombre con magistero alto, infinito
Il Dio dell'Universo, onde più puro
Regno coll'Imeneo l'Amor si avesse.[15]
(Ceroni, *Lettera atlantica*, 1. 82-90).

Relentless walls! whose darksome round contains
Repentant sighs, and voluntary pains:
Ye rugged rocks! which holy knees have worn;
Ye grots and caverns shagg'd with horrid thorn!
(Pope, *Eloisa to Abelard*, 1. 17-20).

In the "Lettera atlantica" the contrast between the real and the ideal,
desire and desolation, is conveyed within the same passage. The entire experience and aspirations of the protagonist are seen with reference to "nudi marmi" alongside "astri che l'azzurra curva smaltano
di Olimpo". The hopes and hopelessness of the lady is seen in terms
of light symbolism — "Con tremola fiamma/Tentano audaci la diurna
luce/Dar'alla notte". Ceroni's aim here is to unite contrasts within
the mind of the individual, and express them with regard to natural
imagery.

Of the six letters the most significant is the fourth, entitled
"Emilia a Rodrigo" — (Lettera iberica). Here once again the conflict
between the religious and secular life is presented along with the subject of vow-taking and an attempt to come to terms with guilt feelings. Early in the poem Emilia expresses her reaction to Rodrigo's
letter:

Lessi, nè profanar gli occhi innocenti
Volea con cifre ignote; incauta lessi
Di sacrilego amor sensi, e parole

327

Che fra i devoti muri, e l'orror santo
Non dovean' unqua penetrar dei chiostri.[16]
(Ceroni, *"Lettera iberica"*, 1. 1-5).

        – Qual mai
Speme ti alletta? e nol sai tu? sull'are
A Dio sacraimi/ osi rapirmi a lui?[17]
(Ceroni, "Lettera iberica" 1. 11-13).

A note of emotion absent from Pindemonte's work is at once apparent in the "Lettera iberica". Ceroni's choice of verbs and his repitition of "lessi" adds dramatic weight to the reading of the letter. It seems to be the poet's intention to excite the reader, to convey that the reaction to the letter will prove turbulent, and the very memory of the words sufficient to inspire from the hand of Emilia a new dramatic reaction. The weakness of the will and the strength of the emotion seem to constitute the cornerstone of the passage. This is seen in the words "nè profanar gli occhi innocenti/Volea"; "incauta lessi". There is the combination of concepts of guilt and innocense rising a climax with the three questions, and the final placing of guilt on the lover:

E nol sai tu? Sull'are
A Dio sacraimi – osi rapirmi a lui?

In common with Eloisa, here Emilia remembers the ceremony of vow taking; Ceroni also refers to the cutting of the hair as symbolic of renunciation of worldly beauty. Unlike those of Eloisa, however, Emilia's memories conjure up an atmosphere of sweetness and virginal innocence, contrasting strangely with the above quoted passage:

Ben mi rimembro quando il crin ricinta
Di virginee ghirlande in lieta pompa
Al celeste mi offria sposo, di avari
Genîtor la esecranda anima, e il labro
Eterni giuri pronunciava i'vidi
Te che pallido il volto in me converso
Tenevi in atto di dolor: . . .[18]
(Ceroni, "Lettera iberica", 1. 21-7.)

Fur recisi i capei biondi; modesto
Velo mi avvolse: con giulivi accenti
Festeggiarmi le suore:[19]
(Ceroni, "Lettera iberica" 1. 29-31).

The tender innocence recalled in the above lines paves the way for a further emotional outburst which poses the question to which Pope's poem gives rise: is it the fault of the individual if over-riding emotions take possession of the mind? Do the emotions control the individual, or is the individual in control of them? And can the inability to control such emotions be defined as moral weakness? Emilia clearly would attempt to place the blame for her disposition on her lover:

> Ma chi agli uomini crede? il desir sculto
> Hanno in fronte; la fè pinta sui labri
> E la frode nel sen. Tal sei tu forse.[20]
> (Ceroni, "Lettera iberica" 1. 63-5).

Ceroni, however, obviously wishes to avoid clear definition and the placing of "forse" at the end of the line contributes a note of uncertainty. Almost similar sentiments are expressed in Conti's translation of *Eloisa to Abelard*, though in fact they do not precisely reflect the original:

> Che si può amar senza peccato intanto
> Tu m'insegnasti; or chi creduto avrebbe
> Che un detto tuo, non fosse casto e santo?
> (Conti, *Lettera di Elisa ad Abelardo*, 1. 76-78).

The cry for pardon in Ceroni's poem reveals once again the complexity and psychological effectiveness of the heroine: the words directly addressed to the lover are coloured by human emotions, they reflect the woman's desire to convince others that she is without blame. In the section of the letter in which momentarily she believes herself to address God, a desire to arrive at self-understanding is spontaneously made:

> ai scellerati accenti
> Gran Dio perdona; è mia colpa se in petto
> Di mie virtù, maggior face divampa?[21]
> (Ceroni, "Lettera iberica" 1. 91-3).

Pope's figure, on the other hand, takes a more analytical and academic approach to her disposition, with the result that the woman Eloisa appears less spontaneous. This is clear from the following lines:

Assist me, Heaven! but whence arose that prayer?
Sprung it from piety, or from despair.
(Pope, *Eloisa to Abelard* 1. 179-80)

Ceroni's poem rises to a heart-rending cry for death or freedom from the thoughts which torment her:

> Dio che m'odi dal ciel fulmina, tuona
> Queste avverse consume are, e delubri,
> O ripiglia il tuo don; dammi la morte
> O alla rapita libertà mi torna;
> Io tua sposa non son: profano il labro
> Temerarj prestò voti; natura
> Non assentia:[22]
> (Ceroni, "Lettera iberica", 1. 77-8).

Both ladies describe their remorse in subdued tones, having passionately declared both love and guilt. As Eloisa, Emilia also envies those who followed another walk of life. Love, remorse and fear are now the attributes of her person. Ceroni has here succeeded in creating the Romantic figure "par excellence":

> Mi è grave intanto il dî; la notte grave
> E coi rimorsi l'amor mio combatte,
> E mi spaventa.[23]
> (Ceroni, "Lettera iberica", 1. 105-7).

> O fortunate voi
> Che avvinte in nodi d'Imeneo seguite
> Facili Leggi; a voi dover supremo
> E il piacer del consorte, e le soavi
> Divider cure.[24]
> (Ceroni, "Lettera iberica", 1. 107-11).

It is clear that Ceroni is indulging in a fashion made popular in Italy by Conti's translation of *Eloisa to Abelard*. It is also clear that he is drawing on Italian eighteenth-century literary tradition in the form of the "poesia di monacazione". The spirit of the work is however totally Romantic, abounding in passionate emotional outbursts and touching on the debate which later is dramatically conceived by Silvio Pellico in his *Francesca da Rimini*. At this point, merely the moral implications of the subject have been bared, whereas Pellico will introduce social and political connotations. However I believe that Ceroni's work, for all its thematic and historical significance is lacking in poetic grace and charm. It never goes beyond the poetry of statement: clear-cut narrative alternates with emotional outburst. The latter are largely expressed by a series of nouns and adjectives which convey the desired mood: "occhi innocenti", "cifre ignote", "sacrilego amor", "devoti muri", "orror santo", "scellerati accenti". Action and finality is achieved in the passage describing the cutting of the hair: the entire world of the religious life is evoked in the use of three verbs "fur recisi", "avvolse", "festeggiarmi", while one witnesses a loss of poetry in a passage of rhetorical questions which probes the disposition of the lover:

> Ma chi agli uomini crede? il desir sculto
> Hanno in fronte, la fè pinta sui labri
> E la frode nel sen. Tal sei tu forse?
> (1. 63-5)

The result is that the letters appear structurally weak. This impression is confirmed with reference to Letter II which describes an unhappy marriage and the memories of vows and promises made in vain. Once again one is aware of the significance of vows, promises and the individual's inability to keep them. Once more one is reminded of the presentation of promise by Pellico and Manzoni, and its significance on a philosophical, psychological, theological and personal level. It can indeed be argued that Pope's popularity in eighteenth-century Italy constitutes a decisive step towards the romantic consideration and exposition of the force and validity of the human will.

The work of Francesco Gianni differs from those of Conti, Pindemonte and Ceroni in that it does not conform to the epistolary genre. The figures of the lovers are contained within a structured framework, and one forms the impression that one is observing from afar the Romantic tragedy. Unlike Pindemonte and Ceroni, Gianni names his protagonists Eloisa and Abelard, and the poem as a whole can be seen as an attempt to sum up the poetic, social and personal implications of the tragedy. Gianni was born in Rome, died in Paris, and his poetry represents for the most part an attempt to fuse and experiment with Arcadian devices applied to Romantic themes within a Neo-Classic framework. Natali, in *Il Settecento* describes him as: "Sarto improvvisatore romano, specie di mulo nato dall 'incrociamento della giumenta arcadia con l'onagro ossianismo nella frega dell'enfasi rivoluzionaria."[25] Carducci also referred to his success in France: "Questo gobbo fremebondo divenne in Francia un curioso campione del cosmopolitismo pontificio trasteverino lustrato di pomice accademica." In the editor's preface to the edition of poems in three volumes, published in Florence in 1827, the following tribute is paid:

> . . .ecco in queste Poesie un Genio, che si rende superiore a tutte le regole, e maggiore di tutti gli ostacoli: a lui suggerisce un momento di riconcentrazione poetica ciò che agli altri appena somministra comunemente la fatica dello studio, e lo stento della lira: l'evidenza delle immagini, la regolarità dell'ordine, la sublimità de'concetti, l'energia della locuzione, l'armonia del numero conveniente all'oggetto, la facilità delle rime, ed il maraviglioso in tutto, par che null'altro lascino a desiderare:[26]

The poem portraying the plight of Eloisa and Abelard is entitled "Eloisa ed Abelardo, argomento con metro obbligato proposto dal chiar, S.P. Prof. D. Antonio Lambertenghi.[27] It consists of 46 three-line stanzas in terza rima. It opens with the poet expressing his intention of unveiling the horrendous details of the love affair of Eloisa and Abelard, and of singing merely of Eloisa's suffering. The latter is depicted in terms of an emotional battle presented in terms of physical and emotional reactions. However, the poem, because of its structure and length is apt to border on the monotonous, and this is aggravated as a result of lack of tone variation. The vision-element, and the detachment of the poet from the details of his subject, is brought out in the opening two "terzine". The poem is to be one of detail of reaction as opposed to one of factual declaration:

> Alunno delle Muse, e del pudore
> D'un vel ricopro l'abborrita scena,
> Trista scena di scandalo, e d'orrore.
>
> Sol d'Eloisa canterò la pena,
> Che sepulta nel buio d'un convento
> Indarno morde la servil catena.[28]
>
> (1. 1-6)

The opening "terzine" reveal Gianni as a talented improvisor whose main concern is the exposition of the story, fluency of expression and variety of vocabulary, and of course correct rhyme scheme. Gianni reveals all of these, but also a reliance, as will be later seen, on the repetition of certain nouns and adjectives: "pudore" and "orrore" certainly meet the demands of the rhyme, as do "pena" and "catena", but the line "Trista scena di scandalo, e d'orrore" to my mind reads rather puerile, as does "indarno morde la servil catena". Description of physical movement preceeds Eloisa's turning of her thoughts towards the past and the presentation of her internal struggle:

> Dell'umil cella muove nell'orrore,
> Quindi s'arresta sovra il freddo letto,
> Nemico a tutti i palpiti d'amore.
>
> Ed il mento abbassando sovra il petto,
> E levando la destra sovra gli occhi,
> Rimembra il lampo del primier diletto;[29]
> (1. 10-15)

The lack of spontaneity is evident from the stilted gesture attributed to the protagonist, and as will be later seen, from the poet's reliance on terms such as "orrore", "amore", "diletto".

The most effective lines of the poem are those in which the anxiety and internal struggle of Eloisa are revealed: Gianni illustrates her violent reaction, her attempt to control herself and her memory of their union and their inability to communicate:

> Pria maledice l'abito abborrito,
> Strappa le bende, e muta poi s'arresta
> Col core dai rimorsi inorridito;
>
> E nell'angoscia intrinseca funesta
> Di nuovi pentimenti, e nuovi affetti,
> Sembra nave premuta in gran tempesta.[30]
> (1. 19-24)

Yet even here it is her movement and exaggerated actions which strike the reader. Nowhere is there evidence of true emotional involvement:

> La vergogna, e il pallor dalle sue gote
> D'Eloisa nel volto allor passaro,
> Che restò con le luci a terra immote.[31]

There is here, however, a note of lyricism in the above lines: "vergogna" yields to "pallor" while the eyes lowered (1. 44-46) to the ground convey simple pathos. Anger, remorse, anxiety and shame have been revealed in the above stanzas — in the following three one witnesses despair alternating with frustrated hopes and tenderness:

> Dai lor occhi sgorgò pianto più amaro:
> Ah! perchè mai per la grata frapposta,
> Quelle lacrime almeno, non si meschiaro!
>
> Rimbalzavano i cor fra costa, e costa.
> E correvano l'alme sulle labbia
> Per gir de'morti alla magion nascosta.
>
> D'amor sospiri, e fremiti di rabbia,
> Disperazion, rimorso, e tenerezza,
> Non sai di lor chi la vittoria s'abbia:[32]
>
> (1. 47-55)

At this point it is clear that the real protagonists of Gianni's poem are not in fact merely Eloisa and Abelard, but their conflicting emotions which rarely rise above the banal. One finds a Romantic theme treated with Arcadian neatness of touch, which however reveals a lack of inspiration and variation. There follows endless repetition of "pudore", "orrore", "pallore", "onore", "angoscia", "rabbia", "tenerezza", "vaghezza", "affetto", "beltade". The final movement of the poem takes the form of a final meeting and union between the spirit of the dead Eloisa and the imprisoned Abelard, bringing about a union between living and dead, life and death, the mortal and the immortal. Abelard in his turn imagines his lover, beatified and more beautiful than ever, in eternity. Three stanzas describe the detachment of Eloisa's soul from her body:

> Ma negli ultimi aneliti ferali
> L'alma si scioglie, e pria di girne al cielo
> Sospende alquanto l'agitar dell'ali;
>
> E dalla testa allontanando il velo
> Si volge indietro a rimirar l'amante.
> E pel seno immortal le scorre un gelo.

Poi sull'arco d'un raggio scintillante,
Come estiva meteora involosse,
Coi segni dell'Amore nel sembiante,
E restò l'altro a lacrimar sull'osse.[33]
(1. 81-90)

All physical attributes have been dispensed with yielding to a delicacy of touch, universality and immortality of concept is conveyed by the expressions conveying space and movement in time: "l'alma si scioglie", "pria di girne al cielo", "allontanando il velo"; "si volge indietro". From the scene of desired physical contact, Gianni moves to a plane of spiritual contemplation. Abelard is carried on wings of thought to contemplate Eloisa in the next world:

E levando i pensieri a vol maggiore
La rivide nel sen d'eternitade
In un vortice immenso di splendore.

Ei va del cielo per le azzurre strade
In alta sua meditazion profonda
Vagheggiando più bella la beltade.[34]
(1. 103-108)

In these "terzine", Gianni enlarges his horizons to embrace the abstractions "pensieri"; "eternitade"; "splendore", "meditazion". He links them to reality by means of verbs of sense and action in a final attempt to unite the physical and abstract, the visual and contemplative, in a poetic world embracing eternity. In this way contemplation and physical sight are identified "levando i pensieri — la rivide", "ei va — in'alta sua meditazion". Bearing in mind these considerations, it is however Gianni's technique which presents itself, rather than its results. The poem closes with a chiselled image of the lover lamenting at the tomb of his beloved:

Lungi dalla città tumultuaria
Ogni notte il meschin tornò alla tomba
Empiendo del suo duol la terra e l'aria,
Siccome in bosco vedova colomba.[35]
(1. 139-142)

That Pope's Eloisa to Abelard is the source of inspiration for the poems of Pindemonte, Ceroni and Gianni cannot be doubted. It is also clear that in the poems of the above mentioned writers one wit-

335

nesses the Romantic treatment of the themes contained in Pope's work. The conflict seen by Pope in philosophic terms is given a social dimension in Pindemonte's poem: the battle is seen not merely between secular and spiritual values, between emotional involvement and rationalism, but also between two different social groups — that of a ruling family and that of the local Lucan nobility. One finds that in Pindemonte's poem, the spiritual values are the most decisive, in an overall analysis of the poem. Ceroni's work brings into play the conflict between innocence and guilt in a setting reminiscent of the eighteenth century poetry of the cloister. In both poems there is a clear attempt to intellectualise human dispositions and tendencies. The same cannot be said however for Gianni's poem: it appears that the Romantic subject, and the opportunity thus afforded to create a linguistically evocative piece, was the prime concern. An Arcadian grace and fluency in treating of themes such as love, joy, despair, and the classically conceived final embrace of Eloisa and Abelard, are the outstanding elements in this poem. One point is quite clear: that the popularity of the epistle form, the sentimental confession of the nun torn between personal and religious loyalties, regarded altogether too daring in the eighteenth century, add a new dimension to the already popular celebration of religious life. During the eighteenth century Pope's *Eloisa to Abelard* was not merely regarded as a great poem in its own right. It was read, studied, translated and imitated. Its theme found its way into various poetic genres, provided a new dimension for the "poesia di monacazione", and in the hands of Francesco Gianni entered the realm of improvisation, assuring a wide hearing and absorption into local tales and culture.

Notes to Chapter V

1 Eustachio Manfredi (Bologna, 1674-1738). Studied law, poetry and mathematics. In 1699 was made Professor of Mathematics at the University of Bologna, was later admitted to the Paris Academy and was greatly admired by Fontenelle. One of his most celebrated works is the "Canzone a Giulia Vanda". See *Rime degli Arcadi*, II (Rome, 1716), p. 21. For a critical assessment of his work see "Il petrarchismo arcadico e la poesia del Manfredi" in *Il Settecento* (Milan, 1970), pp. 375-82.

2 Luigi Cerretti, b. Modena 1738, d. Pavia 1808. In 1758 was appointed secretary to the University of Modena. Five years later was appointed to the chair of Roman History and later to that of eloquence. In 1807 was appointed to an administrative position at the University of Pavia.

3 For a selection of the works of the poets in question see: *Lirici del Secolo XVIII* (Milan, 1877): *Lirici del Settecento* (Milan, 1959).

4 See W. Binni, *L'Arcadia e il Metastasio*, (Florence, 1963).

5 For a detailed discussion regarding imagery in *Eloisa to Abelard* see Rebecca Price Parkin, *The poetic workmanship of Alexander Pope* (Minneapolis, 1955).

6 Giovanni Lenta, *Pope in Italia* (Florence, 1931).

7 Nicola Francesco Cimminio, *Ippolito Pindemonte e il suo tempo* (Rome, 1968).

8 Giovanna Gronda, "Le versioni poetiche di Antonio Conti" in *Giornale storico della letteratura italiana*, LXXXVII (1970).

9 Giuseppe Ceroni, b.S. Giovanni Lupatolo, Verona 1774, d. Governolo 1813. See *Odi* (Verona, 1810); *Poesie* (Mantua, 1813); Mazzoni, *Abati, soldati, autori, attori del Settecento* (Bologna, 1924).

10 Francesco Gianni, B. Rome 1750, d. Paris 1822. See *Poesie* (Pavia, 1795); *Poesie* (Milan, 1807); *Poesie* (Florence, 1827); F.L. Mannucci "Francesco Gianni e la sua patria poetica" in Rivista ligure XXX (1908); N. Bartoli, *Francesco Gianni* (Cava de' Tirreni, 1924); G. Petrocchi, "Francesco Gianni, arcade cattivo soggetto" in *Giornale italiano di folologia*, VII (1954).

11 G. Lenta, Pope in italia, op.cit., p. 72.

12 N.F. Cimminio, *Ippolito Pindemonte e il suo tempo*, op.cit., p. 182.

13 G. Ceroni, *Lettere di sei donne infelici ai loro sposi ad amanti* (Milan, 1803), p. 8.

14 Ibid. p. 10.

15 Ibid.

16 Ibid. p. 35

17 Ibid.

18 Ibid. p. 36.
19 Ibid.
20 Ibid. pp. 37-8.
21 Ibid. p. 39
22 Ibid. p. 38
23 Ibid. p. 39
24 Ibid.
25 G. Natali, *Il Settecento* I, op.cit., pp. 92-3.
26 *Poesie di Francesco Gianni* (Florence, 1827), pp. 10-11.
27 Ibid. pp. 105-12.
28 Ibid. p. 105.
29 Ibid. p. 106.
30 Ibid.
31 Ibid. p. 107.
32 Ibid. pp. 107-8.
33 Ibid. p. 109.
34 Ibid. p. 110.
35 Ibid. p. 112.

CONCLUSION

The purpose of the study was to demonstrate the immense popularity of Alexander Pope's works in eighteenth-century Italy, and to trace the significance of three of his long poems, as regards the literary climate during the century in question. It is concluded that acquaintance with Pope enriched the mock-heroic genre, brought about a vogue for the expression of philosophic ideas through the poetic medium, and effected a complete change of direction in the religious poetry of the cloister. His works also intensified interest in English manners, customs and language, and the praise and eulogies of literary figures provide proof of the esteem in which the English poet was held.

By far the most influential of his works was *The Rape of the Lock*. Readers quickly identified with the "play world" of Hampton Court, and a day in the life of Belinda, or her male counterpart provided delightful and didactic expression, ranging in tone from jovial good humour to biting irony. Belinda's lock appears in a classical setting, enters the realm of the grotesque and finally takes its place in the fairytale world of Pignotti's epic satire.

The poems of Vittorelli, Talassi and Pignotti illustrate three diverse moments in the history of the "poetry of the lock". Vittorelli matches social decadence with poetic decadence. The wig is lifeless, and the emphasis on decorum and decoration serves only to highlight that lifelessness. Talassi's poem provides a lengthy illustration of attack on the object of decorum — the "piuma recisa" carries the preoccupation with the artificial a step further. From the point of view of imagery however, it provides a highly coloured world of silks, tassels and feathers, reminding the objective reader that such social activity is sheer game. Finally in Pignotti's *La treccia donata*, the world of artifice is converted to make-believe, and transported to another planet where, detached from the social order which inspired it, it retains a certain credibility.

Antonio Conti's interest in the dilemma expressed in *Eloisa to Abelard* shows him in the role of translator and creator, whose absorption in his subject demonstrates at least some degree of personal involvement. Conti contrasts the anti-conformism of Eloisa in the translation with the conformism of Abelard in the poem, and the latter's personal guilt feelings resulting from his inability to live up to his own idealistic convictions. A further social dimension is provided by Pindemonte. Ceroni's poem highlights the conflict between guilt and innocence, while Gianni's lighter touch carries the story of the two lovers to the realm of improvisation. In consideration then of the philosophical and emotional implications contained in the figure of Pope's heroine, it is my belief that Antonio Conti's moulding of the figure renders Elisa one of the most significant and far-reaching heroines of eighteenth-century literature.

It must be borne in mind that the eighteenth century witnessed a new-found enthusiasm for translation, both of Classical and European authors. The epic poem was seen as the "genre par excellence" and reproductions varied from faithful versions of Homer and Virgil to lighthearted imitations of mock-heroic satire. During the Italian "Settecento", translations were viewed from two viewpoints; from that of an attempt at exact reproduction in a foreign tongue, and from the point of view of a new art from existing in its own right in its new language. In the latter case one often finds that the hero of the work undergoes a personality change, as was the fate of Conti's Elisa. However, the comparative study of the original and the new version is culturally rewarding. It brings to the fore the demands which are shouldered by the translator as he sets about his work. Far from a faceless individual, lurking in the shadows, and hiding his own inadequacies in the mechanical reproduction of the work of another, the competent translator is of necessity poet, philosopher and linguist. Even more important is his power with regard to the formation of taste. An acceptable or otherwise version of a work of art can make or mar that work for a considerable time, or at least for as long as the translation comes to be regarded as the sole source of acquaintance with a given author, in a given society. It can thus be concluded that the translator-poet was an important figure in eighteenth-century Italy, as he provided the means by which an exchange of ancient and modern cultures could be achieved.

BIBLIOGRAPHY

Manuscript sources:

AMADUZZI, GIOVANNI CRISTOFANO, MS letter to Angelo Talassi, Savignano di Romagna, Biblioteca Comunale, MS 16.99.

ANON. *Il gioco dell'ombra, MS sonnet*, Venice. Biblioteca Marciana, MS CL.9.
no. 404 Col. 7018.

BONDI, CLEMENTE, MS letters, Forlì, Biblioteca Comunale, MS Piancastelli, B;
Bassano del Grappa, Biblioteca Civica, Autografi Remondini, iv. 18.

BONDUCCI, ANDREA, MS sonnet *Per la morte della maestà della regina Anna
d'Inghilterra*, Florence, Biblioteca Nazionale, MS Palatini 1081.

COLPANI, GIUSEPPE, MS letters, Bassano del Grappa, Biblioteca Civica, Autografi Gamba X11, A. 28.

DURANTI, DURANTE, MS letters, Bassano del Grappa, Biblioteca Civica, Autografi Gamba X11, A. 13.

PIGNOTTI, LORENZO, MS letter, Bassano del Grappa, Autografi Remondini
XVIII, 7; MS letter, Autografi Gamba 11. C. 6; MS letters, Florence, Biblio-
teca Nazionale, MS Gonelli 30° no. 228-9.
MS letters, Forlì, Biblioteca Comunale, MS Piancastelli, Aut. 12. P.
MS letters, Pisa, Biblioteca Universitaria, MS 168, 18.

TALASSI, ANGELO, MS letters, Bassano del Grappa, Autografi Remondini XXI.
18; MS letters, Autografi Gamba X11, E. 2.
MS letters Ferrara, Biblioteca Ariostea, MS I. 501. MS letters Forlì, Biblioteca Comunale, Autografi Azzolini, T; MS letters Savignano di Romagna, MS
16. 98.

VITTORELLI, JACOPO, MS letters, Bassano del Grappa, Biblioteca Civica,
Autografi Remondini, XX111 4; MS letters Autografi Parolini X.11;
MS letters Forlì, Biblioteca Comunale, MS Piancastelli, Aut. 22. V.

Printed sources:

ADAMI, ANTON FILIPPO, *I Principi della morale o sia saggio sopra l'uomo, poema inglese di Alessandro Pope, tradotto in versi sciolti italiani. dal Cavaliere Anton Filippo Adami.* (Venice, 1757).

AGNELLI, G. *Precursori e imitatori del 'Giorno'* (Bologna, 1888).

ALEMANNI, V. *Un filosofo delle lettere* (Turin, 1894).

ALLEVI, FEBO, *Fortuna ed eredità del Parini* (Florence, 1970).

AMBROGIO, A. *Intorno all'Algarotti* (Catania, 1924).

ANDRONICO, F. *Alcune osservazioni sopra le poesie d'Ossian* (Florence, 1756).

AUDRA, E. *Les traductions francaises de Pope 1717-1825* (Paris, 1931).

AULT, NORMAN. "Mr. Alexander Pope – Painter" in *New Light on Pope*, (London, 1949).

BABB, LAWRENCE, "The Cave of Spleen" in *Review of English Studies*, vol. XII, no. 46, April 1936.

BADALONI, NICOLA, *Antonio Conti, un abate libero pensatore tra Newton e Voltaire* (Milan, 1968).

BARNARD, JOHN, ed. Pope – *The Critical Heritage* (Suffolk, 1973).

BARTOLI, N. *Francesco Gianni* (Cava de'Tirreni, 1924).

BALLENSPERGER, F. "Le poete Bondi et Jacques Delille" in *Revue de litterature comparée*, 111, 1. (1923).

BENINI, GIAN.-VINCENZO, *Saggio sull'Uomo* (Venice, 1783). *I principi del buon gusto ossia saggio sulla critica* (Padua, 1792); *Il riccio rapito* (1803); *Messia* (1804); *Eloisa ad Abelardo* (Milan, 1804); *Capi d'Opera di Alessandro Pope* (Venice, 1825).

BENJAMIN, WALTER. *Illuminations* (Glasgow, 1973).

BERTANA, E. *Gli intendimenti della satira pariniana* (Verona, 1892); *In Arcadia* (Naples, 1909).

BIANCHINI, G. "Un verseggiatore veronese del secolo XVIII" in *Atti dell'accademia di Verona LXXIV, 2.*

BINNI, WALTER, *La cultura illuministica in Italia* (Turin 1957); *Parini, Saggi* (Turin, 1960); *L'Arcadia e il Metastasio* (Florence, 1963); *Classicismo e Neoclassicismo nella letteratura del Settecento* (Florence 1967, 2nd ed.) *Preromanticismo italiano* (Rome, Bari 1974-1° ed. 1959); "Il Settecento letterario" in *Il Settecento, storia della letteratura italiana* (Milan, 1968).

BONALUME, GIOVANNI, *Parini e la satira* (Bologna, 1958).

BONDI, CLEMENTE, *Poesie diverse di C. Bondi* (Padua, 1776); *Poesie di C. Bondi* (Padua, 1778); *Versi di Bondi* (Lucca, 1778); *Poemetti e rime varie di C.B.* (Venice, 1778); Poesie di C. Bondi (Parma, 1779); *Opere edite e inedite in versi e in prosa di C.B.* vol. 7. (Venice, 1798-1801); *Poesie di C.B. Parmigiano* vol. 2 (Florence, 1808).

BONDUCCI, ANDREA, *Il riccio rapito, poema eroi-comico del Signore Alessandro Pope, tradotto dall'Inglese in verso Toscano* (Florence, 1739).

BRANCA, VITTORINO, *Alfieri e la ricerca dello stile* (Florence, 1947).

BRIZI, O. "Biografia del Dottor Lorenzo Pignotti" in *Almanacco aretino* per gli anni 1841 e 1842 (Arezzo, 1842).

BROGNOLINO, GIOACCHINO, "L'opera letteraria di Antonio Conti" in *L'Ateneo Veneto XVIII* (1893).

BURGADA, G. "Un imitatore del Parini, Lorenzo Pignotti", in *Gazzetta letteraria XVIII*, 37.

CAFFI, F. *Della vita e delle opere di Jacopo Vittorelli* (Venice, 1835).

CALCATERRA, CARLO, *Storia della poesia frugoniana* (Genoa, 1920).

CANTÙ, C. *L'abate Parini e la Lombardia nel secolo passato* (Milan, 1854).

CARDUCCI, G. *Lirici del secolo XVIII.* (Florence, 1871), *Il Parini Maggiore* (Bologna, 1892).

CARETTI, L. *Parini e la critica* (Florence, 1953).

CERONI, GIUSEPPE, *Poesie* (Milan, 1803).

CERRETTI, LUIGI, in *Lirici del Secolo XVIII* (Milan, 1877).

CHIARI, PIETRO, *L'uomo, lettere filosofiche in versi martelliani* (Venice, 1758); *La filosofia per tutti, lettere scientifiche in versi martelliani sopra il buon uso della ragione* (Venice, 1756); *Poesie e prose italiane e latine dell'abate Pietro Chiari* (Venice, 1761); *Eloisa ad Abelardo* (London, 1800).

CLARK, DONALD B. "The Italian Fame of Alexander Pope" in *Modern Language Quarterly* X11 (1961).

COLPANI, GIUSEPPE. *Opere del Cavaliere Giuseppe Colpani di Brescia* (Vicenza 1784 – 89-94).

COMPAGNINO, GAETANO, *Il Settecento* (Rome – Bari 1973).

COMPOSTELLA, B. *Cenni storici e genealogia della famiglia Vittorelli* (Rome, 1906).

343

CONTARI, I. *Il Settecento* (Milan, 1899).

CONTI, ANTONIO, *Prose e poesie*, vol. 2 (Venice 1739-56); *Lettera di Elisa ad Abelardo di A. Pope tradotta liberamente dall'inglese* (Florence, 1760).

CROCE, B. *La letteratura italiana del Settecento* (Bari, 1949).

CUNNINGHAM, J.S. Pope, *The Rape of the Lock* (London, 1961).

DALMISTRO, ANGELO, *Versioni dall'inglese raccolte e date in luce per L'Abate Angelo Dalmistro* (Venice, 1794).

DANDOLO, G. *La caduta della repubblica di Venezia* (Venice, 1857).

DARCIER, Anne "Reflections sur la premiere partie de la preface de M. Pope" (Paris, 1719).

DAVALLE, A. *M. Cesarotti, critico e poeta* (Salerno, 1932).

DEL MAC HAMM, "Antonio Conti and the English Aesthetics" in *Comparative Litterature* VII (1956).

DENNIS, JOHN. *The Critical Works of John Dennis* (Baltimore, 1939-43).

DIAZ, FURIO. *Francesco Maria Gianni: Dalla burocrazia alla politica sotto Pietro Leopoldo di Toscana* (Milan – Naples 1966).

DIXON, PETER, *Alexander Pope* (London, 1972).

DORRIS, GEORGE. *Paolo Rolli and the Italian Circle in London 1715-1744* (The Hague, Paris, 1967).

EDWARD, THOMAS R. Jr. *This Dark Estate* (Berkeley, 1963).

ERSKINE-HILL, HOWARD, *The Social Milieu of Alexander Pope* (Yale, University Press 1975); (Editor) – *The Art of Alexander Pope* (London, 1979).

FERRERO, G.M. *Saggio sull'uomo* (Turin, 1768).

FIDO, FRANCO "Rassegna di studi pariniani recenti" in *Italica* vol. XXXVII no. 4 (1960).

FORD, BORIS. *From Dryden to Johnson* (Middlesex, 1957).

FRANCESCHINI, MOMO. *IUn poeta estemporaneo del Settecento, il ferrarese Angelo Talassi* (Codogno, 1938).

FRASER, GEORGE SUTHERLAND, *Alexander Pope* (London, 1978).

FRITELLI, UGO, *Lorenzo Pignotti favolista, contributo alla storia della favola in Italia* (Florence, 1901).

FUBINI, MARIO, *Studi sulla critica letteraria del Settecento* (Florence, 1934); *Il Parini e 'il Giorno'* (Milan, 1951-2); *Dal Muratori al Baretti* (Bari, 1954);

344

Critica e poesia (Bari, 1956); *La cultura illuministica in Italia* (Radio Italiana, 1957); *Studi di varia umanità in onore di Francesco Flora* (Milan, 1963); *Questioni e correnti di storia* (Milan, 1968); *Saggi e ricordi* (Milan-Naples, 1971).

GENTILE, GIOVANNI, *Frammenti di estetica e di letteratura* (Lanciano, 1921).

GIANNI, FRANCESCO, *Poesie* (Pavia, 1795); *Poesie* (Milan, 1807); *Poesie* (Florence, 1827).

GOLDONI, CARLO, *Memoirs* (Paris, 1946).

GOLDSMITH, OLIVER. *Collected Works* edited by A. Friedman (1966).

GOONERATNE, YASMINE. *Alexander Pope* (Cambridge, 1976).

GOZZI, CARLO *Opere* (Venice, 1758); *Li principi del buon gusto ovvero saggio di critica, poema inglese del Sig. Pope ora per la prima volta fatto italiano* (Venice, 1758).

GRAF, ARTURO. *L'anglomania e l'influsso inglese in Italia nel secolo XVIII* (Turin, 1911).

GRAZIOSI, ANTONIO, *Saggio sopra l'uomo di Alexander Pope, tradotto dall'inglese e diretto a T.B., The Proper Study of Mankind is Man.* (London, 1765).

GRONDA, GIOVANNA, "Antonio Conti e l'Inghilterra" in *English Miscellany* no. 15 (1964); *Antonio Conti, versioni poetiche* (Bari, 1966); "Tradizione e innovazione − le versioni poetiche di Antonio Conti" in G.S.L.I. LXXXVII (1970).

GUERINOT, J.V. ed. *Pope, A Collection of Critical Essays* (New Jersey, 1972).

GUIDI, EGIZIO. *La Dunciade, ossia il poema dell'umana stoltezza* (Ascoli, 1918).

HALOBAND, R. *The Life of Lady Mary Wortley Montagu* (Oxford, 1956).

HORNE, C.J. "Literature of Science" in *From Dryden to Johnson* (Middlesex, 1957).

KNIGHT, DOUGLAS, *Pope and The Heroic Tradition*, (Yale, 1951).

LEAVIS, F.R. *The Common Pursuit* (London, 1952).

LENTA, G. *Pope in Italia* (Florence, 1931).

LEVI − MALVANO, E. *L'elegia amorosa nel Settecento* (Turin, 1908).

LUCATI, V. *La singolare vicenda del 'Giorno'* (Como, 1963).

MAIER, BRUNO. editor, *Lirici del Settecento* (Milan, 1959).

MANNUCCI, F.L. *Il Petrarca in Arcadia* (1905); "Francesco Gianni e sua patria poetica" in *Rivista Ligure* XXX (1908).

MARCHETTI, ALESSANDRO, *Tito Livio Caro, Della natura delle cose* (Milan, 1813).

MARZOT, G. *Il gran Cesarotti* (Florence, 1949).

MAZZONI, MARCELLO, *Fiori e glorie della letteratura inglese* (Milan, 1844).

MICHIELI, A. "Giuseppe Greatti" in *Ateneo Veneto* XXIII.

MOLONEY, BRIAN, *Relazioni fra la Toscana e l'Inghilterra nel Settecento* (Florence, 1969).

MOMIGLIANO, ATTILIO, "Gusto neoclassico e poesia neoclassica" in *Cinque saggi* (Florence, 1945).

MONTI, VINCENZO, *Epistolario* (Florence, 1928).

MUECKE, D.C. *The Compass of Irony* (London, 1969).

MUTINELLI, GIOVANNI BATTISTA, *La sera* (Venice, 1767).

MAC DONALD, W.L. *Pope and his Critics* (London, 1951).

NATALI, GIULIO. *Il Settecento,* 2 voll. (Milan, 1964).

ORTES, GIAMMARIA, *Saggio sopra l'uomo, diviso in quattro lettere d'Alessandro Pope, trasportato dalla poesia inglese nell'italiana* (Venice, 1757); *Scritti editi e inediti* (Milan, 1961).

PAGNINI, GUISEPPE MARIA, *Le stagioni* (Parma, 1780).

PAOLINI, ALDOBRANDO, *Elogio storico filosofico di Lorenzo Pignotti.* (Pisa, 1817).

PARINI, GIUSEPPE, *Il Giorno*, edizione critica a cura di Dante Isella (Milan-Naples, 1969).

PELLEGRINI, GIULIANO, *Il barocco inglese* (Florence, 1953); *La poesia didascalica inglese nel Settecento italiano* (Pisa, 1958).

PETRACCHI, CELESTINO, *Saggio sull'uomo* (Naples, 1742).

PETRINI, DOMENICO, *Dal barocco al decadentismo* (Florence, 1951).

PETROCCHI, G. "Franceso Gianni, arcade di cattivo soggetto" in *Giornale italiano di filologia* (VII (1954).

PETRONIO, G. Giuseppe Parini, *Opere* (Milan, 1957); *Parini e l'illuminismo lombardo* (Milan, 1961).

PEZZANA, A. *Intorno a Clemente Bondi* (Parma, 1821).

PIANCASTELLI, C. *Nel centenario di un olmo* (Bologna, 1923).

PIERI, M. *Ippolito Pindemonte* in *Antologia* n. 98, (February, 1829).

PIERI, SEVERO, *Ippolito Pindemonte, studi e ricerche (aggiunta di liriche inedite e rare)*, (Rocca S. Casciano, 1905).

PIGNOTTI, LORENZO, *La treccia donata* (Florence, 1808); *Il bastone peritole* (Dublin, 1831); *Favole e novelle* (Milan, 1826); *Favole novelle, poesie* (Turin, 1852).

PIGORINI, A. *Il poeta dell'armonia, Angelo Mazza* (Milan, 1930).

PILLORI, ANTONIO, *Saggio sopra la critica* (Florence, 1759); *Saggio sopra l'uomo.*

PINDEMONTE, IPPOLITO, Poesie del Cavaliere Ippolito Pindemonte (Milan, 1833), *Epistole in versi* (Milan, 1829).

PIROMALLI, ANTONIO, *Giuseppe Parini* (Florence, 1966); *L'Arcadia* (Palermo, 1975).

POMA, LUIGI. *Stile e societa nella formazione del Parini* (Pisa, 1967).

POPE, ALEXANDER. The Twickenham Edition of the Poems of Alexander Pope (London & New Haven, vol. 1-X (1939-69); Pope, *Collected Poems* (1924).

PRAZ, MARIO. *Gusto neoclassico* (Florence, 1940); Joseph Addison – *Lo spettatore* (Turin, 1943); *Ricerche Anglo-Italiane* (Rome, 1944); "Rapporti tra la letteratura italiana e la letteratura inglese" in *Letterature comparate* (Milan, 1948); *La civilta veneziana nell'eta romantica* (Florence, 1961); *La letteratura inglese* (Florence, 1968).

PRICE, M. *Interpretations of "The Rape of the Lock"* (New Jersey, 1969).

PRICE-PARKIN, REBECCA, *The Poetic Workmanship of Alexander Pope* (Minneapolis, 1955).

PROSPERO, ADA. *Il poeta del razioncismo settecentesco, Alessandro Pope* (Bari, 1943).

PROVENZAL, DINO. *I riformatori della bella letteratura italiana* (Rocca S. Casciano, 1900).

REEVES, JAMES, *The Reputation and Writings of Alexander Pope* (New Jersey, 1976).

RICOLVI, GIAN-PAOLO, *Saggio sopra la critica, poema inglese di Alessandro Pope, tradotto in versi sciolti italiani da Gian-Paolo Ricolvi* (Turin, 1778).

RODRIGUEZ, F. *Vita di Lorenzo Pignotti* (Florence, 1896).

ROSSI, LUIGI, *La treccia donata, poemetto eroi-comico di Lorenzo Pignotti, raffronti e osservazioni* (Padua, 1906).

ROSSI, VITTORIO, *Storia della letteratura italiana III* (Milan, 1930).

ROUSSEAU, G.S. (Editor) *Twentieth Century Interpretations of The Rape of the Lock* (New Jersey, 1969).

RUBBI, ANDREA. *I conviti raccolta di poemi didascalici* (Venice, 1797).

RUGANI, R. *Vita di Lorenzo Pignotti, e cenni sulla sua favola* (Siena, 1922).

RUMOR, S. *Gli scrittori vicentini dei secoli XVIII e XIX* (Venice, 1905).

SALA di FELICE, E. *Petrarca in Arcadia* (Palermo, 1959).

SALINARI, CARLO, *Sommario di storia della letteratura italiana, 11* (Rome, 1977).

SAVIOLI, LUDOVICO FONTANA, *Amori* (Lucca, 1765); *Amori* (Bassano, 1789); *Amori*, a cura di Momigliano (Florence, 1944).

SALVENINI, GIOVANNI, *Saggio sull'uomo* (Berne, 1761).

SAPEGNO, NATALINO, *Disegno storico della letteratura italiana* (Florence, 1948).

SERENA, AUGUSTO, *Gli amici di Angelo Dalmistro* (Verona, 1889); *Su la vita e le opere di Angelo Dalmistro* (Verona, 1891); *Appunti letterari* (Rome, 1903); *Un altro epigono del Parini* (Treviso, 1903); *Varietà letterarie* (Milan-Rome, 1911).

SIMIONI, A. *Jacopo Vittorelli, vita e scritti* (Rocca San Casciano, 1907).

SISMONDI, *Litterature du midi de Europe* (Paris, 1813).

SOLARIO, FRANCESCO, *Studio critico su Luigi Cerretti* (Florence, 1902).

SUTHERLAND, JAMES. "Poetry in a Polite Society" in *Preface to Eighteenth Century Poetry* (Oxford, 1948).

TALASSI, ANGELO, *La piuma recisa* (Venice, 1778); *L'Olmo abbattuto* (Lisbon, 1789); *Poesie varie* (Venice, 1789).

TERRACINI, B. *Conflitti di lingue e di cultura* (Venice, 1957).

TRENTO, GIULIO, *La coquette* (Treviso, 1732).

UGONI, CAMILLO, *Della letteratura italiana nella seconda metà del secolo XVIII* (Milan, 1856).

ULIVI, F. "Il classicismo del Conti" in *Settecento neoclassico* (Pisa, 1975).

VALSECCHI, F. *L'Italia nel Settecento dal 1714 al 1788* (Milan, 1959).

VARZAN, U.E. "La fortuna di Alessandro Pope in Italia" in *Rivista d'Italia XXIII* (1920).

VIGLIONE, FRANCESCO. "Luigi Cerretti e Alessandro Pope" in *Vittorio Cian, i suoi scolari dell'università di Pisa* (Pisa, 1909); "L'Algarotti e l'Inghilterra, Dai mss del British Museum", in *Studi di letteratura italiana* X111 (1923).

VITTORELLI, JACOPO. *Poemetti e stanze di Jacopo Vittorelli* (Padua, 1773); *Jacopo Vittorelli* (Venice, 1851).

VIVIANI, UGO. *Il medico e poeta Lorenzo Pignotti contro i medici* (Arezzo, 1921); *I guadagnoli poeti aretini* (Arezzo, 1921); "Grossolani errori nelle biografie del medico e poeta Lorenzo Pignotti", *Accademia Petrarca vol. X.* Fasc. 11 (1932).

WARREN, AUSTIN, Alexander Pope, *From Rage for Order* (Chicago, 1948).

WASSERMAN, EARL, R. "The Limits of Allusion in 'The Rape of the Lock' in *Journal of English and Germanic Philology*, LXV (1966).

WIMSATT, W.K. "The game of Ombre in 'The Rape of the Lock' in *Review of English Studies*, N.S.I. (1950).

WORCESTER, DAVID, *The Art of Satire* (New York, 1960).

ZAGHI, CARLO, "Angelo Talassi poeta aulico della regina Maria di Portogallo" in *Corriere Padana* 29 March (1928); "Angelo Talassi, poeta vagabondo" in *Stir*, March (1932).

ZANELLA, GIACOMO, Nuova Antologia (Verona, 1882), *Paralleli letterari* (Verona, 1885).

ZUMBINI, B. *Giornale Napoletano*, 5 february (1882).

Christos S. Romanos

POETICS OF A FICTIONAL HISTORIAN

American University Studies: Series III, Comparative Literature. Vol. 7.
ISBN 0-8204-0088-2   267 pp.   hardcover/lam. US $ 28.—
recommended prices – alterations reserved

This text seeks to re-establish a rigorous dialogue between fiction and historiography. The inquiry is guided by the precepts of phenomenology. It formulates an approach in reference to the oral performance by establishing the historicity of the author-function and by defining the territoriality of the reading experience. (In this experience, the historicity of the author-function and that of the reader converge.) In its application, the approach paves the way for the integration of less known literatures, such as Modern Greek, into the field of comparative literary history. The rise and history of the Greek novel are examined in a comparative context. The fiction of Alé-xandros Kotziás, a contemporary Greek novelist, is considered in relation to other novelists prominent in the European tradition. The novelist is viewed as a fictional historian.

Contents: The text views the novelist as a fictional historian and deals with the historicity of the author-function, the territoriality of the reading experience, and the rise and history of the Greek novel.

PETER LANG AG
New York · Berne · Frankfurt am Main

Steven E. Alford

IRONY AND THE LOGIC OF THE ROMANTIC IMAGINATION

American University Studies: Series III, Comparative Literature. Vol. 13
ISBN 0-8204-0110-2   184 pp.   pb./lam. US $ 19.45
recommended prices – alternations reserved

This study examines romantic irony as a principle of style in the work of Friedrich Schlegel and William Blake. The first half traces Schlegel's critique of the principles of identity and noncontradiction, his developpment of a *romantic* logic, his view of dialectic and rhetoric, and how romantic irony is a stylistic mirror of the results of his critique of formal logic. These findings are tested in a close reading of his essay *Über die Unverständlichkeit* (1800). The second part examines the suggestive relation between Blake and Schlegel's views on logic, dialectic, and rhetoric, and uses these views as the basis for a reading of *The Marriage of Heaven and Hell* (1794). Both thinkers support the conclusion that romantic irony as a principle of style has two moments which can be characterized hermeneutically as negative dialectical and performative.

Contents: This study examines romantic irony as a principle of style in the work of Friedrich Schlegel and Wiliam Blake, using Schlegel's «Über die Unverständlichkeit» and Blake's «The Marriage of Heaven and Hell.»

PETER LANG AG
New York · Berne · Frankfurt am Main

Vernessa S. White

AFRO-AMERICAN AND EAST GERMAN FICTION

A Comparative Study of Alienation, Identity and the Development of Self

American University Studies: Series III, Comparative Literature. Vol. 4
ISBN 0-8204-0016-5   186 pp.   pb./lam. US $ 17.90

recommended prices – alterations reserved

Afro-American and East German fiction point to significant parallels in the pattern of social development among members of both groups, despite the diversities of race, culture and polemical political systems, factors traditionally viewed as barriers. This work compares the social development of contemporary Afro-American and East German counterparts by means of literary analysis.

Contents: Afro-American Literary Images – Racism, Sexism, and Black Identity – Black Identity and the Bourgeoisie – Socialist Humanism vs. Socialist Realism – Morality and Consciousness in *Renata* and *Buridans Esel*.

PETER LANG AG
New York · Berne · Frankfurt am Main